THE APOCALYPSE OF JOHN
A Preterist Commentary on the Book of Revelation

THE APOCALYPSE OF JOHN
A Preterist Commentary on the Book of Revelation

Milton Spenser Terry

Edited by
Kenneth L. Gentry, Jr. and Jay Rogers

Chesnee, South Carolina 29323
"Proclaiming the kingdom of God and teaching those things which concern the
Lord Jesus Christ, with all confidence."
(Acts 28:31)

The Apocalypse of John: A Preterist Commentary on the Book of Revelation
Originally published in 1898 as a chapter in Milton S. Terry, *Biblical Apocalyptics: A Study of the Most Notable Revelation of God*.

Editing, notes, and layout copyright © 2021 by Victorious Hope Publishing.
Second printing with slight corrections (July 2021).

All rights reserved. No part of this book may be reproduced in any form or by any means, except for brief quotations for the purpose of review, comment, or scholarship, without written permission from the publisher.

ISBN: 978-1-7343620-5-3

Published by:
Victorious Hope Publishing
P.O. Box 285
Chesnee, South Carolina 29323

Website: www.VictoriousHope.com

Printed in the United States of America

Cover design: Brian Godawa
Copy editing: Thomas C. Smedley, Ph.D.

Victorious Hope Publishing is committed to producing Christian educational materials for promoting the whole Bible for the whole of life. We are conservative, evangelical, and Reformed and are committed to the doctrinal formulation found in the Westminster Standards.

TABLE OF CONTENTS

Preface (Gentry)... ix
Milton S. Terry Biography (Gentry) xv

INTRODUCTION 1
   1. Authorship.. 1
   2. Date 4
   3. Recent Critical Theories of the Composition................ 9
   4. John in Patmos 15
   5. Scope and Plan of the Apocalypse 19

PART ONE:
THE REVELATION OF THE LAMB (Rev. 1–11).................. 25

Chapter 1: Revelation's Opening (Rev. 1:1–8) 27
   1. Title and Superscription (1:1–3)............................. 27
   2. Salutation (1:4–6)... 29
   3. Apocalyptic Announcement (1:7–8) 32

Chapter 2: Epistles to the Seven Churches (Rev. 1:9–3:22)........ 35
   1. Introductory Christophany (1:9–20)....................... 35
   2. The Seven Epistles (2:1–3:22)............................... 46

Chapter 3: The Opening of the Seven Seals (Rev. 4:1–8:1) 73
   1. The Heavenly Theophany (4:1–11)......................... 73
   2. The Book with Seven Seals (5:1–4)......................... 76
   3. The Lamb at the Throne (5:6–7)............................ 82
   4. The Worship of God and the Lamb (5:8–14) 83
   5. The Opening of the Seals (6:1–8:1) 86

Chapter 4: The Sounding of the Seven Trumpets (Rev. 8:1–11:19) . 107
   1. The Seven Angels (8:2)...................................... 107
   2. The Angel with the Censer (8:3–6)......................... 107
   3. The Trumpets Sounded (8:7–11:19) 109

PART TWO:
THE REVELATION OF THE BRIDE, THE WIFE OF THE LAMB
   (Rev. 12:1–22:21) 151

Introduction to Part Two 153

Chapter 5: The Woman and the Dragon (Rev. 12:1–17) 155
   1. The Woman in Travail (12:1–2) 155
   2. The Great Red Dragon (12:3–4) 156
   3. The Child Caught up to God and the Woman in the
      Wilderness (12:5–6) 158
   4. The War in Heaven (12:7–8) 160
   5. The Dragon and His Angels Cast out (12:9) 161
   6. The Consequent Joy in Heaven (12:10–12) 162
   7. Persecution of the Woman and the
      Rest of Her Seed (12:13–17) 164

Chapter 6: The Two Beasts (Rev. 13:1–18) 169
   1. The Beast out of the Sea (13:1–10) 169
   2. The Beast out of the Land (13:11–18) 174

**Chapter 7: A Sevenfold Revelation of Triumph
   and Judgment** (Rev. 14:1–20) 181
   1. The Lamb and His Thousands on Mount Zion (14:1–5) 181
   2. The Eternal Gospel (14:6–7) 185
   3. The Fallen Babylon (14:8) 186
   4. The Solemn Admonition (14:9–12) 187
   5. The Blessed Dead (14:13) 189
   6. The Harvest of the Earth (14:14–16) 190
   7. The Vintage of Judgment (14:17–20) 193

Chapter 8: The Seven Last Plagues (Rev. 15:1–16:21) 195
   1. The Seven Angels (15:1) 195
   2. The Song by the Glassy Sea (15:2–4) 196
   3. The Procession of the Angels (15:5–8) 197
   4. The Pouring out of the Bowls of Wrath (16:1–21) 199

Chapter 9: Babylon, the Great Harlot (Rev. 17–19:10) 211
   1. The Vision of the Harlot (17:1–6) 211

2. The Mystery Explained (17:7–18). 214
   3. The Angelic Proclamation (18:1–3) 222
   4. The Voice from Heaven (18:4–8) 223
   5. The Dirges and Rejoicing over Her Fall (18:9–20) 224
   6. The Symbolic Act and Word of Doom (18:21–24) 225
   7. The Heavenly Hallelujahs (19:1–8). 226
   [[The Angel's Words to John (19:9–10)]] 229

**Chapter 10: The Millennial Conflict and
   Triumph** (Rev. 19:11–21:8). 231
   1. The Heavenly Conqueror (19:11–16) 232
   2. The Great Supper of Sacrifice (19:17–18) 234
   3. The Beast and False Prophet Destroyed (19:19–21) 235
   4. The Devil Chained and in Prison (20:1–3) 236
   5. The Millennial Reign and Final Overthrow of Satan (20:4–10) 238
   6. The Final Judgment (20:11–15) 245
   7. The New Heaven, New Earth and New Jerusalem (21:1–8). . . 249

Chapter 11: Jerusalem, the Glorious Bride (Rev. 21:9–22:5). 255
   1. The Vision of New Jerusalem (21:9–14) 255
   2. The Measuring of City and Walls (21:15–17) 258
   3. The Materials of its Structure (21:18–21) 259
   4. The Temple and its Light (21:22–23) 260
   5. The Character of its Inhabitants (21:24–27). 261
   6. The River and Trees of Life (22:1–2). 262
   7. The Eternal Reign in Glory (22:3–5) 262

Chapter 12: Conclusion (Rev. 22:6–21) 265
   1. The Angel's Testimony (22:6–7). 265
   2. The Angel and John (22:8–9) 266
   3. The Solemn Admonition (22:10–15) 266
   4. The Personal Testimony of Jesus (22:16) 268
   5. The Great Invitation (22:17). 268
   6. The Prophetic Warning (22:18–20) 269
   7. The Benediction (22:21) 270

APPENDIXES 271
Appendix 1: Approaches to Revelation (Gentry) 273
Appendix 2: A Brief Study on "The Land" in Revelation (Gentry). . . . 291

Appendix 3: Why I Am a Preterist (Rogers) **297**

PREFACE
Kenneth L. Gentry, Jr., Th.D.

The Book of Revelation is undoubtedly the most difficult book of Scripture to interpret. For centuries it has challenged and perplexed the minds of the greatest Christian scholars. And yet, ironically, it is named "Revelation." This is ironic in that the word "revelation" is based on the Greek word *apokalupsis* (hence, "Apocalypse"), which means an "unveiling, uncovering." Such a title would lead anyone opening the book for the first time to think that it will be a clear and straightforward "revelation." But surprisingly, even John himself expresses confusion (Rev. 7:13–14; 17:6–7) or acts confusedly (Rev. 19:10; 22:8–9) in his own book.

Because of this, in *The Devil's Dictionary*, nineteenth-century satirist, Ambrose Bierce amusingly defined "Revelation": "A famous book in which St. John the Divine concealed all that he knew. The revealing is done by the commentators, who know nothing." Our experience in the Christian book market today would lead us to declare that Bierce has actually hit the nail with his head. Too much of what passes for commentary on Revelation is either intolerably trite or altogether misguided.

Terry speaks of John's book by the older nomenclature, calling it *The Apocalypse of John*. But in this Preface I will use the contemporary designation "Revelation," despite maintaining Terry's original title.

Our Interest in John's Book

My interest in Revelation was first piqued when I studied under Greg L. Bahnsen at Reformed Theological Seminary (1975–77). He surprised me, then convinced me of the preterist approach to this glorious book and its early-dating. Since those days, I have invested an enormous amount of time in researching John's perplexing prophecy. I have been hoping to unscrew the inscrutable, you might say. I wrote my 468 page doctoral dissertation on it (1988) and have written four books on it. I have also recently completed a ten-year project in writing a large, two-volume, academic commentary of 1800 pages on it (forthcoming).

My co-editor, Jay Rogers, has written a massive commentary on Daniel (*In the Days of Those Kings*, 730 pages). Anyone familiar with

Revelation will know that Daniel plays a large role in it, perhaps second only to Ezekiel. In fact, John's theme verse, Revelation 1:7, presents us with Daniel's important eschatological statement from Daniel 7:13. Hence, Rogers' strong interest in Revelation.

We clearly have a deep and abiding interest in Revelation. And Milton Terry's work has had a powerful influence on my thinking. Thus, I have long desired to see it back in print and freshened up for a modern audience. The book you are holding is the final result of that desire. I finally was able to get this book back in print due to the help of my computer-savvy, theologically-astute co-editor, Jay Rogers. Jay labored for several weeks in digitizing and correcting digital errors in the final digital version. And he did this while recovering from a heart transplant in mid-2020!

The Significance of Terry's Work

As Christians who are deeply interested in Revelation, it is with great pleasure that Jay and I are releasing Milton Terry's commentary on Revelation as a stand-alone commentary. Since its initial composition in 1898, it has always appeared as a part of his larger volume dealing with the leading apocalyptic passages in Scripture: *Biblical Apocalyptics: A Study of the Most Notable Revelations of God and of Christ in the Canonical Scriptures*. The commentary was the largest chapter in that work, consuming 228 pages of its 512 pages.

Terry's *The Apocalypse of John* is deeply-exegetical, tightly-argued, and clearly-presented. It has been in print for many years due to its strength and clarity. He makes a powerful case for the preterist approach to Revelation. And in doing so, he presents some important angles that are often overlooked even by preterist interpreters of the book. It is time for Terry's book to gain a contemporary hearing in the ongoing Revelation debates.

Some of the distinctive elements in Terry's approach to Revelation are the following.

First, his commentary is a distinctively preterist work. Preterism holds that the great majority of the prophesied events in Revelation were future when John wrote them, but now are in our past. The word "preterist," in fact, means "passed by."

Second, he carefully presents the case for the early dating of Revelation. That is, he shows that it was written prior to the AD 70 destruction of the temple by the Romans. This view was the dominant understanding in the 1800s and the opening decades of the 1900s. Though it lost its dominance in the mid-twentieth century, nevertheless in the past thirty years it has started to press its way back into scholarly discussions (e.g., Revelation commentaries by Stephen S. Smalley and Ian Boxall).

Third, he recognizes that Revelation's theme verse in Revelation 1:7 speaks of Christ's judgment-coming against Israel. This is against the view of most commentators today — including preterist ones — who view it as referring to the Second Coming at the end of history. But Terry presents some strong evidence for the position, which deserves a hearing today.

Fourth, he highlights the important fact that the phrase "the earth [Gk., *tēs gēs*]" may and *should* often be translated "the land," i.e., the Promised Land. This observation throws a flood of light on the whole theme of Revelation and highlights its strong Israel-judgment focus. Most preterist commentators hold that John is focusing almost equally on two first-century enemies of Christianity: Jerusalem and Rome.

Fifth, he presents a strong case for the beast of Revelation being the Roman emperor Nero. Nero was the first imperial persecutor of the early church. He was encouraged to attack the church partly at the instigation of the Jews, who vehemently opposed Christianity.[1]

Sixth, he argues that the Babylonian harlot is an image of corrupt, first-century Jerusalem, rather than ancient Rome or some contemporary phenomenon. By doing this, he is showing how the theme verse applies to the Jews who rejected Jesus as their Messiah. He believes John picked up the harlot imagery from Old Testament denunciations of Israel's idolatrous sins (Isa. 1:21; Jer. 2:20; 3:1–9; Eze. 16:15–41).

Seventh, he is postmillennial in his eschatology. Like preterism, postmillennialism was once dominant in the Church (1600s through the early 1900s). Postmillennialism and the preterist approach to Revelation fit together nicely, thus encouraging the simultaneous rising of the fortunes of both.

Eighth, he recognizes that though Revelation is greatly concerned with first-century events, it is not focused *exclusively* on those events. Terry points out that in the last chapters of Revelation John glances to

---

[1] W. H. C. Frend, *Martyrdom and Persecution in the Early Church: A Study of a Conflict from the Maccabees to Donatus* (Garden City, N.Y.: Doubleday, 1967), 126.

the distant future. This shows the long term consequences of the first-century events prophesied in Revelation.

Terry presents a powerful preterist interpretation, with which we agree. Though we do not agree with every position that Terry presents, we did not "correct" him with our own views. So the reader has the exegetical arguments as Terry originally presented them. Our views can be found elsewhere.

The Preparation of this Commentary

This updated printing of Terry's commentary on Revelation would not have been possible without the diligence of Jay Rogers in digitizing the material. Thankfully, *Biblical Apocalyptics* has remained in print over the years and has included *The Apocalypse of John* as a major portion of it. But the published versions have been created by merely scanning the original text, then printing it "as is." No one attempted resetting the type. Thus, the quality of reproduction was quite low.

In this newly typeset version the reader will find the following improvements.

We are using a modern type-font: AmerigoBT. This makes the text cleaner, being both aesthetically more pleasing in appearance as well as easier on the eyes.

Long paragraphs and sentences have been broken down into smaller sizes according to modern style. When sentences were broken into more comfortable sizes, we sometimes had to add a word or two of transition to make it flow smoothly. We also inserted serial (or Oxford) commas for greater clarity. In addition, we abbreviated parenthetical notes to lighten up the style. This included abbreviating parenthetical verse references (e.g., Matthew to Matt.), using the standard abbreviation "cp." instead of either the bulkier "comp." or the full word "compare," and so forth.

We have also modernized some of the nineteenth-century language, Thus, we replaced some words and phrases with their modern counterparts. This included replacing the following words: "wont to be," "ye," "builded," "must needs," "kine," "wroth," "sware," "anon," "sitteth," "like unto," and so forth. However, we did not change his direct quotations from Scripture, which also involved some antiquated language. For often his argument required a direct citation of the verse. According to Terry's statement in *Biblical Apocalyptics* (Preface, p. 7), the Bible version he used was "in the main" that of the Anglo-American Revised Version of 1881.

The original commentary appeared as a single chapter of 228 pages in one large book. Thus, it was necessary to break down the material into several chapters to present it as a free-standing book. In the process we have unified the layout style which sometimes shifted in the original.

Antiquated Roman numerals have been replaced with Arabic numbers throughout. We have employed modern style for ancient references such as to Josephus, Tacitus, Suetonius, etc. For instance, we changed Josephus' *"Wars,* bk. iv, 4, 5" to *"Wars* 4:4:5."

To make the commentary more accessible to a broader audience, we added English transliterations to the Greek and Hebrew characters found in the original.

We have made it easier to search for a commentary note, not only by breaking up Terry's long paragraphs, but by **bolding** the Revelation quotations being commented on. We also added the Scripture addresses to each newly introduced quote (which was necessary since we broke down the larger paragraphs).

Conclusion

Hopefully our labor will not have been in vain and Terry will be more easily received by a new generation. We trust that you will find Terry as interesting and helpful as we have. He is certainly not inspired, but he is inspiring. He will challenge your thinking.

To supplement your study of Revelation from Terry's basic perspective, we recommend the following commentaries and special studies on Revelation:

- Larry E. Ball, *Blessed Is He Who Reads: A Primer on the Book of Revelation* (2015)
- Alan James Beagley, *The 'Sitz im Leben' of the Apocalypse with Particular Reference to the Role of the Church's Enemies* (1987)
- David Chilton, *The Days of Vengeance: An Exposition of the Book of Revelation* (1990)
- Kenneth L. Gentry, Jr., *The Divorce of Israel: A Redemptive-Historical Interpretation of the Book of Revelation* (forthcoming)
- Kenneth L. Gentry, Jr, *Navigating the Book of Revelation: Special Studies on Important Issues* (2010)
- Douglas Kelly, *Revelation: A Mentor Expository Commentary* (2012)

Sebastian Smolarz, *Covenant and the Metaphor of Divine Marriage in Biblical Thought: A Study with Special Reference to the Book of Revelation* (2011).

BRIEF BIOGRAPHY OF MILTON S. TERRY
by Kenneth L. Gentry, Jr.

Family Background

Milton Spencer Terry was born on February 22, 1840 in the Town of Coeymans, New York. Coeymans was a small town in Albany County with a population of a little over 400 people. He died on July 13, 1914 in Los Angeles, a slightly larger town.

His father John Terry was born on March 13, 1786 in Swansea, R.I.. His mother Elizabeth McLoen (or: MacLaughlin) Terry was born on April 15, 1796 in New York City. At an early period in American history, the Terrys' English ancestors arrived in America and settled in the New England colonies. In 1794, when John Terry was eight years old, he moved with his father Philip Terry and his grandfather George Terry from Swansea to Coeymans.

Milton's parents were farmers who enjoyed reasonable success in their work. Young Milton spent his youth on the farm but is reported to have always been studious, seeking ways to to "advance his mental instruction."[2] He attended district (public) schools as a child in Coeymans.

During an old-fashioned prayer meeting at the home of an old saint, Milton had a remarkable conversion experience which greatly impacted his life. According to a memorial published in the *Official Journal of the New York Conference* (1915): "his heart, like Wesley's, was strangely, divinely warmed, and the ecstasy of that hour he never forgot."

On May 15, 1864, twenty-four year old Milton Terry married Frances Orline Atchinson (b. Oct. 1, 1841) in Delhi, N.Y. They had two children, Minnie Ruth Terry (b. March 29, 1870) and Arthur Guy Terry (May 10, 1878).

---

[2] Robert D. Sheppard, *History of Northwestern University and Evanston* (Chicago: Munsell, 1906), 545.

Both of Milton Terry's children were well-educated. His daughter Minnie was a Phi Beta Kappa at Northwestern University, where she received the A. B. in 1891 and the A.M (in Latin) in 1894. After graduating, she studied in Europe in 1894–95. Then for many years she taught French at Evanston, Illinois, high school. Arthur graduated from Northwestern with a Ph.M. in History in 1902, where he became Professor of History. He also was a Fellow in History at the University of Pennsylvania (1902). Like his father, he was a noted scholar and a published author. For example, he edited the multi-volume series *History Stories of Other Lands: The Modern World* (1915). In this series, he wrote the second volume, which was well-received.

Formal Education

Milton studied briefly at Troy University, but in 1859 he graduated from the New York Conference Seminary in Charlotteville, N.Y. Later he also graduated from Yale Divinity School (1862). He had the D.D. degree conferred on him in 1879 by Wesleyan University in Middletown, Connecticut. He studied for a year in Berlin in 1887. Then in 1895 at the age of fifty-five, he was awarded the honorary LL.D. from Northwestern University in Evanston, Illinois.

He did well in all of his formal academic studies. But he especially excelled in Greek and Latin, then later in Hebrew.

According to a memorial statement in the *Official Journal of the New York Conference* (1915), Milton Terry was a man of "keen intellect and warm heart." He was loved and respected at Northwestern University and in the surrounding area, for he "made for himself a warm place in the hearts of all Evanstonians."[3] He was deemed "very genial and approachable" being "well beloved by the larger number of students who had sat under his instruction, by his colleagues on the Garrett teaching force, and by a host of friends throughout the [Methodist Episcopal] Church."[4]

Ecclesiastical Ministry

Terry was ordained to pastoral ministry in the New York Conference of the Methodist Episcopalian Church. He held various ministerial

---

[3] Frances E. Willard, *A Classic Town: The Story of Evanston* (Chicago: Woman's Temperance Publishing Association, 1891), 278.

[4] "The Death of Dr. Terry," *Western Christian Advocate* (July 22, 1914 [80]: 13.

positions for over twenty years (1863 to 1884). For nineteen years of those years he held pastoral charges in the state of New York.

His first preaching position was for one year in a Hancock, N. Y. church where he filled the pulpit of his recently deceased brother. Following this he engaged in full-time pastoring in New York state in the cities of Hamden, Delhi, Peekskill, Poughkeepsi, Kingston, and New York City. Historical notices on his preaching ministry show he was an effective communicator. He was declared to be "a clear and forceful preacher, very efficient instructor, and profound biblical scholar."

While at the St. Paul's church in Peekskill, N.Y., he began rapidly advancing in his ministerial standing in the conference. During his final four years of ecclesiastical ministry, he was the Presiding Elder of the New District of the New York Conference. In 1880 he was elected as a delegate of the New York Conference to the General Conference of the Methodist Episcopalian Church. He left the pastoral ministry in 1884 when he was elected to the professorship at Garrett Biblical Institute in Evanston, Ill.

Academic Positions

In 1884, Terry was elected to the chair of Old Testament Language and Literature at Garrett Biblical Institute, Evanston, Illinois. He served there for thirty years in various positions from 1884 until his death in 1914. His special interests included apologetics, comparative religion, and Old Testament.

In 1871 he was elected to the American Oriental Society, and in 1883 to the Society of Biblical Literature and Exegesis. He also was a member of the newly established Victoria Institute (London).

Later in 1887 he attended lectures at the University of Berlin, where he picked up Higher Critical concepts that influenced his later thinking. Despite his accepting much of what Higher Critics taught regarding the writing of the Scriptures, he personally maintained a strong commitment to the supernaturalism of the historic Christian faith.[5] Thus, he opens *Biblical Apocalyptics* with these words: "That God

---

[5] He writes in this regard: "For the sake of any who may feel regret that I concede so much to the findings of modern higher criticism I take this opportunity to say that I have in some instances allowed the claims of a radical criticism, which I am personally far from accepting as established, for the very purpose of showing that the great religious lessons of the scripture in question

has at many times and in many ways revealed himself to men is a doctrine fundamental to the Christian faith, and the canonical writings of the Old and New Testaments are believed to be a truthful presentation of such divine revelations."[6]

After serving as Professor of Old Testament Language and Literature at Garrett Biblical Institute, he transferred to the Chair of Christian Doctrine in 1897. He served in this position until his death in 1914.

Published Writings

Terry was not only an accomplished scholar and an effective instructor, but he was also a prolific writer. He wrote extensively on apologetics, philosophy, comparative religions, and dogmatics. He wrote many articles for a variety of publications, including the *Methodist Quarterly Review*, *The Old Testament Student*, *Sunday School Times*, *The Northwestern Christian Advocate*, and others.

He is best remembered today, however, for his books, several of which are still in print. He wrote more than thirty books, including:

The Bible and Other Sacred Books: A Contribution to the Study of Apologetics and Comparative Theology (1890)

Biblical Apocalyptics: A Study of the Most Notable Revelations of God and of Christ in the Canonical Scriptures (1898)

Biblical Dogmatics: An Exposition of the Principal Doctrines of the Holy Scriptures (1907)

Biblical Hermeneutics: A Treatise on the Interpretation of the Old and New Testaments (1883)

Chronicles and the Mosaic Legislation (1888)

Commentaries on the Historical Books of the Old Testament (2 vols. 1873–75)

The Experience according to the Scriptures (1902)

Genesis and Exodus (1889)

Jesus Christ on Marriage and Divorce (1910)

Man's Antiquity and Language (1881)

The Mediation of Jesus Christ: A Contribution to the Study of Biblical Dogmatics (1903)

---

are not affected by critical opinions of the possible 'source,' and date, and authorship, and redaction." Terry, *Biblical Apocalyptics: A Study of the Most Notable Revelations of God and of Christ* (rep.: Grand Rapids: Baker, 1988 [1898]), p. 8.

[6] Terry, *Biblical Apocalyptics*, 3.

Moses and the Prophets: An Essay toward a Fair and Useful Statement of Some of the Positions of Modern Biblical Criticism (1901)

The New and Living Way: An Orderly Arrangement and Exposition of the Doctrines of Christian Experience, according to the Scriptures (1902)

The New Apologetic: Five Lectures on True and False Methods of Meeting Modern Philosophical and Critical Attacks Upon the Christian Religion (1897)

Philosophical and Critical Attacks upon the Christian Religion (1897)

Primer on Christian Doctrine: In the Form of Questions and Answers (1906)

The Prophecies of Daniel Expounded (1893)

Rambles in the Old World (1894)

The Shinto Cult: A Christian Study of the Ancient Religion of Japan (1910)

The Sibylline Oracles Translated from the Greek into English Blank Verse (1899)

The Song of Songs (1893)

His most influential work in evangelical circles was his magisterial *Biblical Hermeneutics* (511 pages; 1883). This has been highly regarded by many scholars and even used in various evangelical colleges and seminaries over the years. Masters' Seminary professor Robert L. Thomas notes that *Biblical Hermeneutics* "was viewed as the standard work on biblical hermeneutics for most of the twentieth century."[7] Thomas goes on to state that Terry's "basic principles of hermeneutics make the most sense" (p. 12). Terry's classic work is still in print today.

The book that you are currently reading was lifted from Terry's *Biblical Apocalyptics*, a large work of 512 pages. *Biblical Apocalyptics*, which is also still in print, was one volume of a three volume set. The first volume in this set was *Biblical Hermeneutics* (1883), which presented interpretive principles that are so important for his study of Revelation, which you have before you in this special volume.

Biblical Apocalyptics was his second volume in this series (1898). Terry explains on p. 8 of that work: "The present treatise is the second in my plan, and, in nature and scope, is supplementary to the *Herme-*

---

[7] Robert L. Thomas, "The Principle of Single Meaning," *Master's Seminary Journal* (Spring 2001): 5 n1.

neutics, being an extended application and illustration of the principles of interpretation set forth therein." The material contained in this book that you have in your hands consumed half of the number of pages in its original source.

The third volume in the set was *Biblical Dogmatics* (604 pages; 1907). His goal in that volume was stated in advance in *Biblical Apocalyptics* as being "an essay toward a luminous, simple and systematic statement of the principal doctrines of the Old and New Testaments" (p. 8). Then in *Biblical Dogmatics* itself he stated that it is a "systematic exposition of religious truth" (p. vi). Thus, he noted, "with [this] publication we complete the trilogy of our contributions to the study of biblical interpretation and doctrine which we began in 1883" (p. viii).

Death and Burial

In February 1914 Terry began an extended sabbatical during the second semester of the school year to gain some much needed rest from his many labors. He went with his wife to Los Angeles, California where he had many friends from among his former students and colleagues.

On Sunday July 12, 1914, he preached at the Methodist Episcopal Church in the city of Covina, which is near Los Angeles. Later that afternoon he suddenly became quite ill. The next morning, July 13, he had a heart attack and died at the age of 74. Just two months before this (May 15), he and his wife had celebrated their fiftieth anniversary.[8]

His wife escorted his body back to Illinois. His funeral was held at Rose Hill Cemetery Chapel in Chicago, on Sunday, July 19, 1914. Rev. Dr. Charles M. Stuart, president of Garrett Biblical Institute conducted the service.

But "though he is dead, he still speaks" (Heb. 11:4) through his many published writings, which have gone in and out of print over the last century.

---

[8] "Death of Dr. Milton S. Terry," *The Christian Advocate* (July 23, 1914), 22.

THE APOCALYPSE OF JOHN

INTRODUCTION

1. Authorship

Available options

The different opinions respecting the authorship of the New Testament books commonly attributed to John may be stated as follows:
1. John, the son of Zebedee, the disciple and apostle of Jesus, was the author of the Apocalypse, the fourth gospel and the three epistles.
2. John the apostle was the author of the Apocalypse, but not of the gospel and the three epistles.
3. John the apostle was the author of the gospel and the three epistles, but not of the Apocalypse.

Those who adopt this third view attribute the Apocalypse either to:
1. A Presbyter John, who is mentioned in early writings.
2. John Mark, the companion of Paul and Barnabas.
3. A John whose only monument is this Book of Revelation and who is otherwise unknown.

Two types of evidence

Our purpose does not call for any extended discussion of these various opinions. But we have discovered no sufficient reason to reject the old and most current tradition that all these Johannean writings are the work of the disciple of our Lord. The external evidence is overwhelmingly in favor of this view and Justin Martyr, Irenæus, Tertullian, Hippolytus, and Origen testify direct testimony that the Apocalypse is the writing of the apostle John. The contrary opinion rests mainly on negative considerations, such as its omission from the early Syriac version and the statement of the Roman presbyter Caius, that it was written by the heretic Cerinthus and published under the name of John in order to obtain for it a claim to apostolic authority.

The more noteworthy objections to the apostolic authorship are based on internal evidence and were well stated by Dionysius of Alexandria (A.D. 250). They have been restated and enlarged by many later writers and have always had weight with critical minds, so that as in the past there will probably ever in the future be not a few who will not be able to concede that the author of the Apocalypse was also the writer of the fourth gospel. The arguments are in substance as follow.

Internal evidences

1. The apostle does not mention himself by name either in the gospel or in the epistles.

This fact, however, may be sufficiently accounted for by the nature and circumstances of each writing. In a book of prophecy, modeled so conspicuously after that of Daniel, there was special reason for using the forms of expression found in the older apocalyptist. As in the older book there is frequent occurrence of the phrase "I, Daniel" (cp. Daniel 7:15, 28; 7:1,15; 9:2), so the New Testament writer of an apocalypse appropriately employs the words "I, John."

2. He calls himself servant, brother and partaker in the tribulation (1:1, 9), but not apostle.

It does not appear evident, however, that an apostle could not have appropriately used these expressions and it may be affirmed with much emphasis that there was no other John in the early Church who could have announced himself simply as "John," and "I, John," without exposing himself to the charge of unseemly arrogance. Furthermore, he is simply bearing "the testimony of Jesus Christ" to the servants of God and accordingly calls himself most appropriately a servant, brother and fellow partaker "in the tribulation and kingdom and patience in Jesus." This is in keeping, too, with the tender sympathy of John, the beloved disciple of Jesus.

3. We find in the Apocalypse no trace of apostolical authority, or of the paternal relation assumed in 1 John 2:1; 5:21; 2 John 1; and 3 John 1.

But such authority would have been notably out of place in a book of prophecy like this; and the epistles to the seven churches are in each case announced as coming from the glorified Christ, not from John, who is merely the reporter.

4. It has been urged by some that the names of the twelve apostles on the foundations of the heavenly city (21:14) would have been incongruous in a vision seen by an apostle.

But in view of what Jesus says of the twelve in Matthew 19:28 and what Paul says of the apostles and himself in Ephesians 2:20 and 2 Corinthians 11:5; 12:11, this objection seems trivial and far-fetched. The writer of the vision says nothing of himself personally, but simply states what was shown him.

5. But the most weighty argument is based on the language and style, which are acknowledged on all hands to be very different from what appears in the gospel and the epistles of John. The language of the Apocalypse is peculiarly Hebraistic and Dionysius long ago said that it was notable for its solecisms and barbarous idioms. The book is distinguished for its numerous symbols and visions of things in heaven and on earth; the addresses to the seven churches are stern and lordly, very unlike the manner of John's epistles.

Instead of the profound, calm and contemplative utterances of the other Johannean writings, we have vivid pictures and symbolic names and numbers. Instead of the spiritual worship taught in the fourth gospel, we have magnificent pictures of cherubim, elders, angels and glorified spirits and all things in heaven and earth and under the earth and on the sea, giving glory to Him who sits upon the throne. The word of God, the Antichrist, the conception of the judgment and the resurrection are all in notable distinction from the same doctrines in the gospel and the epistles. From all these, it is claimed, we must conclude that the author of the Apocalypse is not to be identified with the author of the fourth gospel.

Response to weightiest argument

The weight and force of this argument cannot be ignored. But for the external testimony, no critic would think of ascribing the Apocalypse to the author of the fourth gospel and the three epistles. Yet this argument from the language and style of thought is largely nullified by three considerations:

First, the subject matter and scope of the Apocalypse place it in a totally different class of literature from that of the gospel and of the epistles. It is a book of prophecy. The addresses to the seven churches are not so much epistles as prophetic messages. The series of visions is not designed to inculcate lessons of Christian doctrine so much as to disclose things which were shortly to come to pass.

Second, being essentially a book of prophecy, not a gospel nor an epistle, it is modeled after the apocalyptic portions of the Hebrew Scriptures. There is scarcely a symbol or figure employed that is not appropriated to some extent from the Old Testament. It is, therefore, not to be supposed that the language, or style of thought, or type of doctrine must resemble those of other productions of the same writer.

Third, the difference of language is further accounted for by the supposition that the Apocalypse was written by the apostle at an early period of his ministry and the gospel and epistles some thirty or forty years later. We may easily believe that John, the Galilean fisherman, wrote just such rough Hebraistic Greek soon after he left Palestine. But after thirty years of life in the midst of a Gentile community, he would naturally have acquired such a command of the Greek language as the fourth gospel shows.

Conclusion

We are accordingly of the opinion that the various arguments against the Johannean authorship of the Apocalypse are not conclusive or sufficient to set aside the best testimony of the early Church. It is not necessary, however, to insist upon maintaining the current tradition of the centuries. The exposition of the book is not dependent upon a certain knowledge of its authorship. The question of its origin is one of those problems of criticism on which there will probably never be uniformity of opinion. Dionysius of Alexandria, while disputing the apostolic origin of the Apocalypse, accepted the book as the production of a holy and inspired man of God. Not a few of the ablest exegetes of modern times adopt the views of Dionysius. It would be a singular infatuation to imagine that God could not have sent this "testimony of Jesus Christ" by some other John than the son of Zebedee.

2. Date

Two different opinions have long prevailed respecting the date of the Apocalypse. One rests mainly on a statement of Irenæus, who seems to place the composition in the latter part of the reign of Domitian (A.D. 96). The other is based upon internal evidence and maintains that the book was written before the destruction of Jerusalem. The most recent criticism, which finds documents of different authorship incorporated in the work, assigns some of the documents to an early and some to a later date. Deferring for the present the several hypotheses of the composite origin of the book, we may briefly state the arguments touching the date as follows:

Irenaeus' statement

Irenæus, Bishop of Lyons, says that in his boyhood he had conversed with Polycarp and heard him tell of his personal fellowship with the apostle John (Eusebius, *Eccl. Hist.* 5:20). In speaking of the name of the Antichrist which is concealed in the mystic number given in Revelation 13:18, he says: "If it were necessary to have his name distinctly announced at the present time it would doubtless have been announced by him who saw the Apocalypse; for it was not a great while ago that [it or he] was seen (οὐδὲ γὰρ πρὸ πολλοῦ χρόνου ἑωράθη; *oude gar pro pollou chronou eōrathē*), but almost in our own generation, toward the end of Domitian's reign" (Irenaeus, *Ag. Here.* 5:30).

Here the critical reader will observe that the subject of the verb ἑωράθη (*eōrathē*) "was seen," is ambiguous and may be understood either of John or the Apocalypse. To assert, as some do, that the only grammatical and legitimate construction requires us to understand the *Apocalypse* rather than *John* as the subject of the verb is arbitrary and presumptuous. To say the least, in fairness, one construction is as correct and legitimate as the other.

But why should he say that the book was recently seen? The point he evidently aims to make is that the man who saw the visions of the Apocalypse had lived almost into the times to which Irenæus belonged. Thus, had it been needful to declare the name of the Antichrist, he would himself have done it. The time when John saw the Apocalypse was of no consequence for determining the name of Antichrist so long as the apostle himself was yet alive. There is more reason for believing that the reference is to the Apocalypse [*sic*: "the Apostle"] in the fact that Irenæus elsewhere says that John lived on into the times of Trajan.

Sparse evidence

But admitting that Irenæus refers to the Apocalypse as having been seen near the close of Domitian's reign, his ambiguous statement is the only external evidence of any real value for determining the question. All other testimonies are later and, like the numerous statements of Eusebius, seem to be either repeated from Irenæus or based on mere inferences. And it is notorious that even Eusebius, after quoting Irenæus and others, leaves the question of the authorship of the Apocalypse in doubt.

Heretical sects

It has been claimed that the early date is incompatible with the existence of such heretical sects as the Nicolaitans mentioned in Revelation 2:6,15. This must have required more time for their development. But the most rational explanation of the Nicolaitans indicates the very opposite. For these libertines were the first troublers of the Church and the name itself is a symbolical designation for those destroyers of the people, who, like the Balaamites and Jezebelites of the same chapter (vv. 14, 20), taught the mischievous error of licentious freedom, even "to eat things sacrificed to idols and to commit fornication." These evils were among the earliest with which the Church had to contend (Acts 15:20, 29; 1 Cor. 8:7–13; 6:13–20). There is no conclusive evidence that any sect of this name existed in the early Church. All that writers like Irenæus, Epiphanius, and Tertullian say about their springing from the Nicolas of Acts 6:5, is justly open to suspicion.

Seven churches

It is further argued that the churches of Asia must have existed for some time. Because some had, like Ephesus and Sardis and Laodicea, lapsed from their first love, had become lukewarm, and were ready to die. But such a plea can be allowed no weight in view of the abundant evidence of other defections in apostolic times. How long was it after Paul founded the churches of Galatia that he was compelled to write, "I marvel that ye are so quickly changing from him that called you in the grace of Christ unto a different gospel?" (Gal. 1:6). How soon after his departure did false apostles and deceitful workers and heretical teachers arise in the church of Corinth? See: 1 Corinthians 5:1, 7; 11:18 –21; 15:12; 2 Corinthians 2:17; 11:13; Philippians 3:18; Romans 16:17. There is no apostasy or defection mentioned in connection with the seven churches, which might not have arisen in any Jewish-Gentile church of apostolic times in less than two years after the date of its foundation.

Ecclesiastical bishopric

Some believe that the phrase "angel of the church," employed at the beginning of each of the epistles, implies an advance in ecclesiastical organization beyond the simple constitution of the first period. This is based on the assumption that *angel* means *bishop* and that the Church had no bishops before A.D. 68 who were different from presbyters. But there is no sufficient evidence that some churches were without a special bishop, or responsible pastor, even in apostolic times. And, were this not the case, the opinion that "angel of the church" in the Apocalypse means the pastor, or bishop, is without authority. Much rather is it to be regarded as a symbolical title of the whole Church in its personnel (see our interpretation *in loco*); for the words both of praise and of censure are obviously intended, not for one individual like the pastor, but for the good of all. They are not addressed to the Church as an organic body (the candlestick), but to its personal constituents, who should all be like so many morning stars (Rev. 2:28; cp. 1 Cor. 15:41).

Laodicean Earthquake

The overthrow of Laodicea by an earthquake (Pliny, *Nat. Hist.* 5.41; Tacitus, *Annals* 14.27) has been cited as bearing on this question of date. But, in the first place, it cannot be shown that the church there was destroyed by the earthquake. Furthermore, the statement of Tacitus is that, having been overthrown by an earthquake, the city recovered from its fall in Nero's reign and regained its former glory by means of its own resources. This corresponds notably with what is said in Revelation 3:17 and shows that the place was in a flourishing condition in the time of Nero. Paul's reference to this church in Colossians 4:16, abundantly refutes all arguments against the early date which are based on the destruction of Laodicea by earthquake.

Jewish persecution

A fair weighing of the arguments thus far adduced shows that they all, excepting the statement of Irenæus, favor the early rather than the later date. The facts appealed to indicate the times before rather than after the destruction of Jerusalem. And this opinion is corroborated by the further consideration that the persecutions of the time proceed from the Jews (Rev. 2:9; 3:9). We know that the persecutions of the apostolic age came chiefly through Jewish instigation and even at the time of Polycarp, we read in Eusebius (*Eccl. Hist.* 4:15) that the Christian martyr's death was secured by the fierce zeal of the Jewish population.

Standing temple

The mention, in Revelation 11:1–3, of the temple, the altar, and the court and the mystical designation, in verse 8, of "the great city, which spiritually is called Sodom and Egypt, where also their Lord was crucified," implies that the city and temple of Jerusalem were not yet overthrown. It is singularly futile to plead that these expressions are symbolical. For, whatever the mystical significance, the whole manner of statement supposes such a knowledge of the temple and the altar as would be unnatural and out of place if in fact the city and temple were then in ruins. But, on the other hand, if these were yet existing and the time of their utter demolition was near at hand, the allusions would be most natural and impressive.

Events proximity

The early date is further supported by the emphatic statement, placed in the very title of the book and repeated in various forms again and again: that the revelation was of "things which must shortly come to pass," and the time of which was near at hand (Rev. 1:1, 3; 22:6, 7, 10, 12, 20). If we adopt the early date and the terrible catastrophe of the Apocalypse is understood of the ruin of that great city where the Lord was crucified and on which the Lord himself charged the guilt of all the righteous blood of martyrs from Abel unto Zachariah (Matt. 23:34–37), this prophecy has great force and significance in claiming to foretell things of the near future. The statements are thus seen to be true and appropriate. But it is impossible, without subjecting the language to the most unnatural treatment, to explain these time-allusions as referring to events that were not to take place until centuries after the book was written.

666 cryptogram

Another proof of the early date is found in the mystical number 666 in 13:18. This can be legitimately explained as the number of the name NERO CÆSAR, when written in Hebrew characters (see the exposition *in loco*). This receives additional confirmation in the fact that the book assumes to belong to the period of the sixth king as mentioned in 17:10, ὁ εἰς ἔστιν (*ho eis estin*), "the one that now is." If we follow the most natural method of reckoning the Cæsars and the one which appears in Suetonius and the Sibylline Oracles, we have (1) Julius, (2) Augustus, (3) Tiberius, (4) Caligula, (5) Claudius, (6) Nero. The reign of Nero extended from A.D. 54–68 and somewhere between these dates we may most properly assign the composition of this Apocalypse.

Hebraic langauge

One of the most decisive arguments for the early date is based on the Hebraistic language and style of the author and has been already mentioned in connection with the question of authorship. If the fourth gospel and the Apocalypse are from one writer, the remarkable differences are most naturally explained by supposing the Apocalypse to have been composed many years prior to the gospel. To suppose the contrary is in defiance of all critical observation and experience.

New Testament allusions

There are, finally, several allusions to the Apocalypse in other New Testament writings, which indicate that it must have been one of the earliest written productions of the apostolic times. The contrast of "the Jerusalem that now is and is in bondage with her children," with "the Jerusalem that is above, which is our mother" (Gal. 4:25, 26), sums up in a few words a large portion of the Apocalypse. This may be most easily explained as an allusion to John's well-known visions of the new and heavenly Jerusalem. But it is difficult to suppose that the apocalyptic symbolism was drawn from Paul's brief allegory.

A still more notable allusion appears in Hebrews 12:22–24, which mentions "Mount Zion, the city of the living God, the heavenly Jerusalem, innumerable hosts of angels, the general assembly and church of the firstborn enrolled in heaven and the spirits of just men made perfect." This points to a number of the most familiar pictures of John's Apocalypse. To assume that John borrowed this from the Epistle to the Hebrews would involve a most violent literary judgment. Were it a mere question of citation, or the appropriation of a symbol or of a figure, we might readily believe that the apocalyptic writer borrowed from a New Testament source, as he frequently does from the Old Testament. But in this case it would be making John take the warp and woof of his whole book out of the half dozen expressions found in a single passage of the Epistle to the Hebrews.

Now, there is no contention that Galatians and Hebrews were written before the destruction of Jerusalem. And to say the least, the most natural explanation of the allusions referred to is to suppose that the Apocalypse was already written and that Paul and many others of his day were familiar with its contents. Writers who cite passages from the apostolic fathers to prove the priority of the gospel of John are the last persons in the world who should presume to dispute the obvious priority of the Apocalypse of John to Galatians and Hebrews. For in no case are the alleged quotations of the Gospel more notable or striking than these allusions to the Apocalypse in the New Testament epistles.

3. Recent Critical Theories of the Composition

The unity of the Apocalypse is so apparent and its language and style so uniform, that all schools of critics and interpreters have been, until quite recent times, practically unanimous in admitting its integrity. But since the year 1882, a large number of scholars have essayed to solve the mysteries of the book by a critical analysis and a distribution of its material among a variety of sources.

Daniel Voelter led the way by his work on the *Origin of the Apocalypse* (1882, 2d ed. 1885). He maintained that the present book is the result of a series of redactions. The apostle John (or the presbyter) was the author of the original Revelation, written before A.D. 66, but supplemented by his own hand in subsequent years. The apostle's work underwent several revisions during the first half of the second century. In his *Problem of the Apocalypse* (Freiburg,1893) this writer elaborates his theory with greater fullness, but with some minor modifications. He holds that the entire work, with all the revisions and supplements, is of Christian origin, while most of the recent critics recognize the Apocalypse as a composite of Jewish and Christian elements.[9]

In 1886, Eberhard Vischer published his important essay. In it he thought to show that the Revelation of John is a Jewish apocalypse translated into Greek and worked over with an introduction, some few additions in the body of the work, and a conclusion. This was done by a Christian writer near the close of the first century. Vischer argues that two completely different modes of viewing things run through the entire Apocalypse and that these are so opposite that they cannot be supposed to come from one and the same author.

For example, according to Vischer the vision of the innumerable multitude out of every nation (7:9–17) is opposed to that of the 144,000 out of the tribes of Israel (7:1–8). And the calling Jerusalem "the holy city" in 11:2, is incompatible with the names Sodom and Egypt in verse 8. Aside from the introduction (chs. 1–3) and conclusion (22:6–21), the additions made by the Christian editor appear, however, to be comparatively few. In the entire space of the six chapters (8–13) the following only are attributed to the Christian editor: "in Hebrew "… "and in the Greek he has the name Apollyon" (9:11); "which is called spiritually Sodom and Egypt, where also their Lord was crucified" (11:8); "and of his Christ" (11:15); "and they overcame him because of

---

[9] The theory of Voelter is so fanciful in many of its parts and so minute in its analysis, as to fall by the weight of its own elaborateness. It assumes such a multitude of things which there is now no possibility of proving that one instinctively feels that its author can be no safe guide to trustworthy conclusions.

the blood of the Lamb and because of the word of their testimony and they loved not their life unto death" (12:11); "Jesus" (12:17); "the Lamb that has been slain" (13:8); "if any man hath an ear, let him ear. If any man is for captivity, into captivity he goeth; if any man shall kill with the sword, with the sword must he be killed. Here is the patience and the faith of the saints" (13:9–10).

The hypothesis of Vischer begets distrust by its remarkable simplicity. It outdoes the minute elaborateness of Voelter by an opposite extreme of aiming to show how little the Christian editor has added to the original work. It seems strange that one who took in hand the task of adapting a Jewish apocalypse to a Christian revelation should have confined himself to so few additions. And that he should have retained the parts which this critic believes to be so irreconcilable with the Christian doctrine. Our exposition will show, it is hoped, that all those portions of the book, which are supposed to be peculiarly Jewish, are perfectly compatible with a Jewish Christian authorship. The imagery throughout moves in the line of Old Testament modes of conception and furnishes no doctrine of the Christ, which is not warranted by some corresponding analogy in the gospels. Furthermore, it is exceedingly difficult to believe that a Christian writer, who added the portions, which Vischer assigns him, would have taken it upon himself to record the solemn imprecation of 22:18–19, against any man who should dare add upon or take away from the words of the prophecy of this book.

Weizsäcker, in his *Apostolic Age of the Christian Church*, maintains that the Apocalypse of John is a compilation out of a number of independent prophecies. These are made, not by the apostle, but by some member of his school a short time after his death. Its whole spirit, coloring, and view of the surrounding world make it certain that it all belongs to the first century of our era. Some parts (e.g., 11:1) are earlier than the destruction of the temple (A.D. 70). But other portions (1:9) point rather to the time of Domitian, near the end of the century.

Weizsäcker alleges that the first three chapters and the last two are obviously unsuitable to the main prophecies of the book. And that the three sets of seven symbols (seals, trumpets, and vials) have no natural connection with the subject-matter of these prophecies. The so-called episodes in chapters 7 and 10 are interpolations without any natural relation to the context. And the contents of chapters 17 and 18 have no connection whatever with the seven plagues of chapter 16. The beast from the abyss (11:7) is an unintelligible anticipation of 13:1–2, as is also the form of beast in 12:3. The principal symbols, however, of chapters 11, 12, 13, and 17 are all indicative of historical matters and furnish a clue to the times of the writer. The second beast (13:11–17) cannot be regarded as historical, but is a creation of the writer's imagination.

Against these views of Weizsäcker the following may be fairly affirmed: (1) He unreasonably underrates the unity of scope and plan apparent in the Apocalypse. (2) He indulges in unwarranted assumptions of what the author ought or ought not to have done with his material. (3) He builds too many of his arguments on inferences drawn from doubtful, if not erroneous, interpretations of particular passages. For almost all exegetes acknowledge the unity of the book, and Weizsäcker himself extols the manifest artistic finish as evidence of the author's creative skill and tact. Thus, it is quite insufficient to be told over and over that the visions lack homogeneity, the repetitions are self-contradictory, and the prophecies cannot be fitted into harmony with the plan of the leading sets of symbols. It is scarcely competent for one to declare without qualification what the author ought or ought not to have said touching the three woes referred to in 8:13; 9:12 and 11:14; or touching the arrangement of any of his material.

With other critics Weizsäcker assumes as if it were something clearly settled that the wounded head of 13:3, is Nero slain and that the healing is his supposed return from the dead. He also assumes as a matter of course that the list of seven Cæsars must begin with Augustus, although Suetonius and the Sibylline Oracle begin with Julius (5:12–14). The seven mountains are also quietly assumed to be the *septem colles* of the Latin writers and the woman is the city of Rome, rather than the same great city where the martyrs were slain and the Lord was crucified. In view of the interpretations of these and other passages given in the following pages we need not linger here to argue further against Weizsäcker's hypotheses.

These various theories of the composite structure of the Apocalypse have been taken up, modified, and elaborated by a large number of critics, but no one particular hypothesis has so far succeeded in commanding the general assent of biblical scholars. There are noticeable points of agreement, but no two writers fully agree. Weyland argues for two Jewish apocalypses, both written in Greek, one belonging to the time of Nero, the other to the time of Titus. These were appropriated by a Christian writer in the time of Trajan and wrought into our present book. Pfleiderer supposes two (possibly three) Jewish sources, worked over by two different Christian editors, who interpolated and added a number of passages. Sabatier and his pupil Schoen find, on the contrary, that the groundwork, consisting of chapters 1–11 and the vision of the bowls in 16, is of Christian origin. But the episode in 10:9–11:14, is an interpolation from a Jewish source, as are also 12:1–9,13–17 and chapters 13 and 18.

Friedrich Spitta, in an elaborate volume on the Revelation of John, attempts to show that the three separate visions of the seals, the trumpets, and the vials were originally independent apocalypses. The epistles to the seven churches and the vision of the seals are the work of John Mark, written about A.D. 60. The vision of the trumpets is a Jewish apocalypse of the time of Pompey. That of the vials is another Jewish apocalypse of the time of Caligula. These three, with their related matter, were combined by a Christian compiler about the beginning of the second century and worked out into the plan and order in which the entire book now appears.

C. A. Briggs, in his work *The Messiah of the Apostles*, adopts the documentary theory of the Apocalypse. He argues that the conspicuous unity of the book is due to the skill of the final editor, who combined and arranged in symmetrical form a collection of apocalypses of various dates. He thinks the earliest apocalypse is that of the beasts, now distributed into 10:1b, 2, 8–11; 11:1–13; 12:18; 13; 14:8–13; 18; 19:11–21. Next in order was the apocalypse of the dragon, which now appears in 12:1–17; 20; 21:1–2, 16, 18–21; 22:3–5; 21:3–5.[10] The four apocalypses of the sevens are supposed to have originated in the order of (1) the trumpets, (2) the seals, (3) the bowls, which presuppose both the trumpets and the seals, and (4) the seven epistles, which were the last of the series. These several documents passed through four successive editions, the first of which combined the three separate apocalypses of the seals, the trumpets, and the bowls. The second edition added the seven epistles; the third incorporated the apocalypses of the beasts and the dragon, which perhaps had already been com-

---

[10] Editorial note by Gentry: Briggs actually gives these biblical references and in this order. He does this even though the dragon does not appear in some of them (Rev. 21 and 22), but does appear in others not mentioned (Rev. 13; 16:13). He is arguing for the composite, edited nature of Revelation through four editions. Charles Augustus Briggs, *The Messiah of the Apostles* (New York: Scribner's Sons, 1895), 334.

bined into one work. Then the fourth and final editing must have been done near the end of the first century.

On all these critical theories it is to be observed that their differences are such as are natural to a literary problem of this kind. In any ancient work of a composite character it is not to be expected that critical analysis will be able at once to solve all difficulties or prove to be a task so simple that all critical minds will speedily arrive at one and the same conclusion. We need entertain no hostile prejudice against the hypothesis of compilation and redaction. It is a notable fact that almost all works of this apocalyptic class (all unless it be this Revelation of John and the Shepherd of Hermas) exist under an assumed name and the Greek Daniel, the Book of Enoch, the Apocalypse of Ezra, and the Sibylline Oracles are unquestionably in their present form compilations or modifications of various documents. And it need be no disparagement of the real value of such a production that it has made use of pre-existing material. A writer, inspired or uninspired, may perhaps best accomplish his aim by appropriating and combining various writings which can be made to serve the particular occasion.

But the work of critical analysis may be easily overdone. In the schemes of several of the critics above named, it appears to have been carried to an unwarrantable extreme. No theories of this character can claim high regard which rest conspicuously upon needless conjectures and unreasonable assumptions. Any hypothesis which supposes original documents of diverse authorship and date is bound, above all things, to show in the diverse sources differences of language, style, tone, method, and sentiment. But none of the critics have thus far produced what can be fairly claimed as real examples of incongruity between the different supposed sources. The alleged heterogeneous elements and inconsistencies are imaginary with the critic. In some cases, they arise from a needless, not to say false, interpretation and the varying critical theories suggest more difficulties than they seem able to explain.

We believe that no critic has proven or is able to prove that the Apocalypse is not a Christian work throughout. Its use of Jewish modes of thought and expression no more demand the hypothesis of exclusively Jewish documents than does the Epistle to the Hebrews. A Jewish Christian of the first century could hardly be thought of as incapable of any expression found in this Book of Revelation. It is nothing to the point to show that a Jew might have written much that now appears in this book. The real question is, Whether any portion of it could not have been written by a Jewish Christian? The following exposition will show, we trust, that the work in all its parts is capable of a rational interpretation and that the Domitian date and the Nero legend have occupied far too prominent a place in the critical controversies. If our exposition is correct and defensible, the theories of compilation are both unnecessary and untenable.

4. John in Patmos

John's own testimony is that he "was in the island which is called Patmos on account of the word of God and the testimony of Jesus" (Rev. 1:9). The phrase "on account of the word of God" (διὰ τὸν λόγον του θεου; *dia ton logon tou theou*), according to the well-established usage of διὰ (*dia*) with the accusative, means *for the sake of* the word. It gives the *ground* or *reason* for what is stated. So in chapter 2:3, it is said: "Thou didst endure for my name's sake;" that is, the great objective reason for the endurance in the midst of trials was devotion to the name of Christ. So again in 4:11: "On account of thy will they were and were created;" that is, all things were brought into existence because that was the will of God. The same meaning inheres in this formula in 6:9; 7:15; 12:11,12; 13:14; 18:8, 10, 15; 20:4.[11] Now, according to 1:2, "the word of God and the testimony of Jesus" are no other than this Revelation concerning all things which John saw.

The most obvious meaning, therefore, of verse 9 is that John was in Patmos *for the sake of*, or *on account of*, this Revelation of Jesus Christ. The first and most emphatic thing the writer tells us is that God gave this "revelation" (ἀποκάλυψις, *apokalupsis*) to Jesus and Jesus signified it through his angel unto John, who witnessed it accordingly as God's word and Jesus's testimony (vv. 1–2). It was on this account, not on

---

[11] Whether the reference be expressive of a *consequence* or a *purpose* must be determined from the context or the nature of the case. The examples in 6:9 and 20:4, are commonly cited as proofs of the former. These souls had been *slain* or *beheaded* in consequence of the word of God, etc. But in those passages, as Düsterdieck observes, the determinative expressions slain and beheaded occur and may warrant a construction different from that of 1:9. After the writer so clearly defines in the immediate context what the "word of God and the testimony of Jesus" is, we are not at liberty to give the expressions a different meaning, as that John was in Patmos as a *consequence of his preaching the Gospel*. The exposition which takes διὰ [*dia*] in 1:9, as expressive of purpose, that is, *for the sake* or *purpose of* receiving the word of God, etc., has the strong support of Lücke, De Wette, Bleek, and Düsterdieck.

account of "the tribulation and kingdom and patience" mentioned in the first part of verse 9, that John "was in the island which is called Patmos."

But because John announces himself as a "brother and partaker" in the tribulation of the times, nearly all interpreters have jumped to the conclusion that he must have been in Patmos because of such tribulation. The fact, also, that criminals were banished to that barren island by the Roman emperors has seemed to confirm the tradition that John was dwelling there as an exile when he saw the visions of this Apocalypse. There is certainly nothing improbable in the tradition, but aside from what has been inferred from the single statement of Revelation 1:9, there appears to be no convincing evidence that John was ever an exile in Patmos.

The traditions of the second and third centuries touching the movements of the first apostles are of very little value. Some of them may be true; but none of them are to be accepted as well-attested facts of history. The tradition of John's banishment may be only a specimen of the manner in which a statement like that of Revelation 1:9, was taken up a century after it was written, given a particular meaning, and that meaning propagated without contradiction until it came to be accepted as an unquestionable fact. Aside from this passage there is no more authority for the tradition of John's exile than there is for the statement of Victorinus that he was sent to Patmos to work in a mine; or of Tertullian that he was first plunged into burning oil at Rome and, having suffered no harm, was sent as a captive to Patmos; or of Polycrates that he was a martyr and teacher and also a priest who bore the sacerdotal plate; or of Simeon Metaphrastes that he was shipwrecked off the coast of Ephesus. These and a score of other similar stories illustrate the tendency of early times to take up a word or hint about an apostle and magnify it into a legend. Such legends can have no real value as trustworthy history.

The last reference to John in the Acts of the Apostles is in Revelation 12:2. It is not improbable that after the death of his brother James, there mentioned, John left Jerusalem and proceeded to found Christianity in some of the cities of western Asia. Perhaps one reason why Paul was forbidden of the Spirit to preach in Asia (Acts 16:6) was because John was already on that field. Or possibly John made a journey to Rome, as Tertullian says and was thence banished to Patmos at the time Claudius gave command for all Jews to depart from the imperial city (Acts 18:2). He may have subsequently visited Jerusalem as many times as Paul did.

It is worthy of note that the Muratorian Fragment, a very ancient and important document (A.D. 170), declares that "the blessed apostle Paul, *following the manner of his predecessor John*, wrote in like manner to seven churches expressly by name." This testimony clearly puts John before Paul in writing epistles to the churches and tends to confirm the position taken above that Galatians 4:25–26, is an allusion to John's picture of the heavenly Jerusalem. The apostle John might have been quietly laboring in Smyrna, or in some neighboring parts of Asia Minor, while Paul was at Ephesus. To assume that in such case we must have had some allusion to it in Paul's writings, or in some other New Testament writing, is altogether baseless. The absence of any reference to John in the latter half of the Acts of the Apostles ought to be a sufficient admonition not to presume upon the silence of the New Testament on such matters.

Our object in giving so much space to this question about John's banishment to Patmos is to point out the worthlessness of much that has been written on such matters of little or no importance.[12] Our

---

[12] It is amazing what pages on pages have been written about matters of pure conjecture. Not a few writers on the Apocalypse discuss at great length the question whether John wrote his book while yet in Patmos or after he had returned to Ephesus! Perhaps the best comment one could make on such conjectures would be a travesty somewhat as follows: Assuming that John was in Ephesus when he received his divine call to go to Patmos for the word of God, he probably journeyed on foot to Miletus, over the same route subsequently traveled by the Ephesian elders when they went thither to meet Paul (Acts 20:17). From this place a skillful sailor like the son of Zebedee could row a small boat in less than six hours to the isle of Patmos. Here, in the deep seclusion of the rocky island, he was in visions and revelations of God for forty days and forty nights and was probably supplied with food by ravens, as was Elijah in the wilderness of the Jordan. In that lone spot he first wrote down what he saw; but not satisfied with his first composition, he made a journey to Jerusalem and there revised it. After this he went to his old home in Capernaum and there rewrote the whole book amid the associations of his early life, where he had so often seen the Lord and heard him speak. Then he returned to Asia and published his prophecy first to the church of Philadelphia, probably for the reason that that church alone of all the seven stands without a word of blame in these epistles! Let no one now presume to say that these suppositions are a tissue of worthless and ridiculous conjectures. These conjectures, suppositions, assumptions, fancy-pictures, whatever one

contention is that the question of John's actual residence in Patmos, whether as an exile, or by reason of shipwreck, or otherwise, is of no importance in the exposition of the Apocalypse. But some interpreters seem to think that a whole scheme of exposition might be based upon an inference drawn from such an incidental statement as that of Revelation 1:9 (cf., Alford's *Greek Testament with Notes, in loco*). An impression is made to take the place of proof and often magnified to the neglect of other statements or inferences of equal value. Whether the author of this book went to Patmos as an exile, or for the purpose of receiving this "word of God and testimony of Jesus," ought not to be treated as a question of any serious moment.

One might even go further and maintain that John's being in Patmos may, like Daniel's being "in Shushan the palace, which is in the province of Elam" (Dan. 8:2), have been ideal only. So Ezekiel was "brought in the visions of God to Jerusalem" (Eze. 8:3). John immediately tells us that he was "in spirit," and as the visions he saw of seals, trumpets, beasts, and a woman sitting upon many waters had no external reality in the physical world, so his being in Patmos might be understood as a symbolical expression equivalent to being apart in a lonely desert place.[13]

Whatever, then, the actual facts were, the great divine purpose of John's being in Patmos was to receive this revelation of things then about to come to pass. If he were banished to that desert place be-

---

chooses to call them, are of as much real value as half the hypotheses which are employed in the critical discussions of the Apocalypse. All assumptions of determining the exact time, place, and method of the composition of this book are from their very nature to be regarded with suspicion. And we may venture to add that a considerable part of what has been written in recent years to show the diverse sources out of which the Apocalypse is compiled is of the same fanciful character.

[13] It might indeed be claimed that in a highly wrought apocalyptical composition like this such idealistic method of personal representation is to be presupposed. At the beginning of The Pilgrim's Progress Bunyan writes: "As I walked through the wilderness of this world, I lighted on a certain place where was a den and laid me down in that place to sleep; and as I slept, I dreamed a dream." No well-informed reader ever understood this in its strict realistic import, for in an allegory, "delivered under the similitude of a dream," such formality of statement is part of the art and method of the writer. So, too, in apocalyptical literature, canonical and extra-canonical, the same usage appears.

cause he had made himself obnoxious to the authority of Rome, such fact was but incidental to the great purpose of God thereby effected, namely, the reception of the word of God and the testimony of Jesus Christ which are written in this book.

5. Scope and Plan of the Apocalypse

This remarkable book is the consummation and crown of all the apocalyptical prophecies. Its author has made a most discriminating use of figures, names, and symbols. His imagery belongs to Jewish modes of thought and is appropriated mainly from the Hebrew Scriptures. It is, however, such as a Jewish Christian of the first century might naturally have employed.

The originality of the author is not compromised by such a use of sacred symbols. It takes not from the perfection of the Lord's Prayer that its several petitions had been uttered in many ways before our Lord combined them in the inimitable model, which the churches now possess and use. Originality may be seen in the grouping as well as in the invention of literary material. It is an old saying that "not every collection of straws makes a bird's nest." The highest genius may be displayed in the fresh setting of facts and ideals old as human thought. We feel obliged, in sheer justice, to award this Apocalypse a very high place as a literary composition. It contains the elements of a great epic and every devout reader has been impressed with its sublime imagery as by few other books in the world. Some of the grandest poetry of the Christian ages owes not a little both of its thought and its inspiration to this remarkable prophecy. The language and style are often rough and Hebraistic, but the ideas are of the highest order and the main subject is really the greatest event in human history — the coming and kingdom of the Christ of God.

According to the following exposition, the prophecies of this book are an apocalypse of the fall of Judaism and the rise and triumph of Christianity. The old covenant had "become aged and was nigh unto vanishing away" (Heb. 8:13), but its removal involved a shaking, not only of the earth, but also of the heaven (Heb. 12:26). That transition from the old to the new was an event of unspeakable moment and is depicted as a world-convulsing revolution. The imagery and style of the Old Testament apocalyptists are most appropriately brought into use: sun, moon and stars and the heaven itself, are pictured as collapsing and the crisis of the ages is signaled by voices and thunders and lightnings and earthquake. To insist on a literal interpretation of such imagery is to bring prophecy itself into contempt and ridicule.

In our analysis and exposition we have been guided by the principles of interpretation which have been tested and illustrated in the apocalyptic portions of the Hebrew Scriptures (see *Biblical Apocalyptics*). We thus find that John's Apocalypse is but an enlargement of our Lord's eschatological sermon on the Mount of Olives. It takes up the same line of thought and translates it into the more extended and formal elements of apocalyptic symbolism.

We have endeavored to support our exposition by abundant citation of illustrative analogies from the older scriptures. This shows how the successive revelations depict, in the most perfect harmony with apocalyptic methods, the fearful overthrow of that great city which had become a harlot and the consequent descent from heaven of "the new Jerusalem, made ready as a bride adorned for her husband." The corrupt and outcast Jerusalem, guilty of "all the righteous blood shed on the earth" (Matt. 23:35), is called "Sodom" and "Egypt" and "Babylon" (Rev. 11:8; 17:5). But the heavenly kingdom which shall never be destroyed is appropriately called "the holy city, new Jerusalem" (21:2).

This Apocalypse is not a confused compilation of incongruous fragments. Rather, it is a work of transcendent genius, remarkable for its unity and the admirable symmetry of its arrangement. This is made evident in the following Analytical Outline of its contents.

PART ONE:
THE REVELATION OF THE LAMB (Rev. 1–11)

   a. Title and superscription (1:1–3)
   b. Salutation (1:4–6)
   c. Apocalyptic announcement (1:7–8)

I. **The Epistles to the Seven Churches** (Rev. 1:9–3:22)
   a. Introductory Christophany (1:9–20)
   b. The seven epistles (2:1–3:22)
      1. To the Church in Ephesus (2:1–7)
      2. To the Church in Smyrna (2:8–11)
      3. To the Church in Pergamum (2:12–17)
      4. To the Church in Thyatira (2:18–29)
      5. To the Church in Sardis (3:1–6)
      6. To the Church in Philadelphia (3:7–13)

7. To the Church in Laodicea (3:14–22)

II. The Opening of the Seven Seals (Rev. 4:1–8:1)
    a. The heavenly theophany (4:1–11)
    b. The book with seven Seals (5:1–4)
    c. The Lamb at the throne (5:5–7)
    d. The worship of God and the Lamb (5:8–14)
    e. The opening of the seals (6:1–8:1)
        1. First seal opened: the white horse (6:1–2)
        2. Second seal opened: the red horse (6:3–4)
        3. Third seal opened: the black horse (6:5–6)
        4. Fourth seal opened: the pale horse (6:7–8)
        5. Fifth seal opened: the souls under altar (6:9–11)
        6. Sixth seal opened: the shaking of earth and heavens (6:12–17)
        [[First interlude (7:1–17)
            (1) The sealing of elect Israel (7:1–8)
            (2) The innumerable multitude washed in the blood (7:9–17)]]
        7. Seventh seal opened (8:1)

III. The Sounding of the Seven Trumpets (Rev. 8:2–11:19)
    a. The seven angels (8:2)
    b. The angel with the censer (8:3–6)
    c. The trumpets sounded (8:7–11:19)
        1. First trumpet sounded (earth smitten) (8:7)
        2. Second trumpet sounded (sea smitten) (8:8–9)
        3. Third trumpet sounded (rivers and fountains) (8:10–11)
        4. Fourth trumpet sounded (sun smitten) (8:12)
            [[Eagle makes first announcement of woe (8:13)]]
        5. Fifth trumpet sounded (locust plague) (9:1–11)
            [[Second announcement of woe (9:12)]]
        6. Sixth trumpet sounded (Euphrates armies) (9:13–21)
            [[Second interlude (10:1–11:13)
        (1) The mighty angel from heaven (10:1–7)
        (2) The eating of the little book (10:8–11)
        (3) The measuring of the temple (11:1–2)
        (4) The two witnesses (11:3–13)]]
            [[Announcement of third woe (11:14)]]
        7. Seventh trumpet sounded (the end) (11:15–19)

(1) The kingdom becomes Christ's (11:15)
(2) The song of triumph (11:16–18)
(3) The temple of God in heaven opened (11:19)

PART TWO:
THE REVELATION OF THE BRIDE, THE WIFE OF THE LAMB (Rev. 12–22)

I. The Woman and the Dragon (Rev. 12:1–17)
1. The woman in travail (12:1–2)
2. The great red dragon (12:3–4)
3. The child caught up to God and the woman nourished in the wilderness (12:5–6)
4. The war in heaven (12:7–8)
5. The dragon and his angels cast out (12:9)
6. The consequent joy in heaven (12:10–12)
7. The persecution of the woman and the rest of her seed (12:13–17)

II. The Two Beasts (Rev. 13:1–18)
1. The beast out of the sea (13:1–10)
2. The beast out of the land (13:11–18)

III. A Sevenfold Revelation of Triumph and Judgment (Rev. 14:1–20)
1. The Lamb and his thousands on Mount Zion (14:1–5)
2. The eternal gospel (14:6–7)
3. Fallen Babylon (14:8)
4. The solemn admonition (14:9–12)
5. The blessed dead (14:13)
6. The harvest of the earth (14:14–16)
7. The vintage of judgment (14:17–20)

IV. The Seven Last Plagues (Rev. 15:1–16:20)
a. The seven angels (15:1)
b. The song by the glassy sea (15:2–4)
c. The procession of the angels (15:5–8)
d. The pouring out of the bowls of wrath (16:1–21)
   1. First plague (grievous sores) (16:2)
   2. Second plague (sea turned to blood) (16:3)
   3. Third plague (rivers and fountains turned to blood) (16:4–7)

     4. Fourth plague (sun smitten) (16:8–9)
     5. Fifth plague (throne of beast smitten) (16:10–11)
     6. Sixth plague (Euphrates armies) (16:12–16)
     7. Seventh plague (Babylon doomed) (16:17–21)

V. Babylon, the Great Harlot (Rev. 17:1–19:10)
    1. The vision of the harlot (17:1–6)
    2. The mystery explained (17:7–18)
    3. The angelic proclamation (18:1–3)
    4. The voice from heaven (18:4–8)
    5. The dirges and rejoicing over her fall (18:9–20)
    6. The symbolic act and word of doom (18:21–24)
    7. The heavenly hallelujahs (19:1–8)
      [[Angel's words to John (19:9–10)]]

VI. The Millennial Conflict and Triumph (Rev. 19:11–21:8)
    1. The heavenly conqueror (19:11–16)
    2. The great supper of sacrifice (19:17–18)
    3. The beast and false prophet destroyed (19:19–21)
    4. Satan chained and in pison (20:1–3)
    5. The millennial reign and final overthrow of satan (20:4–10)
    6. The final judgment (20:11–15)
    7. The New Heaven, new Earth and new Jerusalem (21:1–8)

VII. Jerusalem, the Glorious Bride (Rev. 21:9–22:5)
    1. The vision of new Jerusalem (21:9–14)
    2. Measure of city and walls (21:15–17)
    3. Materials of its structure (21:18–21)
    4. Its temple and its light (21:22–23)
    5. Character of its inhabitants (21:24–27)
    6. River and trees of life (22:1–2)
    7. Eternal reign in glory (22:3–5)

Conclusion (Rev. 22:6–21)
    1. Angel's testimony (22:6–7)
    2. John and the Angel (22:8–9)
    3. Solemn admonition (22:10–15)
    4. Jesus' personal testimony (22:16)
    5. The great invitation (22:17)
    6. The prophetic testimony of warning (22:18–20)

7. The Benediction (22:21)

PART ONE:
THE REVELATION OF THE LAMB (Rev. 1–11)

Chapter 1
REVELATION'S OPENING
(Rev. 1:1–8)

1. Title and Superscription (1:1–3)

1 The Revelation of Jesus Christ, which God gave him to show unto his servants, even the things which must shortly come to pass: and he sent and signified it by his angel unto his servant John;
2 who bare witness of the word of God and of the testimony of Jesus Christ, even of all things that he saw.
3 Blessed is he that readeth and they that hear the words of the prophecy and keep the things which are written therein: for the time is at hand.

The first three verses of this book serve the purpose of a title and a superscription. They declare the divine source and object of the revelation and pronounce a blessing on both reader and hearers. We are emphatically told at the outset that this is a **Revelation of Jesus Christ** (1:1). This means, as the context shows, a revelation made known by Jesus Christ. It is not to be explained as a genitive of the object — a revelation concerning Jesus, or belonging to him as a peculiar possession; but a genitive of the subject. For Jesus is "the faithful witness" (v. 5), who made the revelation known to John and through him to the churches.

The original source of this, as of all heavenly revelations, is **God** himself (ὁ θεός, *ho theos*) (1:1). He gave it to Jesus Christ (as John 7:16–17 and 17:7–8, affirm) and Jesus in turn **sent and signified it by his angel unto his servant John**. It was designed to show unto all his servants (that is, servants of Jesus Christ), as well as unto John, the **things which must shortly come to pass**. So John reckoned himself as a fellow-servant along with all who love and worship God and keep his commandments (cp. v. 9 and 22:9). The word *signified* (ἐσήμανεν, *esēmanen*) suggests that this heavenly revelation was communicated through signs and symbols and how God sent and symbolized it is indicated in chapters 5–10. There the sealed book of divine mysteries, seen on the hand of God, is taken by the Lamb. And the seals having been all opened by him, it is given as a little book to John and eaten by him so as to become a word of prophecy to many peoples. **His angel** should here be understood as the angel of Jesus Christ. The particular reference is to the strong angel out of whose hand John took the opened book, as recorded in Revelation 10:8–10.

The subject-matter of the Apocalypse is here said to be **things which must shortly come to pass** (1:1). The word "must" (δει, *dei*) indicates the writer's profound conception of the divine order of the world. The God who rules earth and heaven sees the end from the beginning, determines the times and seasons (Acts 1:7), and secures unfailingly those things which are necessary to the fulfillment of his purposes in the kingdoms of men.

The "things" thus destined to come to pass soon after the composition of this book were in substance the same as those of which Jesus discoursed on the Mount of Olives and which are written in Matthew 24, Mark 13, and Luke 21. They concerned the approaching end of that age, the overthrow of Jerusalem, and with it the old covenant of Mount Sinai, and the coming of the kingdom which is to break in pieces and consume all other kingdoms and never to be destroyed (Dan. 2:44). It was necessary that these things "shortly come to pass," for Jesus had repeatedly declared that the consummation of that age and his coming in his kingdom would take place before that generation passed away (Matt. 16:28; 24:34).

It is next added that this servant John **witnessed the word of God and the testimony of Jesus Christ** (1:2). The aorist tense here used suggests that this title and superscription were written, in the manner of a preface, after the rest of the book was completed. For the moment John contemplates the assembly listening to the reading of the words of the prophecy. To his own mind the entire revelation lies in a definite past and he puts on record the fact that he witnessed, that is, bore testimony to **what he saw**.

The command of verse 19 to write what he saw was strictly obeyed and the book of this revelation is the result and is here spoken of as already completed. The "word of God" (1:2) is here to be understood of this revelation, considered as a word of prophecy originating with God as stated in verse 1; and "the testimony of Jesus Christ" is the same "word of God" as made known by him who in verse 5 is called "the faithful witness." It is the same word and testimony as in verse 9, for the sake of which John was in Patmos and which are thought and spoken of as whatsoever **things he saw** (ὅσα εἶδεν, *hosa eiden*) (1:2).

The mention of **he who reads and those who hear** (1:3) contemplates a public reading and a devout assembly. For **the words of the**

prophecy are here commended as a genuine revelation from God, to be as much heeded as any book of inspired prophecy. "The words of the prophecy of this book" (22:10) do not only furnish a series of wonderful visions, which one may profitably meditate and keep in his heart (cp. Dan. 7:28). Rather they are also full of command, exhortation, rebuke, and warning. And, therefore, the original readers and hearers and those of all time, may **well keep the things which are written therein**.

One immediate motive for observing the words herein written was that **the time was at hand** (1:3). These words, like those of verse 1 and chapter 22:6, 10, 12, 20, declare the imminence of the events predicted in this book. The impending ruin of Judaism and its city and temple was but a few years in the future when John wrote. That world-historical catastrophe was on the one hand a judging and avenging of the blood of the martyrs (Rev. 6:10; 11:18; Matt. 23:31–36). On the other it was a signal that the new word of Jehovah, the gospel of the kingdom, should thenceforth proceed from Jerusalem, untrammeled by the bonds of a local cultus. It will grow until the kingdoms of the world become the possession of Jehovah and his Christ (Rev. 11:15; cp. Psa. 2:8; 1 Cor. 15:25).

2. Salutation (1:4–6)

4 John to the seven churches which are in Asia: Grace to you and peace, from him who is and who was and who is to come; and from the seven Spirits which are before his throne;

5 and from Jesus Christ, who is the faithful witness, the firstborn of the dead and the ruler of the kings of the earth. Unto him that loveth us and loosed us from our sins by his blood;

6 and he made us to be a kingdom, to be priests unto his God and Father; to him be the glory and the dominion for ever and ever. Amen.

The superscription of Revelation 1:1–3 is of the nature of a short preface, or, perhaps, a title-page. After the writer addresses himself to the seven churches of Asia after the manner of an epistolary salutation, he calls himself simply **John** (1:4); in verse 9, "I John" and so again in 22:8. No other John known to the early Church could have announced himself thus so well as the great apostle. Trench writes:

> We instinctively feel that for anyone else there would have been an affectation of simplicity, concealing a most real arrogance, in the very plainness of the title, in the assumption that thus to mention himself

was sufficient to insure his recognition, or that he had a right to appropriate this name in so absolute a manner to himself.[1]

The **Asia** in which the seven churches were located was what is commonly called "proconsular Asia," consisting of the provinces of Mysia, Lydia, Caria, and Phrygia. In these regions ancient tradition places the later life and ministry of the apostle John. There appears no good reason to doubt that, after the martyrdom of his brother James, which was so "pleasing to the Jews" (Acts 12:2–3), he left Jerusalem and repaired to the western part of Asia Minor. It is not improbable that he was the founder of most, if not all, the churches named in verse 11.

The salutation of **grace to you and peace** (1:4) is the same as that of the Pauline epistles (see Rom. 1:7; 1 Cor. 1:3; Gal. 1:3; Eph. 1:2). But the divine source of these mercies is immediately designated in terms peculiar to this Apocalypse. They are from the Eternal One, from the Seven Spirits, and from Jesus Christ. This mention of a trinal fountain of grace and peace should be compared with Matthew 28:19 and 2 Corinthians 13:13.

The one **who is and who was and who is to come** (1:4) is "the God" of verse 1 and "the God and Father" of verse 6. The "seven Spirits" are but an apocalyptic designation of the Spirit who speaks to the churches in chapters 2:7,11,17, etc. The threefold designation of God the Father is an allusion to Exodus 3:14, where God says to Moses that his name is I AM HE WHO IS. This free appropriation and expansion of the words as a proper name may account for the violation of grammar noticeable in the Greek text (ἀπὸ ὁ ὤν, *apo ho ōn*). He is the God who is "from eternity unto eternity" (Psa. 90:2), the ever-living One. But the future manifestation of his being is noticeably represented by the word ἐρχόμενος (*erchomenos*) the one "who is to come," rather than ἐσόμενος (*esomenos*) who "is to be." For the God who is revealed in this Apocalypse is the one who comes in judgment, continually carries on his plan of world dominion, and completes his covenants of promise.

The **seven Spirits** (1:4) are mentioned next, in order to leave the third place for the name, which is also to receive a threefold designation. The Holy Spirit is appropriately given this symbolic title in allusion apparently to the apocalyptic "seven eyes of Jehovah which run to and fro through the whole earth" (Zech. 4:10; cp. Rev. 5:6). The Spirit is manifold in his gifts and operations (1 Cor. 12:4) and the words which

---

[1] Trench, *Commentary on the Epistles to the Seven Churches in Asia*, *in loco*.

are before his throne suggest the teaching of John 15:26, concerning "the Spirit of truth that goeth forth from the Father."

The name of **Jesus Christ** (1:5) is brought in last for the purpose of a special emphasis and because the doxology with which the salutation closes is to be directed conspicuously to him. He is here called **the faithful witness**, the words being appropriated from Psalm 89:37 [38], where the seed of David is said to continue forever, established as the moon, "even a faithful witness in the sky." Christ came into the world to bear witness to the truth (John 18:37) and all the trustworthy testimony which we possess touching God and life and immortality is through him.

He is also the **firstborn of the dead** (1:5) and so has been "declared to be the Son of God in power" (Rom. 1:4). Paul saw the fulfillment of Psalm 2:7, in the resurrection and enthronement of Jesus (Acts 13:33) and in Colossians 1:18, he employs the expression "firstborn from the dead." But in this book the apocalyptist probably uses the word "firstborn" as the chief representative and lord of such as live and reign with Christ in glory (Rev. 20:4, 6; 22:5). He was himself dead, but he says in verse 18, "I am alive for the ages of the ages and I have the keys of death and of Hades."

As "the faithful witness" he is "the truth," and as "firstborn of the dead" he is "the life" (cp. John 14:6). Having himself "been made perfect, he became unto all them that obey him the author of salvation eternal" (Heb. 5:9).

The third title ascribed to him is **Ruler** (or "Prince") **of the kings of the earth** (1:5). The manifest appropriation of the language of Psalm 2:2 and 89:27 implies a recognition of him as the Messiah, the anointed king of Zion, "highest of the kings of the earth." Compare his titles, "King of kings and Lord of lords," in chapters 17:14 and 19:16.

The threefold designation of Jesus Christ prompts many a thought of the unspeakable riches of his grace. It naturally leads the writer to conclude his salutation with a doxology, ascribing **the glory and the dominion** (1:6) through *all the ages* to come (**forever and ever**), unto **him who loves us and loosed us from our sins in his blood** (1:5). Observe that the word "loves" is in the present and "loosed" is aorist. The one points to the continual love which abides as a blessed experience, the other points back to the one great blood-atoning sacrifice for sin by which he "has perfected forever them that are sanctified" (Heb. 10:10, 14).

At the beginning of the sixth verse the writer turns from the participial construction with which he began his doxology and, after the Hebraistic manner so often noticeable in this book, proceeds: **And he made us (to be) a kingdom, priests unto his God and Father** (1:6). This second clause is in apposition with the first and the sentiment is appropriated from Exodus 19:6. There God promises Israel that they shall be a peculiar treasure to him above all people and says, "Ye shall be unto me a kingdom of priests and a holy nation." John here conceives the promise as good as fulfilled, for the revelation of Jesus, communicated to him and the churches, has already assured him of all this. For he has heard "great voices in heaven" saying that Jehovah and his Christ have taken possession of the kingdom of the world (Rev. 11:15; cp. 1 Pet. 2:9) and his saints, made like himself to be both kings and priests, rule over the nations (Rev. 2:26; 3:21; 5:10). Thus the members of this kingdom all become like Melchizedek, uniting the offices of royalty and priesthood. They live and reign with Christ unto the glory of *his God and Father* (1:6), who is also the God and Father of them all. Compare John 20:17 and Revelation 21:3, 7.

3. Apocalyptic Announcement (1:7–8)

7 Behold, he cometh with the clouds; and every eye shall see him and they who pierced him; and all the tribes of the earth shall mourn over him. Yea, Amen.

8 I am the Alpha and the Omega, saith the Lord God, who is and who was and who is to come, the Almighty.

These two verses contain, first, a solemn declaration of the great theme of the book and second, a confirmation of it as a sure word of God. In this twofold aspect the whole announcement follows the style of Old Testament prophets who associate with their oracles the assurance that Jehovah himself is the real speaker. It was the word of Jehovah coming vividly to Ezekiel that enabled him to look into the opened heavens and see the visions of God (Eze. 1:1, 3–4). Amos' announcement that "Jehovah will roar out of Zion and wither the top of Carmel" is immediately followed by "thus saith Jehovah" (Amos 1:2–3; cp. 4:12, 13; Joel 3:16–17; Zeph. 1:1, 2).

The language of verse 7 is in substance identical with that of Jesus in Matthew 24:30: "Then shall appear the sign of the Son of man and then shall all the tribes of the land wail and they shall see the Son of man coming on the clouds of heaven with power and much glory." The image is repeated in Revelation 14:14, but is no more to be understood of a visible phenomenon in the world of sense than is the coming of Jehovah on a swift cloud to destroy Egyptian idolatry, as prophesied in Isaiah 19:1. The emotional style conspicuous in the words **Behold, he cometh with the clouds** (1:7), shows that the writer is in the element of spiritual vision. It betrays a total misconception of apocalyptics to insist that this language can only mean that Christ is to come on a material cloud and display his bodily presence to all men in the world at one moment of time. Such a conception involves a manifest physical absurdity.

The coming is to be understood as we understand Micah 1:3–4: "Behold, Jehovah cometh forth out of his place and he will come down and tread upon the high places of the land; and the mountains shall melt under him." So, too, in Psalm 18:9–11, Jehovah is described as bowing the heavens and coming down, making the thick clouds a pavilion and flying on the wings of the wind.

The language of Revelation 1:7, as well as Matthew 24:30, 26:64, Mark 13:26, and Luke 21:27, is appropriated from Daniel 7:13. And in all these places alike it is to be explained as apocalyptic metaphor and the seeing him by **every eye** must be understood in accord with the same principle of interpretation. The great event and all that it involves from first to last, is conceived as a crisis of ages.

The words **they who pierced him** (1:7) are from Zechariah 12:10. They should here be understood, not so much of the soldiers who nailed Jesus to the cross and pierced his side (cp. John 19:37), as of those Jews upon whom Peter charged the awful crime (Acts 2:23, 36; 5:30) and who had wantonly cried, "His blood be upon us and upon our children" (Matt. 27:25). To the high priests, scribes, and elders who mocked and struck him Jesus himself said, "Hereafter ye shall see the Son of man sitting at the right hand of power and coming on the clouds of heaven" (Matt. 26:64).

The phrase **all the tribes of the land** (1:7) is from Zechariah 12: 12–14. Here as there it has reference to the families of the Jewish people, not to all the nations of the earth. The **mourning** is that of "the great tribulation" of those days of fearful woes when Jerusalem was brought to ruin (Matt. 24:21). It is the long-continued wail of the scattered tribes who wander only to find a grave in foreign lands.

The words **Yea, Amen** (1:7) are best understood as spoken by the Lord himself and in connection with verse 8. The "Yea" is Greek and

"Amen" is its Hebrew equivalent. As the writer combines Greek and Hebrew equivalents in chapter 9:11, so he introduces the statements of verse 8 by a "verily, verily," expressed in each of these two tongues. But coming as they do between the prophetic words of verse 7 and the confirming response of verse 8, they ratify both and give assurance that all these things shall certainly come to pass. In 3:14, the faithful and true witness calls himself THE AMEN.

Revelation 1:8 is the avowed utterance of a **Lord**, (who is) the **God**, the "God and Father" of verse 6 and "the God" of verse 1, who gave this revelation to Jesus Christ to show unto his servants. This is further shown by his calling himself the one **who is and who was and who is to come** (cp. v. 4). He who perpetually exists sees the end from the beginning and so can speak with definite authority and absolute knowledge of things past, present, and to come. All the glorious coming and future of his Messiah's kingdom is seen as in a moment of time. We need not think it strange that he speaks through his prophets of some great events of that reign, which in their development will occupy centuries, as though they were the events of an hour.

He is ὁ παντοκράτωρ (*ho pantocratōr*), the **Almighty**, All-Ruler (1:8). This last word is the Greek equivalent and used in the Septuagint for "Jehovah of hosts" (יהוה צבאות, *Yahweh Tsbaōth*). He calls himself also the Alpha and the Omega, which an ancient gloss has well translated "the beginning and the end." Compare 22:13. The Eternal One is at the beginning and end of all the work of his Messiah. Like the "author and finisher of the faith" in Hebrews 12:2, he is first and last in all the outgrowths of the kingdom of heaven. He created all things and on account of his will they were created (4:11). But he does all these things in and through Christ. Hence the adorable unity, traceable in this book as elsewhere in the New Testament, of Jesus Christ and God. In verse 17, it is the one like unto the Son of man who says, "I am the first and the last."

Chapter 2
THE EPISTLES TO THE SEVEN CHURCHES
(Rev. 1:9–3:22)

1. Introductory Christophany (1:9–20)

9 I John, your brother and partaker with you in the tribulation and kingdom and patience which are in Jesus, was in the isle that is called Patmos, for the word of God and the testimony of Jesus.
10 I was in spirit on the Lord's day and I heard behind me a great voice, as of a trumpet saying,
11 What thou seest, write in a book and send it to the seven churches; unto Ephesus and unto Smyrna and unto Pergamum and unto Thyatira and unto Sardis and unto Philadelphia and unto Laodicea.
12 And I turned to see the voice which spake with me. And having turned I saw seven golden candlesticks;
13 and in the midst of the candlesticks one like unto a son of man, clothed with a garment down to the foot and girt about at the breasts with a golden girdle.
14 And his head and his hair were white as white wool, white as snow; and his eyes were as a flame of fire;
15 and his feet like unto burnished brass, as if it had been refined in a furnace; and his voice as the voice of many waters.
16 And he had in his right hand seven stars: and out of his mouth proceeded a sharp two-edged sword: and his countenance was as the sun shineth in his strength.
17 And when I saw him, I fell at his feet as one dead. And he laid his right hand upon me, saying, Fear not; I am the first and the last and the Living one;
18 and I was dead and behold, I am alive for evermore and I have the keys of death and of Hades.
19 Write therefore the things which thou sawest and the things which are and the things which shall come to pass hereafter;
20 the mystery of the seven stars which thou sawest in my right hand and the seven golden candlesticks. The seven stars are the angels of the seven churches: and the seven candlesticks are seven churches.

As introductory to the epistles to the seven churches, we have first a glorious vision of the Son of man, from whom all the messages proceed. The whole passage readily divides into four parts: (1) John in

Patmos (1:9). (2) Words of the great voice (1:10–11). (3) The vision of Christ (1:12–16). (4) The assuring word to John (1:17–20).

In the expression **I John** (1:9), the writer imitates the style of Daniel (cp. Dan. 7:15; 8:1; 9:2; 10:2; 12:5), the only other biblical writer who employs this form of address. But he takes to himself no special authority as an apostle or a prophet. He is profoundly conscious that he is but a bond slave of Jesus (cp. 1:1) in the communication of these wonderful messages.

He accordingly calls himself **your brother and fellow-partaker in the tribulation and kingdom and patience in Jesus** (1:9). The three words, "tribulation," "kingdom," and "patience" have notable relation to the prophecies of this book. But we need not look for any special significance in the order of the words as here written, nor (as Alford) regard the position of kingdom between the other two words as startling. For verse 6 has already assured us that John conceives the kingdom as good as come. The *tribulation* is the same as that foretold by Jesus in Matthew 24:9. The *kingdom*, although yet to come, was already a mighty power with the disciples of Jesus. They conceived themselves and all who with them were made partakers of the Holy Spirit, as having also "tasted the heavenly gifts and the powers of the age to come" (Heb. 6:5). They were risen with Christ (cp. Eph. 2:6; Col. 3:1) and could be addressed as having already come to Mount Zion and the heavenly Jerusalem (Heb. 12:22).

But the situation was such that they could not expect to enter into the kingdom of God without many tribulations (Acts 14:22) and must meantime run with patience the race set before them (Heb. 12:1). It is unscriptural to maintain that one cannot enter into the kingdom of God and be made a partaker in its heavenly powers and yet speak of its glories and triumphs yet to come. One may be in "tribulation" and in the "kingdom" at one and the same time and this very fact shows the necessity of "patience" and the propriety of placing the word "patience" last in this enumeration.[1]

---

[1] There is much sound sense in the following words of Glasgow: "Those who stickle for a personal coming to Jerusalem in the future are only waiting in weak faith for what stronger faith would teach them that we have already; as the apostate Jews have lingered on for eighteen centuries waiting for the Messiah, not believing that he did indeed come. Personal presence in Jerusalem would not be presence to the saints in all the world. Corporeal visibility to men in the present

The clause **in Jesus** (1:9) qualifies the entire preceding part of the verse. It is only in Jesus Christ, as the personal friend and Saviour, that fraternal fellowship in the tribulation, kingdom, and patience is possible. On the fact and reason of John's being in Patmos, see previous discussion.

I was in spirit (1:10). In the element of visional rapture, in which one obtains revelation of the heavenly mysteries. Compare 4:2; 17:3; 21:10. It involved the conditions of ecstasy (ἔκστασις, *ekstatis*) which fell upon Peter (Acts 10:10) and in which Paul had "visions and revelations of the Lord" (2 Cor. 12:1). Its import is seen by help of the opposite idea expressed in Acts 12:11, "When Peter was in himself" (ἐν ἑαυτω, *en heautō*): that is, when he had recovered his ordinary self-consciousness after the angelic visitation.

In the Lord's day (1:10). This expression has been usually explained as the first day of the week, the day of the Lord's resurrection. We read of this in the Epistle of Barnabas (15:9): "We observe the eighth day in cheerfulness, in which also Jesus rose from the dead." Ignatius, also, in his Epistle to the Magnesians, speaks of "no longer keeping Sabbath, but living κατὰ κυριακήν (*kata kuriakēn*), "according to the Lord's" (day?), in which also our life sprung up through him and his death."

But the critical reader will note that the expressions employed by Barnabas and Ignatius are not identical with this of John and the New Testament phrase for the first day of the week is ἡ μία τῶν σαββάτων (*hē mia tōn sabbaton*) or μία σαββάτου (*mia sabbatou*) (Matt. 28:1; Mark 16:2; Luke 24:1; John 20:1,19; Acts 20:7; 1 Cor. 16:2). But we do have the words ἡ ἡμέρα το κυρίου *(hē hēmera to kuriou)* and ἡμέρα κυρίου (*hēmera kuriou*) as the frequent designation of the day of the Lord's coming (Acts 2:20; 1 Cor. 1:8; 5:5; 2 Cor. 1:14; 1 Thess. 5:2; 2 Thess. 2:2; 2 Pet. 3:10) and this is conspicuously the great theme of this book (see v. 7 and notes thereon). What remarkable difference is there between ἡμέρα κυρίου (*hēmera kuriou*) and κυριακὴ ἡμέρα (*kuriakē*

---

life is a dream, altogether unsanctioned in the New Testament and calculated from age to age to involve feeble believers in disappointment." *The Apocalypse, Translated and Expounded* (Edinburgh,1872), p. 126.

hēmera) that any candid writer should feel called upon to say that the one could not be used as a substitute for the other?[2]

We fail to see how any scheme of apocalyptic interpretation is affected by these words. The great subject of the book is the coming of the Lord to judge his enemies and reward his saints. What difference could it make in the exposition whether John saw his visions on one day of the week rather than another? If he intended to say that his divine ecstasy placed him in the midst of the scenes of the great day of the Lord, we do not see how he could have stated it more emphatically. But if ἐν τῇ κυριακῇ ἡμέρᾳ (*en tē kuriakē hēmera*) merely denotes the day of the week on which he saw the visions, it seems to occupy too prominent a place in the sentence and to receive too much emphasis for such an incidental matter. The only other passage in the New Testament where the word occurs is 1 Corinthians 11:20, in the phrase "Lord's supper" (κυριακὸν δεῖπνον, *kuriakon deipnon*). Will any of those who write so dogmatically on this subject show that the same thought could not have been expressed by τὸ δεῖπνον τοῦ κυρίου (*to deipnon to kuriou*)? Compare the word in Revelation 19:9, 17. The truth is that this whole controversy over the meaning of κυριακή (*kuriakē*) in this passage has no more importance in determining the real meaning of the Apocalypse than the question whether John were corporeally or only in spirit in the isle of Patmos for the sake of this word of God.

Trench very frankly concedes that it is a mistake to suppose "that ἡμέρα κυριακή [*hēmera kuriakē*] was a designation of Sunday already familiar among Christians," although he thinks that "the name had probably its origin here." The plain facts are that the New Testament writers have a well-known phrase to designate the first day of the week. The phrase in question is not so used by them and occurs nowhere else in the New Testament. But its equivalent and closest

---

[2] In Origen's Commentaries on John, *tomus* 10:20 (Migne, *Greek Patrology*, v. 14, col. 372), he discourses on John 2:19, "Destroy this temple and in three days I will raise it up." Here he makes the statement, πᾶς οἶκος Ἰσραὴλ ἐν τῇ μεγάλῃ κυριακῇ ἐγερθήσεται (*pas oikos Israēl en tē megalē kuriakē egerthēsetai*): "the whole house of Israel shall be raised up in the great Lord's (day)." Here certainly κυριακή (*kuriakē*) does not mean the first day of the week. But in the *Teaching of the Apostles* (14:1), the day of meeting to break bread is called κυριακή κυρίου (*kuriakē kuriou*).

parallel, ἡμέρα κυρίου (hēmera kuriou), is of frequent occurrence and everywhere means the day of the Lord's coming, not the day of his resurrection. Since, therefore, this book is not an historical narrative but a record of visions and revelations of God, we incline to regard John's being in Patmos, as well as his being in the "day of the Lord," as a matter of spiritual vision, not of objective reality. In the same manner we understand Daniel's presence in Shushan and by the river Ulai (Dan. 8:2). We do not deny that Daniel may have actually gone to Shushan and John to the island Patmos and that the latter may have seen this vision on a first day of the week and called it "the Lord's day." Yet we think the other interpretation more in harmony with the genius of apocalyptic composition and the purpose of this book.

Adopting this view, we do not, as Alford assumes, render John's language, "I was transported by the Spirit into the day of the Lord's coming." He says nothing about "transportation" either into Patmos or into the day of the Lord. He speaks rather of his visional presence there. He says, I was in Patmos; I was in spirit (not in the Spirit); I was in the Lord's day. To say that, as a matter of visional experience, he was ecstatically in the day of the Lord is as proper and as grammatical as to say that one may "find mercy with the Lord in that day" (2 Tim. 1:18). It would no more be a violence to the language to say that one was in spirit in the wilderness than to say that he "was led in the Spirit in the wilderness" (Luke 4:1). John simply says (not that he was carried away or transported into, but rather) that he was in spirit (that is, visionally) in the Lord's day. He found himself, so to speak, (not coming or going, lifted up or set down, but) in the very midst of visions of the things which were shortly to come to pass. He was visionally in that day as truly as the Lord himself is "glorified in his saints in that day" (2 Thess. 1:10). Compare "So shall the Son of man be in his day" (Luke 17:24).

It is asserted by Alford that "no such rendering would ever have been thought of, nor would it now be worth even a passing mention, were it not that an apocalyptic system has been built upon it." But it is perhaps sufficient to remark that it does not appear to have been first suggested or ever pressed into notice by the exigencies of a system of interpretation. Nor is it conceivable how preterist, historical, or futurist expositor can show it to be more helpful to one scheme than another. With greater sobriety and reason may it be said that the large space given to the discussion of this point is out of all proportion to its importance in any system of interpretation.

Our apology for allowing it so much space in these notes is that it is well, at an early stage of our investigation of this book, to expose the dogmatic air and one-sided partisan pleading which has been the bane of much of the best literature on the Apocalypse. There is little hope of arriving at a trustworthy treatment of such a book of prophecy until men show a willingness to allow due weight to the relative claims of diverse opinions. If one is given to arrogant and reckless assertion on matters of no importance, what confidence can we have in his word or his judgment on matters of fundamental character?

I heard behind me (1:10). No occult meaning is to be sought in the words "behind me." But we recognize an obvious allusion to the phrase as employed in Isaiah 30:21 and Ezekiel 3:12. The great voice came from a point toward which he was not looking; it therefore served to awaken and attract the seer's attention. Many are the great voices mentioned in this book (cp. 5:2, 12; 6:10; 7:2,10; 8:13; 10:3; 11:12,15; 12:10; 14:7, 9, 15, 18; 16:1; 18:2; 19:1,17; 21:3) and they all serve the art and purpose of apocalyptic representation. In most cases we are told from whom the voices proceed, but in this passage it is left indefinite. We might naturally suppose from what immediately follows that it was the voice of the Son of man, but a comparison of 4:1 and what follows there, is not in accord with such a supposition.

The voice was a heavenly call and it seemed to John **great as that of a trumpet** (1:10). Voices, trumpets, angels, and various visional symbols are what may be called the machinery of apocalyptics. The trumpet suggests the signal of a divine revelation or epiphany. Compare Exodus 19:13, 16, 19; Joel 2:1; Matthew 24:31.

What thou seest write (1:11). So he is to be like Daniel, who wrote his dream-visions (Dan. 7:1). The writing is to take the form of a book (βιβλίον, *biblion*) and to be what is called in verse 2 "the word of God and the testimony of Jesus Christ." How this is related to the sealed book of 5:1 and the opened book of 10:2, 8–11, will be interesting to observe in the study of those passages.

The **seven churches** (1:11) call for no extended comment here. The names are those of seven well-known cities of western Asia Minor. And in the absence of any certain information to the contrary, these may be supposed to have all been visited and most of them, perhaps, founded by the writer of this Apocalypse. Those who wish for detailed information concerning Ephesus, Smyrna, and the other cities here named, should consult the large Bible dictionaries under the several names. It has been commonly assumed that these seven were the only churches existing in Proconsular Asia at the time this book was written. Such a supposition is entirely unnecessary and probabilities are against it. Seven seems rather to have been purposely selected in view of the symbolical significance of that number. There is no more reason for assuming that John must have addressed all the existing churches of Proconsular Asia than those of Antioch and Derbe and Lystra, or even those of Corinth and Rome. He writes to whom he is commanded to write and that is all we need know.

The attempts which some have made to determine the exact time and place of John's writing are simply a specimen of exegetical folly. Why should anyone presume to settle such a question when neither the writer himself, nor anyone in a position to know, has put on record one word concerning it? "Whether he wrote it while yet in Patmos, or after he returned to Ephesus," is of no consequence whatever to us now. The vision which John beheld when he **turned to see the voice which spoke with him** (1:12) may be shown in its apocalyptic setting by the following arrangement of its contents:

> Arrangement of the Son of Man Vision (Rev. 1:12–20)
> 1. Seven golden candlesticks (v. 12)
> 2. One like a Son of man (v. 13)
>   (1) Clothed with a garment reaching to the feet (v. 13)
>   (2) Girded with a golden girdle (v. 13)
>   (3) Forehead white as snow (v. 14)
>   (4) Hair white as wool (v. 14)
>   (5) Eyes as a flame of fire (v. 14)
>   (6) Feet like burnished brass (v. 15)
>   (7) Voice like many waters (v. 15)
> 3. Seven stars in his hand (v. 16)
> 4. Sharp sword from his mouth (v. 16)
> 5. Countenance like the sun (v. 16)
> 6. Effect on John (prostration as one dead) (v. 17)
> 7. Words of the Living One (vv. 17–20)
>   (1) Fear not (v. 17)
>   (2) I am the first and the last (v. 17)
>   (3) The Living One (v. 18)
>   (4) Was dead but alive for the ages (v. 18)
>   (5) Hold the keys of death and Hades (v. 18)
>   (6) Write the visions (v. 19)

(7) The mystery of the stars and candlesticks (v. 20)

Such an analytical tabulation of the contents of this vision is perhaps the best comment upon it. The sevenfold forms of statement have no recondite significance that we should seek for some special mystery in each allusion. Rather they altogether serve to impress the grandeur of the Christophany. The seven candlesticks represent the seven churches and the messages about to be given originate with this most godlike Son of man. What could have been more impressive than such a picture of the Living One from whom the faithful testimony and admonitions to the churches come?

One like unto a son of man (1:13–17). It is to be noted that nearly all the details of the picture are taken from Old Testament prophets. The candlesticks recall Zechariah's candlestick, all of gold and seven lamps thereon (Zech. 4:2). The phrase **one like unto a son of man** (1:13) is taken from Daniel 7:13 (cp. also Eze. 1:26). The **clothing and golden girdle** (1:13) are to be compared with Daniel 10:5, Ezekiel 9:2, 3, 11, and Isaiah 11:5. The **hair like wool** (1:14) is from Daniel 7:9 and the flaming eyes and burnished feet from Daniel 10:6 (cp. Eze. 1:7).

The **voice** like the **sound of many waters** (1:15) is appropriated from Ezekiel 1:24, 43:2, and Daniel 10:6. The figure of a **sword going out of his mouth** (1:16) is found in Isaiah 11:4; 49:2 (cp. Heb. 4:12) and the allusion to the **sun shining in his strength** (v. 16) is a reminiscence of Judges 5:31. John's prostration, mentioned in verse 17, was also like that of Ezekiel and Daniel (Eze. 1:28; 3:23; Dan. 8:17). The uplifting words **fear not** (v. 17) are from Daniel 10:12 and the declaration **I am the first and the last** (v. 17) is from Isaiah 41:4, 44:6, 48:12.

All these various parts of the description constitute a composite picture and its majesty is felt only as we contemplate it in the total impression it is designed to make. The author aims to represent this *Son of man* in all the glory in which Daniel beheld the "Ancient of days" (in Dan. 7:9–10) and he freely appropriates from any Old Testament prophet whatever helps to fill up the magnificent outline. When, therefore, interpreters presume to tell us that the girdle was the symbol of his prophetic office (Glasgow) and the white hair the sign of Christ's freedom from sin (Cocceius) and his feet the apostles and ministers of his word (Glasgow), the whole effect of such procedure is to divert attention from the one great purpose of the vision. The different parts simply serve to make up a symmetrical picture. A long flowing robe appropriately has a girdle, but no mystic significance is to be sought in either.

The white head and hair (1:14) are not naturally suggestive of "the beauteous flaxen locks of childhood, thus representing the man Jesus in perpetual youth" (Glasgow). Rather as Daniel 7:9 intimates, they suggest the ancient, the venerable and adorable. The flaming eyes may at once suggest his penetration and intelligence and the sharp sword proceeding from his mouth reminds the biblical student of the Messiah who "shall smite the earth with the rod of his mouth" (Isa. 11:4). Some of these parts have significance when specified separately, as we shall find in some of the messages to the churches. But in this opening Christophany it is better to leave them in their composite relationship and not weaken the grand impression they make as a whole by undue attention to details.

The keys of death and of Hades (1:18). This is an obvious figure for authority over death and the realm of the dead. This glorious Son of man is lord of the citadel, so to speak, where Death seems to reign and he can open and close the gates at will. The gates of this fortress lead to the underworld, the realm of departed souls and over Death and Hades alike this ever-living One has power.

Hence the force of the first words of verse 19: **Write therefore what things thou sawest**. Because the one who **placed his right hand upon** (1:17) John and assured him that he was the arbiter of life and death, is the divine revealer of this Apocalypse. *Therefore* the inspired seer may cast off his sudden fear and with holy confidence write the vision which he has just seen.

The words καὶ ἅ εἰσὶν (*kai ha eisin*) (1:19) what things are, may be understood in two ways: (1) "what things they signify," that is, as explained immediately of the stars and the candlesticks and (2) "what things are now existing," as contrasted with what is to come to pass in the future. On the whole we prefer the latter. For ἅ εἰσὶν (*ha eisin*) followed immediately by καὶ ἅ μέλλει γενέσθαι (*kai ha mellei genesthai*) most naturally means things which now are as distinguished from things which are yet to be. If the writer meant to say "what things thou sawest and what they signify" would he not have used the word σημαίνουσι (*sēmainousi*) (as in Rev. 1:1) rather than εἰσὶν (*eisin*)? As the language now stands, we have the vision itself designated as past, things contemplated in the vision as present, and other things yet to follow after these (cp. 4:1).

As for the mystery of the seven stars (1:20). This verse gives an explanation **of the mystery of the seven stars** and **the candlesticks**. The word "mystery" here means the mystical significance or symbolical meaning of these objects of the vision. The "candlesticks" or "lampstands" (λυχνίας [*luchnias*]; cp. מְנוֹרָה [*minorah*], in Zech. 4:2) are symbols of the churches. As organized bodies of Christian confessors, the churches receive the light of the Lord and reflect the same so as to be the light of the world (cp. Matt. 5:14,16; John 8:12; 9:5).

But a deeper mystery seems to conceal the exact meaning of the seven stars. For, though said to be **angels of the seven churches** (1:20), the import of the word "angels" in such a definition is as difficult to determine as that of **stars**. We reject as unsatisfactory all those explanations which make the angels either messengers, delegates, officers, presbyters, or bishops of the churches. There is no evidence that the word *angel* was ever so employed in the early church. And what especially bears against this view is that the addresses to the several churches are unsuitable for a mere officer, or bishop, or any one individual representative of the church. The responsible and characteristic personnel, embracing the church itself in the main body of its membership, seems to be contemplated in every address to the angel of the church designated. For this reason also we reject the notion that the guardian angel of each particular church is to be understood, for why praise or blame such an angel as personally guilty of the acts of the church itself?

The old view of Andreas and Arethas that the angel of the church is the church itself seems on the whole to be the best supported and in accord with the angel of the altar, the angel of the fire, and the angel of the waters (cp. 14:18; 16:5, 7). The assumption of Alford that "as the *church* is an objective reality, so must the *angel* be, of whatever kind," is a fallacy in apocalyptic interpretation. One might as well maintain that the seals and the trumpets and the bowls of wrath are objective realities. That they have symbolic significance is clear, but that the angels that blow the trumpets have objective reality is as far from the truth as to say that all John's visions had objective reality. To discriminate between the symbol and the thing signified is the task of the interpreter, whose critical judgment should discern what is essentially real and what mere drapery or sign.

The angels of the churches are best explained as an apocalyptic title for the churches, conceived not so much as organized bodies as in the characterizing personal elements and life which distinguish one church from another.[3] So when the Living One says to a church, "I know thy works, thy zeal, thy patience, thy failures, thy poverty and nakedness," the reference is to no one individual, least of all to a bishop or a guardian angel, but to the body of the church itself. Every member of a church so addressed is to feel himself intended and to know that he personally, as well as the whole body associated with him in fellowship, is held in the right hand of him who also holds the keys of death and of Hades.[4] That right hand can lift him up and drive away his fears (1:17) or in righteous judgment remove his candlestick out of its place (2:5).

In passing now to study in detail the messages to the seven churches we note especially the artificial symmetry of form in which they are all cast. Besides the introductory formula, "To the angel of the church write," which is the same in all the epistles, we observe three main divisions in each epistle.

First, the divine source of the message, designated by one or more of the titles of the Son of man already given in the introductory Christophany (1:12–18). The uniform beginning is, "These things saith," virtually the equivalent of the prophetic "Thus saith Jehovah" (cp. Amos 1:3; 2:1; Oba. 1; Zech. 1:4; Mal. 1:2, 9).

Second, the message itself, declaring the speaker's knowledge (οἶδα, *oida*) of the works, character, and condition of the church. With this declaration of knowledge are connected words of praise or blame, admonition or encouragement, according to the condition of each particular church.

Third, the promise to him that overcomes (ὁ νικῶν, *ho nikōn*) associated in each case with the solemn call, "He that hath an ear, let him hear what the Spirit saith unto the churches." In the first three epistles

---

[3] So Düsterdieck: "The angel of the church appears as the living unity of the one organism of the church, which, as it were, in mass clings to the Lord."

[4] Hence the angel of a church is not to be explained as an "ideal reality," or an abstraction of thought, or a personification of the spirit of a community. The word "angel" here, as in analogous passages cited, is a mere apocalyptic title, a symbolical appellative; but it denotes something that is real and conspicuous in each church addressed. "The angel of the church," says Gebhardt, "represents it as a unity, an organized moral person, a living whole, in which one member depends upon and affects the others, in which a definite spirit reigns and by which one church is distinguished from another." *Doctrine of the Apocalypse*, p. 39.

(Ephesus, Smyrna, and Pergamum) these words precede, but in the other four they follow the words of promise.

We also observe a notable correspondence of the contents of these three parts and a striking fitness to each other. The characteristic titles of the Lord who speaks seem to have been chosen with reference to the character of the particular church addressed and the kind of reward promised to the victor.

2. The Seven Epistles (2:1–3:22)
To the Church in Ephesus (2:1–7)
Toiling, enduring, but fallen from her first love

> 1 To the angel of the church in Ephesus write; These things saith he that holdeth the seven stars in his right hand, he that walketh in the midst of the seven golden candlesticks:
> 2 I know thy works and thy toil and patience and that thou canst not bear evil men and didst try them which call themselves apostles and they are not and didst find them false;
> 3 and thou hast patience and didst bear for my name's sake and hast not grown weary.
> 4 But I have this against thee, that thou didst leave thy first love.
> 5 Remember therefore from whence thou art fallen and repent and do the first works; or else I come to thee and will move thy candlestick out of its place, except thou repent.
> 6 But this thou hast, that thou hatest the works of the Nicolaitans, which I also hate.
> 7 He that hath an ear, let him hear what the Spirit saith to the churches. To him that overcometh, to him will I give to eat of the tree of life, which is in the Paradise of God.

The message is from him who **holdeth the stars** and **walketh in the midst** of the candlesticks (2:1; cp. 1:13, 16). In 1:16, the stars were simply "had" in his hand (ἔχων, *echōn*); in 1:20, they were seen "upon" (ἐπί, *epi*) his hand. But here he holds, i.e., "holds fast" or "rules" (κρατῶν, *kratōn*), by his mighty hand (2:1). So, too, in 1:13 he was seen in the midst of the candlesticks, but no motion or activity was noted: here he is "the one who walks" in the midst of the candlesticks. He is a living and active power in the churches, conversant with all that is going on among them.

The contents of the message consist of three main elements: (1) A commendation of the **works**, **toil**, and **patience** of the church (2:2), especially in the trial and conviction of false apostles. (2) Admonition and warning because of leaving their "first love." (3) Their relation to the works of the Nicolaitans. As an example of the evil men, who were too heavy a burden for them to bear, mention is made of **them which call themselves apostles and they are not** (2:2). In what particulars they claimed to be apostles and on what grounds they were proven to be false, we are not told. Compare Paul's words in Acts 20:29–30, to the Ephesian elders about the "grievous wolves," and men of the church "speaking perverse things to draw away the disciples after them."

The **first love** (2:4) from which this church had fallen is to be understood of the first warm affection for Christ which it displayed. There appears to be an allusion to the imagery of Jeremiah 2:2, where Jehovah says of Israel, "I remember thee, the goodness of thy youth, the love of thy espousals."

The notion that such a lapse from the first Christian love and zeal implies a long period after the foundation of the church is altogether untenable. The history of individual churches for nearly two thousand years has shown many an instance of deplorable leaving the first love within less than one year after a most gracious quickening. Paul's epistle to the Galatians ought to silence the partisan pleading which has alleged that this losing of first love by the Ephesians could not have taken place before the end of Nero's reign. Those Galatians, whose first love for Christ was such that they "would, if possible, have plucked out their eyes and given them to" his apostle (Gal. 4:15), fell away from that love so soon that he was obliged to write to them in sorrow, "I marvel that ye are so quickly removing from him that called you in the grace of Christ unto a different gospel" (Gal. 1:6).

Remember ... repent ... do the first works (2:5). The admonition is threefold: "remember," "repent," and "do the first works." The awakening of tender memories leads to repentance and a genuine repentance is evinced by doing the same kind and quality of works as those which displayed the sincerity of the first warm affection. The warning that, in case of failure thus to repent, there would certainly follow a retributive removal of the candlestick itself was but the necessary announcement of him who is emphatically "the faithful witness" (Rev. 1:5).

The Nicolaitans (2:6). These men are only mentioned here, as if their **works** were well known. Their "teaching" is mentioned in verse 15 in connection with that of Balaam, "who taught Balak to cast a stumbling-block before the children of Israel, to eat things sacrificed to idols and to commit fornication." The fact that again in verse 20 "the woman Jezebel" is charged with the same evil teaching and deeds suggests that the names "Nicolaitans," "Balaam," and "Jezebel" are to be understood as symbolical and represent different gradations of one and the same evil.

The church in Ephesus is clear of the evil and commended for hating the works of the Nicolaitans. For in this they have the mind of the Lord who also hates them. But the church in Pergamum had become complicated with the evil and had some who held the "teaching of Balaam" (cf. 2:14) and some who held the teaching of the Nicolaitans (cf. 2:15). That is, the church had different grades of these mischievous teachers, some being more notorious than others. In Thyatira, however, this evil was tolerated by the church and seems to have assumed the boldness of an impious Jezebel, calling for fearful judgment from the Lord.

That the "Nicolaitans" were no heretical sect of this name, as some of the fathers imagined, but that the name is symbolical, may be reasonably concluded from the following considerations.

(1) There is no trustworthy evidence of the existence of a sect of this name. The patristic testimonies from Irenæus downward exhibit a notable vagueness, are in several things self-contradictory, and are evidently based on this passage of the Apocalypse, which they assume to explain. They trace the supposed sect to the Nicolas of Acts 6:5 (apparently for the want of any other person of this name known to the early Church) and report various fanciful stories about the unhappy relations of Nicolas and his wife. The story grows with the lapse of time, until finally Epiphanius says that all the Gnostic sects sprung originally from this same "Nicolas, a proselyte of Antioch." It has been well observed that the patristic knowledge of this sect grew in proportion to the remoteness of the several writers from the times when this Nicolas lived!

(2) The conjunction of Balaamites and Nicolaitans in verses 14 and 15 warrants the inference that if one is a symbolical name so is the other.

(3) The name Nicolaitan (from νικάω [nikaō] and λάος [laos]) is the Greek equivalent of the Hebrew "Balaam" (cf. 2:14),[5] and both alike

---

[5] Balaam may be from בל (bal), "not," or בלע (bal') to "destroy" and עם (yam) "people." If explained as "not the people," it would still suggest hostility to the people, as a foe and an alien. Either derivation sufficiently meets the demands of

denote "destroyer of the people." They correspond as closely as Abaddon and Apollyon in chapter 9:11 and the analogy of that passage in its use of a Greek and Hebrew name of like meaning tends to confirm the view here presented.

(4) But the fact that Balaamites and Jezebelites in these epistles are identical in their teachings and works, as seen by comparison of verses 14 and 20, makes it the more probable that the Nicolaitans are but another class of these same offenders. If this be true, it is easy to trace the obvious gradation of the evildoers in three of these epistles. As dangerous foes of God's people, they are hated in the church of Ephesus; as successors of Balaam, they injure the church of Pergamum, as that ancient soothsayer injured the children of Israel (Num. 31:16). In the church of Thyatira they have become so rooted in the depths of Satan that they are tolerated as an impious harlot, who even claims to be a prophetess.

What hateful evil of the early Church, it may now be asked, is designated by these symbolic names? The answer is furnished both in verses 14 and 20. The eating of things sacrificed to idols and fornication were evils over which the early churches composed of Jews and Gentiles had no little trouble. What Paul writes in Romans 14:15–23 and 1 Corinthians 8:7–13 about eating things sacrificed to idols and his frequent condemning allusions to fornication and other sins of uncleanness (1 Cor. 5:1; 6:13, 18; 2 Cor. 12:21; Gal. 5:19; Eph. 5:3; Col. 3:5; 1 Thess. 4:3–7) is evidence of this. And the first great council of the apostles and elders at Jerusalem was convened to consider matters of this kind.

There were two parties, one stickling over rites and Jewish laws and insisting that the Gentile converts should observe circumcision and other laws of Moses (Acts 15:5). The other contended for greater liberty and argued that the Gentile converts ought not to be brought under the yoke of Judaism. They compromised on four things which were to be enforced as necessary to the peace and prosperity of the Church, two of which were a total abstinence from things sacrificed to idols and from fornication (Acts 15:29). The troubles over these things in churches to which Paul wrote show that the decrees of the Jerusalem council were not everywhere enforced.

---

nominal symbolism.

There were very naturally, as is always the case in such controversies, extremists on both sides. The rigid Jewish party doubtless provoked in many places, like Pergamum and Thyatira, a bold and lawless opposition which carried the liberty for which men like Paul pleaded into impious license. They commanded a following which might well have been likened to Balaam's teaching to cast a stumbling-block before Israel and, in its worst forms, to an idolatry and presumption like that of Jezebel. Such presumptuous libertines may have given the envious Jews occasion to say that Paul's teaching of freedom from the law was responsible for these excesses. And it is notable that "Jews from Asia" excited the multitude against Paul at Jerusalem and cried out, "This is the man that *teacheth all men everywhere against the people and the law*" (Acts 21:28). Such was virtually charging Paul with being a "Nicolaitan" ("foe of the people") in the sense above explained. The charge was a vile slander against Paul, but it may have originated in confounding Paul's real doctrine with the wicked perversion of it in some of the churches of Asia.

To him that overcometh (2:7). This promise is enforced and made quite general by the words which accompany all the promises in the seven epistles: **He that hath an ear, let him hear what the Spirit saith to the churches**. The Spirit is no other than "the seven Spirits which are before the throne" (1:4) and what this universal Spirit here says is not merely for the church of Ephesus, but for all the churches. See more on this at the close of the epistles (3:22). The victor (ὁ νικῶν , *ho nikōn*) in every case is the one who perseveres in all works, toil, patience, conflict, and suffering which the times and situation involve.

He who is faithful to the truth of Christ and maintains his cause unto the end of the struggle, is assured of glorious reward. In this first promise it is the heavenly gift to **eat of the tree of life, which is in the Paradise of God** (2:7). This is a manifest allusion to the tree of life in the garden of Eden as mentioned in Genesis 2:9; 3:22–24. The lost Paradise and its tree of life are to be restored and these Christian victors are to eat of that heavenly fruit. In the New Testament, Paradise is the name of the heavenly abode of disembodied spirits (Luke 22:43; 2 Cor. 12:2, 4). Compare also what is said in chapter 22:2, of the river and "the tree of life, bearing twelve fruits, yielding its fruit every month: and the leaves of the tree were for the healing of the nations."

In studying the symmetry and inner congruity of the several parts of this first epistle of the seven we observe:

1. The propriety of designating Christ in this first epistle by the first and most conspicuous fact which arrested the eye of the seer, his position in the midst of the seven candlesticks and his hold upon the seven stars.
2. He who holds fast and has all power over the seven stars takes occasion in this first address to say how thoroughly he knows all that is good and bad in the personnel of the church. By walking in the midst of the candlesticks and observing all that occurs among them, he will be sure to remove out of its place the candlestick whose representative stars persistently offend.
3. Paradise and the tree of life are a most fitting reward for those who, by toil and patience and doing the first works, recover and retain their first love unto the end. Such will find Paradise restored; they "wash their robes, that they may have the authority over the tree of life" (22:14).

To the Church in Smyrna (2:8–11)
The martyr church

> 8 And to the angel of the church in Smyrna write; These things saith the first and the last, which was dead and lived again:
> 9 I know thy tribulation and thy poverty (but thou art rich) and the blasphemy of them who say they are Jews and they are not, but are a synagogue of Satan.
> 10 Fear not the things which thou art about to suffer: behold, the devil is about to cast some of you into prison, that ye may be tried; and ye shall have tribulation ten days. Be thou faithful unto death and I will give thee the crown of life.
> 11 He that hath an ear, let him hear what the Spirit saith to the churches. He that overcometh shall not be hurt of the second death.

The message to this church comes from Him who is **the first and the last, which was dead and lived again** (2:8). These are titles which he gave himself in 1:17–18, when he laid his right hand upon John and said, "Fear not."

This church is noted for: (1) its **tribulation** and **poverty** (2:9); (2) the **blasphemy by those who say they are Jews and are not, but are a synagogue of Satan** (2:9); and (3) its encouragement in view of imprisonment and bitter trials in the near future (2:10). A part of their affliction may have been the poverty resulting from violent spoiling of their possessions (cp. Heb. 10:34). But they are cheered with the reminder that in spite of such poverty they were truly rich in heavenly treasure, "the crown of life" (2:10; cp. Matt. 5:10–12; 6:20; 2 Cor. 6:10).

The blasphemy of them who say they are Jews (2:9) is to be understood of the calumnious and bitter opposition of fanatical Jews. Those not only at Smyrna, but in all the provinces, were the leaders in the violent persecutions of the Christians (see Acts 13:50; 14:2, 5, 19; 17:5; 21:27; 23:12; 24:5–10; 1 Thess. 2:14–16). Even the martyrdom of Polycarp at Smyrna, a generation later, was distinguished by the fierce zeal with which the excited Jewish calumniators urged it on. Such Jews were unworthy of the name.

Bitterness so malevolent is conspicuously of the devil and hence instead of representing a synagogue of God they are appropriately called a "synagogue of Satan" (2:9). We may well compare "the throne of Satan" in verse 13 and "the depths of Satan" in verse 24. We should note, too, that it is the devil who is about to cast into prison some of the church of Smyrna, so that, thus early in the book, "the old serpent who is called the Devil and Satan" (cp. 12:9; 20:2) appears as the great author of persecutions. The false and unworthy Jews are here his agents, as, at a later stage of the Apocalypse, other agencies appear as instigated and possessed by his infernal genius.

The **ten days** (2:10) are to be taken as a symbolical number, as indicating a limited period of time (cp. Matt. 24:22; Dan. 1:12,14; Gen. 24:55). The exhortation to be **faithful unto death** (2:10) implies in this connection more than fidelity until the time of death; it involves the idea of a martyr's death. Be thou continuously faithful even though that faithfulness subject thee to death. Compare the phrase "unto death" in 12:11 and Acts 22:4. Such a death leads to a crowned life beyond. Compare James 1:12; 1 Peter 5:4; 2 Timothy 4:8. The **crown** (2:10) is that of both victory and royalty.

The single promise to this martyr church is that **he that overcometh shall not be hurt of the second death** (2:11). It is a notable feature of all the promises to the victors, made in these seven epistles, that they anticipate by their allusions the subsequent revelations of this book. Hence the probability that the epistles to the seven churches were written after the prophet had completed the subsequent portions of his Apocalypse. The seven epistles, therefore, are of the nature of an introduction prepared after all the visions and revelations had been fully formulated by the author.

The "second death" is next mentioned in connection with the picture of the enthroned martyrs in 20:4-6: "over them the second death has no power." Their martyrdom leads to heavenly life and enthronement, so that they have a blessed resurrection by reason of their fidelity unto death. As such a resurrection is a second life, so "the lake of fire" a second death. The expression "second death" occurs in the Targum of Onkelos and also in the Jerusalem Targum of Deuteronomy 33:6: "Let Reuben live in eternal life and let him not see the second death." To say, therefore, that one shall not be hurt of the second death is equivalent to saying that with such a one "death shall be no more" (21:4).

In the symmetrical composition of this epistle we observe:

1. How appropriately these words to the martyr church come from the ever-living One, who was dead but lived. It is equivalent to the assurance of John 11:26, that "whosoever liveth and believeth on me shall never die."

2. How appropriately these words "fear not" in verse 10 come from him who laid his right hand upon John and spoke the words recorded in 1:17–18.

3. How appropriate that those who are subjected to great tribulation and trial for Christ's sake and called to die a martyr's death, should be assured of no harm from the second death. Though death seems for a moment to reign over them, much the more gloriously shall they reign in life through Jesus Christ (cp. Rom. 5:17). For them no second death remains, but rather the crown of life, the living and reigning with Christ a thousand years (20:4).

To the Church in Pergamum (2:12–17)
The church near Satan's throne

> 12 And to the angel of the church in Pergamum write;
> 13 These things saith he that hath the sharp two-edged sword: I know where thou dwellest, even where Satan's throne is: and thou holdest fast my name and didst not deny my faith, even in the days of Antipas my witness, my faithful one, who was killed among you, where Satan dwelleth.
> 14 But I have a few things against thee, because thou hast there some that hold the teaching of Balaam, who taught Balak to cast a stumbling-block before the children of Israel, to eat things sacrificed to idols and to commit fornication.

15 So hast thou also some that hold the teaching of the Nicolaitans in like manner.
16 Repent therefore; or else I come to thee quickly and I will make war against them with the sword of my mouth.
17 He that hath an ear, let him hear what the Spirit saith to the churches. To him that overcometh, to him will I give of the hidden manna and I will give him a white stone and upon the stone a new name written, which no one knoweth but he that receiveth it.

To this church the message comes from him **who has the sharp two-edged sword** (2:12). In the vision of 1:16, the sword was seen proceeding out of his mouth. This sharp sword is a symbol of that "sword of the Spirit, which is the word of God" (Eph. 6:17). And in Hebrews 4:12 it is said to be "living and active and sharper than any two-edged sword and piercing even to the dividing of soul and spirit, of both joints and marrow and skillful to judge (κριτικός, *kritikos*) the thoughts and intents of the heart." It is therefore more especially a symbol of conviction and judgment (John 16:8–11). Compare the figure in Isaiah 11:4; 49:2; Hosea 6:5. The Christ who speaks is therefore no other than the divine Judge and Ruler of the world.

The message shows (1) that this church was dwelling **where the throne of Satan** (2:13) is; but (2) was a firm defender of the faith; yet (3) had some Balaamites and Nicolaitans; and therefore (4) is admonished to repent and avert the sword of judgment. The "throne of Satan" is undoubtedly to be understood as some notable stronghold of Satan's power. As another manifestation of Satan was a giving of "his power and his throne and great authority" to the beast out of the sea (13:2), so at Pergamum the great adversary of Christ had in some way established his throne. The fact that the temple and "genuine sanctuary" of Æsculapius was at this place (Tacitus, *Annals* 3:63) may serve at least to suggest that Pergamum was at that time a stronghold of heathenish superstition and idolatry. This fact also helps to account for the pernicious **teaching of Balaam** (2:14) and **of the Nicolaitans** (2:15), which had found some adherents even in the church. To **hold fast** the **name** of Christ and **not deny my faith** (2:13) under such circumstances were high commendation.

We know from Paul's epistles that the church of Corinth was near another throne of Satan. Some in that place were guilty of **eating things sacrificed to idols** and of **fornication** (2:14; 1 Cor. 5:1; 8:1). Such an evil leaven tends to "leaven the whole lump" (1 Cor. 5:6).

As "Balaam" and "Nicolaitan" are symbolic names (see above on v. 6), so we most naturally infer that Antipas is but the mystic name of some one or more faithful witnesses and martyrs of Jesus in that place. The word means "against all,"[6] and may well denote a sufferer like the author of Psalm 22 (vv. 12, 16), around whom the assembly of the wicked formed a circle like so many mad dogs or strong bulls of Bashan. Or like another Jeremiah, who seemed at times to stand alone against a world of evil (Jer.15:10; 20:10). Certain it is that we have no trustworthy account of any early martyr of this name, for the later legends are manifestly fabulous. They are like those of the origin of the Nicolaitans, they have grown out of this word in the Apocalypse and know nothing more than is here written.

The statement of verse 14, that Balaam **taught Balak to cast a stumbling-block before the children of Israel**, accords with the tradition which is recorded in Josephus (*Ant.* 4:6:6). It is also in substance warranted by what is written in Numbers 31:16, compared with Numbers 25:1–2. The teaching of Balaam, as well as that of the Nicolaitans, encouraged loose complicity with idolatrous heathenism. The Balaamites and Nicolaitans, as we have shown above, are best explained as symbolical names of different degrees of the same loose libertinism and freedom with the heathen world. The admonition to **repent** (2:16) is intensified by the threat which follows and is notable for the four words **come, quickly, war**, and **sword**. The whole verse is remarkable as a potent expression of solemn warning.

The promise that follows in 2:17 is also remarkable for its mystic allusions and the correspondence of its symbolism with the situation and conditions of the church in Pergamum. Without detailing the various opinions concerning **the hidden manna, the white stone**, and the **new name** (2:17), we simply observe that the three terms together constitute a trinity of secret gifts. Trench has well admonished us not to look in the realm of heathen customs or in pagan symbolism for our

---

[6] The assertion of Winer (*N. T. Gram.*, §16) and others that Ἀντίπας (*Antipas*) is a contraction from Ἀντίπατρος (*Antipatros*) is of no force in discussing a word which occurs nowhere else in the New Testament and which both the context and the usage of this Apocalypse suggest as a symbolical name. The word is certainly not necessarily a contraction and, if designed as a mystic name, it expresses appropriately the idea of one or a few against many.

explanation and hence not beguile ourselves with the white pebbles of the Greek ballot box or the tessara of the Olympic games.

The **hidden manna** is an allusion to the omer of manna which was deposited as a sacred treasure in the holy of holies in connection with the tables of the law (Exo. 16:32–34). The **white stone** suggests either the pure golden plate on the forefront of the high priest's miter, on which was graven HOLINESS TO JEHOVAH (Exo. 28:36–38), or the URIM AND THUMMIM, which were "put in the breastplate of judgment" and worn "upon the heart" of the high priest (Exo. 28:30). The **new name** is to be compared with 3:12 and 19:12, where it appears to be the symbolic designation of some incommunicable secret known only to Christ and the believing soul. It implies a union and unity with Christ which only he whose life is hidden with Christ in God can know (Col. 3:3–4).

We accordingly understand the threefold allusion of **manna**, **stone** and **name** (2:17) as designed to enhance the thought of the real priesthood of believers (cp. 1:6), to whom "it is given to know the mysteries of the kingdom of heaven" (Matt. 13:11). These victors dwell in the secret place of the Most High. They eat even the treasured manna of the most holy place. They have direct revelations as by the sacred Urim and they know the mysteries of the divine life and the name of their Lord. For that name is in their hearts and they bear the image of the heavenly One (2 Cor. 3:18).

The **new name** (2:17) is a phrase appropriated from Isaiah 62:2 and, like "new song," "new heaven," and "new earth," points to the new kind and quality (καινός, *kainos*) of things which characterize the heavenly kingdom of Christ and of God. Among "the things which must shortly come to pass" (1:1) the Apocalypse gives prominence to the coming down of the "new Jerusalem" to the earth (21:2). For by that glorious coming the Lord will "make all things new" (21:5).

Among the correspondences of this epistle notice:

1. How appropriately the one who has the sharp two-edged sword is represented as making war on evil teachers with the sword of his mouth.

2. He that holds fast the name and faith of Jesus near Satan's throne is appropriately rewarded with the gift of knowing the hidden things of God.

3. The "hidden manna," "white stone," and "new name" suggest a bread of heaven, a prophetic priesthood, and a fellowship with Christ. These would be most inspiring to those who are beset with the snares

and stumbling blocks of a sensual libertinism. Such need and may well desire the gift of prophecy and a knowledge of "all the mysteries and all the gnosis" (1 Cor. 13:2).

To the Church in Thyatira (2:18–29)
The church burdened with Jezebel

> 18 And to the angel of the church in Thyatira write; These things saith the Son of God, who hath his eyes like a flame of fire,
> 19 and his feet are like unto burnished brass: I know thy works and thy love and faith and ministry and patience and that thy last works are more than the first.
> 20 But I have this against thee, that thou sufferest the woman Jezebel, which calleth herself a prophetess; and she teacheth and seduceth my servants to commit fornication and to eat things sacrificed to idols.
> 21 And I gave her time that she should repent; and she willeth not to repent of her fornication.
> 22 Behold, I do cast her into a bed and them that commit adultery with her into great tribulation, except they repent of her works.
> 23 And I will kill her children with death; and all the churches shall know that I am he who searcheth the reins and hearts: and I will give unto each one of you according to your works.
> 24 But to you I say, to the rest that are in Thyatira, as many as have not this teaching, who know not the deep things of Satan, as they say; I cast upon you none other burden.
> 25 Howbeit that which ye have, hold fast till I come.
> 26 And he that overcometh and he that keepeth my works unto the end,
> 27 to him will I give authority over the nations: and he shall rule them with a rod of iron, as the vessels of the potter are broken to shivers;
> 28 as I also have received of my Father: and I will give him the morning star.
> 29 He that hath an ear, let him hear what the Spirit saith to the churches.

Three things distinguish the author of the message to Thyatira: (1) He is called **the Son of God** (2:18); (2) his **eyes** are as **a flame of fire** (v. 18); (3) his **feet** are like **burnished brass** (v. 19; cp. 1:13–15). The title "Son of God," rather than "Son of man," as in 1:13, is designed to remind us of the anointed Son of Jehovah, whose enthronement and world-wide triumphs are celebrated in the second psalm (see especially

Psa. 2:7–9). To this there is obvious reference in verse 27, where see further comment.

The message itself contains three principal declarations: (1) A commendation of the **works, love, faith, ministry, patience,** and increase (πλείονα, *pleiona*) of **good works** (2:19). (2) A statement of the teaching, acts, and doom of **Jezebel** (2:20). (3) A word of encouragement and exhortation to the burdened church (2:19). The chief concern of the exegete is to determine the significance of **the woman Jezebel** (v. 20). The reading "thy wife Jezebel" is now rejected from the leading editions of the Greek Testament (as Tischendorf, Tregelles, and Westcott and Hort, although the last named leaves it in the margin).

The contents of the message show the works, love, faith, ministry and patience (2:19) of **the angel of the church** (2:18) to be on the whole increasingly commendable. These are utterly inconsistent with conjugal union (**to commit fornication**, 2:20) with any woman guilty of the crimes here charged and unwilling to repent. Moreover, as the church itself is always conceived as a bride or a wife, the consort should be represented as a bridegroom or a husband. Accordingly, to speak of the wife of a church is preposterous. The "woman" Jezebel is therefore not to be thought of as having conjugal relation to the church or any of its representatives.

Four things characterize this woman: (1) She **calls herself a prophetess**; (2) she is a seductive teacher; (3) she inculcates and practices **fornication** and eating **things sacrificed to idols** (2:20); (4) she persistently refuses to repent of her foul deeds (2:21). All these facts point to an aggravated form of "the teaching of Balaam" mentioned in verse 14.

Balaam taught Balak to ensnare Israel in sensuality and idolatry, but it does not appear that he himself participated in the sins to which his evil counsels led (Num. 31:16). But Jezebel introduced and vigorously propagated Phoenician idolatry with its abominable sensuality and witchcraft among the children of Israel (1 Kgs. 16:31; 21:25–26; 2 Kgs. 9:22). She was "the daughter of Ethbaal, king of the Zidonians," and, according to Josephus (*Apion* 1:18), her father was not only king but a priest of Astarte. Her marriage with Ahab was a turning point for evil in the history of Israel. Being the daughter of one who was both king and priest, she might naturally call herself a prophetess and feel that her mission was to teach Israel a new religious worship. As for boldness and commanding will-power, Jezebel appears in Old Testament history as the embodiment of all that is terrible in the Clytemnestra of the Greek tragedians and the Lady Macbeth of Shakespeare.

The woman Jezebel is, accordingly, best understood as a symbolic name for powerful heathen influences and customs which beset the church of Thyatira. These formed a controlling tendency toward the foul practices of licentious paganism which were a grievous burden to those who sought to propagate the virtues of the Gospel of Christ. The serious charge against the church of Thyatira was that it had let this woman too much alone in her seductive teaching. It was virtually tolerating a heathen prophetess and thus allowing her pernicious influences to damage many.

She willeth not to repent (2:21). There was a persistent will power back of the Jezebelite leaven, which refused to forsake the customs of a fascinating heathenism and could only be overcome by the penal visitation of God. The persons guilty of the seductive teaching had time to repent, but would not heed the word of truth. They rejected the decree of Acts 15:29.

Cast her into a bed (2:22). Instead of the bed of sensuality she shall be forcibly "cast into a bed" of pain. There may be an allusion to the casting of Jezebel down under the feet of the horses (cp. 2 Kgs. 9:33). The language and connection show that a severe punishment for her sins is intended. And into a similar **great tribulation** those who **commit adultery with her** are also destined to be **cast**, except they repent of her works.

In the next verse Christ proceeds in the same strain and emphasizes the truth that divine retribution is sure to come to everyone **according to your works** (2:23). The killing of **her children with death** is, perhaps, another allusion to the history of Jezebel in the slaughter of the false prophets and the house of Ahab (cp. 1 Kgs. 18:40; 2 Kgs. 10:11, 25). But the great lesson is that all these offenders must reckon with him "who has his eyes like a flame of fire" (v. 18) and is the supreme judge of every man. The language of this verse is largely appropriated from Jeremiah 17:10; Psalm 7:9; and 62:12.

To the rest (2:24). The reference here is obviously to those **that are in Thyatira** who had not accepted the libertine teaching of Jezebel. They are those who were willing to accept and follow the judgment of the apostles and elders touching things sacrificed to idols and fornication. **The deep things of Satan** has been quite generally understood as a caustic reference to the boasts of the Gnostic heretics that they knew the depths of divine mysteries. Incipient Gnosticism and sorcery, as likely to show themselves in apostolic times, may naturally have pretended to such secret knowledge and sorcerers like Simon of Samaria evidently assumed this much (Acts 8:9–11).

But such pretenders would hardly have claimed "to know the deep things of Satan" (2:24). They assumed to "know the deep things," but the writer in sarcasm adds the words "of Satan," as a condemning judgment of the real nature of their mysteries. And yet he charges this claim on the pretenders by appending the words **as they say**. The reference in the phrase **none other burden** seems best explained by comparison with Acts 15:28, when the apostolic council imposes "no greater burden than those necessary things" on the Gentile churches throughout the world.

What ye have hold fast (2:25), That is, retain in firm grasp all the commendable qualities mentioned above in verse 19. **Til I come**. Which the whole trend and teaching of the book represents as an event near at hand. Compare 3:11.

The promise to them that overcome in the church of Thyatira is exceptional. For it adds to the usual words, **he that overcometh**, the words **and he that keepeth my works unto the end** (2:26). The conjunction "and" which introduces the words of promise is also exceptional. It so links the promise to the exhortation of verse 25 as to show that "he that keepeth my works" (contrast "her works," v. 22) **unto the end** is equivalent to "hold fast till I come" (v. 25).

The promise itself includes three things, (1) **authority over the nations**, (2) ruling **them with a rod of iron**, and (3) the gift of **the morning star** (2:27–28). The first two are allusions to the Messianic ideals of the second Psalm, especially verses 7–9. **The morning star** is, according to 22:16, a title of Jesus himself. There is no more impropriety in his saying that he will give himself as a bright light than that he will give his spirit to others. He is the morning star of a new era in the history of humanity and all who, filled with his light and wisdom, let their light shine, become like him the light of the world (Matt. 5:14–16; cp. John 8:12; 12:46).

The promise therefore in substance means that they who overcome shall be identified with the Lord in his kingdom and glory. They shall reign with him and shall be like him. Compare Romans 5:17; 8:17; 2 Timothy 2:12; Colossians 3:4; 1 John 3:2. This same ideal of triumph and glory appears again in Revelation 3:21; 12:5; 20:4. Compare also Matthew 19:28 and Luke 22:29–30.

We observe among the notable correspondences of this message to Thyatira:
1. How appropriately the title "Son of God" stands at the head of a letter in which occur such direct allusions to the enthroned Messiah as portrayed in Psalm 2:7, 12.
2. "He who has eyes like a flame of fire" is a judge who will thoroughly "search the reins and hearts."
3. "His feet like burnished brass" suggest the terrible power with which he will tread down "in death" the impudent Jezebel and her children who do not "repent of her works" (cp. 2 Kgs. 9:33).
4. He who triumphs over the guile and tyranny of such a Jezebel may well reign in authority with the Messianic Son of God and become bimself a "morning star."

To the Church in Sardis (3:1–6)
The nominal but dead church

> 1 And to the angel of the church in Sardis write; These things saith he that hath the seven Spirits of God and the seven stars: I know thy works, that thou hast a name that thou livest and thou art dead.
> 2 Be thou watchful and stablish the things that remain, which were ready to die: for I have found no works of thine perfected before my God.
> 3 Remember therefore how thou hast received and didst hear; and keep it and repent. If therefore thou shalt not watch, I will come as a thief and thou shalt not know what hour I will come upon thee.
> 4 But thou hast a few names in Sardis which did not defile their garments: and they shall walk with me in white; for they are worthy.
> 5 He that overcometh shall thus be arrayed in white garments; and I will in no wise blot his name out of the book of life and I will confess his name before my Father and before his angels.
> 6 He that hath an ear, let him hear what the Spirit saith to the churches.

The message to this church is from him who **hath the seven Spirits of God and the seven stars** (3:1). These "seven Spirits" are the same which in 1:4, are said to be "before the throne;" in 4:5, they appear as "seven lamps of fire burning before the throne," and in 5:6, as "seven eyes sent forth into all the earth." These are all so many different apocalyptic conceptions of the one Holy Spirit, proceeding from God and Christ, whose operations are defined profoundly in John 16:7–14. The Christ possesses this sevenfold Spirit in all fullness (John 3:34; Col. 1:19) and hence all spiritual life and activity in the churches must proceed from this divine source. He accordingly has also "the seven stars" (cp. 1:16). Holding them in his right hand, he searches them through and through as by the light of so many lamps of fire and with the intelligence of so many watchful eyes. Nothing, therefore, in the personnel of the churches can escape his gaze and his judgment. Compare note on 1:20.

The message itself is a notable mixture of severe judgment, warning, exhortation, and promise. Christ levies several charges against the church: (1) It is nominally alive but **thou art dead** (3:1). (2) It has some **things that remain** (τὰ λοιπά, *ta loipa*) but that were **ready to die** (3:2). (3) It has **no works** complete before God (3:2). Nevertheless, (4) there were a few who **did not defile their garments** and are pronounced **worthy to walk with me** in white (3:4). (5) The others are admonished (a) to **watch** (3:3), (b) to establish what good **remains** (3:2), and (c) to **remember** . . . **how thou hast received and didst hear and keep it and repent** (3:3). (6) In their failure to watch, the Lord **will come as a thief** in an unexpected hour (3:3). This last admonition is to be compared with chapter 16:15 and Matthew 24:43–44; 1 Thessalonians 5:2; 2 Peter 3:10.

In the **how** (πῶς [*pōs*]) of verse 3 we note a vivid reminder of the hearty and joyful manner of their first reception of the Gospel, as contrasted with the spiritual deadness of their present condition (cp. 1 Thess. 1:5–10; Gal. 4:13–15). A notable failure to go on to perfection results in spiritual stagnation. The gravest charge, perhaps, against the church of Sardis is, **I have found no works of thine perfected before my God** (3:2). Nothing had been brought to completion (πεπληρωμένα [*peplērōmena*]). There was such an apathy that any strong conflict with the irreligious world was impossible. There is no trouble at Sardis with Nicolaitans, Balaamites, or Jezebelites; the church itself is but another world.

In Revelation 3:5 the promise to him **that overcometh** is threefold: (1) He shall be arrayed in **white garments**; (2) **his name** shall not be **blotted out of the book of life**; and (3) his name shall be confessed by **My Father and before his angels**. The "white garments" indicate that they are found worthy and "meet to be partakers of the inheritance of the saints in light" (Col. 1:12; cp. Matt. 13:43) and to enter upon the blessedness of heavenly life.

The **book of life** is a familiar biblical figure (cp. Exo. 32:32; Psa. 69:28; Dan. 12:1; Luke 10:20; Phil. 4:3; Heb. 12:23). The words of this promise are to be compared with the mention of "the Lamb's book of life" in Revelation 13:8; 17:8; 20:12, 15; 21:27. The pure and good in the sight of God are conceived as having their names enrolled in a book, like a registry of citizens kept by the proper magistrate. From such rolls the names of deceased citizens are erased. The apocalyptist conceives the names of the true living citizens of heaven as "written in the book of life from the foundation of the world" (17:8).

The words **I will in no wise blot his name out** (3:5) are analogous with "shall not be hurt of the second death" in 2:11 and both passages are to be compared with 20:14–15. The confession **of his name before my Father and before his angels** (3:5) is a thought appropriated from Mark 8:38; Luke 9:26: "If any man serve me, him will the Father honor" (John 12:26; cp. Rom. 2:10; 8:17).

The correspondences between the different parts of this epistle to Sardis are numerous and suggestive:

First, it is appropriate that a dead and dying church should be addressed by him who has the seven Spirits of God. Those lamps of fire (cp. 4:5) illumine the regions of death-shade and have power to revive the dying and the dead.

Second, he who holds the seven stars must be cognizant of everything about them and knows alike the names of the dead, the dying, and the worthy. For the powers of his Spirit are as manifold as the stars.

Third, those who in the midst of such contagion of death keep their garments undefiled (cp. "wash their robes" in 22:14) are fittingly rewarded with white garments and closest fellowship with Christ in heaven.

Fourth, he who has a name to live while he is dead will find no registry of his name in heaven. But he who is bold to confess the name of Jesus before men will have his own name confessed by Jesus before God and the angels of heaven (cp. Matt. 10:32).

To the Church in Philadelphia (3:7–13)
The faithful and stable church

> 7 And to the angel of the church in Philadelphia write; These things saith he that is holy, he that is true, he that hath the key of David, he that openeth and none shall shut and that shutteth and none openeth:
> 8 I know thy works (behold, I have set before thee a door opened, which none can shut) that thou hast little power and didst keep my word and didst not deny my name.
> 9 Behold, I give of the synagogue of Satan, of them who say they are Jews and they are not, but do lie; behold, I will make them to come and worship before thy feet and to know that I have loved thee.
> 10 Because thou didst keep the word of my patience, I also will keep thee from the hour of trial, that hour which is to come upon the whole world, to try them that dwell upon the earth.
> 11 I come quickly: hold fast that which thou hast, that no one take thy crown.
> 12 He that overcometh, I will make him a pillar in the temple of my God and he shall go out thence no more: and I will write upon him the name of my God and the name of the city of my God, the new Jerusalem, which cometh down out of heaven from my God and mine own new name.
> 13 He that hath an ear, let him hear what the Spirit saith to the churches.

The source of this message is (1) **he that is holy**, (2) **he that is true**, and (3) **he that has the key of David** (3:7). These titles are not found in the Christophany of Revelation 1, but the "holy" and the "true" occur again in 6:10 (cp. "faithful and true" in 19:11). And the key of David correlates with "Root of David" in 5:5 and "root and offspring of David" in 22:16. The latter part of the verse is appropriated from Isaiah 22:22 and designates Jesus as the Messiah, the true son and successor of David, who holds the key as the symbol of power and authority.

Thus, the true house of David is perpetuated in the new kingdom of God and "the King of the ages" (15:3), who is "King of kings and Lord of lords" (19:16). He not only inherits "the throne of his father David," but is also destined to "reign over the house of Jacob forever; and of his kingdom there shall be no end" (Luke 1:32–33). He accordingly holds "the keys of the kingdom of heaven" (Matt. 16:19) and has all authority over its administration. His opening and shutting are final and decisive. For, as Trench well observes, "Christ has not so committed the keys of the kingdom of heaven, with the power of binding and loosing, to any other, but that he still retains the highest administration of them in his own hands."

The contents of the epistle to this church are notable for the absence of anything like rebuke or blame. The Lord seems to have found nothing against this church, the only one of the seven to receive such honor. (1) It is first of all distinguished for having set before it a **door opened** (3:8). The Lord has thus made use of the key of David just referred to and opened a door of opportunity for that faithful church to make converts to the new kingdom of God. For the figure of an opened door compare Acts 14:27; 1 Corinthians 16:9; Colossians 4:3. This great and effectual door no enemy of the truth was to close up.

(2) Another fact to be noticed is the statement **thou hast little power** (3:8). This is best explained as equivalent to 1 Corinthians 1:26–28. This church made no show of "many wise after the flesh, many mighty, many noble;" it was not what the world would call a strong and influential church. But (3) Jesus notes its real strength consisted in: thou **didst keep my word**. He further adds that this was in such faithful adherence to the truth that, when put to test, thou **didst not deny my name**.

(4) As a consequence and reward of such unwavering confession, the Lord will bring some of their Jewish enemies to **worship before thy feet and to know that I have loved thee** (3:9). Thus shall be fulfilled in them the prophetic promise of Isaiah 49:23; 40:14; and 43:4. **The synagogue of Satan** has been already mentioned in connection with the church of Smyrna (2:9). But in that case it was only presented as a persecuting power. Here some of that synagogue are made to come and worship along with the faithful servants of him who has the key of David. This shows further what a door is opened at Philadelphia and how Satanic foes are made to come through it and acknowledge and worship Jesus Christ as Lord. Those who thus come and worship meet the condition imposed in Matthew 23:39.

Revelation 3:10–11 contains a most encouraging word of promise and of exhortation: **Because thou didst keep the word of my patience, I also will keep thee from the hour of trial** (3:10). We best understand "the word of my patience" as the word which reveals and inculcates the patience of Christ, namely, the Gospel itself. To "keep" that word is to abide steadfast in the same meekness and patience which were exemplified in the Lord himself. And to be kept "from the hour of trial" is, not to be exempted from affliction and temptation, but to be saved from failure in that hour. Thus, it is not to be taken out of the world, but kept from the evil (John 17:15).

That hour which is to come upon the whole world, to try them that dwell upon the earth (3:10) is the same as the "great tribulation" spoken of by Jesus in Matthew 24:21, 29 and Mark 13:19. In the midst of enemies and bitter persecution the disciples were counseled by the Lord to stand firm and true and he assured them that not a hair of their heads should perish, but that in patience they should win their souls (Luke 21:18–19). These of Philadelphia are given substantially the same assurance and are exhorted to **hold fast** (3:11) the good confession and noble record they had already made. This is so that **no one** [might] **take thy crown**; that is, get the better of them in good deeds and so obtain a crown of glory which might have been their own (cp. Col. 2:18). Here we have a fore-glimpse of them who come out of the great tribulation (7:14).

The promise to the victor in Revelation 3:12 is worthy of special study: (1) **I will make him a pillar in the temple of my God.** (2) **He shall go out thence no more.** (3) **I will write upon him** [a] **the name of my God**, [b] **the name of the city of my God**, and [c] **mine own new name**. All this indicates that such steadfast confessors as in Philadelphia kept the word of Jesus and did not deny his name are to be built into the living temple of God.

With little change of imagery this promise is substantially like that of our Lord to Peter when, by revelation of God the Father, he confessed his name: "Thou art Peter and upon this *petra* I will build my church" (Matt. 16:18). That promise was from him who held the keys of the kingdom of heaven and could give authority to open and to shut. Zechariah's Messianic prophecy declared not only that "the man whose name is Branch" should "build the temple of Jehovah," but also that they who were afar off should come and "build in the temple of Jehovah" (Zech. 6:12, 13, 15).

The temple of my God (3:12) is that "habitation of God through the Spirit," that "household of God," of which we read in Ephesians 2:19–22 and 1 Corinthians 3:16. It is the church of the new dispensation conceived under the figure of a building. It is misleading to dispute, as some have here done, whether the reference in this promise is to the Church militant or the glorified Church in heaven. For the apocalyptist does not distinguish these two conditions of the temple, but thinks of it only as God's building for time and eternity. Those who are made pillars therein are to remain so and **shall go out thence no more** (3:12).

We cannot here anticipate the symbolism of the temple of God as measured off for preservation in 11:1 and, after the sounding of the seventh trumpet, opened in the heaven (11:19). Nor does the statement of 21:22, that the new Jerusalem contains no temple but the Almighty and the Lamb, conflict with the imagery of this promise to the church of Philadelphia. For, as Alford well says, "that glorious city is all temple and Christ's victorious ones are its living stones and pillars."

That **the temple of my God** and **the new Jerusalem** (3:12) are essentially one is inferred from the threefold name which the victors are to have written upon them: **the name of my God**, of **the new Jerusalem**, and **mine own new name**. This threefold inscription makes them citizens of heaven (cp. Phil. 3:20) and those who stand with the Lamb on Mount Zion (14:1) and serve God and the Lamb forever (22:4) have his name written upon their foreheads. The new name here mentioned is to be compared with 2:17 and 19:12 and suggests the deep mysteries of the kingdom of God, which are hidden from the wise and understanding, but graciously revealed to babes (Matt. 11:25). In the inner correlations of this epistle we observe:

First, how appropriately the words of comfort and encouragement to a steadfast church come from him "who is holy and true."

Second, he who holds the key of David speaks naturally of "a door opened" and of pillars fixed in "the temple of my God."

Third, he who denies not the name of Jesus shall bear his "own new name."

Fourth, the church before which is set an opened door may well bear the name of "the new Jerusalem which cometh down out of heaven," and whose gates of pearl are never closed (21:25).

To the Church in Laodicea (3:14–22)
The lukewarm and self-conceited church

> 14 And to the angel of the church in Laodicea write; These things saith the Amen, the faithful and true witness, the beginning of the creation of God:
> 15 I know thy works, that thou art neither cold nor hot: I would thou wert cold or hot.

16 So because thou art lukewarm and neither hot nor cold, I will spew thee out of my mouth.

17 Because thou sayest, I am rich and have gotten riches and have need of nothing; and knowest not that thou art the wretched one and miserable and poor and blind and naked:

18 I counsel thee to buy of me gold refined by fire, that thou mayest become rich; and white garments, that thou mayest clothe thyself and that the shame of thy nakedness be not made manifest; and eyesalve to anoint thine eyes, that thou mayest see.

19 As many as I love, I reprove and chasten: be zealous therefore and repent.

20 Behold, I stand at the door and knock: if any man hear my voice and open the door, I will come in to him and will sup with him and he with me.

21 He that overcometh, I will give to him to sit down with me in my throne, as I also overcame and sat down with my Father in his throne.

22 He that hath an ear, let him hear what the Spirit saith to the churches.

The threefold title here is (1) **the Amen,** (2) **the faithful and true witness,** and (3) **the beginning of the creation of God** (3:14). The first occurs in 1:7 and is a frequent word in John's gospel (John 1:51; 3:3; 10:1); the second is found in part in 1:5 and the third has its parallel in Colossians 1:15. The first two are in substance one and serve to attest the trustworthy character of what is written. Compare the statement of 22:6, "These words are faithful and true."

The words "beginning of the creation of God" (3:14). are another way of saying that Christ is the "Alpha," "the first," as he is represented in Revelation 1:8, 18. He is the beginning as well as the end, the first as well as the last. The language, considered by itself alone, may be construed to mean, as the Arians teach, that Christ is himself a creature. But such an interpretation is inconsistent with the constant teaching of this book, which so identifies God and the Lamb that what is predicated of one is also attributed to the other. Jesus Christ is subordinate to the Father, but not a creation of his power, for every created thing in heaven and earth is represented as worshiping him (5:13). It is appropriate that titles which appear in the introduction of the book (1:5, 7–8) and are repeated again at the close (22:6, 13), should stand at the head of this last of the seven epistles to the churches.

The message to this church contains no word of commendation, but charges two offenses: (1) **Thou art neither cold nor hot** (3:15) and (2) **Thou sayest, I am rich and have gotten riches and have need of** nothing (3:17). The lukewarmness which constitutes the first offense is a condition of spiritual indifference and indecision. Such a moral state is worse than hostile coldness. For there is more hope of winning such an open-faced sinner to Christ than one who has tasted some benefits of grace and then settled down into a feelingless indifference. If one is not "hot" (ζεστός [*zestos*]), that is, glowing with fervent love for Christ, it were better for him to be cold than to be void of all keen spiritual sensibility. Hence the significance of the words **I would thou wert cold or hot** (3:15).

The imagery is from different conditions of water. Water either cold or hot may be pleasant to the taste, but that which is lukewarm produces nausea and one spews it out of his mouth in loathing and disgust. But spiritual insensibility begets pride and self-conceit. This lukewarm church boasts of acquired riches and of having no sense of need. In this respect it resembled Ephraim (Hos. 12:8) and the Corinthians to whom Paul wrote in a strain of holy irony (1 Cor. 4:8). This fact shows up still more clearly the fearful evil of indecision and unconcern about one's relation to God.

Such a one imagines himself **rich**, when in fact he is of all men **the wretched one and miserable and poor and blind and naked** (3:17). In view of this, their true condition, the counsel (συμβουλεύω [*sumbouleuō*]) which now follows is especially telling. Those who say they are "rich" and "have need of nothing" (3:17) are in perishing need of some good counsel. And this counsel comes in the form of searching rebuke and condescending advice from the Lord. What they need is a supply (1) of the true riches (cp. Luke 12:21; 1 Cor. 1:5), (2) of **white garments** to cover their spiritual nakedness, and (3) of **eyesalve** that they may truly see (3:18). In their apathy and self-conceit, the Laodiceans had become really "miserable and poor and blind and naked" and the only power sufficient to supply their wants was the Christ who was and is "the beginning of the creation of God" (3:14).

Those needy ones must come to him and buy, for though his mercies are without money or price, the arrogant and self-conceited must surely pay the heaviest of all prices — the humiliation and surrender of themselves. They must renounce their self-conceit and pride and be made to feel that they are indeed poor and needy. When they acquire such a spirit they may obtain the pure **gold refined by fire** (3:18; cp. 1 Pet. 1:7) and be clothed in the "white garments" of a living and active righteousness (Col. 3:10) and receive that divine anointing which removes the blindness of one's spiritual vision and teaches him all things (1 John 2:11, 27).

I love ... reprove ... chasten (3:19–20). The three things go together (cp. Job 5:17; Psa. 94:12; Prov. 3:12; Heb. 12:6). This statement in connection with the other things said to the lukewarm and self-conceited church shows how much the faithful and true Witness loves and yearns to save those who show indifference toward him. It becomes still more conspicuous by the touching figure of the next verse: **Behold, I stand at the door and knock** (3:20). To those who ought to be the suppliants and to be themselves doing what is enjoined in Matthew 7:7, he who was with God in the creation of the world approaches as a seeker and knocks for admission to their hearts. **I will come in** (cp. John 14:23).

The promise to the victor is quite analogous to that in the epistle to the church in Thyatira (2:26–27). They who overcome are to be associated with Christ on his throne. Having suffered with him and triumphed through his grace, they shall also reign with him (cp. 2 Tim. 2:12; Rom. 5:17; 8:17; Col. 3:4). And thus will be answered the prayer of Jesus in John 17:22–24. The resurrection, ascension and enthronement of Jesus Christ are the last and highest ideals of triumph which the church may share. It is, accordingly, appropriate that this promise should come last in the manifold promises made to the seven churches.

The correspondences of thought noticeable in this last of the seven epistles are the following:

First, he who is the Amen appropriately appeals to such as are false and self-deceived.

Second, the faithful and true Witness imparts appropriate counsel and fails not to expose the self-delusion of those who are really blind and naked.

Third, he who is the first (as well as the last) and at the very beginning of the creation of God, appropriately concludes the promises to such as overcome with the final glory of reigning in triumph with Christ and God.

Fourth, it is most encouraging counsel to know that the love which faithfully reproves and chastens is able to refine and clothe and enlighten the miserable and poor and blind and naked so as to make them suitable to sit in the very throne of God.

At the conclusion of our notes on these seven epistles we record the following observations:

1. We find so much that is truly conspicuous and commanding in these messages that it seems like carrying interpretation too far into

fanciful conjectures when we seek for deeper mysteries than those to which we have called attention. The notion that we have in these seven epistles a prophetic outline of seven chronological periods of Church history traceable through the Christian centuries may be safely discarded as the fiction of extremists. Their great error consists in spending more effort to discover what may possibly be made out of a sacred writer's words than to make sure of that which the scope and language most naturally require.

2. The seven Spirits before the throne represent the one holy universal Spirit of God. Thus, it may be admitted that the seven churches represent in good measure the universal Church of Jesus Christ. And the conditions of life, labor, patience, trial, and hope are in substance such as may be seen somewhere in the Church of all time.

3. As the entire Apocalypse has much in common with our Lord's eschatological discourse in the synoptic gospels, so we notice in the personal addresses and appeals to the seven churches much that corresponds in substance to that which Jesus addressed personally to his disciples (e.g., Matt. 24:9, 11–13, 21, 42–51). The whole book has a purpose of comforting and encouraging the church of that first period — the apostolic age.

4. These epistles are so full of references to things which follow in subsequent portions of the Apocalypse that we may well believe they were not completed in their present form until the rest of the book was written. They appear on close analysis to be of the nature of a preface or introduction to the Revelation, but too thoroughly interwoven with its ideas and method to be attributed to a different authorship. If the interpretation we give of John's Revelation is correct, there is no sufficient ground or reason for supposing that the book was constructed by combining two or more different apocalypses.

Chapter 3
THE OPENING OF THE SEVEN SEALS (Rev. 4–6)

1. The Heavenly Theophany (4:1–11)

1 After these things I saw and behold, a door opened in heaven and the first voice which I heard, a voice as of a trumpet speaking with me, one saying, Come up hither and I will show thee the things which must come to pass hereafter.
2 Straightway I was in the Spirit: and behold, there was a throne set in heaven,
3 and one sitting upon the throne; and he that sat was to look upon like a jasper stone and a sardius: and there was a rainbow round about the throne, like an emerald to look upon.
4 And round about the throne were four and twenty thrones: and upon the thrones I saw four and twenty elders sitting, arrayed in white garments; and on their heads crowns of gold.
5 And out of the throne proceeded lightnings and voices and thunders. And there were seven lamps of fire burning before the throne,
6 which are the seven Spirits of God; and before the throne, as it were a glassy sea like unto crystal; and in the midst of the throne and round about the throne, four living creatures full of eyes before and behind.
7 And the first creature was like a lion and the second creature like a calf and the third creature had a face as of a man and the fourth creature was like a flying eagle.
8 And the four living creatures, having each one of them six wings, are full of eyes round about and within: and they have no rest day and night, saying, Holy, holy, holy, is the Lord God, the Almighty, who was and who is and who is to come.
9 And when the living creatures shall give glory and honor and thanks to him that sitteth on the throne, to him that liveth for ever and ever,
10 the four and twenty elders shall fall down before him that sitteth on the throne and shall worship him that liveth for ever and ever,
11 and shall cast their crowns before the throne, saying, Worthy art thou, our Lord and our God, to receive the glory and the honor and the power: for thou didst create all things and because of thy will they were and were created.

The messages to the seven churches were appropriately introduced by a sublime Christophany. For they were specific counsels of Christ himself, the Son of man, to the churches of that time and, indeed, of every period and place which exhibit similar conditions. But what follows, even to the conclusion of the book, consists mainly of symbolic revelations and they are appropriately introduced by a Theophany, seen in the opened heaven. The contents of this vision, minutely analyzed, may be thus arranged:

1. Vision of the throne and the One sitting thereon (4:1–3)
2. The twenty-four elders (4:4)
3. The lightnings, voices and thunders (4:5)
4. The seven lamps of fire (4:5)
5. The glassy sea (4:6)
6. The four living creatures (4:6–8)
7. The heavenly worship (4:8–11)
8. The book with seven seals (5:1–4)
9. The Lamb in the midst of the throne (4:5–7)
10. The worship of God and the Lamb (4:8–14)
    a. Song of the living creatures and the elders (4:8–10)
    b. Song of myriad angels (4:11–12)
    c. Song of the whole creation (4:13)
    d. Response of the living creatures and elders (4:14)

Such heaven-scenes appear in the earliest fragments of apocalyptic writing, as in Genesis 1:26; 3:22; 6:3, 7. But the most notable Old Testament models, after which the visions of these two chapters have been patterned, are the visions of Isaiah 6:1–4 and Ezekiel 1:4–28; 10:1–22. It detracts not from the inspiration and originality of John that he made himself a profound student of the Hebrew prophets and cast his own visions in the forms long consecrated to the purposes of holy revelation. The noblest human element as well as the divine in sacred scripture is manifest in such appropriation of metaphor and symbol.

After these things (4:1). After the visions and testimonies recorded in the preceding chapters. How long after is not said and is of no importance in our study of this book. It is pitiable to note what long paragraphs and even pages have been written on such a trivial question. Whether it was "soon after," or "sometime after," or "after he had written down the previous visions," matters not. These are all questions which probably never seriously occupied the thoughts of the sacred writer.

Door opened in heaven (4:1). Heaven is the place of God's throne and the source of all true revelations. Therefore, in order to see and know the mysteries of God, the door of his heavenly temple must be opened (cp. Gen. 28:17; Eze. 1:1; Matt. 3:16; Acts 7:56; 10:11; 2 Cor. 12:1–4).

The most exact translation of the words which follow is: "And the voice the first which I heard (was) as of a trumpet speaking with me" (4:1). The obvious reference is, to the first voice heard after the vision of the opened door. John heard other voices after this first one (cp. 4:5, 8, 10; 5:2, 9, 11, 13). Some think it was the same voice mentioned so similarly in 1:10 and to be understood as the voice of Christ. But it is only by inference that the "great voice" of 1:10, is supposed to be that of Christ, since Christ has been speaking continuously through the seven epistles of chapters 2 and 3. But it is by no means so evident as some assume that **the first voice which I heard** is intended to refer to the voice spoken of in 1:10, or that it was the voice of Christ. There are many and great voices which are heard speaking in this Apocalypse and it is not important to determine whether this first voice is the same as that of 1:10, or the first one heard after the heavenly door was opened. It is in any case the voice of heavenly authority and may well be supposed to have come from him that sat upon the throne.

Come up hither (4:1), i.e., ascend into this realm of heavenly vision and revelation. John was thus caught away in spirit like Ezekiel to behold "visions of God" (cp. Eze. 3:12; 8:3; 11:1). This first verse of Revelation 4 begins and ends with the same words, **after these things** (μετὰ ταῦτα [meta tauta]) and the reference seems to be in each case substantially the same. That which **must come to pass** is something to take place necessarily after the things thus far shown. And in the last occurrence, the phrase may well be translated simply **hereafter**. In view of the meaning in 1:19 and the form of words in 1:1, we can hardly adopt the punctuation of Westcott and Hort, who connect the words with what follows in verse 2.

I was in the Spirit, better: "I was in spirit" (4:2; as in 1:10). This language implies a new uplift of divine rapture. But it need not be supposed to imply that the seer had meanwhile lost his inspiration, or lapsed from the state of ecstasy in which he beheld things already described. He must have been "in spirit" to see the "door opened in heaven," and to hear the **voice as of a trumpet** (4:1). But upon seeing and hearing these things, immediately a special rapture seized him.

This enabled him to look through the opened door of heaven and behold the wonderful theophany about to be described.

A throne set in heaven (4:2). This was in the same heaven (ἐν τῷ οὐρανῷ [*en tō ouranō*]) the door of which he had seen already opened (4:1). The "throne" was seen as "set," or already placed, in the heaven, when first the seer beheld it and at the same time he saw **one sitting upon the throne** (4:3; cp. Isa. 6:1; Dan. 7:9). The one who sat upon the throne is not named, but he is described much after the manner of the unnamed one in Ezekiel 1:26–27.

Like a jasper stone (4:3). A precious stone of various colors, as purple, blue, green, yellow. **Sardius** is a similar stone of carnelian hue; red, or flesh-colored. These comparisons serve here, as in Ezekiel 1:4, 26–27, to give a powerful impression of the intense splendor of him who sat upon the throne. The **rainbow round about the throne** (4:3) is a symbol of covenanted mercy (Gen. 9:12–17). This rainbow was **in appearance like an emerald** (4:3) that is, a precious stone of a light green color. Aside from its symbolic suggestiveness, this stone serves in the picture as a screen or veil to soften the intense brightness proceeding from the throne.

Thrones ... elders (4:4). These are ruling elders, for they occupy thrones after the manner of those who execute judgment (cp. 20:4; Dan. 7:9, 18, 22, 27). There are as many thrones as elders, so that each one sits upon his own separate throne. Here we naturally recall the words of Jesus to his disciples in Matthew 19:28: "In the regeneration, when the Son of man shall sit upon the throne of his glory, ye also shall sit upon twelve thrones, judging the twelve tribes of Israel." John, however, saw not twelve but **four and twenty thrones** (4:4). The **four and twenty elders** (4:4) who sat upon the thrones were arrayed in white garments, symbolical of their heavenly purity and glory (3:5). And on their heads were **crowns of gold**, additional emblems of their royal dignity.

The whole picture indicates a glorious company of enthroned nobles. They sit on thrones as so many kings and therefore cannot here be thought of as ministering angels or servants. The twenty-four may have been chosen in reference to the twenty-four courses of priests (1 Chron. 24) and in that case the enthroned elders may be regarded as a symbol of the kingdom which is constituted of those who are priests unto God (1:6). But as the gates of the new Jerusalem bear the names of the twelve tribes of Israel and the foundations the names of the twelve apostles (21:12, 14), we may well believe that these twenty-four enthroned elders symbolize the glorified Church of the Old and New Testaments as represented by the twelve tribes and the twelve apostles. All these are conceived as exalted into regal splendor and associated like Daniel's "saints of the Most High" (Dan. 7:18, 22, 27) with the King on the throne (cp. 3:21) as so many heavenly princes.

Lightnings ... voices ... thunders (4:5). These are signs of the terrors and omnipotence of the Most High in the heaven as well as of his manifested presence on earth (cp. 11:19; Exo. 19:16). The procession of these from the throne suggests that the throne of God is the source of all revelation and power. The **seven lamps of fire burning before the throne** (4:5) are another symbol of the **seven Spirits of God** (4:6; cp. 1:4), who is that one universal Spirit from whose presence no man may hide (Psa.139:7). They are like so many flaming eyes which search the whole world (5:6; Zech. 4:10; Prov. 15:3) and bring every man's work into judgment before God.

A glassy sea (4:6). This is not "a sea of glass," as translated in the common version. Nor is it to be identified with the "glassy sea mingled with fire" in 15:2; nor the same as the river of life in 22:1. Rather it is simply the broad open space before the throne, the polished floor, such as is to be seen in any great throne-chamber. This appeared in the vision to be so large and so polished into the brightness of a precious stone like **unto crystal**, after the manner of a tessellated pavement, that the writer could not describe it more appropriately than by comparing it to a "glassy sea like unto crystal."

The seer describes the position of the four *zoa*, or **living creatures**, as in **the midst of the throne and round about the throne** (4:6). They do not appear to support the throne as in Ezekiel's vision (Eze. 1:22, 26). For one stands at the middle point of each of the four sides of the throne and so facing the throne (cp. Exo. 25:20, 22). This is so that the seer could observe the multitudinous eyes before and behind, which symbolize remarkable intelligence. The faces of these intelligent beings were like those of Ezekiel's vision (Eze. 1:10) and resembled those of a **lion**, a **calf**, a **man**, and a **flying eagle** (4:7). Thus, they represent the four highest types of animal life.

As in Isaiah's vision (Isa. 6:2), the living creatures had **each one of them six wings** and they were **full of eyes** (4:8). Their eyes are not only **before and behind** (4:6), as seen in their attitude toward the throne, but also **round about and within** (4:8) when viewed in reference to the wings. Outside and under the wings they were also full of eyes and like Isaiah's seraphim they are continually repeating the trisagion. In Isaiah they cry: "Holy, holy, holy, Jehovah of hosts: the whole earth is full of his glory." In our Apocalypse the formula is enlarged into a characteristic parallelism:

Holy, holy, holy Lord, the God, the Almighty,
He who was and who is and who is to come (4:8).

It is evident that this whole picture is modeled after the vision of the seraphim in Isaiah 6:1–4 and of the cherubim in Ezekiel 1:4–14. The **living creatures** (4:6) contribute largely to the glory and impressiveness of the scene. They may be regarded simply as parts of a great composite picture of the presence-chamber of the Almighty. They do not have special symbolical import other than suggesting, perhaps, the ministers and attendants suitable for a throne-chamber so heavenly and holy. Viewed in this light they are merely the bodyguard or immediate attendants of the King, such as are to be seen about the throne and person of every great sovereign when he appears in state.

Thus understood they would have no more symbolical meaning than the glassy pavement before the throne. But the detailed description of their forms and their essential identity with the cherubim of the Old Testament, leave it hardly doubtful that, like the four and twenty elders, these four *zoa* are symbols of some intelligent beings, or of the whole creation, as active and worshipful in the presence of God. The name clearly indicates *living* creatures, their wings symbolize *rapidity* of movement and their innumerable eyes suggest *wisdom* and continual *watchfulness*. With good reason, therefore, have many of the best interpreters concluded that the cherubim are symbols of the highest ideal of the living creation in its relation to its God.

Any really satisfactory explanation of the cherubim must present one predominant idea traceable alike in the Edenic symbols (Gen. 3:24), in those which spread their wings over the mercy seat (Exo. 25:20), and in those which appear in the visions of Isaiah 6, Ezekiel 1, and this Apocalypse of John. As the sword of flame at the gate of Eden was a symbol of the righteousness which demands the punishment of sin, the cherubim may well, on the other hand, symbolize the intelligent and active love that ever worships Him that is holy. Whether hovering over the mercy seat in the holy of holies, or appearing in the temple of heaven, or executing the divine purposes of God, the cherubim represent the highest ideal of created beings glorified before the holy One who rules the heavens and the earth.

While the twenty-four elders represent "the church of the firstborn who are enrolled in heaven," the living creatures may symbolize a still higher concept of the ultimate glorification of "the spirits of just men made perfect" (Heb. 12:23). The elders and the cherubs may therefore represent, not different orders of created beings, but the whole body of the redeemed at different periods of glorification. The elders might well denote the saints of the Most High as enthroned to receive and possess the Messianic kingdom (cp. Dan. 7:9, 18, 27). The seraphim would then picture the glorified and perfected creation of God, including all saints, when the Christ "shall have abolished all rule and all authority and power." This would be when he shall have "delivered up the kingdom to the God and Father," and the Son himself shall become so subjected "that God may be all in all" (1 Cor. 15:24–28). Then the last enemy shall have been destroyed and there shall be no more death, nor tears, nor pain, nor night, nor curse (Rev. 21:4; 22:3, 5).

In this symbolic portraiture of the throne of God it certainly was fitting to introduce representations of such ideals of power and wisdom and judgment as are ever traceable in the divine administration of the world. But also of such progressive glorification of the saints as shall take place "unto the ages of the ages." Hence, in accord with the explanation of the cherubim we have suggested, these exalted and glorified beings appropriately cry, without pause day or night:

"Holy, holy, holy Lord, the God, the Almighty,

He who was and who is and who is to come." (4:8)

The worship here recorded is to be compared with that described in 5:8–14. Here it is solely from **the living creatures** (4:9) and **the four and twenty elders** (4:10). They act in concerted harmony, so that when the cherubim lead off in ascribing **glory and honor and thanks to him that sitteth on the throne, to him that liveth unto the ages of the ages** (4:10), the elders also join in the worship and **fall down before him that sitteth on the throne** (4:10) and **cast their crowns before the throne** (4:11). The worship of the four living creatures before the throne of the Eternal is, like the cherubim at the gate of paradise and in the holy of holies, a pledge of the final glorification of the creation of God and hence it is said in verse 11, **Thou didst create all things and because of thy will they were and were created.**

We should understand that the elders and the cherubim alike symbolize that which is from the seer's point of view an ideal of the future ages of the kingdom of God and his saints. Thus, the future tense of the verbs, "shall give," "shall fall," "shall worship," "shall cast" (δώσουσιν, πεσοῦνται, προσκυνήσουσιν, βαλοῦσιν [*dōsousin, pesountai, proskunēsousin, balousin*]), has a noticeable significance. The falling down and casting their crowns before the throne, as well as the words of adoration and praise, are so many becoming forms of humiliation before God. Thus the redeemed and glorified saints of the Most High shall acknowledge his glory and honor and power through all the ages to come.

In this heavenly worship we note the threefold forms of expression in the trisagion of 4:8, the **glory and honor and thanks** of 4:9, in the **fall** and **worship** and **cast crowns** of 4:10 and the **glory, honor,** and **power** of 4:11. A threefold allusion seems to be designed in the closing words of 4:11, **thy will, they were and were created**. Back of all things, as the source and ground of their existence, is the will of God. It is *on account of* that will (not *by means* of it) that all things *were* and are. "They were" because God willed it. The ἐκτίσθησαν (*ektisthēsan*), "were created," adds to ἦσαν (*ēsan*) the thought that **all things** (τὰ πάντα [*ta panta*]) not only were in existence by reason of God's "will," but were also *brought into existence* because God so willed and brought it to pass by his act of creation.

2. The Book with Seven Seals (5:1–4)

> 1 And I saw in the right hand of him that sat on the throne a book written within and on the back, close sealed with seven seals.
> 2 And I saw a strong angel proclaiming with a great voice, Who is worthy to open the book and to loose the seals thereof?
> 3 And no one in the heaven, or on the earth, or under the earth, was able to open the book, or to look thereon.
> 4 And I wept much, because no one was found worthy to open the book, or to look thereon.

This sealed book is a part of the vision **of him that sat on the throne** (5:1) and is not to be thought of as a separate and independent revelation. The division of chapters at this point is unfortunate and tends to mislead the common reader. Having described the throne and him who sat thereon as the Holy One, to be adored by crowned elders and living cherubim through all the ages, the seer proceeds to record additional features of the same adorable Theophany. **On the right hand** (ἐπὶ τὴν δεξιάν [*epi tēn dexian*]), that is, as if it were lying on the open palm of the enthroned Sovereign) appeared **a book written within and on the back, close sealed with seven seals** (5:1). This imagery is taken from Ezekiel 2:9, 10 (cp. also Isa. 29:11).

The book is to be thought of as a scroll, a book-roll, like the Hebrew מְגִלָּה (*megillah*), and written on both sides. Just how the "seven seals" were adjusted we are not told. But from the opening of one seal after another, as described in chapter 6, it may be inferred that the roll was composed of seven leaves or sections, each one of which was fastened by a seal.

The meaning of this sealed book appears from the opening of its several seals. It is a symbol of the mystery of God which is about to be revealed by the Lamb, consisting of "the things which must come to pass hereafter" (4:1). The unsealing of the book is the apocalypse itself, "the revelation of Jesus Christ, which God gave to him to show unto his servants the things which must shortly come to pass," and which "he sent and signified by his angel unto his servant John" (1:1). For we shall see (what too many expositors have failed to note) that after the seals have been opened, the revelation appears as "a little book opened" (10:2). Then John takes from the mighty angel's hand and eats and is commissioned to publish "over many peoples and nations and tongues and kings." The sealed βιβλίον (*biblion*) of this vision thus becomes the opened book (τὸ βιβλίον τὸ ἠνεῳγμένον [*to biblion to ēneōgmenon*]) in the hand of the angel, who gives it unto John and commands him to eat it (10:8–11).

A strong angel proclaiming (5:2–3). It must have been a strong angel, who was able amid "lightnings and voices and thunders" (4:5), to proclaim with such a **great voice** as to be **heard in the heaven** and **on the earth** and **under the earth.** (5:3).The entire universe is thus denoted and no one was found in heaven or earth or Hades **worthy to open the book** (5:3–4). There is a suggestiveness in the word ἄξιος (*axios*), "worthy," in this connection. He must certainly be one of high rank and dignity who can take the book of mystery from the hand of God and open its secret things to the knowledge of others. He who is "worthy" to do a work like this must be possessed of something more than mere knowledge or intellectual ability.

I wept (5:4). As if in disappointment of what was promised by the voice of 4:1.

3. The Lamb at the Throne (5:5–7)

> 5 And one of the elders saith unto me, Weep not: behold, the Lion that is of the tribe of Judah, the Root of David, hath overcome, to open the book and the seven seals thereof.
> 6 And I saw in the midst of the throne and of the four living creatures and in the midst of the elders, a Lamb standing, as though it had been slain, having seven horns and seven eyes, which are the seven Spirits of God, sent forth into all the earth.
> 7 And he came and he taketh it out of the right hand of him that sat on the throne.

One of the elders (5:5). It is appropriate that a representative of the exalted and glorious Church of God should comfort the weeping seer. **Lion ... Judah ... David** (5:5). All these terms are remarkably expressive of the Messianic hero, the hope and consolation of Israel (Luke 2:25), the blessed Christ of God (cp. Gen. 49:9; Isa.11:1, 10). **Hath overcome** (5:5), as in 3:21. This Lion of Judah, this Root of David, overcame, conquered (ἐνίκησεν [enikēsen]) by the passion of the cross and the power of his resurrection, so as to be worthy as well as able to open the book and the seven seals thereof. Compare the sentiment of 5:9.

We have an obvious Hebraism in the words **in the midst of the throne and of the four living creatures and in the midst of the elders** (5:6). The meaning is: between the throne and the living creatures on the one side and the elders on the other. But the **Lamb** here seen was so in mid-view of the throne and so related to the throne, that in 22:1, it is called the throne of the Lamb as well as of God. And so in the song of praise which here follows (vv. 8–13) the Lamb is honored even as the one who sits upon the throne. It is all because he "overcame and sat down with his Father in his throne" (3:21).

It is a most remarkable thing that when the seer looked to behold the conquering Lion of Judah, of whom the elder spoke, he saw a little lamb standing as though it had been slain. The word ἀρνίον (*arnion*) is strictly a diminutive and means a little lamb. It occurs nowhere in the New Testament outside this book except in the one instance of John 21:15 and there in the plural.

The striking contrast between the lion and the lamb is further enhanced by representing the lamb standing as slain. The fact of his standing shows that he was truly alive; but something in the vision showed just as clearly that he **had been slain** (5:6). How this was made to appear we may not certainly determine. But the two descriptive participles (ἑστηκός — ἐσφαγμένον [*estēkos* — *esphagumenon*]) taken together express the same great truth as the Lord himself proclaims in 1:18: "I was dead and behold I am alive unto the ages of the ages." That which was seen was a symbol of the crucified and risen Lord, whom Paul set forth as "delivered up for our trespasses and raised up for our justification" (Rom. 4:25). The great trouble with Judaism was that it looked for a mighty lion and was scandalized to behold, instead, a little lamb. The "veil upon their heart" (2 Cor. 3:15) hindered their seeing that the slain lamb was also the lion of Judah.

This lamb, moreover, had **seven horns and seven eyes** (5:6). The *horns* are here, as elsewhere, symbols of power and the seven suggests the perfection of power possessed by the *lamb*. The "seven eyes" are symbols of a corresponding perfection of wisdom and are defined to be identical with **the seven Spirits of God** (5:6), which have already been described as so many "lamps of fire burning before the throne" (4:5). He who has these seven eyes is competent to "search all things, even the deep things of God" (1 Cor. 2:10). It is especially worthy of notice that the seven Spirits of God are here identified with the eyes of the Lamb. Hence the inference that the Spirit as well as the throne of God is in some profound and wonderful sense the Spirit of the Lamb (cp. also 1:4 and 3:1).

He came and has taken (5:7). This use of the perfect instead of the aorist may be charged to the inaccurate grammar peculiar to the Apocalypse. His coming and taking the book from **the right hand of him that sat upon the throne** evinced that though he had been slain he was now alive and active and powerful to reveal the deep things of God. In the vision of Revelation 10 we shall see how the book, when opened, is given to John to be eaten.

4. The Worship of God and the Lamb (5:8–14)

> 8 And when he had taken the book, the four living creatures and the four and twenty elders fell down before the Lamb, having each one a harp and golden bowls full of incense, which are the prayers of the saints.

9 And they sing a new song, saying, Worthy art thou to take the book and to open the seals thereof: for thou wast slain and didst purchase unto God with thy blood men of every tribe and tongue and people,
10 and nation and madest them to be unto our God a kingdom and priests;
11 and they reign upon the earth. And I saw and I heard a voice of many angels round about the throne and the living creatures and the elders; and the number of them was ten thousand times ten thousand and thousands of thousands;
12 saying with a great voice, Worthy is the Lamb that hath been slain to receive the power and riches and wisdom and might and honor and glory and blessing.
13 And every created thing which is in the heaven and on the earth and under the earth and on the sea and all things that are in them, heard I saying, Unto him that sitteth on the throne and unto the Lamb, be the blessing and the honor and the glory and the dominion, for ever and ever.
14 And the four living creatures said, Amen. And the elders fell down and worshiped.

The act of taking the book out of the hand of the Most Holy One called forth at once the worship of all the hosts of heaven and earth, for the entire universe was interested in this sublime act of the Lamb. The worship as here described consists of four parts: (1) The song of the cherubim and the elders (vv. 8–10). (2) The worship of myriads of angels (vv. 11–12). (3) Worship of the entire creation (v. 13). (4) Response of the cherubim and the elders (v. 14).

The worship of **the four living creatures and the four and twenty elders** (5:8) is represented as one, just as in 4:9–11, they are seen to act in concert. Four different expressions serve to indicate the homage they pay, namely, **fell down, each one a harp, bowls of incense**, and **a new song** (5:8–9). Harps and bowls full of incense have been thought unsuitable for cherubim and are supposed by some expositors to be understood only of the elders. But the text makes no such distinction and predicates all that is here said alike of living creatures and elders. And this is perfectly consistent with the view of the cherubim and elders as presented in the foregoing notes. The symbolic representatives of redeemed humanity may, as kings and priests before the throne, present the symbols of the prayers of the saints (cp. 8:3 and Psalm 141:2). The new song they sing is something new in kind (καινή [*kainē*]), as if prompted by a new and fuller revelation of the Lamb of God.

His worthiness to open the sealed book is celebrated as resting upon three acts of unspeakable love: (1) **Thou wast slain**, (2) **didst purchase ... with thy blood**, (3) and **madest them to be a kingdom and priests** (5:9–10). And these three are virtually one, for the sacrificial death, the redeeming efficacy of the blood, and the consummation of this redemption in the heavenly kingdom constitute the infinitely meritorious work and triumph of the Son of God. The direct object of the verb "didst purchase" (ἠγόρασας [*ēgorasas*]) is not expressed except by implication (for the reading ἡμᾶς [*hēmas*] is omitted in the best accredited texts). But the redeemed ones are said to be from **every tribe and tongue and people and nation** (5:9). This fourfold designation is frequent in this book (cp. 7:9; 10:11; 11:9; 13:7; 14:6; 17:15). In 5:11 the words **they reign upon the earth** (i.e., "they are reigning on the earth") show that the conquest and judgment are conceived as present and continuing (cp. 2:27; 20:4–6; 1 Cor. 15:25).

The **many angels**, whom John both **saw and heard** (5:11) seem to have formed a kind of circle round about the throne. And **the living creatures and the elders** and their innumerable multitude is designated by the impressive but indefinite terms **ten thousand times ten thousand** (*myriads* of *myriads*) and **thousands of thousands** (*chiliads* of *chiliads*) (5:11). The expression is an imitation of Daniel 7:10, but fuller and more striking. The angelic worship is notable for its sevenfold ascription to the Lamb of **power, riches, wisdom, might, honor, glory, and blessing** (5:12). How infinitely worthy must he be who receives from all the angels homage like this!

Finally, **every created thing** is heard to join in this worship (5:13). And the realms of their being are named under four heads, **heaven, earth, under the earth**, and **on the sea** (5:13). And then, by way of repetition and emphasis, it is added: even **all things that are in them** (5:13). Thus to the song of cherubim and elders and the great voice of innumerable angels, the entire creation itself, with every part and portion of the same, is represented as responding. They respond with like words of adoration, addressing their worship unto **him that sitteth on the throne and unto the Lamb** (5:13). The previous strains of worship mention only the Lamb, but this response of all creation mentions first the enthroned Ruler of the universe and ascribes to him and to the Lamb **blessing, honor, glory,** and **dominion** (5:13), which four terms should be compared with the seven of verse 12.

The antiphonal response of the four living creatures is simply **Amen** (5:14). This is eminently fitting and impressive and the last act noticed of **the elders** was apparently one of silent adoration, as they **fell down and worshiped** (5:13).

5. The Opening of the Seals (6:1–8:1)

The contents of Revelation 4 and 5 are thus seen to be an apocalyptic introduction to what follows in chapters 6 to 11 and, indeed, to the entire sequel of the book. Its most striking features are modeled after the visions of Isaiah 6 and Ezekiel 1, but the New Testament seer shows his own penetration and originality in the fullness and variety of his descriptions. What more magnificent introduction can be imagined than this elaborate picture of the throne of God and of the Lamb? From thence "proceed lightnings and voices and thunders," symbolic signs of momentous revolutions in the world. And while the vision of these two chapters is essentially a Theophany, the most conspicuous person revealed therein is the Lamb in the midst of the throne. It is worthy of note that in 22:1–2, the last object seen by John is the river of life "proceeding out of the throne of God and of the Lamb."

In the artificial arrangement of the book we observe that the first four seals are closely related to each other and form a class by themselves. The fifth and sixth seals form a striking contrast, as if answering one to the other. Between the sixth and seventh seals comes a double vision of the salvation of God's servants and martyrs (ch. 7). The seventh seal itself issues in the sounding of the seven trumpets (chs. 8–11), which are again capable of division into four and three, as will be pointed out in the proper place. The first four seals are rapidly opened one after another and disclose a fourfold picture of impending judgments. They reveal in each case what one of the four living creatures calls forth and the imagery is evidently modeled after the four chariots and horses of Zechariah 6:1–8, with which Zechariah 1:8–11, is also to be compared.

First seal opened (white horse) (6:1–2)

> 1 And I saw when the Lamb opened one of the seven seals and I heard one of the four living creatures saying as with a voice of thunder, Come.
> 2 And I saw and behold, a white horse and he that sat thereon had a bow; and there was given unto him a crown: and he came forth conquering and to conquer.

And I saw (6:1). What he saw is stated in verse 2 and the words are repeated at the beginning of that verse by way of resumption, after having stated what he **heard** when **the Lamb opened one of the seals** (6:1). The word **come**, which each of the four cherubim utters **with a voice like thunder** (6:1) is not addressed to John, for he was already in position to behold (4:1–2). Nor was it addressed to Christ, as Alford and Glasgow imagine by comparing 22:17, 20, for Christ is present as opener of the seals. Rather, it is addressed to that which, in the first four seals, at once responds and comes forth in obedience to the command, namely, first the white, next the red, third the black, and last the pale horse and his rider.

A white horse (6:2). Symbol of victorious war. The entire imagery of this first picture points suggestively to the opening of the Roman war against Jerusalem, which was irresistible in its movements (νικῶν [nikōn]) and destined to prevail (ἵνα νικήσῃ [hina nikēsē]). The fact that the victorious rider had a bow suggests that in the first stages of this bitter and decisive war the fighting was at a distance, not a close hand-to-hand struggle, such as a use of the sword implies. The war began by capturing the outlying towns of Palestine, preparatory to the siege of the great central city, Jerusalem.

There was given unto him a crown (6:2). It is a notable fact that Vespasian, who began and Titus, who completed the Jewish war, both obtained the imperial crown.

Second seal opened (red horse) (6:3–4)

> 3 And when he opened the second seal, I heard the second living creature saying, Come.
> 4 And another horse came forth, a red horse: and to him that sat thereon it was given to take peace from the earth and that they should slay one another: and there was given unto him a great sword.

A red horse (6:4). One having the color of fire (πυρρός [*purros*]), or of blood symbolizing the terrible bloodshed inseparable from bitter and relentless war. Such bloody warfare will necessarily **take peace from the earth** (6:4), i.e., the land, which is laid waste by its disastrous progress. The great sword is a fitting additional symbol, suggesting, as in contrast with the bow of the preceding rider, the closer and more bloody conflict of hand-to-hand struggle. Thus each successive symbol of the fourfold picture intensifies the terrible impression designed to be made.

Third seal opened (black horse) (6:5–6)

> 5 And when he opened the third seal, I heard the third living creature saying, Come. And I saw and behold, a black horse; and he that sat thereon had a balance in his hand.
> 6 And I heard as it were a voice in the midst of the four living creatures saying, A measure of wheat for a penny and three measures of barley for a penny; and the oil and the wine hurt thou not.

A black horse (6:5). Symbol of deadly famine. Black is naturally suggestive of something to be dreaded as a calamity. The **balance in his hand** (6:5) suggests the scarcity of times when the most necessary articles of food are difficult to obtain and, when obtained, are to be weighed out with strictest care.

I heard as it were a voice (6:6). Observe how the art of the apocalyptist makes voices from a mysterious source help to intensify the import of his visions. "That the cry sounds forth **in the midst of the four living creatures** is, in itself, natural, since the unsealing of the book occurs at the throne of God, which is in the midst of the four beings" (Düsterdieck).

The prices of wheat and barley are extortionate when a *choinix* (about a quart measure) of the one is held for a *denarius* (a "penny"), the usual payment for a full day's work (Matt. 20:2). And the wheat is only three times that amount of the more common article, barley, for the same price. In a time of famine the most common and necessary articles of food become scarce and costly.

The command not to **hurt** or injure (ἀδικέω [*adikeō*]) **the oil and the wine** (6:6) is supposed by some interpreters to be addressed to the rider on the black horse and to put a limit to the famine. These luxuries are not to be injured, but rather to remain plentiful, as a mitigation of the suffering when the more common articles are cut off. But a more congruous explanation of the command is that which regards it as a general maxim for the time. It is addressed to any and all whom it might concern, not to waste and destroy that which, though commonly a luxury, may be the only food obtainable.

Fourth seal opened (pale horse) (6:7–8)

> 7 And when he opened the fourth seal, I heard the voice of the fourth living creature saying, Come.
> 8 And I saw and behold, a pale horse: and he that sat upon him, his name was Death; and Hades followed with him. And there was given unto them authority over the fourth part of the earth, to kill with sword and with famine and with death and by the wild beasts of the earth.

A pale horse (6:8) The word translated "pale" is χλωρός [*chlōros*] which is a pale-green color (cp. the word as used in 8:7 and 9:4). The rider is named **Death** (*Thanatos*), and reminds one of Horace's familiar *pallida mors* in *Odes* 1:4, 13:

Pallida Mors æquo pulsat pede	Pale death with impartial foot, at
pauperum tabernas	the door of the poor man's cottage,
Regumque turres	and at the prince's gate

But in John's picture Death was not the only figure. For another personification, **Hades followed with him** (6:8), as if the two were joined together in the appointed work of terrible judgment. Hades is here to be understood as the underworld, the realm of disembodied souls, which swallows down all those whom Death destroys. So Death and Hades are associates (cp. 20:13).

To both of these awful powers was **given authority over the fourth part of the earth** (i.e., land; 6:8), a notably large portion. Compare the "third part" in 8:7–12 and the "tenth part" in 11:13. The work of destruction for which these awful personages are sent out is accomplished by means of **sword, famine, death,** and **wild beasts** (6:8). These are no other than the "four sore judgments" of Jehovah, by which he threatened Jerusalem through the ministry of Ezekiel (Eze. 14:21; cp. the language of Eze. 5:12; 6:11, 12; Jer. 14:12; 21:7; 24:10; 44:13).

We are not to understand the **sword** (ῥομφαία [*romphaia*]) as referring back to the "sword" (μάχαιρα [*machaira*]) of 6:4, nor the famine as a designed allusion to what is symbolized in 6:5–6. We are rather to recognize in the symbolism of the fourth seal a general portraiture of the fearful consummation of all the preceding and a designed aggravation of them all. The word **death**, in the latter part of this verse (6:8), as associated with the other three destructive agencies, is best understood as corresponding with the דֶּבֶר (*deber*), deadly "pestilence," in Ezekiel 14:21 (so translated there by the Septuagint). It is not referring to the specific figure of the rider on the pale horse.

Throughout the entire picture of the first four seals we note the prominence of this symbolic number and should keep in mind the prevailing habit of biblical apocalyptics to represent wide-sweeping judgments in a fourfold way. The symbols of these seals are to be understood as representing one combined set of events and not as prophecies of calamities far separated in time. "It is not war in one age of the world, famine in another, death and carnage in another, but war, famine and death in dread combination, all conspiring to plague the men of some one generation. For these things *naturally go together*. You cannot have the white horse of victory and conquest through the bow without war; you cannot have the red horse of war without having also the black horse of famine and the pale horse, death, in his immediate train." (Cowles)

The true interpretation of these first four seals is that which recognizes them as a symbolic representation of the "wars, famines, pestilences and earthquakes" which Jesus declared would be "the beginning of sorrows" in the desolation of Jerusalem (Matt. 24:6, 7; Luke 21:10, 11, 20). The attempt to identify each separate figure with some one specific event misses both the spirit and method of apocalyptic symbolism. The aim is to give a fourfold and most impressive picture of that terrible war on Jerusalem, which was destined to avenge the righteous blood of prophets and apostles (Matt. 23:35–37) and to involve a "great tribulation," the like of which had never been before (Matt. 24:21).

This is like the four successive but closely connected swarms of locusts in Joel 1:4. It is also like the four riders on different colored horses in Zechariah 1:8, 18 and the four chariots drawn by as many different colored horses in Zechariah 6:1–8. These four sore judgments of Jehovah move forth at the command of the four living creatures by the throne. They execute the will of Him who declared the "scribes, Pharisees and hypocrites" of his time to be "serpents and offspring of vipers," and assured them that "all these things should come upon this generation" (Matt. 23:33, 36). The writings of Josephus abundantly show how fearfully all these things were fulfilled in the bloody war of Rome against Jerusalem.

Fifth seal opened (souls under altar) (6:9–11)

> 9 And when he opened the fifth seal, I saw underneath the altar the souls of them that had been slain for the word of God and for the testimony
> 10 which they held: and they cried with a great voice, saying, How long, O Master, the holy and true, dost thou not judge and avenge our blood on them that dwell on the earth?
> 11 And there was given them to each one a white robe; and it was said unto them, that they should rest yet for a little time, until their fellow-servants also and their brethren, who should be killed even as they were, should be fulfilled in number.

The **fifth seal** (6:9) opens a martyr scene and serves to relieve from the spell of horror begotten by the visions of the first four seals. Here again we note the studied method of the writer to vivify and enhance his prophecy by means of revelations of opposite character. We are not to regard this martyr scene as the prediction of an historical event to follow in chronological order after the events depicted in the first four seals. It serves rather for the encouragement and comfort of all who were exposed to martyrdom "in the tribulation and kingdom and patience in Jesus" (Rev. 1:9). It corresponds to Jesus's words in Matthew 24:9 and Luke 21:16, which admonished the disciples of the tribulation and death which many among them must suffer during the apostolic period. Again and again in this Apocalypse we shall notice visions of similar import and purpose.

I saw, under the altar the souls (6:9). The vision finds its explanation in the custom of pouring out the blood of sacrificial victims at the basis of the altar (Lev. 4:7; 5:9). "The life (or soul) of the flesh is in the blood," according to Leviticus 17:11. So in the seer's vision, the souls which went forth in the blood of them **that had been slain for the word of God** are conceived as so many sacrifices of life for the **testimony** which they held (testimony here in the same sense as Rev. 1:2, 9). Each life cries out from the blood "at the bottom of the altar," where the victim had been slain.

They cried with a great voice (6:10). Like the blood of Abel crying from the ground unto God (Gen. 4:10). This cry of the martyr-souls may be understood as arising from "all the righteous blood shed upon the earth, from the blood of righteous Abel" to the last victim of Jewish persecution (cp. Matt. 23:35–37). **How long** (6:10). Compare Zechariah 1:12.

O Master (6:10). Observe that the word here employed is not the more common and general κύριος (*kurios*), "lord." Rather, it is the more specific δεσπότης (*despotēs*), "master," which implies the ownership of slaves. Compare the word σύνδουλοι (*sundouloi*) in the next verse and δοῦλοι (*douloi*) in Revelation 11:18. The Master to whom these martyrs pray is God, **the holy and the true** (6:10). The cry for judgment and vengeance is not to be understood as the expression of bitter and vindictive feelings. Rather it is a call for the Judge of all the earth to do that which is due to his holiness and truth. He who forbids men to avenge themselves on one another declares that vengeance belongs unto him (Rom. 12:19). He will surely avenge his chosen ones who cry to him day and night (Luke 18:7–8).

To each one a white robe (6:11; cp. Rev. 7:9, 13–17). The white robes and the rest assured the martyrs correspond with Jesus's pledge to his followers that in their patience they should win their souls (Luke 21:19) and that "whosoever shall lose his life for my sake and the gospel's shall save it" (Mark 8:35).

Yet for a little time (6:11). This is equivalent to the ἐν τάχει (*en tachei*) "speedily," of Luke 18:8. Before that generation passed away, the accumulated vengeance was to come upon that same generation (Matt. 23:35–36).

Until their fellow-servants ... should be fulfilled in number (6:11). That is, until the number of martyrs who were about to be killed, even as they were, should be complete. These others yet to be killed may be recognized in the two witnesses of Revelation 11:3–13, for when the seventh trumpet sounded "the time for the dead to be judged came and the time to give the reward to the prophets and saints" (Rev. 11:18). Meanwhile, until that time should come, these martyr-souls are each one robed in the garment of heavenly victory. And as we are to learn from subsequent visions, they will be guided by the Lamb "unto fountains of waters of life," where "God shall wipe away every tear from their eyes" (Rev. 7:17).

Sixth seal opened (shaking of earth and heavens) (6:12–17)

> 12 And I saw when he opened the sixth seal and there was a great earthquake; and the sun became black as sackcloth of hair and the whole moon became as blood;
> 13 and the stars of the heaven fell unto the earth, as a fig tree casteth her unripe figs, when she is shaken of a great wind.
> 14 And the heaven was removed as a scroll when it is rolled up; and every mountain and island were moved out of their places.
> 15 And the kings of the earth and the princes and the chief captains and the rich and the strong and every bondman and freeman, hid themselves in the caves and in the rocks of the mountains;
> 16 and they say to the mountains and to the rocks, Fall on us and hide us from the face of him that sitteth on the throne, and from the wrath of the Lamb:
> 17 for the great day of their wrath is come; and who is able to stand?

The opening of the **sixth seal** (6:12), as described in this passage, seems somewhat like an immediate answer to the cry of the souls under the altar. The imagery is in the main identical with that of Matthew 24:29–31, which describes the coming of the Son of man "immediately after the tribulation" spoken of in the preceding context. The descriptions in both passages are an apocalyptic portraiture of the great and terrible day of the Lord and the several images and allusions are appropriated from Old Testament prophecy, as the subjoined references show.

A great earthquake (6:12). Symbolic signal of divine visitations of judgment. Compare Isaiah 29:6 and also Revelation 8:5; 11:13, 19; 16:18. **Sun became black … moon became as blood** (6:12). Compare Joel 2:10, 31; 3:15; Isaiah 13:10; 24:23; Ezekiel 32:7–8; Amos 8:9; Matt. 24:29.

The stars of the heaven fell (6:13). Compare Joel 2:10; 3:15; Isaiah 13:10; Ezekiel 32:7. **As a fig tree**, compare Isaiah 34:4; Nahum 3:12.

Heaven was removed as a scroll (6:14). Compare Isaiah 34:4. **Every mountain and island were moved** (6:14). Compare Jeremiah 4:24; Habakkuk 3:6; Ezekiel 26:15, 18; 38:20; Nahum 1:5; Isaiah 64:1, 3; 40:15; 41:5.

Fall on us and hide us (6:16). Compare Hosea 10:8; Isaiah 2:19, 21; Luke 23:30.

Who is able to stand. Compare Nahum 1:6; Psalm 76:7.

A careful comparison of these different Old Testament passages in connection with the imagery and language of the sixth seal shows how freely our author appropriates the older scriptures to suit the purpose of his own book of prophecy. The great day of the Lord is thus set forth after the manner of Isaiah 13:6–9; Zephaniah 1:14–18; and Joel 1:15; 2:1–2. And as the language of the older scriptures referred to impending judgments of Jehovah on wicked men and nations, so 6:12–17 is to be understood as a like description of fearful judgment impending at the time when this book was written. And the appalling calamities involved in the overthrow of Jerusalem and their relation to the kingdom of God, were surely of a magnitude equal to any of those depicted by the apocalyptic writers of the Old Testament, whose language our author appropriates.

We have now seen that the first six seals, as opened by the Lamb, form a closely connected series and appropriate the apocalyptic imagery of the Hebrew prophets. The first four find fulfillment in the war which began about A.D. 66, swept over Galilee and Samaria, and laid waste all the cities and villages of Palestine. The first four seals became intensified with all those scenes of blood and famine and woe which made the siege and final overthrow of Jerusalem by the Romans one of the most horrible events of human history.

It must be kept in mind that these calamities of the Jewish people were announced in most explicit terms by Jesus as a judgment upon that wicked generation for its guilt in shedding the righteous blood of saints and prophets (Matt. 23:34–38). Hence the significance of placing the martyr scene of verses 9–11 in the midst of these pictures of retributive judgment. The first four seals disclose the conjoined forces of war, carnage, famine, and aggravated mortality, moving forth at the command of the four living creatures. But the opening of the fifth seal enables us to hear the cry of the martyrs for judgment and vengeance and then, as if in immediate answer to that cry, the sixth seal is opened and all the signs and terrors of the day of wrath appear. These are all apocalyptic disclosures of things which were to "come to pass quickly."

[[First Interlude (7:1–17)]]

The Sealing of Elect Israel (7:1–8)

> 1 After this I saw four angels standing at the four corners of the earth, holding the four winds of the earth, that no wind should blow on the earth, or on the sea, or upon any tree.
> 2 And I saw another angel ascend from the sunrising, having the seal of the living God: and he cried with a great voice to the four angels, to whom it was given to hurt the earth and the sea, saying,
> 3 Hurt not the earth, neither the sea, nor the trees, till we shall have sealed the servants of our God on their foreheads.
> 4 And I heard the number of them who were sealed, a hundred and forty and four thousand, sealed out of every tribe of the children of Israel.
> 5 Of the tribe of Judah were sealed twelve thousand:
> Of the tribe of Reuben twelve thousand:
> Of the tribe of Gad twelve thousand:
> 6 Of the tribe of Asher twelve thousand:
> Of the tribe of Naphtali twelve thousand:
> Of the tribe of Manasseh twelve thousand:
> 7 Of the tribe of Simeon twelve thousand:
> Of the tribe of Levi twelve thousand:
> Of the tribe of Issachar twelve thousand:
> 8 Of the tribe of Zebulun twelve thousand:
> Of the tribe of Joseph twelve thousand:
> Of the tribe of Benjamin were sealed twelve thousand.

After the opening of the sixth seal, with its tremendous signs of judgment, one might naturally expect the seventh seal to be immediately opened and the final consummation to be told. But such is not the method of this Apocalypse. As between the fourth and sixth seals the heavenly victory and comfort of the martyrs were revealed, so between the sixth and seventh seals there intervenes a glorious vision of the sealing and salvation of the true servants of God. The martyr scene of the fifth seal is here enlarged so as to take in all the servants (δοῦλοι [douloi]) of God. Including the brethren who have been "partakers in the tribulation and kingdom and patience which are in Jesus" (1:9) and who "washed their robes and made them white in the blood of the Lamb" (7:14).

In order to appreciate this method of the book the more clearly, we may here anticipate the subsequent revelations so far as to observe

the seven instances in which the writer introduces such visions of triumph and glory between appalling scenes of woe.
1. The martyr scene of 6:9–11, between the fourth and sixth seals.
2. The sealing and salvation of God's servants between the sixth and seventh seals (7:1–13).
3. Triumph and ascension of the two witnesses between the sixth and seventh trumpets (11:3–12).
4. The hundred and forty-four thousand with the Lamb on Mount Zion and the world-wide proclamation of the Gospel, between the persecutions of the two beasts (13:1–18) and the fall of Babylon and torment of those who worship the beast (14:1–6).
5. The victorious company, singing the song of Moses and the Lamb, between the bloody harvest (14:17–20) and the seven last plagues (15:2–4).
6. The great multitude, singing Hallelujah, between the fall of Babylon and the last great battle with the beast and his followers (19:1–10).
7. The vision of the enthroned martyrs between the binding and imprisonment of Satan (20:1–3) and his release for final war against the saints (20:4–6).

Thus again and again, in the midst of scenes of tribulation and judgment, we are lifted up by some corresponding picture of glory and triumph. This feature of the book cannot reasonably be regarded as accidental. Rather, it is part of the plan and method of the inspired writer, who was divinely guided so as to set the several revelations in most telling form.

After this I saw (7:1). There was a pause in the progress of disclosures. The terrors of the sixth seal were adapted to appall and leave the seer in a spell of amazement and confusion. The scenes which followed were of a nature to compose and cheer him. The contents of this seventh chapter are, in fact, an answer to the question with which the sixth chapter ends, "Who is able to stand?" We are herein assured that the awful judgments impending shall not harm those whom God seals as his own servants.

How this corresponds with our Lord's words as recorded in Luke 21:18–19, is noticeable: Some of them were to suffer death and they were all to be hated and persecuted; but "not a hair of their head should perish," for in their patience they should possess (κτάομαι [ktaomai]) their souls. Hence the blessed truth of Matthew 10:39: "He that loseth his life for my sake shall find it." The entire picture of this seventh chapter seems also to correspond with the words of Jesus in Matthew 24:31: "He shall send forth his angels with a great trumpet-sound and they shall gather his elect from the four winds, from one end of heaven to the other."

To interpret these words literally and insist that this gathering of the elect is a visible phenomenon, taking place at one moment or brief period of time, is but to perpetuate an error in biblical exegesis which results only in confusion. The same observation holds in respect to the visions of the sealing of God's servants in 7:1–8 and the great multitude out of all peoples in 7:9–17. The apocalyptic picture must be instantaneous, like any object presented symbolically to our thought. But the facts depicted are not therefore to be supposed as occurring at any one particular period or place. Unless the time and chronological order are expressly stated they need form no essential feature of the vision.

Consequently, nnnthis sealing of God's elect and the glorification of the countless multitude before the throne, are to be understood of events extended through an indefinite period and designed to furnish a vivid picture of the glory of those that inherit the salvation of God in Christ. The period which the date and scope of this book imply is that of the first apostles and servants of Jesus — the apostolic age.

Four angels ... four corners ... four winds (7:1). These three sets of fours are noticeable, as accordant with a scheme of symbolical numbers, but need not be supposed to have specific significance. It is an irrelevant fancy which finds in the four angels the four emperors, Maximian, Severus, Maxentius, and Licinius, who hindered the preaching of God's word (Lyra). It is scarcely outdone by the notion of Bengel that **the earth ... the sea ... any tree** (7:1) mentioned in this same verse, are to be understood, respectively, as Asia, Europe, and Africa! We have had so many occasions to notice that world-judgments and their agents move, so to speak, by fours that we need not stop to emphasize this additional example.

The **winds** are God's messengers and agents to execute his will (Psa. 104:4; Heb. 1:7) and the four points of the compass are appropriately called **the four corners of the earth** (7:)1. The **earth, sea,** and **tree** are naturally mentioned as objects affected by the wind and also in anticipation of the things to be smitten by the coming plagues (see 8:7, 8). It accords with the spirit and style of apocalyptics that all the forces of the world should be conceived as committed to the charge of angels. Compare "the angel of the waters" in 16:5.

Another angel (7:2). The ministry of innumerable angels constitutes what may be called the machinery of apocalyptic writings (cp. Zech. 2:3). **Ascend from the sunrising** (7:2). "It is appropriate and significant that the angel, coming for a victorious employment which brings eternal life, should arise from that side from which life and light are brought by the earthly sun. The angel himself, who does not descend from heaven, but ascends from the horizon, is represented after the manner of the rising sun" (Düsterdieck).

The seal of the living God (7:2) is here conceived as a sort of signet ring by which the name of God and the Lamb (cp. 14:1) was to be stamped upon the foreheads of his servants (7:3; cp. 9:4). This imagery of sealing God's servants in view of impending calamities is taken from Ezekiel 9:4. There an angel is commissioned to "go through the midst of Jerusalem and set a mark upon the foreheads of the men that sigh and that cry over all the abominations that are done in her midst." This mark was to save them from the slaughter about to be executed on the guilty. In a similar way the mark of the blood of the paschal lamb on the dwellings of Israel turned away the destroying angel from the door (Exo. 12:7, 13).

The purpose of the sealing was to preserve the true Israel of God as a holy seed. It was not designed to save them from tribulation, but to preserve them in the midst of the great tribulation about to come and to glorify them thereby. Though the old Israel be cast off, a new and holy Israel is to be chosen and **sealed** with the Spirit of the living God (7:3). Though the old Jerusalem perish, a new and heavenly Jerusalem will come forth to take its place. The glory of the new dispensation will be that the true Israelites will come, not to fire and blackness and trumpet and words of terror, but to Mount Zion, the city of the living God, the church of those enrolled in heaven and the spirits of just men made perfect (Heb. 11:18–24).

I heard the number (7:4). The process of the sealing is passed over without mention and the result announced. A **hundred and forty and four thousand** (7:4). A symbolical number made up of twelve times twelve, allowing each tribe an equal number. This number appears again significantly in Revelation 14:1 and the new Jerusalem has twelve gates, guarded by as many angels and bearing the names of the twelve tribes (21:12). It measures twelve thousand furlongs and its wall is a hundred and forty and four cubits (21:16–17). Compare the "twelve pillars, according to the twelve tribes of Israel" (Exo. 24:4), the twelve cakes of showbread (Lev. 24:5), the twelve memorial stones "according to the number of the tribes" (Josh. 4:5), and the "twelve bullocks for all Israel" (Ezra 8:35).

In Revelation 7:5–8, twelve names are here written after the manner and spirit in which the twelve tribes are often enumerated in the Old Testament (cp. Gen. 46; Exo. 1:1–4; Num. 1;13; Eze. 48). No special significance is to be attached to the names or the order in which they occur. **Judah** was naturally placed first, as the great leader and prince from whom the "Root of David sprang" (5:5) and **Benjamin** is named last because he was the youngest.

Why Dan is omitted is now as impossible to explain as why **Simeon** is omitted in Deuteronomy 33. Some think the tribe of Dan had become extinct, for while mentioned in 1 Chronicles 2:2, his name does not appear in the lists of 1 Chronicles 4–8. Inasmuch as he would not omit **Levi**, nor fail to recognize the double portion of **Joseph** (whose name is substituted in v. 8 for Ephraim), he must omit one name to secure exactly twelve. And who more suitable to be omitted than the firstborn son of Rachel's handmaid? The omission is of no significance.

The "one hundred and forty-four thousand" (7:4) are thus far presented to our thought only as sealed of God and numbered. The purpose of the sealing was, at least in part, to preserve them from the judgments about to fall upon the earth. The relation of this sealed and numbered company to the "great multitude which no man could number" (7:9–17) will be discussed at the end of the chapter.

The Innumerable Multitude Washed in the Blood (7:9–17)

> 9 After these things I saw and behold, a great multitude, which no man could number, out of every nation and of all tribes and peoples and tongues, standing before the throne and before the Lamb, arrayed in white robes and palms in their hands;
> 10 and they cry with a great voice, saying, Salvation unto our God who sitteth on the throne and unto the Lamb.
> 11 And all the angels were standing round about the throne and about the elders and the four living creatures; and they fell before the throne on their faces and worshiped God, saying, Amen:
> 12 Blessing and glory and wisdom and thanksgiving and honor and power and might, be unto our God forever and ever. Amen.
> 13 And one of the elders answered, saying unto me, These who are arrayed in the white robes, who are they and whence came they?

14 And I say unto him, My lord, thou knowest. And he said to me, These are they who come out of the great tribulation and they washed their robes and made them white in the blood of the Lamb.

15 Therefore are they before the throne of God; and they serve him day and night in his temple: and he that sitteth on the throne shall spread his tabernacle over them.

16 They shall hunger no more, neither thirst any more; neither shall the sun strike upon them, nor any heat:

17 for the Lamb who is in the midst of the throne shall be their shepherd and shall guide them unto fountains of waters of life: and God shall wipe away every tear from their eyes.

After these things (7:9). Another stage of the interlude (cp. v. 1), so that the visions of 7:1–8 and 9–17 are to be recognized as distinct and successive.

A great multitude, which no man could number (7:9). Obvious contrast with the twelve times twelve thousand who were sealed (7:4). **Out of every nation and tribes and peoples and tongues** (7:9). These are therefore not confined to the "tribes of the children of Israel" (7:4).

Standing before the throne and before the Lamb (7:9). This is a heavenly, rather than an earthly, scene. The circumstances of sealing the one hundred and forty-four thousand clearly implied that they were on the earth and exposed to danger, but these before the throne have evidently passed all such exposure to harm.

Arrayed in white robes (7:9). White robes are an appropriate vesture of those who have passed into heavenly triumph and blessedness (cp. 3:4; 6:11). **Palms in their hands** (7:9). This is an emblem of triumphant peace and joy. The word φοίνικες [phoinikes], "palm branches," occurs only here and in John 12:13. Compare 1 Maccabees 13:51; 2 Maccabees 10:7; 14:4.

Cry with a great voice (7:10). The united audible worship of such a countless throng must be with a great sound. **Salvation unto our God** (7:10). The word "salvation" in the Greek has the article, thus, it is "the salvation." All the life, triumph, glory, and blessedness of their being and position are contemplated in this salvation and they ascribe it all to God and to the Lamb. In these two verses observe the fourfold expressions:

Nation, tribes, peoples, tongues;
Standing, arrayed, palms, cry.

All the angels were standing (7:11; cp. 5:11). The verb εἱστή-κεισαν (*eistēkeisan*) is strictly pluperfect and if translated "had been standing" might perhaps suggest that the angels had been there before these white-robed multitudes came (cp. 1 Pet. 1:12). And now they joined in the heavenly worship by responding to the "great voice" (7:10) of the innumerable saints.

Blessing ... glory ... wisdom ... thanksgiving ... honor ... power ... might (7:12). Seven chosen words of praise and the same as those employed by the angels in 5:12, except that "thanksgiving "is here substituted in place of "riches."

One of the elders (7:13). Just as in 5:5, this is a most appropriate one to act as John's interpreter, being a representative of the Church of the living God. **Answered** (7:13) is an idiomatic use of this word, as in Matthew 11:25. The angel spoke relevantly to the occasion and so answered the expectant inquiry of John's enraptured gaze (cp. Zech. 3:4; 4:4, 11–12). The question of the elder and John's answer in verses 13–14 are to be compared with those in Zechariah 1:19, 21; 3:2; 4:11–13. This form of question and answer serves to give dramatic life to the description.

These are they who come out (7:14). Not "who came out"; nor "who shall come out" of the tribulation, although this is necessarily implied by logical inference. But "they who come" (οἱ ἐρχόμενοι [*hoi erchomenoi*]), that is, "they who are about to come." The vision contemplates them as one great company already before the throne (7:15).

The great tribulation (7:14). This is not to be understood as all the trials which may ever befall those who are counted worthy at last to enter the glory of God in heaven. This comforting assurance may indeed be allowed as a doctrine certainly tenable by reason of necessary inferences from such a picture of salvation and from other teachings of Holy Scripture. But our prophet's field of vision contemplates a definite tribulation of the near future, that bitter "hour of trial which was about to come upon the whole world, to try them that dwell upon the earth" (3:10). It is the same "great tribulation" spoken of by Jesus in Matthew 24:21, immediately after which the "sign of the Son of man" is to appear in heaven (Matt. 24:29).

But from the tribulation thus definitely contemplated we need not exclude any of the trials incident to the apostolic period, such as those referred to in John 16:33; Acts 14:22. The entire period between John's writing and "the consummation of that age" (referred to in Matt. 24:3) was for the Church a time of affliction, as Matthew 24:9 implies.

Washed ... white (7:14). Compare 1:5; 22:14; Ephesians 5:26–27; 1 John 1:7.

They are before the throne (7:15) like ministers of his presence. They **serve him** (7:15) so that their heavenly glory is not a repose of idle inactivity, but a service of delight. They serve him **day and night** (7:15) for day and night are alike to "the spirits of just men made perfect." In fact, there is no such thing as night to them (21:25).

In his temple (7:15). Their service is that of "priests unto God" (1:6). This temple of God is doubtless the same which, in 11:19, is seen "opened in the heaven." It is the triumphal outcome of what is measured in 11:1 and destined to survive the ruin of the great city which crucified the Lord. In a later vision this temple is identified with "God the Almighty and the Lamb" (21:22). All this is intimated in the statement that he who sits upon the throne shall **spread his tabernacle over them**, so that they shall dwell with him and he with them (cp. 21:3; Exo. 29:45; Lev. 26:11; Isa. 4:5, 6).

This mention of "throne," "temple," and "tabernacle" (7:15) in one verse is suggestive and shows how all three are virtually one. The profoundest symbolism of tabernacle and temple points out how God will dwell with men and men with God.

They shall no longer suffer from **hunger ... thirst ... sun ... heat** (7:16). This imagery is appropriated from Isaiah 49:10 (cp. Psa. 121:6). This implies utter absence of all plague and pestilence and such calamities as were about to come at the sound of the first four trumpets of woe (8:7–12).

The Lamb ... their shepherd (7:17) shall act the part of a good shepherd, as suggested by such scriptures as Psalm 23:1; Isaiah 40:11; John 10:11. **Fountains of waters of life** (cp. Psa. 23:2; 36:8; Isa. 49:10). **Wipe away every tear** (7:17). More expressive and tender than "all tears" (cp. Isa. 25:8; 35:10).

It remains for us here to inquire into the relation of the visions of 7:1–8 and 9–17 to each other. It is evident that the two companies are *represented* as distinct. But it does not therefore follow that they are of different nature and destiny. The distinctions are quite noticeable: (1) The one company are sealed with some stamp of the living God, while no such mark is mentioned of the others. (2) The one are out of "every tribe of the sons of Israel" (7:4); the other out of "every nation and all tribes and peoples and tongues" (7:9). (3) The one comprise a definite number; the other is innumerable.

(4) Nothing is affirmed of the first class except that they were "sealed out of every tribe of the children of Israel" (7:4). But the other appear in "white robes," with "palms in their hands" (7:9), and ascribe praise to God and the Lamb (7:10). The angels respond to their cry and one of the elders tells who they are and from where they come. They speak in terms of description closely analogous to those of Revelation 21:3–7 and 22:1–5. This shows that the innumerable company of 7:9–17 are the same as those blessed ones who wash their robes and have the right of the tree of life and to enter into the new Jerusalem (22:14). They are "the bride, the wife of the Lamb" (21:9) and though here they are not spoken of as sealed, there they are "written in the Lamb's book of life" (21:27) and "his name is on their foreheads" (22:4).

We observe further that in Revelation 14:1–5, we have a vision of "the Lamb standing on Mount Zion and with him a hundred and forty and four thousand, having his name and the name of his Father, written on their foreheads." They also sing "before the throne and before the four living creatures and the elders." They are defined as "virgins," who "follow the Lamb whithersoever he goeth," and "were purchased from among men (as a kind of) first-fruits unto God and unto the Lamb." These as certainly correspond to the select and sealed Israel of 7:4–8, as "the bride, the wife of the Lamb," in Revelation 21 and 22, corresponds to the white-robed multitude of 7:9–17.

We must interpret 7:4–8 in the light of 14:1–5 and 7:9–17, and in the light of what is seen in Revelation 21 and 22 as constituting the new Jerusalem. Thus, we need not suppose the sealed and numbered Israelites of the first vision to be excluded from the greater multitude of the second. If we adopt the view of many expositors in regarding the one hundred and forty-four thousand as Jewish Christians (the Church of the circumcision, Gal. 2:9, 10), we need not thereby exclude them from the innumerable company "out of every nation and from all tribes and peoples and tongues" (7:9). After all, these terms clearly include the Jewish as well as all other peoples.

It is most consonant with the language of the passage and the method of the book to understand these two companies as not so much composed of entirely different persons as contemplated in different relations and from different points of view. If we inquire how the souls under the altar to whom white robes were given (6:9–11) are related to this innumerable company arrayed in white robes and palms in their hands, our problem would be very much the same. The greater number may well include the smaller, but the smaller are nevertheless to be regarded as constituting a special class, so distinguishable as to call for a separate description. The martyrs who "were slain for the word of God" (6:9) receive special recognition and appear again as enthroned with Christ in exceptional glory (20:4–6). And no one would imagine them excluded from the company that inherit the new Jerusalem. So the hundred and forty-four thousand may be included in the innumerable multitude of 7:9–17, but they are first viewed as a special class chosen out of the twelve tribes of Israel. We need not suppose them any more worthy, or noble, or exalted than others. But the definitions of 14:1–5 set them before us as the "first fruits unto God and unto the Lamb."

We accordingly understand the company "sealed out of every tribe of the children of Israel" as an apocalyptic picture of that "holy seed" of which Isaiah speaks in Isaiah 6:13. That is, they are the surviving remnant which was destined to remain like the stump of a fallen oak after cities had been laid waste and the whole land had become a desolation. It was that "remnant of Jacob," which was to be preserved from the "consumption determined in the midst of all the land" (Isa. 10:21–23). It is the same "remnant according to the election of grace" of which Paul speaks in Romans 9:27–28; 11:5. God will not destroy Jerusalem and make the once holy places desolate until he first chooses and seals a select number as the beginning of a new Israel. The first Christian Church was formed out of chosen servants of God from "the twelve tribes of the dispersion" (Jms. 1:1). The end of the Jewish age was not to come until by the ministry of Jewish Christian apostles and prophets the gospel of the kingdom had been preached in the whole world for a testimony unto all the nations (Matt. 24:14). The same great fact is again symbolized in 11:1–2, by the measuring of the temple of God.

Viewed in this light, the contents of Revelation 7 are placed most impressively between the sixth and seventh seals. The old dispensation is about to come to an end: the city and temple are about to be destroyed by the judgment of God, as foretold by Jesus in Matthew 23:36–38. But before the end is disclosed by the opening of the seventh seal with its trumpets of woe, we have a vision, first, of that chosen remnant out of all Israel, composed of such Jews as were "sealed with the Holy Spirit of promise" (Eph. 1:13; 4:30; 2 Cor. 1:22). They were marked with that circumcision of the heart which is "in spirit, not in letter; whose praise is not of men, but of God" (Rom. 2:28–29). But the revelation does not stop with this vision of a new Israel, surviving as the nucleus of a new age and church. Rather it adds the larger picture of 7:9–17, as showing unto what that chosen first fruits will ultimately expand. The "remnant according to the election of grace" was but the beginning of a "holy seed." This seed is destined to become an innumerable company before the throne of God and of the Lamb and thus fulfill in the highest sense the ancient promise made to Abraham (Gen. 15:5; 22:17–18).

The assertion that these correlated visions are so incongruous that they could not have originated with one author, but must be fragments of lost apocalypses, is thus seen to be without valid ground. It would reflect most unwarrantably on the literary sense of the final compiler or redactor of our book. The genius for symmetry and tact displayed in the arrangement of the contents of this entire book justifies us in the belief that what recent critics imagine to be dislocated fragments of various preceding works are all well-considered and artistically planned portions of one great apocalypse, designed to encourage and comfort the earliest Christian churches.

Seventh seal opened (8:1)

> 1 And when he opened the seventh seal, there followed a silence in heaven about the space of half an hour.

The opening of the seventh seal reveals seven angels, who proceed to sound seven trumpets as so many signals of the end. The imagery of the whole section which now follows (Rev. 8–11) appears to have been suggested by the record of the seven trumpets which sounded the fall of Jericho. Those trumpets sounded the doom of the first great Canaanitish city which stood in the way of the conquest of the promised land; these sound the doom of "the great city, which spiritually is called Sodom and Egypt" (11:8, 13) and which stood in the way of the free progress of the word of God and the testimony of Jesus Christ. Jerusalem and her temple, then in bondage with her children," must give way before "the Jerusalem that is above and free" (Gal. 4:25–26).

The seven trumpets included in the seventh seal serve, after the manner of apocalyptic repetition, to intensify the terrors of the great day of wrath which were seen at the opening of the sixth seal (6:12–17). The revelation of that great and terrible day of the Lord here proceeds to bring forward a more exhaustive appropriation of Old Testament metaphor and symbol. This is in order to make a profounder impression upon the seer and his readers and also to show that these judgments were ordained of God and shortly to come to pass (cp. Gen. 41:32). So Daniel's apocalypse, in the vision of chapter 8, repeats in various details and with greater precision the latter portion of the vision of chapter 7.

Silence in heaven (8:1). How much learned folly has been displayed in fanciful expositions of this silence in heaven! It has been made to signify the repose of the Church after the Diocletian persecution (Lord); the liberty granted the Church by Constantine (Daubuz); the silent forbearance of Christians under Jewish persecution (Alcazar); the thousand years' rest before the end of the world (Vitringa). The source of such far-fetched notions is in the main a failure to recognize a rhetorical element in Holy Scripture and the art of the sacred writers in their studied efforts to make impressions by means of analogies and contrasts which exist in the very nature of images. What is thus merely incidental and suggestive in a certain context is magnified into a mystic meaning of far-reaching significance.

This "silence" is in the heaven where all these related visions appear. And, as all the preceding seals were accompanied by voices (cp. 6:1, 3, 5, 7, 9, 12, 16), this last one is distinguished by the contrast of silence. It was simply the silent expectation and awful suspense before the final scene. The mention of it by the writer serves to enhance the solemnity of the vision about to be disclosed.

About half an hour (8:1). This would be a short time, but sufficiently long to enhance the awful solemnity of the occasion. Perhaps the idea of this silence was suggested by the cessation of singers and trumpets when King Hezekiah and those with him bowed themselves in reverent worship (2 Chron. 29:28–29). The "half an hour" may have some reference to the offering of incense described in 8:3 and 4. For that would be about the length of time necessary for a priest to enter the temple and offer incense and return (cp. Lev. 16:13–14; Luke 1:10, 21).

Chapter 4
THE SOUNDING OF THE SEVEN TRUMPETS
(Rev. 8–11)

1. The Seven Angels (8:2)

2 And I saw the seven angels which stand before God; and there were given unto them seven trumpets.

The seven angels which stand before God (8:2). The well-known presence-angels familiar to those versed in current Jewish angelology (see Tobit 12:15: "I am Raphael, out of the seven angels who stand ready and enter before the glory of the Lord."). But no special significance attaches to these seven angels more than to the four angels of 7:1.

Were given unto them seven trumpets (8:2). By whom these are given is not recorded. In the corresponding vision of the seven bowls of wrath, the bowls were given by one of the four living creatures (15:7). Each one of these angels received a trumpet, just as in 15:1 and 16:1 each angel had a bowl of plagues. The trumpets serve as signals of so many successive scenes of a terrible series of judgments, while the bowls are symbols of so many vessels of woe.

2. The Angel with the Censer (8:3–6)

3 And another angel came and stood over the altar, having a golden censer; and there was given unto him much incense, that he should add it unto the prayers of all the saints upon the golden altar which was before the throne.
4 And the smoke of the incense, with the prayers of the saints, went up before God out of the angel's hand.
5 And the angel taketh the censer; and he filled it with the fire of the altar and cast it upon the earth: and there followed thunders and voices and lightnings and an earthquake.
6 And the seven angels which had the seven trumpets prepared themselves to sound.

And another angel came (8:3; cp. 7:2; Zech. 3:2). All such ministration of angels is part of the machinery of apocalyptics and the writer introduces as many angels as seem appropriate to perform the various parts of the symbolic picture. As the angel of the sunrise in 7:2 had charge of the sealing of God's servants, so this one acts the part of an officiating priest in the offering of incense.

Stood over the altar (8:3). Compare the vision of Amos 9:1. The great temple of God in heaven is before the eye of the seer and, like the earthly tabernacle and temple patterned after it (Exo. 25:40; 26:30; Heb. 8:5), has its golden altar of incense before the throne. So in the tabernacle the position of the altar of incense was immediately in front of the veil, behind which was the ark, with its mercy seat and cherubim where Jehovah was enthroned (Exo. 30:6; 25:21–22; 1 Kgs. 6:20, 22; Psa. 80:1; 99:1).

The **much incense** (8:3) is a fitting symbol of the prayers of all the saints. It is said that the incense was given to the prayers, that is, added to the prayers as a sign that they were presented and heard before the throne of God. Compare the mention of incense in Revelation 5:8 and Psalm 141:2. These prayers of all the saints are to be understood as in harmony with the cry of the souls under the altar (6:9, 10). They are superadded to them and are of the same character as the cry of God's elect ones referred to in Luke 18:7–8. In answer to these many prayers the judgment and vengeance prayed for are about to be executed.

The smoke … with the prayers (8:4). The dative of ταῖς προσευχαῖς (*tais proseuchais*) may be translated "with the prayers," as their accompanying symbol. Or it can be translated "for the prayers," as indicative of their acceptability before the throne of God.[1]

The angel has taken (8:5). This is apparently an inaccurate use of the perfect for the aorist, as in 5:7.

Filled it with the fire of the altar (8:5). The same fire of the altar which had burned the incense. So speedy is the answer to the prayers that the same fire which consumes the incense returns in burning coals of judgment upon the murderers of the saints to destroy both their land and city.

---

[1] So Winer: "The ascending smoke had reference to the prayers, was designed to accompany them and render them more acceptable." G. B. Winer *Grammar of New Testament Greek* (Edinburgh: 1882), 270.

Cast it upon the earth (8:5). A symbolic act, signifying that God was about to answer the prayers of his saints and would avenge them speedily (Luke 18:8).

Thunders and voices and lightning and an earthquake (8:5). This is a fourfold sign of approaching judgments. These terminate the silence of half an hour (8:1), which was sufficiently long for the symbolic scenes just described to make their full impression. The fourfold signals serve also to notify the trumpet-angels to proceed.

3. The Trumpets Sounded (8:7–11:19)

The sounding of the seven trumpets occupies the rest of Revelation 8–11. As in the case of the seven seals, the first four form a class by themselves and are noticeably distinguished from those which follow. The seven trumpets correspond in substance to the seven φιάλαι (*phialai*), "bowls" or "vials" of wrath in Revelation 16 and the imagery is appropriated in part from the plagues of Egypt. The entire picture is to be understood as an apocalypse of the same woes referred to by Jesus in Luke 21:25–26: "There shall be signs in sun and moon and stars; and upon the earth distress of nations, in perplexity for the roaring of the sea and the billows; men fainting for fear and for expectation of the things which are coming on the world: for the powers of the heavens shall be shaken."

Any attempt to interpret such language literally, or to find in each separate allusion and figure an allegorical meaning, must end in confusion. The entire description moves in the element of apocalyptic symbolism and aims to produce an impression of the fearfulness of divine judgments on wicked men and nations. We find an Old Testament parallel in Ezekiel 38:18–23, where Jehovah speaks in fury and jealousy and fire of wrath and announces:

> a great shaking in the land of Israel; so that the fishes of the sea and the fowls of the heaven and the beasts of the field and all creeping things that creep upon the earth and all the men that are upon the face of the earth, shall shake at my presence and the mountains shall be thrown down and the steep places shall fall and every wall shall fall to the ground.... Every man's sword shall be against his brother. And I will plead against him with pestilence and with blood; and I will rain upon him and upon his hordes and upon the many peoples that are with him, an overflowing shower and great hailstones, fire and brimstone.

It would be an arbitrary and puerile distortion of this passage in Ezekiel to give distinct allegorical significance to the fishes and fowls and beasts and men and mountains and hailstones and fire. Likewise it seems equally absurd to search through the history of modern Europe for events answering to the imagery of the seven trumpets. The language and method of the biblical apocalyptists, as seen in the Hebrew scriptures, abundantly prepare us for understanding all the trumpet-woes of Revelation 8–11. They are in substance identical with the great signs and terrors of Luke 21:25–26, which our Lord assured the disciples would all take place before that generation passed away (Luke 21:31). The imagery of trumpets is, as we have seen, constructed in allusion to the trumpets which sounded the fall of Jericho (Josh. 6).

First trumpet sounded (earth smitten) (8:7)

> 7 And the first sounded and there followed hail and fire, mingled with blood and they were cast upon the earth: and the third part of the earth was burnt up and the third part of the trees was burnt up and all green grass was burnt up.

Hail and fire, mingled with blood (8:7). Hail and fire were mingled together in one of the Egyptian plagues (Exo. 9:23–24). Our author intensifies the picture by adding to the imagery thence derived the element of blood (cp. Eze. 5:17; 38:22; Joel 2:30).

Third part (8:7). As in the symbolic picture of Ezekiel 5:2, 12, each of the first four trumpet-plagues destroys a third of something.

Earth ... trees ... grass (8:7; cp. 7:1, 3). Three objects naturally associated together are specified as the subjects of the plague. This is just as in the next plague, where sea, creatures of the sea, and ships are put together (8:8–9).

Second trumpet sounded (sea smitten) (8:8–9)

> 8 And the second angel sounded and as it were a great mountain burning with fire was cast into the sea: and the third part of the sea became blood;
> 9 and there died the third part of the creatures which were in the sea, even they that had life; and the third part of the ships was destroyed.

As it were a great mountain (8:8). That is, something that looked like a great burning mountain. The image may have been suggested by Jeremiah 51:25; but the mountain has no significance here as a separate symbol. It merely appears a moment as the instrument employed by heaven to turn the third part of the sea into blood. Like the fire cast upon the earth in 8:5, it resulted in the bloody sea and so brought a judgment like another one of the Egyptian plagues (Exo. 7:20–25).

The consequent death of **the third part of the creatures which were in the sea** and the destruction of **the third part of the ships** finishes out the picture (8:9). This is just as the mention of trees and grass in 8:7 fills up the picture of destruction contemplated in the first trumpet-woe. To find special meanings in the living creatures of the sea and the ships is as uncalled for as to do the same in the trees and grass of the previous picture. The one plague affects the earth and what naturally belongs to it; the other affects the sea and what naturally belongs to the sea.

Third trumpet sounded (rivers and fountains) (8:10–11)

> 10 And the third angel sounded and there fell from heaven a great star, burning as a torch and it fell upon the third part of the rivers and upon the fountains of the waters;
> 11 and the name of the star is called Wormwood: and the third part of the waters became wormwood; and many men died of the waters, because they were made bitter.

A great star, burning as a torch (8:10). This pictures an immense meteor glowing as with the luminous flame of a lamp (λαμπάς [*lampas*]). The star in this plague served the same purpose as the burning mountain in the previous plague. The effect produced suggests that the star in falling burst into mineral fragments and changed into poisonous bitterness the third part of the rivers and the fountains of which men were apt to drink.

Wormwood ... bitter (8:10–11; cp. Exo. 15:23). The effect of this plague is different from that on the sea and more disastrous to men. **Many men died of the waters** (8:11), which were rendered poisonous by the deadly wormwood.

Fourth trumpet sounded (sun smitten) (8:12)

> 12 And the fourth angel sounded and the third part of the sun was smitten and the third part of the moon and the third part of the stars; that the third part of them should be darkened and the day should not shine for the third part of it and the night in like manner.

Sun ... moon ... stars (8:12). The effect of this fourth stroke was like that of the ninth plague of Egypt (Exo. 10:21–22). This completes the cycle of the first four judgments on land, sea, rivers and fountains and luminaries of heaven. Apocalyptic parallels of this fourth trumpet-plague are found in Joel 2:10, 30–31; Ezekiel 32:7–8; Matthew 24:29; Luke 21:25.

These first four trumpets sound the coming of sorrows and tribulation essentially like those symbolized by the first four seals (6:1–8). We need not seek to trace minute analogies between them, but should rather look upon them as another set of symbols pointing to the same calamities. They foretokened the earthquakes, famines, pestilences, terrors, and carnage which were to be a part and parcel of the woes attendant upon the destruction of Jerusalem. Thus by repetition under different symbols and by means of all analogous images of plague and wrath, the sacred writer aims to make the most profound impression of the great and terrible day of the Lord which is near at hand.

[[Eagle Makes First Announcement of Woe (8:13)]]

> 13 And I saw and I heard an eagle, flying in mid heaven, saying with a great voice, Woe, woe, woe, for them that dwell on the earth, by reason of the other voices of the trumpet of the three angels, who are yet to sound.

An eagle (8:13). This is not an angel, as in 14:6. The eagle is here introduced as the swift messenger of woe (Hos. 8:1; cp. Deut. 28:49; Jer. 4:13). **The great voice**, with its awful notes of **woe, woe, woe** (8:13) is a part of the art of this book to make use of every figure and symbol which will serve to enhance the impressiveness of the word of the prophecy. How fearful the plagues foretokened by the sounding of the first four trumpets!

But these are only a beginning of woes as compared with the things to come **by reason of the other voices of the trumpet of the**

three angels, who are yet to sound (8:13). Expectation is thus raised to its highest pitch and the three remaining woes may be supposed to reach the consummation of the age and show its end.

Fifth trumpet sounded (locust-plague) (9:1–11)

> 1 And the fifth angel sounded and I saw a star from heaven fallen unto the earth: and there was given to him the key of the pit of the abyss.
> 2 And he opened the pit of the abyss; and there went up a smoke out of the pit, as the smoke of a great furnace; and the sun and the air were darkened by reason of the smoke of the pit.
> 3 And out of the smoke came forth locusts upon the earth; and power was given them, as the scorpions of the earth have power.
> 4 And it was said unto them that they should not hurt the grass of the earth, neither any green thing, neither any tree, but only such men as have not the seal of God on their foreheads.
> 5 And it was given them that they should not kill them, but that they should be tormented five months: and their torment was as the torment of a scorpion, when it striketh a man.
> 6 And in those days men shall seek death and shall in no wise find it; and they shall desire to die and death fleeth from them.
> 7 And the shapes of the locusts were like unto horses prepared for war; and upon their heads as it were crowns like unto gold and their faces were as men's faces.
> 8 And they had hair as the hair of women and their teeth were as the teeth of lions.
> 9 And they had breastplates, as it were breastplates of iron; and the sound of their wings was as the sound of chariots, of many horses rushing to war.
> 10 And they have tails like unto scorpions and stings; and in their tails is their power to hurt men five months.
> 11 They have over them as king the angel of the abyss: his name in Hebrew is Abaddon and in the Greek tongue he hath the name Apollyon.

A star from heaven fallen unto the earth (9:1). Observe the perfect πεπτωκότα (*peptōkota*) "fallen," as indicating that the star was already fallen from heaven when John first saw it. The personification of this star from heaven, which is implied in his being given the key of the pit of the abyss, warrants the interpretation according to which the star denotes an angel. That it represents an evil and not a good angel is inferred from the word "fallen," as well as from his unloosing the plague of infernal locusts upon the earth. We may well compare Isaiah 14:12: "How art thou fallen from heaven, O brilliant star (הילל [*hallel*]; Septuagint, ἑωσφόρος [*eōsphoros*]; Vulgate, *Lucifer*), son of the morning!" Also Luke 10:18: "I beheld Satan fallen as lightning from heaven."

Alford well suggests a connection of imagery between this passage and 12:9. Note that the dragon drew after him "the third part of the stars of heaven" (12:4) and the king of the infernal locusts is "the angel of the abyss" (9:11). Thus, we may well infer that the king of these locusts is designed to be thought of as a fallen star.

The pit of the abyss (9:2) is here as elsewhere to be understood of the infernal world, the prison of evil spirits. Compare Luke 8:31. In 20:1 "the key" is held by an angel, who also has "a great chain" to bind Satan.

As the smoke of a great furnace (9:2). This figure is appropriated from Genesis 19:28 and Exodus 19:18. **Sun ... darkened** — Compare the similar effect of the locust-plague in Joel 2:10.

Locusts upon the earth, i.e., "the land" (9:3). This woe corresponds to the Egyptian plague described in Exodus 10:12–15, but the imagery descriptive of these locusts out of the abyss is appropriated from Joel 1:6; 2:4–10.

As the scorpions of the earth (9:3). We take the words of "the earth" (or "the land") not as serving to distinguish land-scorpions from sea-scorpions. Rather they set up a contrast with these scorpion-locusts from the abyss. Though coming out of the infernal world they have a power like that of the well-known creature of the land, which is a terror and torment to those who live in certain hot climates (Deut. 8:15). The scorpion has many feet and eyes like the spider. But its deadly power is in its tail (cp. 9:10), which has many joints and is provided at the extremity with a crooked point with which it strikes its victim. This point of the tail is like the sting of a bee, secreting at its base a poisonous fluid. When it strikes a man, the poison, like that of a deadly serpent, is injected into the wound and, if not fatal, causes unspeakable torment.

Not hurt the grass shows that they are quite unlike ordinary locusts, which devour **every green thing** and **every tree** which comes in their way (9:4). These had been sufficiently injured by the plague of the first trumpet (8:7; cp. 7:3).

Such men as have not the seal of God (9:4; cp. 7:3 and Eze. 9:4–6). The disciples were gifted with power over unclean spirits (Mark 6:7) and all who received the Gospel were turned from the power of Satan unto God (Acts 26:18).

They should not kill (9:5). Though armed with stings like scorpions, these locusts were not permitted to take the life of their victims. **Five months** (9:5) covers the usual period, from May to September, during which locusts appear. We need seek no mystical time-reference here. If anything unusual is to be noticed it is that this infernal plague is continuous during the whole period of five months. Ordinarily they come in swarms during any of the five months, but soon pass away. But these locusts, whose work is to torment men, not vegetation, continue their terrible work through the whole five months.

Their torment (9:5), i.e., the torment of the men receiving the poisonous stroke. **The torment of a scorpion** (9:5) employs the genitive of the subject, meaning the torment inflicted by a scorpion when it strikes a man. The stroke of the scorpion's tail, like the sting of a great hornet, causes an intense pang of agony.

Seek death and shall in no wise find it (9:6). Like those depicted by Job, who would prefer death to such miserable life (Job 3:21).

Shapes of the locusts like horses (9:7). This comparison is from Joel 2:4. But our writer adds to Joel's picture and represents the infernal locusts as wearing golden crowns and human faces. These suggest the qualities of royalty and intelligence. They may well symbolize spiritual hosts of wickedness such as Paul describes by the words "principalities," "powers," and "world-rulers of darkness" (Eph. 6:12; cp. Col. 2:15).

Hair as the hair of women (9:8). These locusts were like the "hairy locust" mentioned in Jeremiah 51:27 (ילק סמר [*yeleq samar*]), a young devouring locust bristling with hair; not "rough caterpillars," as A.V., nor "rough cankerworm," as R.V.). But the hair of these was long and flowing and so arresting attention because of its unusual quantity (cp. 1 Cor. 11:14–15).

Teeth as of lions (9:8). So in Joel 1:6.

Breastplates (9:9). The word so rendered (θώρακας [*thōrakas*]) may mean either "breasts" or "breastplates." But as "the shapes of the locusts were like unto horses prepared for war" (9:7), it comports with the whole picture that they also wear what has the appearance of breastplates of iron, thus shielded by a strong coat of mail. Compare the breastplate of fire and hyacinth and brimstone in 9:17.

As the sound of chariots (9:9). An eyewitness of a plague of locusts in Palestine writes: "The locusts passed over the city in countless hosts, as though all the swarms in the world were let loose and the whirl of their wings was as the sound of chariots." Compare the same figure in Joel 2:5 and the rest of the description given in the footnote below.[2]

Tails ... stings ... hurt men five months (9:10). These statements reiterate in more specific form what has been already stated in verse 5. While most of the imagery is appropriated from Joel these features are peculiar to the picture created by our apocalyptist.

Abaddon ... Apollyon (9:11). These words, appropriated from the two original languages of the Holy Scriptures, signify alike, "Destroyer." They are each an appropriate title for the ruler of this monstrous army from the abyss.

We recognize in the woe of the fifth trumpet an apocalyptic symbolizing of the demoniacal possessions and mad fury which came upon the Jewish people and especially upon their leaders, during the last bitter struggle with Rome. That this is the most obvious import of the symbols and the most natural interpretation of the whole passage, may be seen in the following facts:

1. The abyss is the acknowledged prison of demons, or unclean spirits (cp. 20:1–3 and Luke 8:31).
2. The imagery of smoke, darkness, and tormenting of men fitly symbolizes the demoniacal possessions of New Testament times. It also pictures all that infernal fury and rage which take possession of wicked men when they yield to the power of the devil and give themselves over to believe a lie.

---

[2] On this entire description we have a striking comment in the following testimony of one who saw a plague of locusts in Palestine in 1866: "From early morning till near sunset the locusts passed over the city in countless hosts, as though all the swarms in the world were let loose, and the whir of their wings was as the sound of chariots. At times they appeared in the air like some great snowdrift, obscuring the sun, and casting a shadow upon the earth. Men stood in the streets and looked up, and their faces gathered blackness. At intervals those which were tired or hungry descended on the little gardens in the city, and in an incredibly short time all that was green disappeared. They ran up the walls, they sought out every blade of grass or weed along the ground, or on the tops of the house. One locust found near Bethlehem measured more than five inches in length. It was covered with a hard shell, and had a tail like a scorpion." *Journal of Sacred Literature for 1866*, p. 89.

3. The angel-king of the abyss, who is called the Destroyer, is satisfactorily explained only of Satan, "the prince of the demons" (cp. Matt. 12:24–27). He is the same evil angel that appears again in this book as the dragon, the old serpent, the devil, cast down with his angels to the earth, chained and shut up in the abyss, and finally cast into the lake of fire.
4. The words of Jesus in Matthew 12:43–45, are a prophecy of woe to come upon that generation through the agency of unclean spirits. The fallen spirit which is cast out of a man is there represented as going and gathering to himself seven other evil demons and with them entering into the house from which he had been ejected and making it worse than ever before. "Even so shall it be also unto this wicked generation," said Jesus. That generation had been visited by the Saviour and he had shown his power to cast out Satan. But the Jewish people rejected his teaching, continued empty of his truth and persisted in Pharisaic washings and garnishing of self-conceit and hypocrisy. It remained, therefore, as a fitting work of the devil to call up a host of his kindred spirits and take possession of a house so vacant and inviting. We have only to change the figure slightly to make the allegory of Matthew 12:43–45, a duplicate picture of the trumpet-woe of Revelation 9:1–11.
5. Finally, we have in the writings of Josephus (*Wars* 5:10:5; 5:13:6) a remarkable confirmation of this interpretation. "No age," says he, "ever bred a generation more fruitful in wickedness than this from the beginning of the world." "I suppose," he observes in another place, "that had the Romans made any longer delay in coming against these villains, the city would either have been swallowed up by the ground opening upon them, or been overwhelmed by water, or else been destroyed by such thunder as the country of Sodom perished by; for it had brought forth a generation of men much more atheistical than were those that suffered such punishments; for by their madness it was that all the people came to be destroyed."

[[**Second announcement of woe (9:12)**]]

> 12 The first Woe is past: behold, there come yet two Woes hereafter.

This verse, like 8:13, is designed to enhance the expectation of the woes about to follow. The words, like those of 11:14, are the words of the writer of the book, not those of an eagle or an angel. And the three announcements are an incidental evidence of the unity of plan in Revelation 8–11.

Sixth trumpet sounded (Euphrates-armies) (9:13–21)

> 13 And the sixth angel sounded and I heard a voice from the horns of the golden altar which is before God,
> 14 one saying to the sixth angel, who had the trumpet, Loose the four angels which are bound at the great river Euphrates.
> 15 And the four angels were loosed, which had been prepared for the hour and day and month and year, that they should kill the third part of men.
> 16 And the number of the armies of the horsemen was twice ten thousand times ten thousand: I heard the number of them.
> 17 And thus I saw the horses in the vision and them that sat on them, having breastplates as of fire and of hyacinth and of brimstone: and the heads of the horses are as the heads of lions; and out of their mouth proceedeth fire and smoke and brimstone.
> 18 By these three plagues was the third part of men killed, by the fire and the smoke and the brimstone, which proceeded out of their mouths.
> 19 For the power of the horses is in their mouth and in their tails: for their tails are like unto serpents and have heads; and with them they do hurt.
> 20 And the rest of mankind, who were not killed with these plagues, repented not of the works of their hands, that they should not worship devils and the idols of gold and of silver and of brass and of stone and of wood; which can neither see, nor hear, nor walk:
> 21 and they repented not of their murders, nor of their sorceries, nor of their fornication, nor of their thefts.

The imagery of the fifth trumpet is taken largely from Joel's picture of the fourfold locust-plague (Joel 1:4, 6). Likewise also the imagery of the sixth trumpet corresponds notably to that of Joel 2:1–11. There we have the terrible picture of a rushing army of horsemen spreading fiery destruction before them and behind them. The two successive pictures have a close relation to each other both in Joel and in this Apocalypse. And in the latter we note the mention of horses, heads, breastplates and tails in both visions.

Voice from ... the golden altar (9:13). And so like an answer from before the throne of God to the prayers of all the saints (cp. 8:3–5).

Loose the four angels (9:14). Notice four angels here as in 7:1. There they "hold the four winds of the earth;" here they are to be let loose from the restraint which had so far bound them. The number four in both cases has no other significance than that of being the apocalyptic number of world-judgments. That the angels are to be regarded as evil rather than good is inferred from the fact of their having been bound and from the character of the army which they lead. Compare the warlike angelology of Daniel 10:13, 20.

The great river Euphrates (9:14) is here employed as a symbolic name. It alludes to the well-known fact that from the regions of that river came those rods of Jehovah's anger (Isa.10:5): the great armies of Assyrians and Chaldeans which swept over the land of Israel like a destructive flood. Compare Isaiah 7:20; 8:7–8; Jeremiah 46:10; Habakkuk 1:6–11.

Prepared for the hour and day and month and year (9:15). Notice the article with the first noun only, as if equivalent to the hour of the day, etc. They have been held fast as in bonds, so to speak, only waiting for the appointed hour of summons to march forth upon their work of ruin.

Kill the third part of men (9:15). Compare the first four trumpets as destroying each a third (8:7–12). The tormenting locusts were permitted only to hurt men, but there was no restriction to a third. Now these angels of the Euphrates are sent forth to kill men, but in the same proportion as the earth, trees, sea, fountains and sun were smitten at the sounding of the first four trumpets.

The number of the armies (9:16). Observe how suddenly the four angels assume the form of an immense army. The angels of the army, like the angels of the seven churches, thus seem to be resolved into the army itself (cp. note on 1:20). The idea of angelic princes or leaders of armies, however, is traceable in Daniel 10:13, 20–21.

Twice ten thousand times ten thousand (9:16), or two hundred millions. An apocalyptic number, definite, as suggestive of an accurately numbered host and yet so immense as to appear like an innumerable multitude (cp. Psa. 68:17).

I heard the number (9:16). Some voice, therefore, must have proclaimed the number.

Thus I saw the horses (9:17). That is, in the manner about to be narrated. **In the vision** (9:17). This word (ὅρασις [*horasis*]) serves to admonish us that all this picture of woe is but a vision. Therefore it is not to be treated as a detailed record of material things. The symbolism of the sixth seal (6:12–17) is not to be interpreted literally. Likewise the symbolism of this sixth trumpet is not to be subjected to such a method of exegesis as would find in horses, riders, breastplates, heads, and tails an accurate description of something to appear in actual life and form like these.

Having breastplates (9:17). These seem to have been so adjusted as to shield both the horses and the riders. The **fire, hyacinth,** and **brimstone** here denote the colors of the breastplates. They correspond to the **fire and smoke and brimstone,** which **proceedeth** out of the leonine **mouth** of each of the horses. The fire would represent red, the hyacinth a dark blue like that of smoke, and the brimstone a yellow color.

As the heads of lions (9:17). These have the appearance of hideous monstrosities, like the beast of 13:1–2 and that of Daniel 7:7.

These three plagues (9:18). Namely, the fire and the smoke and the brimstone, a threefold symbol of the terrors of destructive war.

The power ... in their mouth and in their tails (9:19). They spread destruction before them and behind them for the tails also have heads. The notable difference being that the heads of the horses resemble the heads of lions and the heads of the tails are like those of serpents. As serpents they have power to do harm not unlike the stings of scorpions (9:10). So the destructive work of this great army is like that depicted in Joel 2:2: "A fire devoureth before them and behind them a flame burneth; the land is as the garden of Eden before them and behind them a desolate wilderness."

Repented not ... and they repented not (9:20–21). These two verses make a double assertion of the impenitence and the wickedness of the survivors of these plagues. Those who were not killed were two-thirds of all the wicked men exposed to the terrors of this second woe.

The **works of their hands** are immediately defined as idolatrous objects of worship made **of gold and of silver and of brass and of**

stone and of wood (9:20). To do homage to such was no better, according to Leviticus 17:7 and Deuteronomy 32:17, than to worship demons (cp. 1 Cor. 10:20). The language of our writer is here appropriated from such passages as Deuteronomy 4:28; Psalm 135:15–17; Isaiah 17:8; Daniel 5:4.

The four crimes mentioned in 9:21 are to be noted as the flagrant crimes of Jezebel (cp. 1 Kgs. 21:14–15; 2 Kgs. 9:22). They are all violations of the second table of the decalogue, as the idolatry contemplated in verse 20 is a violation of the first table. Thus **the rest of the men who were not killed in these plagues** (9:20) are conceived and fittingly characterized as apostate Israelites, guilty of persistent violation of both tables of the law. These sins are typically representative of apostasy from the law of God as promulgated at Sinai. In the interpretation we are consistently to keep in mind that we are dealing with a complex symbol seen in vision. Therefore, particular acts of idolatry or of crime are as little to be looked for in Jewish history (as a corresponding detailed fulfillment of the prophecy) as are horses with lions' heads, breathing fire from their mouths, and destroying men with their tails.

The total picture presented in 9:20–21 is, accordingly, appropriate for the Jewish people, who "denied the Holy and Righteous One and killed the Prince of life" (Acts 3:14–15). They became "full of hypocrisy and iniquity" so as to merit the title of "offspring of vipers" (Matt. 23:28, 33). And among them false prophets arose and led many astray (Matt. 24:11, 24).

This occurred in the latter time of the period which ended with the fall of Jerusalem and even while yet the apostles lived to warn and admonish. Yet some departed from the faith and gave heed to seducing spirits and doctrines of demons and were guilty of all manner of wickedness (cp. 1 Tim. 4:1; 2 Tim. 3:1–6). To represent all such guilt and apostasy of the Jewish nation at that time as a flagrant violation of both tables of their fundamental law is in perfect accord with the methods of biblical apocalyptics.

In clearest harmony, therefore, with the scope and methods of this Apocalypse, we understand the immense army of cavalry depicted in the symbols of the sixth trumpet to be no other than the overwhelming military forces of the Roman empire. The imperial forces marched against Jerusalem and pressed the terrible siege to the utter overthrow of city and temple. A comparison of Matthew 24:15 and Luke 21:20, shows that the compassing of Jerusalem with armies was a placing of "the abomination of desolation in a holy place" and a sign that her desolation was at hand. This abominable desolation was spoken of in Daniel the prophet. For it was of the same destructive character, if not the same calamity, as that which, in Daniel 9:26–27, is represented as overwhelming city and sanctuary in awful ruin and bringing down a determined divine judgment "upon the desolate."

It is a well-attested fact that the Euphrates formed the eastern boundary of the Roman empire at the time of the Jewish war and that four legions of soldiers were stationed there (Tacitus, *Annals*, 4.5; Dio Cassius, 4:23). Josephus states that Titus was followed by "three thousand drawn from the river Euphrates" (*Wars* 5:1:6). But to see in these facts a striking fulfillment of "the four angels at the great river Euphrates" (in 9:14) would be wrong. It would be to follow the erroneous methods of those literalists who pay more attention to such an accidental correspondence of details than to the main purpose of a great symbolic picture. In the explanation of such a picture it is of the first importance to keep in view the one great total impression designed to be made. Undue attention to incidental features of the larger picture tends to divert from the main purpose of the whole.

As an exhibition of the incongruous and misleading interpretations which have been put upon this passage, we give space to the following. These have been current with many of the "continuous historical" expositors for a century past. The armies described in Revelation 9:17–19 are the Turkish hordes, which are said to have started out on a career of western conquests extending from Bagdad to Constantinople. They completed their work in the capture of the last named city. Great stress has been laid upon the following points as evidences of the truthfulness of the exposition:

1. These hordes went forth from the region of the Euphrates.
2. They were composed largely of cavalry.
3. Their myriads were so great that, according to Gibbon, they overspread a frontier of six hundred miles.
4. The breastplates represent the characteristic warlike apparel of the Turks, which is scarlet, blue, and yellow (that is, fire, hyacinth and brimstone).
5. The heads like those of lions represent both the fierceness and the nominal titles of the leaders.
6. The fire, smoke, and brimstone out of their mouths is a reference to the use of powder in the siege of Constantinople.
7. The tails like unto serpents are the horsehair military ensigns, worn as symbols of authority by the Turkish pashas.

8. The hour, day, month, and year of verse 15 are resolved by mathematical calculation into three hundred and ninety-six years and one hundred and thirty days (from January 18, 1057 to May 16 or 20, 1453).

On this interpretation we make the following observations:

First, so far as the warlike imagery of the vision of 9:17–19 goes, it may symbolize Turkish armies as well as any other armies. But one is left to wonder what the Turkish invasion and the capture of Constantinople had to do with John and his contemporaries. And how the events of 1057–1453 A.D. are to be truthfully included among "the things which must shortly come to pass" (Rev. 1:1). It is also singular that if the seer really attempted to foretell so many of the minute features of that Turkish war, he should have mentioned the Euphrates by name, but made not the slightest allusion to Byzantium and the Bosporus.

Second, it is a most remarkable use of symbolism to make *breastplates* of fire, hyacinth, and brimstone represent merely the colors of the apparel worn by the Ottomans.

Third, to make the horses' heads emblematic of mere popular titles of the *leaders* (when the number of them is 200,000,000) is in the last degree far-fetched and incongruous. But if the lion heads represent the fierceness and strength of the *leaders*, should they not have been put on the riders rather than on the horses?

Fourth, if the horsemen especially represent cavalry, as is claimed, it is difficult to perceive the propriety of making the gunpowder used in the siege of Constantinople come from the horses' mouths.

Fifth, to make the tails mere horsehair symbols of authority worn by chieftains is not only to involve the same incongruity as that noticed in respect to the heads (number 3 above), but also to allow no sufficient significance to the serpent form and heads of the tails.

Sixth, to resolve "the hour and day and month and year" of 9:15 into a long period of centuries is to pay no proper respect to the grammatical import of the language (see note on 9:15). But it also makes the entire picture involve the confusion of supposing one and the same army to continue in existence four hundred years. We need not here comment further on the exegetical jugglery which turns years into centuries and days into years.

[[**Second interlude** (10:1–11:13)]]

The visions of this passage are of the nature of an interlude between the sounding of the sixth and seventh trumpets. The writer thus displays consummate art in bringing forward a number of important revelations before the final stroke of doom. In this respect he follows the method of an epic poem or of a great tragedy and brings in by way of episode all that can as well be introduced before the final crisis. In this way he enhances expectation and makes the catastrophe of the end the more impressive when it comes. Accordingly, when he comes to record the sounding of the last trumpet (11:15–19), he is able to do so in few words, representing the end as signally decisive and unspeakably sublime.

By means of this interlude four things are presented to view: (1) The mighty angel coming down from heaven (10:1–7); (2) the eating of the little book (8:11); (3) measuring the temple of God (11:1–2); and (4) the two witnesses (11:3–13).

The mighty angel from heaven (10:1–7)

1 And I saw another strong angel coming down out of heaven, arrayed with a cloud; and the rainbow was upon his head and his face was as the sun and his feet as pillars of fire;
2 and he had in his hand a little book open: and he set his right foot upon the sea and his left upon the earth;
3 and he cried with a great voice, as a lion roareth: and when he cried, the seven thunders uttered their voices.
4 And when the seven thunders uttered their voices, I was about to write: and I heard a voice from heaven saying, Seal up the things which the seven thunders uttered and write them not.
5 And the angel which I saw standing upon the sea and upon the earth lifted up his right hand to heaven,
6 and sware by him that liveth forever and ever, who created the heaven and the things that are therein and the earth and the things that are therein and the sea and the things that are therein, that there shall be delay no longer:
7 but in the days of the voice of the seventh angel, when he is about to sound, then is finished the mystery of God, according to the good tidings which he declared to his servants the prophets.

Another strong angel (10:1). One leading purpose of this angel is to deliver the little book to John. Thus, the most obvious reference of the word "another" is to the strong angel of 5:2, who made the proclamation there recorded concerning the sealed book. One strong angel inquired in heaven and earth and underneath the earth (5:3) for someone worthy to open the sealed book and now another strong angel descends from heaven, with a little book laid open in his hand.

Arrayed with a cloud (10:1). This angel is not sitting on a cloud, as in 14:14, nor descending on a cloud, as one coming for the execution of judgment (Isa. 19:1; Matt. 24:30). Rather, he is wearing a cloud as a garment. This is like the cloud of glory which filled the tabernacle and covered the appearance of Jehovah above the mercy seat (Exo. 40:34–38; Lev. 16:2). Compare in 12:1, "a woman arrayed with the sun."

The rainbow upon his head (10:1). This is a symbol of covenanted mercy (cp. 4:3; Eze. 1:28). It is another sign that the appearance of the "strong angel" is not for judgment, but for the announcement of "good tidings" (cp. 10:7).

His face (10:1), not his countenance (ὄψις [*opsis*]) as in 1:16. **As the sun**, which is a source of light and life (cp. John 1:9; 8:12). "It is God that said, Light shall shine out of darkness, who shined in our hearts unto illumination of the knowledge of the glory of God in the face of Jesus Christ" (2 Cor. 4:6).

His feet as pillars of fire (10:1). As if to give light to his ways, like the pillar of fire that illumined the way of Israel out of Egypt (Exo. 13:21–22). It also showed the presence and guidance of Jehovah's Angel (Exo. 14:19; 23:20; 32:34). Compare the "feet like unto burnished brass" in 1:15.

In his hand a little book open (10:2). In 5:7, the Lamb was seen to take the sealed book "out of the right hand of him that sat on the throne." Then after a pæan that sounded through all the universe, he proceeded to open the seals. They are all opened now and the last trumpet is about to sound. The book of mystery is therefore no longer a sealed book. It now seems to John like a little book (βιβλαρίδιον [*biblaridion*]) and opened (ἠνεῳγμένον [*ēneōgmenon*]) and it is about to be given to him as a word of revelation and prophecy.

Right foot upon the sea ... left upon the earth, i.e. "land" (10:2). As if he were truly Lord of sea and land.

Cried with a great voice as a lion roareth (10:3). This shows that the little Lamb (ἀρνίον [*arnion*]) that took the book from the hand of God is truly the Lion of the tribe of Judah, who "conquered to open the book and the seven seals thereof" (cp. 5:4–7). So the revealer of the heavenly mysteries, who was first announced as the Lion of Judah and then appeared as a slain Lamb, now comes down from the heaven as a glorious, mighty Angel to declare the nearness of the end (vv. 6 and 7) and to transmit the opened book "unto his servant John" (cp. 1:1).

The seven thunders uttered their voices (10:4). Signs of revolutions and wonderful events about to be inaugurated, but which John was forbidden to record. Compare 12:19.

Seal up ... the seven thunders (10:4). This command is to be compared with Daniel 8:26; 12:4, 9, where the seer is told that the vision is shut up and to be kept concealed for many days, even to the time of the end. This is an apocalyptic method of saying that the thunder voices signified many "unspeakable words, which it is not lawful for a man to utter" (2 Cor. 12:4). What these voices uttered and why the thunders were seven in number, must remain a mystery. He would be very presumptuous who should at this time undertake to declare what John was forbidden to write.

But one might, perhaps, be permitted to suggest something for the benefit of a certain class of "continuous-historical" interpreters, like Elliott. He discerns in the seven thunders a symbol of the papal bulls. But these mystic thunders may much more probably have contained "a complete revelation of the history of Christianity from the days of Jesus on to the end of the world." And inasmuch as the long periods of that history covered so many events which could not be truthfully said to "come to pass shortly," the prophet was wisely forbidden to attempt the impracticable task of writing them all down!

Lifted up his right hand to heaven and sware (10:5). Compare the notably analogous language of Daniel 12:7. The objection that such an oath is inconsistent with the idea that this strong angel is designed to represent Christ is nullified by the fact that the entire vision of 10:1–7 is symbolical. If it is proper at all to represent Christ under the form of a strong angel, it certainly violates no law of propriety to represent him as an angel lifting up his hand and swearing according to the customary form. But even aside from this consideration, why is it not as fitting for Christ thus to swear as for Jehovah to swear by himself? Compare Genesis 22:16; Isaiah 45:23; Jeremiah 49:13; Amos 6:8. The form of lifting up the right hand could hardly have been omitted from such a symbolic picture.

Who created the heaven ... earth ... sea (10:6). Compare Psalm 146:6; Nehemiah 9:6; and Exodus 20:11.

Shall be delay no longer (10:7). The immediate context and comparison with 6:11, warrants our translating χρόνος [*chronos*]) in this passage by "delay." The "yet a little time" (ἔτι χρόνον μικρόν [*eti chronon mikron*]) of 6:11, is now about to end, for the seventh trumpet is to sound the ἐτελέσθη (*etelesthē*), **it is finished**. Compare the γέγονεν (*gegonen*) of 16:17 and the τετέλεσται (*tetelestai*) of John 19:30. The prayers of the martyr-souls and of all saints are now about to be answered and so there shall be no more delay in bringing in the long-expected consummation.

The days of the voice of the seventh angel (10:7). That is, the days immediately preceding the blast of the seventh angel; the last days of the old dispensation, **when** the last trumpet is **about to sound**, and (when) the **mystery of God** was **finished**. This mystery of God is the "gospel and the preaching of Jesus Christ, according to the revelation of the mystery which hath been kept in silence through times eternal, but now [in Paul's time] is manifested and by the scriptures of the prophets, according to the commandment of the eternal God, is made known unto all the nations unto obedience of faith" (Rom. 16:25–26). This mystery is further defined in Ephesians 1:9; 3:3–9; and Colossians 1:26–27. The verb ἐτελέσθη (*etelesthē*), "was finished," is in the aorist tense. It conveys the idea that when the seventh angel sounds the last trumpet the mystery of God is to be thought of as a definite revelation of the past.

The seventh trumpet, as we understand this book, is the symbolic signal of the end of the old dispensation and the consequent beginning of the new era of the kingdom of Christ on earth (cp. 11:15). But the Old Testament prophets contemplated the appearance of the Messiah and the going forth of the new word of Jehovah as occurring "in the end of the days" — that is, the last days of the eon or dispensation under which they were living (cp. Isa. 2:2; Mic. 4:1 and, for like use of the phrase, see Gen. 49:1; Num. 24:14; Dan. 10:14).

In the same manner the New Testament writers consider themselves as living near the end of the age and making known the mystery of God in Christ, "who was manifested at the end of the times" (1 Pet. 1:20). This "end of the times" belongs, not to the era of the new dispensation, but to the concluding days of the old. So God spoke in fulfillment of Messianic promises "in the end of these days in his Son" (Heb. 1:1). The appearance of Christ and the first preaching of his Gospel are thus uniformly represented as occurring at a certain "fullness of times" (Gal. 4:4; Eph. 1:10). Christ was manifested by the sacrifice of himself "once for all at the end of the ages" (Heb. 9:26). Paul understood that he and his contemporaries were they "upon whom the ends of the ages have come" (1 Cor. 10:11).

It is a serious error, therefore, when learned exegetes persist in assuming that the phrase "the last days," as employed in the Scriptures, means the period of the new Christian dispensation. Current chronology helps to perpetuate this error by dating the Christian era from the birth of Christ; but our current chronology is no competent interpreter of the language or concepts of the prophets and apostles.

According to the good tidings which he declared to his servants the prophets (10:7). This is a free but accurate translation of what the Greek idiom expresses much more briefly: "as he evangelized his servants the prophets." But our English idiom does not employ this transitive use of the verb in the sense here intended. The prophets of the Old Testament are here referred to and all Messianic revelations made known to them were a declaration of good tidings, a gospel of good things to come.

The eating of the little book (10:8–11)

> 8 And the voice which I heard from heaven, I heard it again speaking with me and saying, Go, take the book which is open in the hand of the angel that standeth upon the sea and upon the earth.
> 9 And I went unto the angel, saying unto him that he should give me the little book. And he saith unto me, Take it and eat it up; and it shall make thy belly bitter, but in thy mouth it shall be sweet as honey.
> 10 And I took the little book out of the angel's hand and ate it up; and it was in my mouth sweet as honey: and when I had eaten it, my belly was made bitter.
> 11 And they say unto me, Thou must prophesy again over many peoples and nations and tongues and kings.

The voice ... again speaking (10:8). The same voice as that mentioned in verse 4. **Go, take the book which is open** (10:8). Observe that it is called by the heavenly voice τὸ βιβλίον (*to biblion*), "the book," as in 5:1–5. But John calls it in this chapter (vv. 2, 9, 10) **the little book** (τὸ βιβλαρίδιον [*to biblaridion*]) (10:9). The imagery of taking and eating the book as detailed in this passage (10:8–11) is based upon Ezekiel 2:9–3:7, 14. The Old Testament seer was commanded to take the roll of the book, which had been spread out before him, and eat it and go and speak unto the house of Israel. He found it in his mouth "as honey for sweetness," but when the Spirit lifted him up and took him away upon his mission he went in bitterness and heat of spirit.

Eat it (10:9). Compare the figure of eating the words of Jehovah and finding them a joy to the heart in Jeremiah 15:16.

Sweet ... bitter (10:10). Notice the reverse order of these words in verse 9. The angel spoke of the bitterness first, but in the actual experience the seer tells us: **It was in my mouth sweet as honey: and when I had eaten it, my belly was made bitter** (10:10). The most natural explanation of this is that the reception of the word of prophecy is a sweet and precious experience; the eating of this word, as in the case of Jeremiah (15:16), produced immediate joy and rejoicing of heart. But that word contained so many announcements fraught with "lamentations and mourning and woe," and destined to be treated in so many instances with derision and defiance (cp. Eze. 2:9; 3:7) that the sympathetic heart would often be made bitter by reason of the burden.

They say unto me (10:11). Who those are who thus speak is not recorded, but the plural suggests that the saying came from many voices. **Thou must prophesy again** (10:11). John's prophetic ministry is not to end with the reception of this Apocalypse. He is "again" (πάλιν [*palin*], i.e., *further* and *anew*) **to prophesy over** (or concerning) **peoples and nations and tongues and kings**. John was destined to survive the catastrophe of Jerusalem and to proclaim the passing away of the old darkness and the shining of the new and true light of the Gospel (1 John 2:8).

It is not in point to make the word "again" allude to one portion of this Apocalypse as contrasted with another part for John has not yet in this book prophesied at all. He has only been receiving revelations. And the eating of the little book is but one symbolic act in the midst of many others. It is not the end of the revelations he is to receive before he will go forth to resume his ministry as a servant and prophet of Jesus Christ. This apostle had, like Peter and other disciples (cp. Acts 2:14–36; 3:18–21), already proclaimed the coming and kingdom of Christ. But after receiving these impressive revelations of the end of the old system and the coming in of a new age, he will be able to preach and prophesy again a word of God concerning all nations and peoples.

We may now revert to what is observed in the note on 5:1, that the sealed book of that former vision is the opened book of 10:8–11. The Lamb took it out of the hand of him who sat upon the throne (5:7); having opened the seven seals, he now has given it as a little book to John, who takes it out of the angel's hand and eats it as a word of prophecy (10:10–11). So when this servant of Jesus goes forth again to prophesy he will have become possessed of "the Revelation of Jesus Christ, which God gave him (that is, Jesus)," and which he in turn "sent and signified by his angel unto his servant John" (1:1).

It remains to add a further word in defense of the position assumed throughout this chapter that the strong angel who gives the book to John is designed to represent Jesus Christ himself:

1. The description accords noticeably with that of the Christophany of 1:12–18.
2. He is the same as the Lamb who took the book out of the hand of him that sat on the throne and now holds it open in his own hand.
3. He speaks as Lord in 11:3 and throughout the vision appears to exercise a power and authority unsuitable to a created being.
4. It accords with the habit of apocalyptic repetition and especially with the method of this book, to present Christ under various forms. We are first told the revelation is from Jesus Christ (1:1); then we have the glorious Christophany of 1:12–18; then he is announced as the Lion of Judah and appears as a Lamb that had been slain. After this angelophany he appears again as Michael (12:7); then again as the Lamb on Mount Zion (14:1); then as the Son of man on a white cloud (14:14); then as the rider on a white horse (19:11). In view of this variety of revelation the objection that he could not be presented under the form and name of an angel loses all its force.
5. Finally, the purpose of this interlude (10:1–11:13) makes it particularly appropriate that the Christ's appearance should be under the symbolism of an angelophany; for he appears not as God, or as judge, but as the rainbow-crowned angel of the covenant, who commits the word of God to his servant and apostle.

The measuring the temple (11:1–2)

> 1 And there was given me a reed like unto a rod: and one said, Rise and measure the temple of God and the altar and them that worship therein.
> 2 And the court which is without the temple cast without and measure it not; for it hath been given unto the nations: and the holy city shall they tread under foot forty and two months.

The first eleven verses of this chapter furnish a double picture, just as chapter 10 has done. And as it is impossible to disconnect the angelophany of 10:1–7, from the eating of the book in 10:8–11, so it is impossible for us to make the measuring of the temple in 11:1–2, independent of the figure of the two witnesses in 11:3–12.

The two pictures of the eleventh chapter stand also in most intimate relation to those of the tenth chapter. The appearance of Christ as the light of the world and the angel of the covenant announced the near end of the old age and commissioned his disciples to proclaim his word to all the nations (Matt. 28:19–20; Mark 16:15). This was immediately followed by that apostolic ministry which gathered out of the Israelitish people the "remnant according to the election of grace." But it was a ministry so hateful to the great body of the Jewish people that their testimony was despised and rejected. And consequently, they were persecuted unto death (cp. Matt. 24:9). This intimate connection of the four pictures of the interlude will appear more fully further on.

There was given me a reed (11:1). It is noticeable that the seer himself is ordered to take part in this symbolical act, but no account is given of his doing what was commanded him.

Saying (11:1). No new speaker has been introduced and the close connection of what is here written with the preceding vision leaves us the most natural inference that the mighty angel who ordered John to take and eat the book is still the speaker.

The command **to measure the temple of God** and to **cast** the court **without** (11:2) is followed in one connected discourse with the account of the two witnesses. This is as if the one implied and involved the other. So there was no particular opportunity to record the doing of what was commanded. It further displays the consummate art of the writer to concentrate attention upon the great thought intended by the symbol and to avoid narration of details.

The **reed like unto a rod** (11:2) was to serve as a measuring rod, like the "measuring reed" of Ezekiel 40:3. The imagery here is taken in substance from Ezekiel 40. The entire conclusion of Ezekiel's prophecy, from the fortieth chapter to the end, is a symbolic portraiture of the glorious future of God's true Israel, a detailed Jewish ideal of the restored church and kingdom of God. John appropriates only a few ideals.

In his picture, only the temple proper, the ναός (*naos*), with its altar and worshipers, is measured off for preservation. The ναὸν τοῦ θεοῦ (*naon to theou*), translated **temple of God**, is strictly only that portion of the entire sanctuary (ἱερόν [*hieron*]) which constituted the holy place and the holy of holies. **The altar** (τὸ θυσιαστήριον [*to thusiastērion*], 11:1) which belonged to this part was the golden altar of incense which stood before the veil.

The symbolical character of the passage is seen in the further command to measure them that **worship therein**. Only the consecrated priests were permitted to enter and minister in the holy place. But while the priest offered incense on the golden altar, the devout people of Israel were apt to pray without (Luke 1:10). And the priest's act of offering the incense was an impressive symbol of their prayers (cp. 8:3–4 note) and truly represented all the devout worshipers among God's Israel. The holy places and all that was symbolized by them and those who truly worshiped therein, are, accordingly, measured off for preservation from the impending destruction.

In these we have another symbol of "the remnant according to the election of grace." We have already shown how this was represented by the sealing of an elect Israel out of every tribe (cp. 7:1–8 and notes there and at the end of Rev. 7). Earlier between the opening of the sixth (6:12) and seventh (8:1) seals, a chosen number out of the tribes of Israel are sealed so as not to perish in the oncoming judgments (7:4–8).

Similarly, here between the sounding of the sixth (9:13) and seventh (11:15) trumpets, a measured portion of the sanctuary of Israel is marked off for preservation from the impending woe. This chosen remnant is to be the nucleus of a new Israel of God, a temple of the Spirit. For after the seventh trumpet sounds (11:15) and the destructive judgment falls (11:18) and the kingdom of Christ is inaugurated (11:17), "the temple of God which is in heaven was opened" and in it once more appears the long-lost "ark of his covenant" (11:19).

The court (11:2). The uncovered courtyard (αὐλή [*aulē*]) outside the temple proper and inclosing it on all sides. It is to be **cast without** (11:2). That is, treat it as destined to destruction and so already given over to be trodden down. Compare the casting off (ἀπωθέω [*apōtheō*]) of unbelieving Israel in Romans 11:1–2. As the activity of John is conceived as merely symbolical, he is appropriately addressed as if actually doing that which is to come to pass by the judgment of God.

Measure it not (11:2). Earlier those who received not the seal of God were given over to destruction (8:5–12). So likewise those who are represented by the portions of the sanctuary not measured are, along with the holy places, **given over to the nations** to **tread under foot** (11:2). For the unmeasured portion is conceived as already given unto the nations by divine decree. Thus, John's not measuring it is therefore virtually a casting it out as doomed.

The holy city (11:2). Thought of and spoken of here as "holy" because associated in the immediate context with the holy remnant out of whom God is to build the new Jerusalem. So in Isaiah 64:10–11 the cities of Judah and the temple, although desolate and burned with fire, are called "holy cities" and "our holy and beautiful house," because of their past association with saintly fathers.

Tread under foot (11:2; cp. Isa. 63:18; Luke 21:24). **Forty and two months** (11:2). Compare 13:5 where the same number is given for the period of the authority of the beast. Forty-two months are to be resolved into days by reckoning thirty days to the month. This is the same as "twelve hundred and sixty days" ($42 \times 30 = 1260$), which is mentioned in the next verse as the period during which the two witnesses prophesy (cp. also 12:6). The twelve hundred and sixty days appear in 12:14 to be equivalent to the mystic number "a time and times and half a time," which is appropriated from Daniel 7:25; 12:7.

There is no good reason to doubt that these several designations are but examples of apocalyptic variety in the use of terms. And all such serve to denote, not so much the same exact period of time, as a period of one and the same character. In every case, it should be observed, this mystic number points to a period of apparent triumph for the enemy of God's people and of humiliation, trial, and persecution for the saints. Even the three and a half days of 11:9 are of like character, being a period of cruel exposure and shame.

Seven is so often suggestive of something sacred that we may well think of three and a half as a broken seven, a ruptured covenant, a temporary triumph of the enemy of God (cp. Dan. 9:27). We accordingly understand this mystic number, not as a mathematical problem which we can reduce to a specific chronology of times in order to tell the day and hour of historical events. Rather, it is symbolical of a comparatively short period of trial and disaster to the people of God.

These "forty-two months" (11:2) during which the nations shall tread the holy city under foot are identical with the "times of the nations" referred to in Luke 21:24: "They shall fall by the edge of the sword and shall be led captive into all the nations; and Jerusalem shall be trodden down by nations until the times of the nations be fulfilled." These "times of the nations" are obviously the period allotted to the nations to tread down Jerusalem. Those times are fulfilled as soon as the nations shall have accomplished their work of treading down the holy city. It is a misleading fancy, a catching at the mere sound of words, to confound these "times of the nations" with the "fullness of the nations" in Romans 11:25. The "times of the nations" in Luke are times of judgment on Jerusalem, not times of salvation to the Gentiles.

Revelation 11:1 and 2, then, are a symbolical picture. They are quite analogous to the sealing of the one hundred and forty-four thousand in 7:1–8 and the implied visitation of judgment on the unsealed Israel left out of the enumeration there detailed. There, however, the people of the twelve tribes are more particularly placed in view. Here it is rather the temple and the city that are suggested as corresponding objects of thought.

The two witnesses (11:3–13)

3 And I will give unto my two witnesses and they shall prophesy a thousand two hundred and threescore days, clothed in sackcloth.
4 These are the two olive trees and the two candlesticks, standing before the Lord of the earth.
5 And if any man desireth to hurt them, fire proceedeth out of their mouth and devoureth their enemies: and if any man shall desire to hurt them, in this manner must he be killed.
6 These have the power to shut the heaven, that it rain not during the days of their prophecy: and they have power over the waters to turn them into blood and to smite the earth with every plague, as often as they shall desire.
7 And when they shall have finished their testimony, the beast that cometh up out of the abyss shall make war with them and overcome them and kill them.

8 And their dead bodies lie in the street of the great city, which spiritually is called Sodom and Egypt, where also their Lord was crucified.
9 And from among the peoples and tribes and tongues and nations do men look upon their dead bodies three days and a half and suffer not their dead bodies to be laid in a tomb.
10 And they that dwell on the earth rejoice over them and make merry; and they shall send gifts one to another; because these two prophets tormented them that dwell on the earth.
11 And after the three days and a half the breath of life from God entered into them and they stood upon their feet; and great fear fell upon them which beheld them.
12 And they heard a great voice from heaven saying unto them, Come up hither. And they went up into heaven in the cloud; and their enemies beheld them.
13 And in that hour there was a great earthquake and the tenth part of the city fell; and there were killed in the earthquake seven thousand persons: and the rest were affrighted and gave glory to the God of heaven.

The contents of Revelation 11:1–2 correspond to those of 7:1–8. Similarly, the description of the Two Witnesses (11:3–13) has a corresponding relation to the vision of the great multitude who come out of the great tribulation and enter into the heavenly felicity of God and the Lamb (11:9–17). As this latter vision comes immediately before the opening of the seventh seal, so the picture of the Two Witnesses immediately precedes the sounding of the seventh trumpet. Compare note at the beginning of Revelation 7.

And I will give unto my two witnesses (11:3). Note how the discourse of him who speaks in 11:1 and commands the seer to measure the temple, proceeds without interruption directly to the description of the witnesses. Neither the temple, city, nor witnesses of this chapter appear to John in vision. Rather, all are presented as the word of the strong angel who has delivered the opened book to John. When, therefore, he speaks of "MY two witnesses" he assumes an authority and rank that virtually makes him equal with God. And we have already seen abundant evidence that, like the angel of the covenant, Jehovah's name was in him (Exo. 23:21).

"I will give" (11:3). This verb is not followed by a direct object. But it implies that to the witnesses will be imparted wisdom and ability to testify through their appointed time. Moses, God's great prophet to Israel, was assured that Jehovah himself would be with his mouth and teach him what to say in the hour of trial (Exo. 4:12). Similarly, the disciples of the Lord Jesus were told that, when brought before governors and kings for his sake and to bear witness against them and the nations, it should be given them in the very hour what they should speak (Matt. 10:19; Mark 13:11; Luke 12:12).

They shall prophesy (11:3). These witnesses are essentially prophets. They do the very work to which the seer himself was appointed (10:11) after he had eaten the book of the revelation of Jesus. The apostolic prophesying "over many peoples and nations and tongues and kings" was one of the most important things of the closing period of the old dispensation. For the end of that age was not to come until "the gospel of the kingdom should have been preached in all the world for a the nations" (Matt. 24:14).

A thousand two hundred and threescore days (11:3). This is not to be identified with the "forty-two months" of verse 2, as if covering the same chronological period of time. Rather, as explained above, it is symbolical of a like period of persecution and suffering among the saints of God. During an appointed time of trial and while many souls under the altar of sacrifice cry out, "How long, O Lord, dost thou not avenge our blood?" (6:10) these witnesses and prophets of Jesus are faithfully to declare the whole counsel of God. Compare Daniel 9:26–27, where the Messiah is to confirm a covenant with many for one week. Then in the midst of that week, the desolating abomination pours its destructive flood upon the city and the sanctuary.

Clothed in sackcloth (11:3). This is the appropriate garb of prophets at a time of impending woes (Isa. 20:2; Jer. 4:8; Zech. 13:4).

These are the two olive trees (11:4). This is a direct allusion to the symbols of Zechariah 4. There the golden candlestick was seen to be fed with oil by two olive trees standing one upon the right and the other upon the left of the candlestick. In that vision the candlestick represented, as always, the Church or people of God, whose defense and triumph are not to be sought by means of the might and power of the world, but by the Spirit of Almighty God. The two olive trees or olive branches represented Zerubbabel and Joshua, who for their time were declared to be "the two anointed ones that stand by the Lord of the whole earth." Through those two anointed leaders God for the time communicated his divine power to his people and it was a time of peril.

Appropriating these symbols in their broader import, the speaker here calls the Two Witnesses both **olive trees** and **candlesticks** (11:4). They represent what was symbolized by the one candlestick and the two trees. They are in some sense both the light of the world and the builders and defenders of God's true temple. That there should be **two candlesticks** as well as **two** "olive trees" is probably owing to the fact that the witnesses are spoken of as two. The "two" is thus emphasized as a symbolic number, the number of witnesses always necessary to establish testimony (Deut. 17:6; 19:15; Matt. 18:16; 2 Cor. 13:1).

But these Two Witnesses, being candlesticks as well as olive trees, are representative of the Church itself, the whole body of God's people, as well as their anointed leaders. The original New Testament Church constituted the true "household of God, being built upon the foundation of the apostles and prophets, Christ Jesus himself being the chief corner stone; in whom each several building, fitly framed together, groweth into a holy temple (ναόν [*naon*]) in the Lord" (Eph. 2:20–21). And that which was the distinguishing character and glory of the first Christian household of God was the fact that it was a witnessing Church, a Church of martyrs (μάρτυρες [*martures*]).

Revelation 11:5–6 describe the Two Witnesses as gifted with miraculous power and divinely defended from harm until their work is done. The allusions are to well-known facts in the lives of Moses and Elijah. Thus for the time of their ministry, the Two Witnesses are as potent to repel harm, smite their enemies, and do wonderful works as were those two most distinguished prophets of the olden time.

If any one desireth [wills] **to hurt them** (11:5). That is, to act toward them like the hostile forces which in successive companies marched against Elijah (2 Kgs. 1:9, 12) as if to do him harm.

Fire proceedeth out of their mouth and devoureth their enemies (11:5). In Elijah's case "the fire of God came down from heaven and consumed the enemy" (2 Kgs. 1:10, 12). This is conceived as a terrible and real fulfilling of what Jehovah said to his prophet Jeremiah: "Behold, I will make my words in thy mouth fire and this people wood and it shall devour them" (Jer. 5:14; cp. Jer. 1:10; Psa. 97:3). But in accord with the symbolism of 1:16 and 2:12, the language may be taken metaphorically. It would thus suggest how the word of these prophetic witnesses was as a savor of death unto death unto the enemies of God and his people.

In this manner must he be killed (11:5). That is, by the devouring judgments of God, as announced by the witnesses. They have **power to shut the heaven** (11:6), as did Elijah in 1 Kings 17:1. In that they have **power over the waters to turn them to blood** (11:6), they are like

Moses and Aaron in Exodus 7:17, 19. They can also **smite the earth with every plague** (11:6). This alludes to all the other plagues of Egypt, as brought on by Moses and Aaron (cp. 1 Sam. 4:8). Note Christ's promise to his disciples in Luke 10:19 and Mark 16:17–18.

When they shall have finished their testimony (11:7). Observe that no power in earth or hell is able to prevail against them until their work is done. But, although the supernatural powers above referred to interpose to aid them in their work, they fall at last and die the death of martyrs.

The beast that cometh up out of the abyss (11:7). This beast has not yet been described, but the reference is an anticipation of what is written in 13:1–2 and 17:8. This is just as in 3:12, where the writer anticipates "the new Jerusalem which cometh down out of heaven." But this beast is no other than the kingly angel of the abyss mentioned in 9:11 and whose name and nature there pointed him out as the Destroyer.

Make war ... overcome (11:7). The language in which the beast is here described is suggested in Daniel 7:3, 21. The dragon from the abyss appears later to take possession of the Roman power (13:1–2). Thus, it may, perhaps, be well to note that capital punishment, even when demanded by Jewish law, must be executed by authority of the empire. This is seen in the case of Jesus (John 18:31). In cases of violence, when an offender was put to death by a Jewish mob, as in the case of Stephen, we may still believe that the Roman power winked at the illegality and was thus in fact to blame. The Roman empire was thus chargeable with executing the penalty of death. Thus, like the beast of Revelation 13, it may be said to have made war on the early Christians and killed them. But the inspiration of all such cruel persecutions and death came from the prince of hell.

Their dead bodies in the street (11:8). So that they were made an open spectacle of shame. The mad vindictiveness of their enemies has often thus exhibited itself on the dead bodies of martyrs; but their deadly hate could only "kill the body" (Matt. 10:28).

The great city (11:8) is the same great city as that mentioned in 14:8; 16:19; 17:5, 18. It is **called spiritually** as indicating its spiritual or moral character: **Sodom and Egypt** (11:8). This double name is employed symbolically to designate the great city under description as characterized by what the words "Sodom and Egypt" would most naturally suggest to a Jewish mind.

In biblical history, the words "Sodom and Egypt" are synonymous with flagrant wickedness and oppressive persecution. In Genesis 18 and 19 we read of the enormous sin of Sodom, that cried to heaven for judgment. And the whole story of the exodus of Israel out of Egypt shows the bitter oppression of that "house of bondage." In Isaiah 1:10, the prophet addresses the leaders of the Jewish people of Jerusalem as "rulers of Sodom." In Jeremiah 23:14, the prophets of Jerusalem and all the people are said to be unto God as Sodom and Gomorrah. In Ezekiel 16:46–52, Jerusalem is charged with corruption and sins even worse than those of Sodom. Egypt figures frequently in the Old Testament as the house of bondage and the seat of abominable idolatry (Exo. 1:13–14; 13:3; 20:2; Deut. 15:15; Jer. 43:12–13; 46:25; Eze. 20:7; 23:3, 8). No more suitable names, therefore, could have been employed, spiritually, to designate that great city upon which Jesus charged the crimes specified in Matthew 23:34–37 and Luke 13:34 (cp. also Acts 7:52).

But, to put the matter beyond all question, it is further added that the city in which the witnesses were exposed to shame was the same city **where also their Lord was crucified** (11:8). There is only one city that comes to mind at this specific statement and that answers perfectly to the description of this verse. Jesus himself said to his disciples "that he must go unto Jerusalem and suffer many things of the elders and chief priests and scribes and be killed" (Matt. 16:21; 20:18; Mark 10:33; Luke 18:31). It was he who said, "It cannot be that a prophet perish out of Jerusalem" (Luke 13:33). It was the people of Jerusalem that madly cried, "His blood be on us and on our children" (Matt. 27:25).

In view of these statements and the well-known facts, it is a remarkable exhibition of partisan pleading to allege, as does Alford (*Greek Testament, in loco.*) that Christ "was crucified, not in, but outside the city and by the hands, not of Jews, but of Romans!" And yet this expositor and others like him have much to say about our duty to be governed by the obvious import of the language of Scripture. Yet they can thus presume to nullify the statement that Jerusalem was the place where the Lord was crucified and insist that this "great city" must be understood of some unknown and unnamed city, "which will be the subject of God's final judgments." And Lange can gravely write that the city where the Lord was crucified (ἐσταυρώθη [*estaurōthē*]) means a "divine establishment, embracing Church and State, as a mock-holy fallen theocracy!" (*Commentary, in loco.*)

One chief trouble with those interpreters who try to explain away this obvious reference to Jerusalem is that they consider it impossible to identify this "great city, which spiritually is called Sodom and Egypt," with "the holy city" of 11:2. These, they insist, cannot be the same. But others will incline to think that half the ingenuity employed on their own visionary expositions of the place where the Lord was crucified might have shown them that, in strict accord with Old Testament usage, both designations suit Jerusalem. How is it that Isaiah could call this same Jerusalem a "faithful city" and a "harlot" in one breath? The answer is very simple: Once "righteousness lodged in her, but now murderers" (Isa. 1:21). Similarly Jeremiah speaks in Jeremiah 2:20.

The simple fact is that in verses 2 and 8 of this chapter, Jerusalem is viewed in different relations. This mentions in the first instance "the temple of God and the altar and them that worship therein." Then its being measured off for preservation (cp. 2 Sam. 8:2) made it proper in that connection to speak of the city which was about to be trodden down by the nations as "the holy city." For he is contemplating it there as a place of hallowed associations about to be ruined. The wickedness of the city does not in that connection come into view at all, but rather the destruction of a venerable shrine. Hence the designation of the city is naturally and properly like that of Isaiah 64:10–11, where the prophet cries: "Thy holy cities are a wilderness, Zion is a wilderness, Jerusalem a desolation. Our holy and beautiful house, where our fathers praised thee, is burned up with fire and all our pleasant things are laid waste."

Furthermore, in verses 1 and 2, the thought is primarily directed to that reserved and chosen remnant out of whom God is to build a new Jerusalem. Hence there is a touch of pathos in the accompanying allusion to the desecration of "the holy city." But after the description of the death of the Two Witnesses and the shameful exposure of their dead bodies and in immediate connection therewith, the place and people guilty of their blood may well be called "Sodom and Egypt." That "great city" was enormously great in wickedness and doomed to a judgment of retribution for "all the righteous blood shed on the earth, from the blood of righteous Abel unto the blood of Zacharias" (Matt. 23:35). A city or a people is great or small in proportion to its importance from the prophet's point of view.

From among the peoples and tribes (11:9). Jerusalem was often thronged with such (cp. Acts 2:5–13).

Three days and a half (11:9). Their ascending "into heaven in the cloud" (11:12) is after the manner of the ascension of their Lord and a symbol of their triumph. Likewise this subjection of their dead bodies to their enemies for "three days and a half" accords proximately with the period when his dead body lay in the grave. Compare the sign of the prophet Jonah (Matt. 12:39–40).

But the three and a half days are as truly a symbolical number as the forty-two months of 11:2 and not to be understood as a specific designation of computable time. Like the "time, times and half a time" (see 11:2 note), it seems to be intended to suggest a broken seven and to indicate a short period of calamity and shame. It is something worthy of note in this connection that Jesus himself speaks, in Luke 13:33, in a like singularly mystic way. There before addressing Jerusalem as the murderer of prophets, he says: "I must walk to-day and to-morrow and the day following: for it cannot be that a prophet perish out of Jerusalem."

Rejoice ... make merry ... send gifts (11:10). Customary expressions of great hilarity. The enemies of God show great rejoicing when they imagine they have gained a victory. But their triumphing is usually short. **Tormented them** (11:10). Wicked men, like demons, are usually tormented by the presence and word of Christ and his true prophets. So the words of Peter and Stephen cut to the heart when they, as witnesses of Jesus Christ, declared his truth to their Jewish enemies (Acts 5:32–33; 7:54).

Breath of life ... and they stood (11:11). The language is mainly from Ezekiel 37:10 and appropriately pictures a resurrection of dead bodies. **Great fear fell** (11:11). A notable change occurs from the merriment described in 11:10. Their rejoicing is suddenly turned into trembling.

They went up into heaven in the cloud (11:12; cp. Acts 1:9). As they had suffered like their Lord, so also are they glorified with him (Rom. 8:17; 2 Tim. 2:11). The imagery and allusions are throughout to the ascension of Jesus, but the similar ascension of Elijah is not to be excluded. As Elijah's power as a prophet is alluded to in 11:5–6, so his final glorification may also be naturally associated with that of Jesus.

We observe that (according to the best sustained reading) the witnesses heard **a great voice from heaven** (11:12) calling them up on high. But it is not said that their enemies heard that voice, but rather that they **beheld them** (11:12). Contrast the companions of Saul who heard the heavenly voice but beheld no one (Acts 9:7). In all this description of the power, prophesying, death, resurrection, and ascension of the Two Witnesses we recognize an apocalyptic picture. And that picture is of the work, sufferings, and triumph of the apostles and prophets of Jesus, who laid the foundations of the Christian Church.

The careful reader of the foregoing notes on the Two Witnesses will have seen that the exposition has led naturally and logically to the conclusion just announced. A very large proportion of those who founded and built the New Testament Church were called to seal their work and testimony with their blood. That these apostles and prophets are truthfully portrayed in 11:3–12 may be more clearly seen by the following considerations:

1. They were preeminently *witnesses* (μάρτυρες [*martures*]). Compare Luke 24:48; Acts 1:8; 2:32; 3:15; 5:32; 10:39, 41; 13:31.
2. They are represented as Two Witnesses rather than any other number for two reasons. First, because of the analogy of the two olive trees and, second, especially because it requires two witnesses to establish testimony (Deut. 17:6; 19:15; Matt. 18:16; 2 Cor. 13:1).
3. They were anointed, like Joshua and Zerubbabel, to build the new Church. And they were in fact the candlestick that was destined to supplant and supersede the old defunct Judaism.
4. They were notably gifted with power to work miracles and were divinely supported until their work was finished (Mark 16:17–18; Luke 10:19; Acts 5:12; 28:5). Hence the obvious allusions in verses 5 and 6 to the miraculous power exercised by Moses and Elijah.
5. Their resurrection and triumphant going up into heaven is an apocalyptic picture of what Jesus had repeatedly assured his followers (Matt. 10:16–32; 24:9–13; Luke 21:12–19). It corresponds to the triumph of the martyrs in Revelation 20:4–6, which is there called "the first resurrection."

This account of the Two Witnesses concludes the fourfold picture of what we have entitled the second interlude (10:1–11:13). We do well to pause here, before proceeding to the grand finale and, even at the risk of some repetition, emphasize the relations and significance of this section of the Apocalypse. We have explained the four parts of the section as (1) a manifestation of Christ as the great covenant angel; (2) a revelation and commission given to John to prophesy to the nations; (3) a calling of the chosen remnant of true Israelites to be the nucleus of the future Church; and (4) the work, power, suffering and glory of the founders of Christianity.

The significance of these revelations, as coming between the sixth and seventh trumpets, must be studied as a part of the artistic scheme of the Apocalypse. Their position here may be seen to indicate that the manifestation and ministry of Christ and the witness of his new Gospel in the world must precede the overthrow of Jerusalem and of the cultus which centered in the temple. Christ's proclamation of the approaching end of the age and of his own kingdom at hand was magnificently symbolized in this strong angel from heaven, who declared the mystery of God about to be finished.

Interpreters and theologians have in general strangely failed to note the uniform teaching of the Scriptures that both the incarnation of Christ and the apostolic ministry took place in the end of the age. Christ's own testimony was that "the kingdom of heaven is at hand," and that the Gospel of his kingdom must be preached "in the whole world for a witness unto all the nations" before "the end" should come (Matt. 24:14). Peter at Pentecost recognized that the outpouring of the Spirit was to be "in the last days" (Acts 2:17). God spoke in the last days by his Son (Heb. 1:1); for though Christ was foreknown before the foundation of the world he was manifested "at the last of the times" (1 Pet. 1:20). In Hebrews 9:26, the manifestation and sacrifice are said to occur "at the end of the ages." It is therefore a serious error of exegesis to maintain that the centuries of Christian history belong, in the biblical sense of the words, to "the last days" or "the end of the age."

This Apocalypse depicts the end of the Old Testament cultus and the consequent beginning of the new kingdom of God among men. It was, therefore, in striking harmony with the scheme of the book that a manifestation of Christ and the commission and prophetic witnessing of the first generation of martyrs should be set forth in appropriate symbols before the sounding of the seventh trumpet. Hence we may well admire the consummate genius and art displayed by the writer in presenting all these things in an impressive episode between the sixth and seventh trumpets.

With this view of the plan and purpose of the writer, observe now the fitness of the four pictures as presented in this interlude. The appearance of the strong angel, his holding a book opened, his authority over sea and land, his leonine cry, the response of the seven thunders (cp. John 12:23–32), the declaration that there shall be no more time-delay in finishing the mystery of God as spoken by the prophets — all this is a wonderful setting forth of the substance of Jesus's testimony to the world. Nothing is more firmly fixed in the common record of the synoptic gospels than the assertion of Jesus that the generation then living should not pass until all these things should be fulfilled.

The giving of the book to the seer and the assurance that he must prophesy over all the nations is a most admirable symbolizing of the apostolic commission of Matthew 28:19–20; Mark 16:15; and Acts 1:8. The measuring of the holy places and true worshipers of the temple and the casting out of the rest, depicts the election of the true Israel. Around her the new building of God would grow into a holy temple (Matt. 16:18; 1 Cor. 3:9; Eph. 2:21) and abide in heavenly places after the old one had passed from human view.

The foregoing notes have sufficiently shown how the Two Witnesses symbolize the witnessing Church of the apostolic age. As the innumerable multitude in chapter 7:9–17 may include the sealed Israel of 7:4–8, so these witnesses may also include the measured worshipers of 11:1.

In that hour (11:13). This is the hour of the triumph of the witnesses. It is the last lingering hour of the sixth trumpet, when it became evident to the most desperate Jewish zealots that their city was doomed.

A great earthquake (11:13). A literalist might well appeal here to the narrative of Josephus:

> There broke out a prodigious storm in the night, with the utmost violence and very strong winds, with the largest showers of rain, with continued lightnings, terrible thunderings and amazing concussions and bellowings of the earth, that was in an earthquake. These things were a manifest indication that some destruction was coming upon men, when the system of the world was put into this disorder and anyone would guess that these wonders foreshowed some great calamities that were coming. (*Wars*, 4:4:5)

But we need no such exact correspondences of statement or description in order to show the fulfillment of apocalyptic symbols. The figures point to a great political upheaval, a signal revolution in human affairs.

The tenth part of the city fell (11:13). This represents a conspicuous portion of the city. The number is to be taken symbolically, like the fourth part in 6:8 and third part in 8:7–8.

Seven thousand persons (11:13). Another symbolical number, indicative of a noticeably large number of persons. It amounts to a calamity so great that overwhelming fear begins at once to take possession of the rest of the populace.

The fact here recorded that **the rest were affrighted** (11:13) shows that there is a notable change from the picture presented in 9:20–21. The effect produced is like that upon the centurion at the earthquake which accompanied the death of Jesus on the cross (Matt. 27:54). The statement that they **gave glory to the God of heaven** (11:13; cp. Dan. 2:19) affords a gleam of light and hope amid the gathering darkness, prophetic of what the seventh trumpet will inaugurate.

[[Announcement of third woe (11:14)]]

14 The second Woe is past: behold, the third Woe cometh quickly.

The third woe cometh quickly (11:14). The final catastrophe, toward which all things have been moving on, is now about to be reached. With inimitable art the sacred writer has heightened expectation and prepared the way for this great consummation. As epic and dramatic poets, who arrange all that can enhance the final scene in episodes and statements that beget expectation and awe, so this writer has prepared us for the sublime finale. This enables him to state the outcome in a few effective sentences.

The seventh trumpet sounded (the end) (11:15–19)

The preceding revelations have sufficiently indicated what we are to expect at the sounding of the seventh and last trumpet. The mighty angel also expressly declared in 10:7 that the sounding of the seventh trumpet would serve to announce the finishing of "the mystery of God, according to the good tidings which he declared to his servants the prophets." The completion of that mystery was the special mission of Christ and his apostles. It occupied the transition period between the old dispensation and the full inauguration and establishment of the kingdom of Jehovah and his Messiah.

With the fall of Jerusalem and the ruin of the temple, Christianity became thoroughly liberated from the fetters of effete Judaism. And it entered upon its world-wide career of leavening the civilizations of the earth with a higher spirit and of bringing the kingdoms of the world into subjection to the law of Christ.

Having prepared the way for the signal announcement of the end of the old age and the beginning of the new, our author displays the highest art in making the sublime description very brief. The great word-picture consists of (1) the heavenly announcement that the kingdom is become Christ's, (2) the heavenly song of triumph, and (3) the vision of the opened temple of God in the heaven.

The kingdom becomes Christ's (11:15)

15 And the seventh angel sounded; and there followed great voices in heaven and they said, The kingdom of the world is become the kingdom of our Lord and of his Christ: and he shall reign forever and ever.

Great voices in heaven (11:15). It is not said from whom these voices came, but they seem to have been a united chorus of all the hosts of heaven. It is the art of the writer to make voices from heaven declare the issue of the seventh trumpet.

The kingdom of the world (11:15). That is, "the kingdom and dominion and the greatness of the kingdom under the whole heaven," spoken of by Daniel the prophet (see Dan. 7:14, 27). **Is become that of our Lord** (11:15). Compare the language of Psalm 22:28 and Obadiah 21. **And of his Christ** (11:15). An imitation of the language of Psalm 2:2.

He shall reign forever and ever (11:15). This is literally "unto the ages of the ages" (εἰς τοὺς αἰῶνας τῶν αἰώνων [eis tous aiōnas tōn aiōnōn]). Compare the language of Exodus 15:18; Psalm 10:16; and Daniel 2:44; 7:14, 18, 27.

There is joy in heaven that the kingdom of Jehovah and of his Messiah is now at last established. The witnesses (of 11:3–12) have already made it known "in all the world." And it has for a generation been "bearing fruit and increasing;" for already in Paul's day it "was preached in all creation under the heaven" (Col. 1:6, 23).

This is the "kingdom that cannot be shaken," spoken of in Hebrews 12:28. There it seems to be a reference to the shaking of earth and heaven by these last trumpets. And this involves "the removing of those things that are shaken," that is, the old covenant of Sinai, represented in the Jerusalem that was in bondage with her children (cp. Gal. 4:25). It is shaken "that those things which are not shaken may remain" (Heb. 12:27). The shaking down of obsolete Judaism by the thunders of God made way for the complete inauguration of the kingdom of Christ.

The song of triumph (11:16–18)

16 And the four and twenty elders, who sit before God on their thrones, fell upon their faces, and worshiped God,
17 saying, We give thee thanks, O Lord God, the Almighty, who art and who wast; because thou hast taken thy great power and didst reign.
18 And the nations were wroth and thy wrath came and the time of the dead to be judged and the time to give their reward to thy servants the prophets and to the saints and to them that fear thy name, the small and the great; and to destroy them that destroy the land.

Elders who sit before God on their thrones (11:16; cp. note on 4:4). It is very appropriate that these enthroned representatives of the Old and New Testament Church should utter forth the pæan of thanksgiving and triumph contained in 11:17–18. From their exalted position at the throne of God they see, as it were, the end from the beginning. And like the voices of 11:15, they contemplate the kingdom as fully come.

Who art and who wast (11:17), or "the one who is and who was." Observe the omission of the ὁ ἐρχόμενος (*ho erchomenos*), "who is to come" of 1:8 and 4:8. For the mystery of God is now conceived as finished. From the elders' point of view, the kingdom has come. So they say, **Thou hast taken thy great power and didst reign** (11:17). The kingdom is no longer "at hand," but has appeared.

The nations were angry and thy wrath came (11:18). This is an allusion to Psalm 2:1–2, 5, as having now been fulfilled (cp. Acts 4:24–30). All the strifes and jealousies and ambitious self-seeking; all the threatenings and oppressions and persecutions; all the mad revolts and sedition of "Herod and Pontius Pilate and the nations and the people of Israel," were overruled to the glory of God and the accomplishment of his purposes.

The time of the dead to be judged (11:18). The time has come to avenge by divine judgments of wrath those dead martyrs, for they "had been slain for the word of God" (6:9–11). And for avenging the faithful witnesses whose dead bodies were exposed in that great city where their Lord was crucified (11:7–8). The "little time" of 6:11 is now finished; the martyr-blood is now avenged (cp. Matt. 23:35). It only remains, as the elders say, **to give their reward to thy servants the prophets and to the saints and to them that fear thy name** (11:18).

Observe, the apocalyptist does not stop to picture the ruin of the rest of the city (cp. 11:13) and to narrate details of the final woe. These have been all sufficiently implied and it would detract from the power of this concluding passage to thrust such details in. The higher art is shown by making the glorified elders say or sing the assured triumph and eternal glory of God's "servants the prophets." This phrase is appropriated from Daniel 9:6–10; Amos 3:7; and Zechariah 1:6. The additional words, **the small and the great,** are taken from Psalm 115:13: "He will bless them that fear Jehovah, the small along with the great."

Destroy them that destroy the land (11;18). Namely, those "inhabitants of Jerusalem and men of Judah" who had so culpably neglected the vineyard of the Lord entrusted to their care (cp. Isa. 5:1–7 and Matt. 21:33–46). Jesus warned the chief priests and elders of the Jewish people that the Lord of the vineyard would "miserably destroy those miserable men and let out the vineyard to other husbandmen" (Matt. 21:41).

God's temple in heaven opened (11:19)

> 19 And there was opened the temple of God that is in heaven; and there was seen in his temple the ark of his covenant; and there followed lightnings and voices and thunders and an earthquake and great hail.

There was opened the temple of God that is in the heaven (11:19). This temple is the heavenly reproduction of what was measured off for preservation in 11:1–2. It is "the true tabernacle, which the Lord pitched, not man" (Heb. 8:2; cp. Heb. 9:8–13 and 10:9). The writer does not stop here to describe this heavenly temple, for he proposes by a second series of revelations to present the same subject from another point of view and by means of other symbols. This temple will appear again at the close of the book as Jerusalem the golden, which has for its temple "the Lord God the Almighty and the Lamb" (21:22). There will dwell forever "those who are written in the Lamb's book of life" (21:27).

The ark of the covenant (11:19). Nothing could more effectively enhance this vision of God's temple in the heaven than to behold in it that most precious and holy of all the treasures of the old tabernacle and temple, that is, "the ark of the covenant of Jehovah." This was not mentioned in 11:1. It had long been lost and the Jewish temple of

John's time contained no ark within the veil. But in that temple of the living God, which was to supersede the temple made with hands, there appears again this holiest symbol of the mystery of God in Jesus Christ. In this temple the saints are given to know the mysteries of the kingdom of heaven.

The statement that **there followed lightnings and voices and thunders and an earthquake and great hail** (11:19) is a sign that the revelations now made to John are not all that he is to behold. These great signs may be regarded as echoes of the great crisis just past, but they are no less intimations that there is much more to follow. The reader also is thus admonished that the heaven of these visions is yet open (cp. 4:1) and he may expect to see and hear yet other things pertaining to the coming and kingdom of Christ.

John Huss contended not with the evil, but with the temple of the living God, which rose to supersede the temple made with hands; these appears again the oldest symbol of the worship of Jesus Christ; but in ten simple thousands are given up to love the protection of the kingdom of heaven.

Jno. also tells that there followed him in long processions and countless ones, nor thousands and great hail (11:19), meaning that the revelation was to John are not all bar there to behold. These facts described as a colony of things which are not yet seen, but they will appear. It mentions that if we is made to receive yellow. The reader is admonished that the nearer to there visions is yet more and he is not enabled to see and hear more. Things are having to run divine and higher's place.

PART TWO
REVELATION OF THE BRIDE, THE WIFE OF THE LAMB
(Rev. 12–22)

Introduction to Part Two

Joseph's second dream of the sun, moon, and stars bowing down to him was in its essential import only a repetition, under other symbols, of his first dream of the sheaves in the field (Gen. 37:5–11). And Pharaoh's double dream of the cattle and the ears was explained as but one in significance. Yet it was repeated unto the king twice in order to deepen the impression and assure him that the matter was established of God and destined to come to pass quickly (Gen. 41:18–26, 32). Similarly, the second half of this Apocalypse is another portraiture of the same great subject which has been set before us in the foregoing chapters.

The "great red dragon" (12:3) is not to be regarded as different from the "angel of the abyss" (9:11). The "hundred and forty-four thousand" on "Mount Zion" (14:1) are the same as the "sealed" Israelites (7:4–8). The "seven last plagues" (Rev. 15 and 16) correspond noticeably to the "seven trumpets of doom" (8:2–9:21). "Babylon the great" (14:8) is the same as "the great city where the Lord was crucified" (11:8). And the "new Jerusalem" (21:1) filled with "the glory of God" (21:11) and the Lamb (21:23) is but another symbol of "the temple of God that is in heaven" (11:19).

In all this elaborate recapitulation, John follows the manner of the prophet Daniel. The Old Testament prophet's vision of the four beasts (Dan. 7) is but another presentation of the same four kingdoms symbolized in Nebuchadnezzar's dream (Dan. 2). Similar repetitions, as we have pointed out in *Biblical Apocalyptics,* appear in the apocalyptic portions of Zechariah and Joel, which constitute a notable feature of the biblical apocalypses.

Part First has revealed the Lamb of God under various symbols, glorious in power, opening the book of divine mysteries, avenging the martyred saints, and exhibiting the fearful judgments destined to come upon the enemies of God. Everything is viewed as from the throne of the King of heaven, who sends forth his armies and destroys the defiant murderers of his prophets and burns up their city (cp. Matt. 22:7).

Part Second reveals the Church in conflict with infernal and worldly principalities and powers, surviving all persecution, and triumphing by the word of her testimony. And, after Babylon the harlot falls and passes from view, she appears as the wife of the Lamb, the tabernacle of

God with men, glorious in her beauty, and imperishable as the throne of God.

Chapter 5
THE WOMAN AND THE DRAGON
(Rev. 12)

The Woman in Travail (12:1–2)

1 And a great sign was seen in heaven; a woman arrayed with the sun and the moon under her feet and upon her head a crown of twelve stars;
2 and she was with child: and she crieth out, travailing in birth and in pain to be delivered.

A great sign was seen (12:1), that is, a symbolical figure of remarkable attributes, such as the seer proceeds immediately to describe. The phrase, **in heaven** (12:1), which locates so many visions of the Apocalypse, may well be understood as a mystic designation of that element of exalted life and fellowship in which the things of God are spiritually discerned. True Christians have their citizenship (πολίτευμα [*politeuma*]) in this heaven (Phil. 3:20). And they sit together with Christ and one another "in the heavenlies" (ἐν τοῖς ἐπουρανίοις [*en tois epouraniois*], Eph. 2:6). In a similar way we are to think of the New Testament Church as in some sense the kingdom of heaven. Into this same element Satan and his angels carry war (12:3, 7).

A woman (12:1). Here to be understood as a symbol of the apostolic Church, which Paul in Galatians 4:26, calls "Jerusalem which is above, which is our mother." **Arrayed with the sun** (12:1) means clothed with the glory of God, who covers himself with light as with a garment (Psa.104:2; cp. Isa. 60:1). **The moon under her feet** (12:1) serves to enhance our conception of her exalted position. And the **crown of twelve stars** (12:1), while being a possible allusion to the twelve apostles, is intended rather to give additional splendor to the vision. Compare Song of Songs 6:10 and the description of the Son of man in Revelation 1:13–16.

Any attempt to find distinct allegorical meanings in the sun, moon, and stars as here presented tends to obscure the vision. The picture is composite and these luminaries are naturally mentioned as giving their glory to the appearance of the woman in the heaven. The sun enrobes her; the moon, not the earth, appears as her footstool; and the stars form a crown for her head.

She crieth out, travailing in birth and pain to be delivered (12:2). This language and imagery are in substance from Isaiah 66:7–8, where the reference is expressly to Zion: "As soon as Zion travailed, she brought forth her children. Before she travailed she brought forth; before her pain came, she was delivered of a man child." As the Old Testament Church thus brought forth children, so the New Testament Church, but not without many outcries of pain.

The Great Red Dragon (12:3–4)

> 3 And there was seen another sign in heaven; and behold, a great red dragon, having seven heads and ten horns and upon his heads seven diadems.
> 4 And his tail draweth the third part of the stars of heaven and did cast them to the earth: and the dragon standeth before the woman who is about to be delivered, that when she is delivered, he may devour her child.

Another sign in heaven (12:3). This is another symbol, as in 12:1, and in the same element of vision. This sign was seen in the same heaven from which Jesus beheld Satan fall (Luke 10:18).

A great red dragon (12:3). In 12:9 he is said to be "the old serpent, he that is called the Devil and Satan, the deceiver of the whole world." Representing "the old serpent," he may well be pictured as a dragon, a monster which in ancient sculpture and painting is often represented as a winged crocodile. But this monster of John's vision is not said to have been supplied with wings, but **has seven heads and ten horns** (12:3). The redness of his appearance may suggest that, like the red horse of 6:4, his work was to take away peace from the earth. In John 8:44, he is said to have been a manslayer from the beginning.

It is added that there were upon his **heads seven diadems** (12:3). These heads, horns and diadems are thought by some to be here mentioned in anticipation of what is written in 13:1 and to be interpreted by means of 17:9–12. But such a procedure is scarcely necessary at this stage of our exposition. It is, rather, to be remembered that the Lamb was seen to have seven horns and seven eyes (5:6). So why should not his great antagonist, the Antichrist, appear with like symbols of power?

The **ten horns** (12:3) of this dragon may be regarded as symbols of his great power, just as we have explained the seven horns of the Lamb. And the heads and diadems are in like manner symbols of the regal resources and splendor of the prince of the devils. He is thought of as presuming to sway authority and power like the King of heaven and to say like the proud Babylonian oppressor: "I will exalt my throne above the stars of God. I will ascend above the heights of the clouds; I will be like the Most High" (Isa. 14:13–14; cp. vv. 3–4).

His tail draweth the third part of the stars (12:4). This imagery, like that of 9:10 and 19, shows him to have a great power for destruction behind him. Thus, with his tail he accomplishes what the little horn of Daniel 8:10 did with his whole strength. No special importance is to be attached to the fact that the dragon's tail does this work of dragging down the stars. For like the infernal locusts (9:10) and many another monster of the dragon type, the tail is a most potent weapon of their power to do harm. Such a dragon in the heaven might naturally be expected to sweep down many of the stars with the angry lash of his tail and cast them to the earth. The whole picture is to be treated as a highly poetic description of Satan's presumption and power. It is not to be taken in pieces with the idea of finding some separate allegorical significance in each particular part.

The "third part of the stars" is, accordingly, to be understood in the same general way as in 8:12. A large proportion of the luminaries of the heaven seemed to be dragged down by the power of the dragon's tail. But he is not especially aiming to destroy the stars. The object of his deadly rage is rather the woman and the child about to be born of her. For now the seer beholds that the dragon is standing (ἕστηκεν [*estēken*]). Thus, he has taken his position and remains there waiting before the woman who is about to bring forth. He does this so that **when she is delivered, he may devour her child** (12:4). His attitude is therefore like that of the king of Egypt watching to destroy every male Israelite as soon as born (Exo. 1:16, 22).

The Child Caught up to God and the Woman in the Wilderness
(12:5–6)

5 And she was delivered of a son, a man child, who is to rule all the nations with a rod of iron: and her child was caught up unto God and unto his throne.
6 And the woman fled into the wilderness, where she hath a place prepared of God, that there they may nourish her a thousand two hundred and threescore days.

A son, a man child (12:5). The Greek of this phrase is υἱόν ἄρσεν (*huion arsen*). It is peculiar in making the appositive ἄρσεν (*arsen*, "man child," neuter) a kind of additional definitive of υἱοῦ (*huiou*), "son." Like the change from masculine to feminine in Matthew 16:18 *(*πέτρος > πέτρα [*petros to petra*]), it may suggest that the man child here, as in Isaiah 66:7, is not an individual, but a collective body.

It has been the error of many interpreters to insist that this man child represents the Messiah. But the son in this symbol is no more a single person than the mother. Like the seed of the woman in Genesis 3:15 (cp. Rev. 12:17), it need not exclude the Messiah, but it certainly does include those who are Christ's. The time-limits and scope of this book require us to refer it particularly to the firstborn or first fruits of the apostolic Church. Thus, while the woman's seed in Genesis 3:15 most naturally includes the Messianic victor, the man child of this symbol most naturally excludes the person of the Messiah.

Those who think that the man child is the Christ seem to be misled by the statement that he **is to rule all the nations with a rod of iron** (12:5). They forget what was said to those in Thyatira: "To him that overcometh will I give power over the nations and he shall rule them with a rod of iron" (2:26–27). The language and imagery here, as there, are taken from Psalm 2:9. Compare also the picture of the enthroned martyrs reigning with Christ a thousand years (20:4–6). So also the two witnesses, like their Lord, went up to heaven in a cloud (11:12). These symbolic representations were given as a comfort and assurance to all those in the early Church who were called to suffer with their Lord and who were compelled to say, "If we suffer, we shall also reign with him" (2 Tim. 2:12).

Moreover, the statement that **her child was caught up unto God and unto his throne** (12:5), as from before the face of the dragon, does not accurately describe the ascension of Christ. It does, however, appropriately symbolize the triumph of the martyrs who "overcame because of the blood of the Lamb and because of the word of their testimony and loved not their lives unto death" (12:11). The apocalyptist here makes no account of physical death. The fact that the dragon did kill the children of the Church (11:7) amounts to nothing in this vision in view of their immediate exaltation to the throne of God. They realize what Jesus said of himself as "the resurrection and the life," and that "he that believeth on me, though he die, yet shall he live: and whosoever liveth and believeth on me shall never die" (John 11:25–26). See also Luke 21:18–19: "Not a hair of your head shall perish. In your patience ye shall win your souls."

The woman fled into the wilderness (12:6). This is an appropriate symbol of the scattering of the church in Jerusalem by reason of great persecution (Acts 8:1). Jesus himself commanded a similar flight in Luke 21:21; Matthew 24:16. According to Eusebius (3: 5), "the whole body of the church in Jerusalem, commanded by a divine revelation," fled to Pella, beyond the Jordan. This place at that time, according to Josephus (*Wars* 3:3:3), was mostly a desert. But we should err in confining the symbolic flight of this woman to any such single event of the time before the fall of Jerusalem.

This flight is rather the general scattering abroad of all those who were driven by persecution to forsake their homes and go into greater retirement. Like the prophets that fled from the persecutions of Jezebel, many of the early Christians hid themselves in caves and dens of the earth (cp. 1 Kgs. 18:4; Heb. 11:38).

Where she has a place prepared by God (12:6). This is like the Israelites when they fled out of Egypt before the persecution of Pharaoh and became "the church in the wilderness" (Acts 7:38).

A thousand two hundred and threescore days (12:6). The same symbolic number as that which denoted the period during which the two witnesses prophesied (11:3), a notable period of oppression and trial (cp. 12:14).

Revelation 12:7–12 constitute a side picture to show that the dragon would not be permitted to maintain his position "in the heaven." It is not to be thought of as a chronological sequel of what has been presented in 12:1–6. Rather it is designed to furnish additional information concerning the character and history of the dragon.

The War in Heaven (12:7–8)

7 And there was war in heaven: Michael and his angels going forth to war with the dragon;
8 and the dragon warred and his angels; and they prevailed not, neither was their place found any more in heaven.

War in heaven (12:7). This war is in the same element in which the woman and the dragon have thus far appeared.

Michael and his angels (12:7). These are obviously the heavenly antagonists of the dragon and his angels. As the one class represents the powers of darkness, the others must represent the forces of light. It would have been incongruous to introduce Christ, or the Lamb, by name, as the great opponent of the dragon. And equally so to have portrayed the seed of the woman as going to war with the dragon as soon as they were born.

But while incongruous in the apocalyptic imagery and scheme, it is still true in fact that Christ and his holy angels are the real antagonists of Satan. The mention of the rest of the woman's seed in 12:17 and the statement of 12:11 that they who overcame the great adversary "loved not their life even unto death," are evidence that the redeemed "first fruits unto God and the Lamb" (14:4) also take part in this great war.

We accordingly understand "Michael and his angels" to be here a symbolic designation of Christ and his apostles, together with all the angelic forces in sympathy and cooperation with them. The name "Michael" is taken from Daniel 10:13, 21; 12:1, where he is spoken of as "the great prince who standeth over the children of thy (Daniel's) people." We compare also with this "the prince of the host of Jehovah" (Josh. 5:14), who assisted the children of Israel in the overthrow of Jericho.

As we have shown in the note at the close of Revelation 10, it accords with the apocalyptic scheme of this book to introduce Jesus Christ under various names and symbols. Having appeared in 10:1 as the strong covenant angel of light, he now appears as Michael the archangel, the great leader of the hosts of heaven against the prince of hell.

The anomalous infinitive construction τοῦ πολεμῆσαι (*tou polemēsai*, i.e., "to wage war") is apparently appropriated from the Septuagint of Daniel 10:20. But it is without proper grammatical connection with the preceding phrase. The ἐπολέμησαν (*epolemēsan*) of the *textus receptus* is translated "fought against" in the Authorized Version. But it is destitute of manuscript authority and evidently an attempted emendation. Probably the best solution of the solecism is the supposition that some word corresponding to the ἐπιστρέψω (*epistrepsō*) of Daniel 10:20, has fallen out of the text and the Anglo-American revisers have done well to supply the words going forth.

They prevailed not (12:8). That is, the dragon and his angels prevailed not, but were cast down, as the next verse states. **Neither was their place found any more in heaven** (12:8). The ministry of Christ and his apostles was to clear the spiritual heaven and effectually break Satan's power.

The Dragon and His Angels Cast Out (12:9)

> 9 And the great dragon was cast down, the old serpent, he that is called the Devil and Satan, the deceiver of the whole world; he was cast down to the earth and his angels were cast down with him.

The great dragon was cast down (12:9). We interpret these words and the whole passage in the light of Luke 10:18. There Jesus said to the seventy who returned with joy and declared that the demons were subject unto them in his name, "I beheld Satan fallen as lightning from the heaven."

We are not to suppose that Jesus beheld this sight as an objective fact in the physical world. As little to the purpose would it be to suppose a reference to the original fall of Satan as an angel of light. Rather, in the ministry and triumph of the seventy Jesus was beholding (ἐθεώρουν [*etheōroun*]) as in vision the glorious outcome of the apostolic ministry. He exulted with them, not so much in what they had already done, as in the anticipation of greater works to follow.

Jesus accordingly said to them that they should rejoice, not so much in the subjection of the evil spirits as in the assurance that their names were written in the heavens (Luke 10:20). They were already enrolled in the heavenly army of the great Captain of their salvation. They might therefore understand, not only that the God of peace would bruise Satan under their feet shortly (Rom. 16:20), but that they should be partakers with the Lord in his work, sufferings, triumph, and glory.

Another passage to be cited in this connection is John 12:31: "Now is there a judgment (κρίσις [*krisis*], "a crisis") of this world: now shall the prince of this world be cast out." Here we recognize another anticipation of triumph on the part of Jesus. His exaltation through suffering and death was destined to draw all men unto him (John 12:32). As the dragon's tail drew many stars down and cast them to the earth, so on the opposite side would Christ and his angels cast out Satan and draw all men up from the earth into the heaven, there to become the stars of God. In his comments on John 12:31, Alford says: "Observe, it is *shall be cast* out, not *is cast out*, because the casting out shall be gradual, as the drawing in the next verse. But after the death of Christ the casting out began and its first fruits were the gathering of the Gentiles into the Church."

This apocalyptic "war in heaven" may also be understood to include all such "wrestling against the principalities, against the powers, against the spiritual hosts of wickedness in the heavenlies," as is referred to in Ephesians 6:12. To be "able to quench all the fiery darts of the evil one" (Eph. 6:16) is to partake in the spiritual and supernatural triumphs which all Christly souls enjoy in vital fellowship with their Lord.

The Consequent Joy in Heaven (12:10–12)

> 10 And I heard a great voice in heaven, saying, Now is come the salvation and the power and the kingdom of our God and the authority of his Christ: for the accuser of our brethren is cast down, who accuseth them before our God day and night.
> 11 And they overcame him because of the blood of the Lamb and because of the word of their testimony; and they loved not their life even unto death.
> 12 Therefore rejoice, O heavens and ye that dwell in them. Woe for the earth and for the sea: because the devil is gone down unto you, having great wrath, knowing that he hath but a short time.

I heard (12:10). The art of description is displayed by turning from further detail of the "war in the heaven" and presenting the outcome of the struggle by means of **a great voice in the heaven**. This one "great voice" celebrates the victory much like the many "great voices" in 11:15. The exclamation, **now is come the salvation** (11:10), should be compared with "now is there a crisis of this world" in John 12:31. In both passages there is a prophetic anticipation of the glorious result, a welcome of it as if already come.

Notice the fourfold expression, the **salvation, the power, the kingdom,** and **the authority** (12:10). These come to view whenever the power of Satan is broken and his character as κατήγωρ (*kategor*), "accuser," is exposed. The word *Kategor* (קטיגור) is found in rabbinical writings as a designation of Satan, as *Sabeegor* (סביגור) is of Michael.

When he is called **the accuser of our brethren** (12:10), it is implied that the heavenly voice represents all brethren and partakers in "the tribulation and kingdom and patience of Jesus" (1:9). It may have proceeded from the twenty-four elders, representatives of the glorified Church. He **accuseth them before our God day and night** (12:10). This is a reference to the persistent going up and down of Satan and acting the part of a destructive enemy of such servants of God as Job (cp. Job 1:7; 2:2; 1 Pet. 5:8; and Matt. 12:43).

They overcame (12:11). The "they" (αὐτοί [*autoi*]) are "our brethren" of the preceding verse. They are here contemplated as having already conquered (ἐνίκησαν [*enikēsan*]) and witnessed even unto death. This warrants our including them all in the great host of Michael.

Because of the blood of the Lamb and ... the word of their testimony (12:11). Not "by the blood," as in the King James Version. Although it may seem proper to conceive their victory as accomplished by means of the blood of Jesus and especially by means of the word of their testimony. But the writer views both the blood and the testimony as the *ground* or *reason* of their triumph, rather than the *means*. It was for the sake of the Lamb and for the sake of their testimony and for what these were destined to accomplish in the world, that they overcame. The telic idea attaches to the language here as in 1:9. And the inspired apocalyptist is subjectively controlled with the idea of divine purpose to be accomplished in accord with the words of this book of prophecy.

Unto death (12:11). That they "loved not their life even unto death" evinced the wisdom presented in Matthew 16:25 and displayed the fidelity which, according to 2:10, ensures "the crown of life." All those who are included among these conquerors follow the Christ in conquest and glory. And as we contemplate their heavenly triumph we may well recall the promise of 3:21: "To him that *overcometh* I will give to sit down with me in my throne, as I also *overcame* and sat down with my Father in his throne."

Rejoice, O heavens (12:12). These words are appropriated either from Isaiah 49:13 or Psalm 96:11. The heavenly places are delivered of the evil spirits, so that now they are contemplated as a tabernacle in which all who "sit together in the heavenlies" have blissful fellowship (cp. Eph. 2:6; Col. 3:1).

Woe for the earth and the sea (12:12). For these, instead of the heavens, are now about to become the scene of Satan's new activity and mischief (see 13:1, 11). **Having great wrath** (12:12). His wrath is due to his failures and his being cast down to the earth. Such defeats intensify his rage.

He hath but a short time (12:12). The binding of the dragon and the casting of him into the abyss (20:1–3) are among the things which, according to this book, "must shortly come to pass" (1:1; 22:6).

The Persecution of the Woman and the Rest of Her Seed
(12:13–17)

> 13 And when the dragon saw that he was cast down to the earth, he persecuted the woman who brought forth the man child.
> 14 And there were given to the woman the two wings of the great eagle, that she might fly into the wilderness unto her place, where she is nourished for a time and times and half a time, from the face of the serpent.
> 15 And the serpent cast out of his mouth after the woman water as a river, that he might cause her to be carried away by the stream.
> 16 And the earth helped the woman and the earth opened her mouth and swallowed up the river which the dragon cast out of his mouth.
> 17 And the dragon waxed wroth with the woman and went away to make war with the rest of her seed, who keep the commandments of God and hold the testimony of Jesus: and he stood upon the sand of the sea.

When the dragon saw (12:13). This resumes from 12:9. **He persecuted the woman** (12:13). The triumphs in the heavenly places do not prevent continued persecution and trials of the Church of God.

She was given **the two wings of the great eagle** (12:14). The metaphor of Exodus 19:4 (cp. also Deut. 32:11–12) is more fully expressed. As Jehovah bore his people away from the face of Pharaoh and the Egyptians and carried them as on the strong wings of an eagle to himself, so he cares for this persecuted woman. Contrast "the wings of a stork" by which the woman called Wickedness was carried to the land of Shinar (Zech. 5:9).

This flight of the woman into the wilderness is not different from that mentioned in 12:6. But the matter is here again presented to show the further action of the serpent toward her. The **time and times and half a time** (12:14) is equivalent to the "twelve hundred and sixty days" of 12:6. And like it, this expression also denotes a period of humiliation and trial, like that of exile. This mystic number seems to have been resolved by reducing 1260 days into times approximating a year of 360 days each. See note on 11:2.

Serpent cast out ... water as a river (12:15). The one figure from the story of the Exodus seems to have suggested another. And the host of Pharaoh which pursued the flying Israelites out of Egypt (Exo. 14:8–9) and were swallowed up in the Red Sea (Exo. 14:28), served to construct the image of a stream of water cast forth out of the dragon's mouth. The waters are here a symbol of the forces at the command of the serpent, just as the chariots and horsemen were at the command of Pharaoh and sent forth to overtake and overwhelm the flying Israelites. Others, however, may prefer to explain the figure of overwhelming waters more generally, as in Psalm 18:16–17 and 124:2–5. If one prefer this more general allusion, there is certainly no controlling reason for insisting on the more particular reference. The imagery is no more to be explained literally or allegorically than the two wings of the eagle.

The earth helped the woman (12:16). In the development of the figure it is naturally the earth, not the sea, that **opened her mouth and swallowed up the river** (12:16). The earth helped the woman by opening her mouth and swallowing the stream of water that issued from the dragon's mouth. Here again we may see an allusion to Numbers 16:32, where it is written that "the earth opened her mouth and swallowed" the wicked men who rebelled against Moses and against God. The great thought in all these images is that the divine power is put forth to deliver and sustain the New Testament Church of God in the day of her persecution. This is the same power that of old caused the miracles of Egypt and of the Red Sea and of the wilderness.

Waxed wroth with the woman (12:17). The "wrath" mentioned above in 12:12 became intensified because of the obvious divine help by which the Church was defended.

Went away to make war with the rest of her seed (12:17). Satan went up and down in the earth, as he often does, and sought new devices by which to carry on his war. The words **the rest of her seed** (12:17) refer to those other children of the Church who had not yet been caught up to the throne of God (cp. 12:5). This reference serves to show that the man child of 12:5 is not to be understood as the Christ-child, Messiah. Rather it pictures the special "first fruits unto God and the Lamb" (14:4), who receive preeminent attention in this book.

Thus far the symbol of the woman and her offspring has exhibited three things, which are to be discriminated as follows:
1. The woman, a symbol of the mother church at Jerusalem.
2. The man child, the first fruits (ἀπαρχή [aparxē]), consisting of such apostles and martyrs as the two witnesses of 11:3–12 and the martyr souls of 6:11 and 20:4, who receive exceptional distinction and glory.
3. The rest of the woman's seed, who suffer persecution and great tribulation, but are not slain for the testimony of Jesus, which they in common with the others hold.

These distinctions are easily made and maintained. The Church, considered as an institution and an organic body, is distinguishable from her children. We see this clearly in Isaiah 66:7–8 and Galatians 4:22–26. The children of the Church, the individual members, are here thought of as two classes: (1) the first fruits of martyrs and witnesses, caught up unto God and sitting on his throne (cp. 2:26–27; 3:21) and (2) the rest who suffer persecution on the earth. We accordingly observe that the Church is in one point of view the totality of all her members or children. Yet in other ways, familiar to the Scripture, her individual members are thought of as related to her as children to a mother.

At 12:17 this chapter ends with what appears in the common text as a part of verse 1 of Revelation 13: "**And he** [the dragon] **stood upon the sand of the sea**" (13:1). He stood as if looking for some new ally or instrument by means of which he might the better persecute the rest of the woman's seed.

The entire symbolism of Revelation 12 may thus be seen to have a rational and satisfactory explanation by means of suggestions and parallels found in the Old Testament. A New Testament writer, familiar as was Paul or the author of the Epistle to the Hebrews with the Scriptures, could have developed all this symbolism from that divine storehouse of apocalyptic ideals. But current Jewish thought may also have taken up some elements of ancient mythology and the images of leviathan and the dragon in such passages as Psalm 74:13–14; Isaiah 27:1; and Ezekiel 29:3. These are doubtless to be understood as allusions to mythical monsters of the deep. But the New Testament apocalyptist need not be supposed to have sought for his imagery outside the Scriptures of the Jewish people.

Chapter 6
THE TWO BEASTS
(Rev. 13)

The symbolism of the two beasts is appropriated in great part from Daniel's vision of the four great beasts from the sea (Dan. 7). But while in Daniel the beasts represent separate and successive world-powers, the two beasts of John's vision are contemporaneous. The second is a mere satellite of the first, exercising the authority of the first beast as if in his immediate presence. Hence while appropriating the symbols from Daniel, our author shows his independent mastery of the materials by his construction of a symbolic picture quite distinct from any of those in Daniel.

The Beast out of the Sea (13:1–10)

1 And I saw a beast coming up out of the sea, having ten horns and seven heads and on his horns ten diadems and upon his heads names of blasphemy.
2 And the beast which I saw was like unto a leopard and his feet were as the feet of a bear and his mouth as the mouth of a lion: and the dragon gave him his power and his throne and great authority.
3 And I saw one of his heads as though it had been smitten unto death; and his death-stroke was healed: and the whole earth wondered after the beast;
4 and they worshiped the dragon, because he gave his authority unto the beast; and they worshiped the beast, saying, Who is like unto the beast?
5 and who is able to war with him? and there was given to him a mouth speaking great things and blasphemies; and there was given to him authority to continue forty and two months.
6 And he opened his mouth for blasphemies against God, to blaspheme his name and his tabernacle, even them that dwell in the heaven.
7 And it was given unto him to make war with the saints and to overcome them: and there was given to him authority over every tribe and people and tongue and nation.

8 And all that dwell on the earth shall worship him, every one whose name hath not been written from the foundation of the world in the book of life of the Lamb that hath been slain.
9 If any man hath an ear, let him hear.
10 If any man is for captivity, into captivity he goeth: if any man shall kill with the sword, with the sword must he be killed. Here is the patience and the faith of the saints.

A beast (13:1). Here, as in Daniel's visions, the beast symbol is of a great world-power inimical to the Church of God.

Coming up out of the sea (13:1). The conclusion of the preceding picture, where the dragon was seen standing upon the sands of the sea, prepared the way for this new vision. As in Daniel 7:1–3, the beasts were seen to come up from the storm-tossed sea. And as the "many waters" of Revelation 17:1, 15 represent "peoples and multitudes and nations and tongues," it is legitimate to trace the analogy of great kingdoms arising out of the commotion and strife of nations.

Thus the great empires of the world have arisen and come to power. But the reference to the "sea" here and to the "earth" in 13:11 appropriately follow after the woe for earth and sea pronounced in 12:12. Sea and land thus appear to represent all the world over which the authority of the beast is exercised.

Ten horns ... seven heads ... ten diadems (13:1). This is like the image of the great dragon in 12:3, except that the diadems are ten in number and placed, not on his heads, but on his horns. We look for no secret mystery in such incidental variations. In general we regard the beast as a symbol of worldly empire: the "horns" represent kings (cp. Dan. 7:24) and the "diadems" upon them are the natural symbol of royalty and rank belonging to a king. The "heads" most naturally suggest the different seats or centers of the royal resources and power.

The numbers "ten" and "seven" are symbolical here as in 5:6 and 12:3 and need not be pressed into definite significance. For nothing in the context calls for any such search after seven periods, or seven forms of government, or ten kings, as many expositors have presumed to find in these numbers. They serve here to denote the extent and completeness of the beast's power and authority.

Upon his heads names of blasphemy (13:1). In all the seats of his power he perpetrates and encourages such blasphemy as is referred to in 13:5–6 (cp. 17:3).

Leopard ... bear ... lion (13:2). A monstrosity made up of different parts of the first three beasts of Daniel's vision (Dan. 7:4–6), but stated in reverse order. This is somewhat like the fourth beast of Daniel (Dan. 7:7–8). As the fourth beast of Daniel represented the empire of Alexander and his successors, this first beast of the New Testament Apocalypse represents the Roman empire.

We are immediately told that to this Roman beast **the dragon gave him his power and his throne and great authority** (13:2). Accordingly, we should keep in mind that in all this prophetic symbolism we have before us the first-century Roman empire as a persecuting power.

This Apocalypse is not concerned with the history of Rome. It is as irrelevant to its scope to search among its revelations for a synopsis of the history of mediæval Europe as to look therein for mystic prognostications of the history of the Church in India or China. We do not find anywhere in the book a reference even to "the eternal city" by the Tiber.

The beast is not a symbol of the *city of Rome*, but of the great *Roman world-power*, conceived as the organ of the old serpent, the Devil, to persecute the scattered saints of God. The empire was represented in the reigning Cæsar. Having failed in the struggle of the spiritual forces of wickedness in the heavenly places (12:7–9, 13), the dragon is now represented as appropriating the forces of worldly empire to further his Satanic plans. The empire, possessed of the power and throne of Satan, must wield a **great authority** (13:2) for evil in the world.

One of his heads as ... smitten unto death (13:3). Observe that it is "one of his heads," not one of his horns, that is thus smitten. Hence we infer that it is no one king, emperor, or ruler that is referred to. Were the reference to an individual ruler we should, according to all analogies of biblical symbolism, have had one of the horns smitten and subsequently restored. We are told that though this head was smitten with a stroke that seemed likely to result in death, **his death-stroke was healed** (13:3).

The heads of a symbolic beast are best understood as the chief seats of power and dominion. The four heads of the third beast of Daniel's vision seem to have implied the dominion it possessed in the four quarters of the earth (Dan. 7:6) and especially the rule and authority it maintained in the different places.

We accordingly see in the wounded head of this Roman beast a reference to some temporary loss of power in one of its many seats of authority. According to 13:14, it was a "stroke of the sword" by which the wound was given, indicating that it was some military conquest (cp. 6:4). The Roman dominion over Palestine is especially within the scope of this book. Therefore, it was not irrelevant for the author to make a symbolical recognition of the grievous wound the empire received in this quarter during the civil wars and troubles that followed the assassination of Julius Cæsar.

At this time the Parthians overran all of western Asia and Palestine and captured Jerusalem (see Josephus, *Antiquities* 14:13; *Wars* 1:13). This was truly a smiting of one of the strongholds of Roman supremacy as if it were unto death and erecting over Jerusalem for the time the dominion of a totally different world-power. "For a full year," says Rawlinson, "western Asia changed masters; the rule and authority of Rome disappeared and the Parthians were recognized as the dominant power" (*Sixth Oriental Monarchy*, p. 189). But the subsequent conquests of the Roman armies healed this notable wound of the empire and her power over that land was restored to her again.

The whole earth wondered after the beast (13:3). So widespread was the dominion of the empire and so complete its control of all the nations under its sway, that every subject land might well be filled with admiration and awe in the thought of a world-power so apparently omnipotent.

They worshiped the dragon ... and they worshiped the beast (13:4). They worshiped the one in the other. And the reverence required to be paid to the image of the reigning emperor was, from the standpoint of our apocalyptist, a blasphemous idolatry.

According to Josephus the honors which were demanded by the Cæsars included among other things that all subjects of the empire, in all the provinces, should build altars and temples to him, treat him as they would treat the other gods, and even swear by his name (*Antiquities* 18:8:1). It is matter of well-known record that Julius Cæsar was apotheosized after his death (Suetonius, *Cæsar* 88; Dio, 47:18). Augustus had temples and altars erected to his honor (Suetonius, *Octavius* 52). Caligula called himself the brother of Capitolian Jupiter (Josephus, *Antiquities* 19:1:1) and had an image of his own head placed upon a statue of Olympian Jupiter (Suetonius, *Caligula* 22). Nero received the most abject worship of the senate and the people of Rome. Pliny's letter to Trajan evinces the extent to which the worship of the emperor's image was required in the provinces (Pliny, *Epistles* 10:96; see also Tacitus, *Annals* 15:29:74).

A mouth speaking great things and blasphemies (13:5). This description is taken from Daniel's portrait of the impious Antiochus Epiphanes (Dan. 7:8, 20, 25; 11:36). It applies with even greater force to such impious representatives of empire as Caligula and Nero.

Authority to do (13:5). The ποιῆσαι (*poiēsai*) of the Greek text here seems to have been modeled after the Theodotion version of Daniel 11:28, where the same form appears without any direct object following. The verb in its connection implies some such object as his own will. Compare also Daniel 8:12, 24; 11:36. The beast had power and authority to do what he pleased for the mystic period of **forty and two months** (13:5) the same or a similar time of calamity as in 11:2.

The blasphemies against God, besides all other forms they may have taken, were directed also against **his name and his tabernacle, even them that dwell in the heaven** (13:6). There seems to be an allusion here to "the temple of God and the altar and them that worship therein," mentioned in 11:1. This idolatrous world-power, which commanded the armies destined to "tread down the holy city forty and two months" (11:2) and execute divine judgment on an apostate nation, made little or no distinction between Jews and Christians.

The "holy seed" is chosen out of all Israel to be the nucleus of "God's tabernacle with men" (21:3) and exalted to dwell in the heavenlies in Christ Jesus (Eph. 2:6). It suffered many things from the blasphemous impiety and persecutions of the Roman power. "No blasphemy can surpass that of arrogating the homage due to God alone. This was practically blaspheming God and his worshipers. To receive such worship from men is most emphatically to decry both God and all his true worshipers in heaven"(Henry Cowles).

It was given unto him to make war with the saints (13:7). In this respect he was another manifestation of persecuting power like the little horn of Daniel's vision (cp. Dan. 7:21), from which passage these words are taken. The "saints" here are to be understood as equivalent to "the rest of her seed" in 12:17. The "dragon" (13:4) is conceived as having usurped the powers of worldly empire in order to make war upon the children of the Church.

Authority over every tribe ... people ... tongue ... nation (13:7) is equivalent to universal empire. **All shall worship him** (13:8). Repetition in substance of what has been stated in verses 3 and 4. Not written in the book of life i.e., the book referred to in 3:5 and 20:12, 15 (cp. Dan. 12:1).

From the foundation of the world (13:8). Whether this clause is designed to connect with **slain** immediately preceding, or with **written** near the beginning of the sentence, is an open question. Either construction is possible. The former is favored by the nearness of the word "slain" to the qualifying clause. The latter is favored by the statement of 17:8 and, perhaps, the general sense and scope. Doctrinally considered both sentiments are true, for 1 Peter 1:20 sustains the one and Ephesians 1:5, 11 and Romans 8:29 confirm the other. The context favors the connection with **written** (13:8) for it is not particularly relevant to speak here of the slaying of the Lamb from the foundation of the world. But it does notably enhance the exceptional glory of those who worship not the beast to be admonished that their names were written of old in heaven (cp. Luke 10:20).

Let him hear (13:9). This admonition calls attention to what is about to be said, after the manner of 2:7, 11, 17.

For captivity ... with the sword (13:10). The language and sentiment are mainly from Jeremiah 15:2 and Matthew 26:52. Two forms of persecution are specified, as those wherein **the patience and the faith of the saints** are to be chiefly exhibited. And at the same time the admonition is given not to resort to the use of carnal weapons, **the sword**, for the propagation of God's truth. Herein the counsel of Jesus in Matthew 26:52, is affirmed. At the same time the words give assurance that retribution will come in due time to the persecuting power.

Here is the patience (13:10). That is, here is the opportunity for the exercise of "the patience" and **the faith of the saints** who will be called to suffer by **captivity** and **sword** (13:10).

The Beast out of the Land (13:11–18)

> 11 And I saw another beast coming up out of the earth; and he had two horns like unto a lamb and he spake as a dragon.
> 12 And he exerciseth all the authority of the first beast in his sight. And he maketh the earth and them that dwell therein to worship the first beast, whose death-stroke was healed.
> 13 And he doeth great signs, that he should even make fire to come down out of heaven upon the earth in the sight of men.
> 14 And he deceiveth them that dwell on the earth by reason of the signs which it was given him to do in the sight of the beast; saying to

them that dwell on the earth, that they should make an image to the beast, who hath the stroke of the sword and lived.
15 And it was given unto him to give breath to it, even to the image of the beast, that the image of the beast should both speak and cause that as many as should not worship the image of the beast should be killed.
16 And he causeth all, the small and the great and the rich and the poor and the free and the bond, that there be given them a mark on their right hand, or upon their forehead;
17 and that no man should be able to buy or to sell, save he that hath the mark, even the name of the beast or the number of his name.
18 Here is wisdom. He that hath understanding, let him count the number of the beast; for it is the number of a man: and his number is Six hundred and sixty and six.

The distinguishing features of this second beast are somewhat numerous and seemingly sufficient to identify the power intended without much difficulty. The chief points to be noted are: (1) that he comes up out of the land rather than the sea; (2) that he has two horns like a lamb; (3) but he speaks as a dragon; (4) he exercises all the authority of the first beast, as if he were the mere agent and representative of the same; (5) he compels the worship of the first beast, and (6) he works all sorts of lying wonders to secure the most thorough subjection to his authority. So it is particularly noticeable that this second beast is but a satellite of the great power denoted by the first beast.

The two most current explanations of the beast from the "earth," i.e., land, are: (1) That which sees in it a description of the pagan priesthood as allied to the Roman state and including all its divination, witchcraft and various magical arts. And (2) that which identifies it with the Latin Church, the Roman papacy, considered especially as a priestly persecuting power.

But neither of these views seems in perfect accord with the analogous symbolism of beasts, which everywhere stand for some organized world-power. The rise of the Roman papacy, moreover, was far beyond the scope of this revelation which was of "things shortly to come to pass." Aside from the great unspeakable future of the kingdom of God and of Christ, the beginnings of which are celebrated in this book (e.g., 11:15; 20:4; 21:2–3), our prophecy makes no note of particular events of the distant future. Why should John have been gifted to foretell the rise and fall of the papacy rather than the discovery of America and the founding of the great western republic of religious liberty?

The best way of setting aside an erroneous interpretation is to present a better one in its place. Some elements of truth attach to that view which recognizes in the symbol the witchcraft and magical arts of paganism. But faithful adherence to the analogies of biblical symbolism requires that this second beast be a real political power. It is an organized dominion, not a mere function or attribute of such power and dominion.

We find all the requirements of the symbol met in the provincial governments of Judæa and Palestine by the procurators (commonly called "governors" in the New Testament, ἡγεμόνες (hēgemones). Thus, Pilate is called the "governor" (ἡγεμών [hēgemōn]) in Matthew 27:2, 11, 27; and Luke 20:20. And the authority of Rome, as exercised by him in the crucifixion of Jesus, is an example of the power of such a provincial ruler. Felix and Festus also bear the same title (Acts 23:24, 26; 24:27; 26:30). These rulers were the immediate representatives of the emperor and held from him the power of life and death over their subjects (Josephus, *Wars* 2:8:1). How the dominion exercised by these provincial governors meets all the conditions of the beast described in 13:11–17 will appear in the following notes.

Another beast ... out of the earth, i.e., the land (13:11). Observe that **land** (or "earth") here is contrasted with "sea" in 13:1. In view of the fact that Jerusalem is the main center of operations in this book, we may most naturally understand the reference to the *land* of Judæa. That is, the particular *land*, or province, with which this Apocalypse is concerned. If, however, one sees in the "sea" of 13:1 a symbol of the confusion and strife out of which great empires rise, the "land" of this verse may denote the more quiet and established conditions under which local governments with delegated powers have their origin.

Two horns like a lamb (13:11). No special significance need be sought in these "two horns," inasmuch as a horned lamb would naturally have two horns. But if particular significance is sought we should expect to find it in two kings or governors of exceptional notoriety. These, in fact, appear in Albinus and Gessius Florus, the last two procurators of Judæa. Josephus says of them:

> Albinus concealed his wickedness and was careful that it might not be discovered to all men; but Gessius Florus (who was sent by Nero as successor to Albinus), as though he had been sent on purpose to show his crimes to everybody, made a pompous ostentation of them to our nation, as never omitting any sort of violence, nor any unjust sort of punishment; for he was not to be moved by pity and never was

satisfied with any degree of gain that came in his way.... It was this Florus who necessitated us to take up arms against the Romans, while we thought it better to be destroyed at once than by little and little. (*Antiquities* 20:11:1; cp. *Wars* 2:14:15)

Spake as a dragon (13:11). The same infernal spirit possessed this second beast as that which prompted the blasphemies mentioned previously of the first beast in 13:5–6. The beast which has the horns of a lamb and the speech of a dragon is also a striking symbol of the false prophet, who is like a ravenous wolf in sheep's clothing (Matt. 7:15).

All the authority of the first beast in his sight (13:12). He is therefore the subordinate and servant of the higher power of Rome. Thus, all he does is under the oversight of his master, as if in his immediate presence. He exercised all local power in the name and authority of the empire. Such exercise of power on the part of the provincial governor of Judæa is illustrated by the statement of Tacitus: "While Tiberius was reigning emperor, Christ was put to torture by the procurator Pontius Pilate" (*Annals* 15.44).

Maketh the earth (i.e. the "land," which is put under his power) **and them that dwell therein to worship the first beast** (13:12). How procurators and proconsuls enforced the worship of the empire in the image of the reigning emperor is especially witnessed by the famous letter of Pliny to Trajan, (*Epistles* 10:97). He declares to the emperor that he gave over to capital punishment those Christians who persisted in their faith, but adds: "When at my instance they would call on the gods and by incense and wine would supplicate thy image, which for this purpose I had ordered brought along with the likenesses of the deities and would besides curse Christ, ... I thought that they ought to be dismissed."

Doeth great signs (13:13). In this respect the beast made use of such lying wonders as the magicians of Egypt employed when they opposed the ministry of Moses and Aaron (cp. 2 Tim. 3:8). As regards the "great signs" mentioned in this verse and the following, they may be supposed to include those foretold by Jesus in Matthew 24:24 (cp. 2 Thess. 2:9–10). Nor is it improbable that men like Gessius Florus, intent on carrying out the imperial mandates of such a beast as Nero, would have turned to their nefarious purposes the magical arts of impostors like Simon (Acts 8:9) and Elymas (Acts 13:8). After all, such sorcerers seem to have been numerous in all the provinces of the empire (cp. Acts 19:19).

He deceiveth (13:14). Compare this to the statement in 2 Thessalonians 2:11. There it is said in connection with "the signs and lying wonders and all deceit of unrighteousness" practiced by the Satanic Antichrist that "God sendeth them a working of error (πλάνη, *planē*) that they should believe a lie."

Make an image to the beast (13:14). This was one of the ways by which he deceived **them that dwell on the earth** (i.e., "land"). The image of the reigning emperor was virtually the image of the beast as represented by that emperor. Düsterdieck observes that "all images of deified emperors must have appeared to the Christian conscience as images of the beast, the more certainly as all those individual emperors were possessors of the same antichristian secular power."

To give breath to the image of the beast (13:15). That is, to give a spirit to the image or make it appear to be alive. It was the work of the local governors to make the Roman authority a very living thing to all its subjects. And the vigorous exercise of such power might in symbolic description be spoken of as a giving of life to the image of imperial sovereignty. There may also in this connection be an allusion to such well-known claims and feats of miraculous power by Simon Magus. In *Recognitions of Clement* (3:47) he is represented as saying: "I have flown through the air; I have been mixed with fire and been made one body with it; I have made statues move; I have animated lifeless things."

Causeth all ... mark on their right hand (13:16). This verse and the following describe in a form suitable to the symbolic portrait of the entire passage (13:11–17) the absolute power and rigor with which Rome enforced her claims on all the subject provinces. All who failed to conform to the imperial orders and receive the mark (χάραγμα [*charagma*]) of such passive submission were proscribed and the procurators were charged with enforcing the interdict.

Here is wisdom (13:18). That is, here is opportunity for the exercise of wisdom, namely, in the solution of the riddle about to be propounded. Compare the like form of expression in 13:10.

The number of the beast (13:18). It is obviously the number of the first beast which is here intended, for the reference is continually to that beast in 13:12, 14, 15, and 17. This fact shows still more clearly that the second beast has no independent authority of his own. Rather, he is at most the minion and satellite of the first beast. He is a subordinate power through whom the beast "out of the sea" (13:1) exercises his authority on the land. And the spirit of "the old serpent" (12:9), the "dragon" (13:1, 2, 4, 11), i.e., "Satan" (12:9; 20:2), possesses and actuates them both.

It is the number of a man (13:18). This most naturally means that the number about to be given, when set in the proper numerical letters, will represent the name of a man. The apocryphal apocalypses contain numerous examples of such designations of proper names.[13] Less satisfactory is the explanation, which, citing 21:17 and Isaiah 8:1 as parallels, makes the number of a man equivalent to "according to human reckoning" or "counted as men count." In either case it is agreed that the number is to be resolved into letters that will spell out the name intended.

It is a question what alphabet, Hebrew or Greek, is to be understood. The assumption of some that we must look to the Greek alphabet because the book is written in Greek is quite untenable in view of 9:11, where the Hebrew name of the angel of the abyss is placed first. The Hebrew cast and style of the whole book makes it further probable that the tongue of the Hebrews would be the language specially appropriate for such a mystic riddle as is here propounded to the wise.

But if a double designation, one Hebrew and one Greek, both pointing out the same great beast, can be produced, the solution will be all the more entitled to credit. We have such a solution in the Hebrew appellation *NERON CÆSAR* (נרון קסר) and in the Greek word Λατεῖνος (*Lateinos*) long ago propounded by Irenæus. The plea sometimes made that these names were sometimes written with one letter more or less is worthless in view of the fact that they were also written as in the preceding.

The further fact that scores of names in many different languages can be made to represent numerically **six hundred and sixty and six** (13:18) ought to admonish us that *not any possible solution* of the name, but rather a *relevant solution*, is required. Having already shown that the Roman empire is the beast described in 13:1–8, we naturally look for some name that gives specific designation of that power. In 17:11, we observe that the beast is conceived as identical with any one of the reigning kings, who for the time represents the empire and commands

---

[13] See *Sibylline Oracles*, Terry's English translation, book 1, lines 167–171, 383–387. In book 5, lines 15–70, the emperors from Julius Cæsar to the Antonines are similarly designated. Compare also the frequent use of numbers and letters in this enigmatical way in books 12 and 14.

its forces. It will be further shown in our notes on that passage that Nero was the sixth of the list of Cæsars there referred to.

Hence it would seem that no solution of this number of the beast could be more conclusive or relevant than the name נרון קסר (*Neron Qsr*) *Neron Cæsar*. After all, this is a form of the name actually found in rabbinical writings. The numerical value of the Hebrew letters forming this name is as follows: נ=50; ר=200; ו=6; נ=50; ק=100; ס=60; ר=200. And when these seven numbers are added together they equal the numerical sum of 666.

It is also worthy of note that Irenæus mentions the number six hundred and sixteen (616) as the reading of some of the ancient manuscripts of his time. Significantly, another form of writing the name Nero Cæsar, נרו קסר (*Nrn Qsr*), gives this very number. The fact that both forms are legitimate ways of spelling Nero's name in Hebrew characters suggests that this ancient diversity of readings arose from a current understanding that Nero was the man intended. Some spelled the name one way and some another. No interpreter ought to demand a more fitting solution of this mystic number.

The Greek word Λατεῖνος (*Lateinos*) is also entitled to consideration, because it also points to the great *Latin* world-power. It is less specific and therefore less satisfactory than the Hebrew name above given. Yet it was the ancient and current appellation of the great empire which had its chief seat in ancient Latium.

Chapter 7
A SEVENFOLD REVELATION OF TRIUMPH AND JUDGMENT
(Rev. 14:1–20)

The revelation of the three great foes, the dragon, the beast from the sea, and the beast from the land, is followed immediately by a sevenfold disclosure of victory and judgment in the heavens. The purpose of these visions and voices from heaven is obviously to show that the powers of the heavens are mightier than those of the infernal serpent and his associates.

The trinity of hostile forces, armed with many lying wonders, might seem from a human point of view invincible. But John is like the young servant of Elisha when confronted with the horses and chariots and immense host of the king of Syria. Here he is admonished that they which are with the persecuted Church are more and mightier than they which make war against her (cp. 2 Kgs. 6:15–17).

The contents of this chapter are a vivid apocalyptic setting of much that is written in the second psalm. There we read that the enemies may rage and do their worst, but he who sits in the heavens shall have them in derision (Psa. 2:1–4).

The Lamb and His Thousands on Mount Zion (14:1–5)

> 1 And I saw and behold, the Lamb standing on the mount Zion and with him a hundred and forty and four thousand, having his name and the name of his Father, written on their foreheads.
> 2 And I heard a voice from heaven, as the voice of many waters and as the voice of a great thunder: and the voice which I heard was as the voice of harpers harping with their harps:
> 3 and they sing as it were a new song before the throne and before the four living creatures and the elders: and no man could learn the song save the hundred and forty and four thousand, even they that had been purchased out of the earth.
> 4 These are they which were not defiled with women; for they are virgins. These are they which follow the Lamb whithersoever he goeth. These were purchased from among men, to be the first fruits unto God and unto the Lamb.
> 5 And in their mouth was found no lie: they are without blemish.

The Lamb (14:1). This is the same Lamb who received the divine worship of 5:9–13 and opened the book of seven seals. He is seen **standing on the mount Zion** (14:1). The Mount Zion is here to be understood as the heavenly Zion, the seat of the new Jerusalem which is above and which is our mother (Gal. 4:26). On this holy mountain is to rise the new temple of God in the heaven (11:19).

The hundred and forty and four thousand (14:1) are not different from "them that worship therein," who are measured in 11:1. Being the **first fruits unto God and unto the Lamb** (14:4), they are the same as the twelve times twelve thousand of 7:4–8. In that earlier vision they were represented as sealed on their foreheads as the servants of God (7:3). Here they appear as standing with the Lamb on Zion, **having his name and the name of his Father, written on their foreheads** (14:1).

The purport of the vision is to show that the old dragon is making war with the woman's seed (12:17) and even employing the proscriptive force of worldly empire to secure his foul designs. Nevertheless, a new and holy congregation is gathering on Mount Zion. They are learning there to sing a "new song" known only to the redeemed, i.e., that select "first fruits" whose excellency is here extolled.

A voice from heaven (14:2). Three comparisons are given to enhance in our minds the wonderful qualities of this voice: it was like **many waters**, like **a great thunder**, and **like harpers harping with their harps** (14:2). Its loudness did not seem to take anything from its charming melody. Altogether it was a sound of heavenly song so magnificent and harmonious as to imply new triumphs of God and of the Lamb.

They sing as it were a new song (14:3). New triumphs, new revelations, new eras in the kingdom of God call for new songs. We see this in 5:9, as well as in Psalm 33:3; 40:3; and 144:9. **Before the throne** (14:3). This new song was sung in that holy heaven where John had previously seen the throne and him that sat on it and **the four living creatures and the elders** (4:2–11). It was where he heard the sound of the worship being paid to God and the Lamb (5:13).

It is not here written by whom this new song was sung. But it is said that **no man could learn the song save the hundred and forty and four thousand** (14:3). Only the skilled ear and the understanding heart that were versed in the mysteries of the kingdom of God were competent to learn the song of redemption. The thought here suggested is that the one hundred and forty-four thousand comprised a select company, whose common trials, dangers, and final triumphs enabled them to appreciate and learn the heavenly song. They **had been purchased out of the earth** (14:3) and therefore they belonged to heaven. Hence the reason why they alone could learn the new song. Observe that when one is purchased out of the earth he becomes an associate of the heavenly host that worship one common Lord.

Not defiled with women ... virgins (14:4). This is to be understood figuratively of spiritual purity. These are free from all that is associated in thought with carnal uncleanness. As fornication, harlotry, and adultery stand in this book (2:20–22; 17:2, 4; 18:3; 19:2) for all abominations of idolatry and uncleanness. Thus, these undefiled ones are called virgins to denote their separateness from all such contaminations. The word for "virgins" (παρθένοι [*parthenoi*]) is here masculine and is used also in other Greek writings for men as well as women.

They ... follow the Lamb (14:4) through all exposure and trial in this life and to the living fountains in the heavenly glory (cp. 7:17). Their abiding and intimate relations with the Lamb are thus emphasized here after the statement above: they were **with him** (14:1).

These were purchased (14:4). This is repeated in substance from 14:3. But it is defined more particularly as **from among men** rather than "from the earth." This indicates their elect and precious character as a **first fruits unto God and unto the Lamb**. The confessors and martyrs of the apostolic Church, who overcame by reason of their testimony and the blood of the Lamb, are thus declared to be a first fruits (ἀπαρχή [*aparxē*]). They are a choice selection out of the innumerable company of saints. The purpose of this Apocalypse was to give special comfort and encouragement to these virgin spirits.

In their mouth was found no lie (14:5). For, like their Lord, they are holy and true (3:7). There seems here to be an appropriation of language and thought from Zephaniah 3:13: "The remnant of Israel shall do no iniquity, nor speak lies; neither shall a deceitful tongue be found in their mouth" (cp. Isa. 53:9). **They are without blemish**. This completes the description and gives it a most admirable finish. No spot of any kind is found in them. Contrast the murders, sorceries, fornication and thefts of 9:21.

The question expositors have raised is whether the foregoing picture of Mount Zion was in heaven or on earth. It may well be answered by reference to Hebrews 12:22–24, a passage which seems to us clearly to have been written with this vision of the Apocalypse in mind.

The heaven of our apocalyptist is the visional sphere of the glory and triumph of the Church and no marked distinction is recognized between the saints on earth and those in heaven. They are conceived as one great company and death is of no account to them. So the writer of Hebrews 12:22, says, "Ye are come unto Mount Zion." That is, you who have entered into the life of faith and are made "partakers of a heavenly calling" (Heb. 3:1). These have already come (προσελη-λύθατε [*proselēluthate*]) to Zion. This is the mountain and city of the living God, the heavenly Jerusalem, on which John saw the one hundred and forty-four thousand with the Lamb.

Thus, the writer of Hebrews says you have come as so many additional members of the general assembly and Church of the firstborn, who are enrolled in heaven. You have also come to the innumerable company of angels, whose voices John heard like the sound of many waters and of a great thunder and of harpers singing a new song. "The spirits of just men made perfect" in Hebrews 12:23, is but another designation of the undefiled, who are without blemish and are therefore called virgins.

Thus, the entire passage here in Revelation 14 serves to illustrate how saints "dwelling in heavenly places in Christ Jesus" (Eph. 1:3) are all one in spirit and triumph, no matter what physical locality they may occupy. The entire picture is one of vision and therefore questions of physical locality are out of place. Hence we are to understand the vision of 14:1–5, as we do the visions of 11:19 and 12:1. Indeed, this is how we are to understand all the other pictures by which the apocalyptist discloses the real position and victories of those "who follow the Lamb whithersoever he goeth" (14:4). The redeemed children have passed from death into life. They live though they die and their life of faith and hope is so hidden in God that they are conceived and spoken of as never dying (John 11:25–26).

> The Church triumphant in thy love,
> Their mighty joys we know:
> They sing the Lamb in hymns above,
> And we in hymns below.

The Eternal Gospel (14:6–7)

> 6 And I saw another angel flying in midheaven, having eternal good tidings to proclaim unto them that dwell on the earth and unto every nation and tribe and tongue and people;
> 7 and he saith with a great voice, Fear God and give him glory; for the hour of his judgment is come: and worship him that made the heaven and the earth and sea and fountains of waters.

Another angel (14:6). This angel is to be distinguished from the angelic harpers mentioned in 14:2. **Flying in midheaven** (14:6). This is contrasted to the flying eagle and his message of woe in 8:13.

Having eternal good tidings (i.e., the gospel) **to proclaim** (14:6). The order of the words in the Greek is worthy of note. Having "eternal good tidings to announce as good tidings" (εὐαγγελίσαι [euaggelisai]). Although without the article, this gospel eternal is no other than "the gospel of the kingdom" which Jesus declared should be "preached in the whole world for a testimony unto all the nations" before the end of the Jewish cultus and temple should come (Matt. 24:14).

It is appropriately called an "eternal gospel," for it was declared of old as a blessed hope to the fathers and prophets (10:7). It "was preached in all creation under heaven" by the apostles (Col. 1:23) and its saving truths are the comfort and joy of the Church through all ages.

The proclaiming of the Gospel **unto them that dwell on the earth** (i.e., the land; 14:6) seems to be a reference to the first preaching of the apostles to the Jews of Palestine. This is distinguished from the later proclamation of Christ **unto every nation and tribe and tongue and people** (14:6) after it became manifest that "to the Gentiles also God granted repentance unto life" (Acts 11:18). Compare also the seer's commission in 10:11 of this book.

So we are assured, in the face of all the dragon's persecution of the woman's seed, that the Lamb and his followers triumph on Mount Zion. And also that the Gospel of the kingdom is proclaimed among all the nations.

Fear God and give him glory (14:7; cp. 11:13). The Gospel has its message of fear as well as of joy. The terrors of the Lord are one means of persuading men (2 Cor. 5:11). And the near approach of **the hour of his judgment** was an important part of the preaching of the apostolic age (Acts 10:42; 17:31; 24:25). **Worship him who made the heaven**. Not the beast and his image (cp. 14:9 and 13:12, 15). He alone who created all things is worthy to receive the glory and honor (cp. 4:11 and Isaiah 40:12). The division of the physical universe into **heaven, earth, sea**, and **fountains** is characteristic of the writer of this book (cp. 5:13; 8:7 –12; 16:2–8).

The Fallen Babylon (14:8)

> 8 And another, a second angel, followed, saying, Fallen, fallen is Babylon the great, which hath made all the nations to drink of the wine of the wrath of her fornication.

Another, a second angel (14:8). Each announcement has its special angel. Scarcely has the angel of the eternal Gospel made his proclamation than another **followed**, announcing the fall of **Babylon the great**. This great Babylon is mentioned here proleptically, as was the beast out of the abyss in 11:7. But the fuller portrait is reserved for a special revelation in Revelation 17 and 18. A similar proleptic allusion is again made in 16:19.

The language is appropriated from Isaiah 21:9 and Jeremiah 51:7–8. It is to be understood here as a decree of doom, announced with prophetic assurance as if the fall had already occurred. The name "Babylon" is employed symbolically. Like "Sodom and Egypt" in 11:8. it must be explained by means of the historical associations which the great city of the Euphrates would most naturally suggest to Jewish thought.

Babylon is depicted in the Old Testament prophets as the proud oppressor, the insolent persecutor, full of abominable idolatries and of all manner of wickedness. The name is, accordingly, employed in this book to designate the woman of 17:3–4. She is "the mother of harlots and of the abominations of the earth" (17:5) and is "drunken with the blood of saints" (17:6). She is presented as committing fornication with "the kings of the earth" (18:3) and becoming a "habitation of demons and a hold of every unclean spirit and of every unclean and hateful bird" (18:2). She does this while "having dominion over the kings of the earth," i.e., the land (17:18).

That this great city is no other than Jerusalem, the murderer of the prophets (16:6; 18:24; cp. Matt. 23:31). She is full of hypocrisy and extortion and all uncleanness (17:4), the hold of a generation of vipers and drunken with superstition and spiritual idolatry and schemes of worldly power, as will be shown in the notes on Revelation 17. Jesus said that the end of this city and the pre-Messianic age (Matt. 24:2–3) would follow the preaching of the Gospel among the nations (Matt. 24:14). Likewise in this Apocalypse the proclamation of the fall of "Babylon the great" (17:8) follows immediately after that of the eternal Gospel (17:6).

The wine of the wrath of her fornication (14:8). This peculiar expression is an addition to Jeremiah's language. That prophet speaks of "Babylon, a golden cup in Jehovah's hand, that made all the earth drunken: the nations drank of her wine; therefore the nations are mad" (Jer. 51:7). Some accordingly explain the words **wine of the wrath of her fornication** as equivalent to "inflammatory wine of her fornication." Her foul sins are conceived as so much heating and inebriating wine which made others drunken as herself. But it is better to understand the word wrath (θυμός [thumos]) here as in 14:10 of "the wrath of God," so that we have the double thought that the wine of her fornication is also the wine of God's wrath.

The Solemn Admonition (14:9–12)

9 And another angel, a third, followed them, saying with a great voice, If any man worshipeth the beast and his image and receiveth a mark on his forehead, or upon his hand,
10 he also shall drink of the wine of the wrath of God, which is prepared unmixed in the cup of his anger; and he shall be tormented with fire and brimstone in the presence of the holy angels, and in the presence of the Lamb:
11 and the smoke of their torment goeth up forever and ever; and they have no rest day and night, they that worship the beast and his image and whoso receiveth the mark of his name.
12 Here is the patience of the saints, they that keep the commandments of God and the faith of Jesus.

Another angel, a third (14:9; cp. vv. 6, 8). The announcement of Babylon's fall is appropriately followed by a warning against the worship of the beast, as if that sort of idolatrous worship had been the ruin of the great city. The warning is emphasized with **a great voice**, so that all may hear and be duly admonished. The worshiping of **the beast and his image** and receiving **his mark on** ... (the) **forehead** are direct allusions to what has been written in 13:12–17. It was the work of the second beast to enforce this worship of the first beast upon "the land and them that dwell therein" (13:12). Now the warning is sounded aloud that anyone who participates in this worship must necessarily come to fearful judgment as surely as did Babylon the great.

Drink of the wine of the wrath of God (14:10; cp. the language of Isa. 51:17; Jer. 25:15–16; and Psa. 75:8). **Prepared unmixed in the cup of his anger.** This figure suggests anger in its most intense fury, like a cup of strong drink undiluted with any mixture of water. **Tormented with fire and brimstone** (cp. 20:10). This is the writer's way of designating the gehenna of fire.

In the presence of the holy angels and ... of the Lamb (14:10). The torment is conceived as inflicted before the eyes of the angels and of the Lamb. This accords with the concept of Mark 8:38; Luke 9:26; 16:23. Thus the dire punishment is depicted as an act of judgment to be administered in the very presence of the Lamb and the angels of his power.

The smoke of their torment (14:11). The smoke of the fire and brimstone which causes their torment. And it **goeth up forever and ever** (14:11). This statement, which is designed to add horror to the thought of the torment is repeated again in 18:18 and 19:3. It is appropriated from Genesis 19:28, where Abraham is said to have looked toward Sodom and Gomorrah, "and, behold, the smoke of the country went up as the smoke of a furnace." The figure is enlarged and intensified in Isaiah's prophecy of the desolation of Idumea in the day of Jehovah's vengeance (Isa. 34:9–10).

The doctrinal significance of this passage is not to be overlooked. So far as it has any bearing on the question of the duration of the punishment of the wicked it speaks without any hint of limitation. It accords with the teaching involved in Matthew 25:46 and also with the "certain fearful expectation of judgment and a fierceness of fire which shall devour the adversaries" spoken of in Hebrews 10:27. A torment that runs through "ages of ages" (αἰῶνας αἰώνων [$ai\bar{o}nas\ ai\bar{o}n\bar{o}n$]) is a most fearful conception (14:11).

They have no rest (14:11). That is, from their torment. They have no release or recreation from their doleful lot (cp. 20:10).

Here is the patience of the saints (14:12; cp. 13:10). Here is opportunity for the exercise and display of saintly patience. The refusal to worship the beast and his image demanded the martyr's firmness and a patience in persecution which only a true keeping of God's commandments and faith in Jesus could secure.

The Blessed Dead (14:13)

13 And I heard a voice from heaven saying, Write, Blessed are the dead who die in the Lord from henceforth: yea, saith the Spirit, that they may rest from their labors; for their works follow with them.

I heard a voice from heaven (14:13). The precious revelation of this verse is given through **a voice from the heaven**, not by a vision and the special commandment to **write** serves to enhance the value of this particular communication.

Blessed are the dead who die in the Lord (14:13). This comes as a most encouraging word immediately after the admonition of 14:9–12. For that solemn warning implied the putting to death of multitudes who counted not life on earth so dear that they would keep it by violation of "the commandments of God and the faith of Jesus" (14:12). Dying in vital fellowship with the Lord Jesus involved with many a martyr's death of violence and torture. But the Lord had already instructed his followers that "whosoever would save his life shall lose it; and whosoever shall lose his life for my sake and the Gospel's shall save it" (Mark 8:35).

It is worthy of note, perhaps, that the only other beatitude of the Apocalypse is that pronounced on him that "has part in the first resurrection" (20:6). The special emphasis of the sentence lies in the closing words ἀπ' ἄρτι (*ap arti*), **from henceforth**. These words most obviously mean "from this time onward" and are best construed with μακάριοι (*makarioi*), "blessed": "Blessed from now onward are the dead who die in the Lord" (14:13). They are immediately introduced into the presence of the Lord himself, so that, as in the case of Paul, for them "to die is gain" (Phil. 1:21).

The consolation afforded by this assurance of immediate and continuing blessedness is like that which Paul writes to the Thessalonians "concerning them that fall asleep." So far from losing any glory or blessedness, those fallen asleep in Jesus have the precedence, being already with the Lord and so occupying a position of preeminence in every signal manifestation of his presence (1 Thess. 4:13–18). Those who "die in the Lord" are blessed at once and forever thereafter. They are not required to wait until the dragon and the beast have finished their persecution of the Church on earth, Nor do they linger in longing expectation of some future reward. But, having fallen asleep in Jesus, they find him to be the resurrection and the life and though dying, they live (John 11:25). And they are blessed "from henceforth," that is, from the moment of death onward, forever.

The blessedness is indicated by the further statement that **they shall rest from their labors** (14:13). The Greek word for "labors" (κόπων [*kopōn*]) involves the idea of fatiguing toils and may include that of sufferings. The blessed dead rest from all such labor and are blessed in that they may and shall thus rest.

For (14:13). This is the best attested reading and is less likely to have been substituted for δέ (*de*) than vice versâ. It introduces another reason for pronouncing them "blessed." And at the same time, it enhances the thought of their rest from the toils of earthly life and persecution.

Their works (ἔργα [*erga*]) **follow with them** (14:13). This refers to all the good works they have wrought in fellowship and suffering with Christ. These are conceived as accompanying them, like so many attendants and witnesses of their keeping "the commandments of God and the faith of Jesus." (14:12). **They rest from their labors.** but their works abide with them as things of precious memory (cp. 1 Thess. 1:3).

The Harvest of the Earth (14:14–16)

> 14 And I saw and behold, a white cloud; and on the cloud I saw one sitting like unto a son of man, having on his head a golden crown and in his hand a sharp sickle.
> 15 And another angel came out from the temple, crying with a great voice to him that sat on the cloud, Send forth thy sickle and reap: for the hour to reap is come; for the harvest of the earth is over-ripe.
> 16 And he that sat on the cloud cast his sickle upon the earth; and the earth was reaped.

Revelation 14:14–20 contains two distinct visions. The one (vv. 14–16) shows a son of man reaping "the harvest of the earth." The other (vv. 17–20) shows an angel gathering "the vintage of the earth." But the two pictures have so much in common that they seem to have been designed to accompany and supplement each other. Their relevancy to what precedes is seen in that they are an assurance that God will bring every work into judgment, whether good or evil . And by this he will thus vindicate his own servants "in the presence of the holy angels and in the presence of the Lamb" (14:10 above). The two descriptions present the following notable correspondences:

The Harvest	The Vintage
1. Son of man on a white cloud	1. Angel from the temple in heaven
2. Having a sharp sickle	2. Having a sharp sickle
3. Another angel from the temple crying with a great voice to send forth the sickle and reap	3. Another angel from the altar calling with a great voice to send forth the sickle and gather the clusters of the vine
4. The harvest is over-ripe	4. The grapes are fully ripe
5. He that sat on the cloud cast his sickle upon the earth and it was reaped	5. The angel cast his sickle into the earth, gathered the vintage and cast it into the wine press of God's wrath
[Nothing is said as to the character of the harvest.]	6. The wine press when trodden overflows with blood amounting to a vast sea — symbol of fearful retribution

The two closely related figures of harvest of grain and vintage of grapes appear in Joel 3:13: "Put ye in the sickle, for the harvest is ripe: come, get you down; for the press is full, the vats overflow; for their wickedness is great." This association of the two illustrations of judgment warrants us in referring both the harvest and the vintage to the impending judgment of God upon the wicked.

The habit of apocalyptic repetition is for the purpose of showing that the vision is established of God and shortly to come to pass (Gen. 41:32). It also allows us to refer these visions of harvest and vintage both alike to the execution of the wrath of God upon his enemies. It may also be argued that if the harvest of Revelation 14:14–16 represents an ingathering of saints, rather than a judgment on the wicked, something ought to have been added after 14:16, or elsewhere, in order to acquaint us with a distinction so important.

It may, however, be maintained that in such apocalyptic symbolism too many formal definitions are out of place and much is left to inference. The harvest reaped may alone be sufficiently suggestive of gathering the wheat into the garner (cp. Matt. 3:12; 13:30). After the benediction on the blessed dead and the reference to their rest and works there was no need of further specification to inform us that the ingathering of the ripe harvest is symbolic of the blessed reward of the saints.

We incline, therefore, to the view of 14:14–16, which makes the harvest represent the ingathering and blessed reward of the saints. The double picture of harvest and vintage may well be regarded as an apocalyptic amplification of the parable of the wheat and the tares (Matt. 13:24–30, 37–43). The harvest gathered by the sickle (cp. Mark 4:29) corresponds to the gathering of the wheat into the storehouse (Matt. 13:30). But the vintage trodden in the wine press corresponds to the binding of the tares and the casting of them into a furnace of fire. Everything in language and allusion fits this interpretation of the double vision.

A white cloud (14:14). Compare the white horse of 6:2 and 19:11, as symbolic of a triumphant procedure. **On the cloud ... one like a son of man** (cp. Dan. 7:13; Matt. 24:30). This "son of man" is no other than the Christ of 1:7. His heavenly royalty is further indicated by his having on his head a **golden crown**. The **sickle** is the instrument alike of reaping and of vinedressing.

Another angel came out from the temple (14:15). The machinery of apocalyptics, as elsewhere observed, makes use of any number of angels which the various visions may require. The word **another**, as in 14:6, refers in a general way to angels mentioned or implied in the preceding context.

The angel cried with a **great voice** to "the son of man" to thrust in the sickle and reap (14:15). This does not necessarily imply his superiority. For he is himself but a messenger out of God's heavenly **temple**, serving to utter a signal cry. **Send forth thy sickle**. This language is taken from Joel 3:13. Compare the expressions "cast his sickle" (14:16, 19) and "send out thy sickle" (14:15; cp. Mark 4:29). The allusion is to the reaper's habit of putting forth his sickle with a swing of the arm in the act of reaping.

The harvest is over-ripe (14:15). Or, as the aorist implies, "was dried up." But the word here seems to have no other meaning than that the harvest was fully ripened for the sickle. The time of harvest was fully come.

The Vintage of Judgment (14:17–20)

17 And another angel came out from the temple which is in heaven, he also having a sharp sickle.
18 And another angel came out from the altar, he that hath power over fire; and he called with a great voice to him that had the sharp sickle, saying, Send forth thy sharp sickle and gather the clusters of the vine of the earth; for her grapes are fully ripe.
19 And the angel cast his sickle into the earth and gathered the vintage of the earth and cast it into the wine press, the great wine press, of the wrath of God.
20 And the wine press was trodden without the city and there came out blood from the wine press, even unto the bridles of the horses, as far as a thousand and six hundred furlongs.

Another angel ... from the temple (14:17). The same temple as that mentioned in verse 15 and which was opened to the seer's vision in 11:19. These angels come forth from the temple **which is in heaven**, for there is the throne of God and they are the ministers of his judgments. The Son of man does his will by the angels of his power (cp. Matt. 13:30, 41; 25:31; 2 Thess. 1:7–8).

Another angel ... from the altar (14:18). Compare the angel "over the altar" in 8:3–5, who added incense to the prayers of the saints. For he cast the fire of the altar into the earth (8:5), as if in answer to the prayers of the souls under the altar to avenge their blood (6:10). The same angel seems to be here denoted by the statement that it was **he that hath power over the fire** (14:18). That is, he is the one who in the former vision filled the censer with the fire of the altar and cast it down upon the earth. It was fitting that the same angel **called** (φωνέω [phōneō]) **with a great voice** (14:18) the signal for the thrusting in of the sickle into the clusters of grapes **fully ripe** for the wine press of bloody judgment.

The great wine press of the wrath of God (14:19). Compare this "wine of the wrath of God" in 14:10. These words, together with what is added in the next verse, show that the entire picture of verses 17–20 is one of terrible retributive judgment. But the extent of the judgment, or the particular objects of the divine wrath, are not specified. We may think of the dragon and of the two beasts and of Babylon the great, for they were all acting the part of enemies of God and the Lamb. But the repeated mention of the "earth" (that is, the "land;" 14:15, 16, 18, 19) and the city in 14:20 (cp. 11:8) point us most naturally to the land and city of the Jewish people. For throughout this book they are the most notable objects of the wrath of God.

Trodden without the city (14:20). We understand the city here referred to as the "Babylon the great" of verse 8 and identical with the city which is called "Sodom and Egypt" in 11:8. Without and around this city the Roman armies gathered to tread down Judah and Jerusalem until her times of judgment were fulfilled (Luke 21:20–24). Those armies were under God the agents of divine retribution and by them was the wine press of his wrath trodden. On this figure of treading the wine press, compare Isaiah 63:3, from which the imagery is partly drawn (cp. Lam. 1:15).

Blood ... even unto the bridles (14:20). The picture of blood is made purposely appalling by the extravagance of the hyperbole. It seemed to the seer as if **the horses** (cp. 9:16–17 and 16:12–16) that trod the land of this vine waded in a sea of blood. And that sea extended **as far as a thousand and six hundred furlongs** (14:20). This number, like all others in the book, is symbolical, made up of forty times forty, the number of judgment and penalty (Num. 14:34; Gen. 7:12). It thus suggests a retribution fearfully intensified.

The distance indicated is equivalent to two hundred miles. That is approximately the length of Palestine from north to south. This may incidentally point to the fact that this whole land was, figuratively speaking, deluged with blood during the Jewish war which ended in the destruction of Jerusalem. This fearful vision of judgment stands in relation to the seven last plagues of Revelation 15 and 16, as does the symbolism of the sixth seal (6:12–17) to that of the seven trumpets.

Chapter 8
THE SEVEN LAST PLAGUES
(Rev.15:1–16:21)

The contents of Revelation 15 are of the nature of an introduction to the pouring out of the seven bowls of wrath (Rev. 16), which will be found to correspond strikingly to the seven trumpets. After the announcement of the seven last plagues in 15:1 there is a vision of victors singing a song of triumph (15:2–4). This artistic feature corresponds to the introduction of the multitudes, sealed by the living God and arrayed in white robes, singing with the angels round the throne (Rev. 7). That one was brought in between the opening of the sixth and seventh seals and just before the seven angels were sent forth to sound the seven trumpets of woe.

The Seven Angels (15:1)

> 1 And I saw another sign in heaven, great and marvelous, seven angels having seven plagues, which are the last, for in them is finished the wrath of God.

Another sign in heaven (15:1). This is an allusion to the great signs seen in 12:1, 3. **Seven angels having seven plagues**. Compare the opening of the seventh seal which issued in the seven trumpets (8:1–2). See also the language of Leviticus 26:21.

The last (15:1). This is called such because in them is **finished the wrath of God**. In them is consummated the utter overthrow of "Babylon the Great" (16:19). Immediately after the seventh plague (16:17–21) "one of the seven angels that had the seven bowls of plagues" showed John the special apocalypse of the fall of this Babylon the harlot (17:1). And, still further on, one of the same seven angels showed him the corresponding vision of the new Jerusalem, "the bride, the wife of the Lamb" (21:9).

The Song by the Glassy Sea (15:2–4)

2 And I saw as it were a glassy sea mingled with fire; and them that come off victorious from the beast and from his image and from the number of his name, standing by the glassy sea, having harps of God.
3 And they sing the song of Moses the servant of God and the song of the Lamb, saying, Great and marvelous are thy works, O Lord God, the Almighty; righteous and true are thy ways, thou King of the ages.
4 Who shall not fear, O Lord and glorify thy name? for thou only art holy; for all the nations shall come and worship before thee; for thy righteous acts have been made manifest.

A glassy sea mingled with fire (15:2). This is quite different from the "glassy sea like unto crystal" (4:6) which formed the open space before the throne. This had, like that, a smooth, glittering surface, as if it were of glass. But it had also the appearance of being "mingled with fire," as if reflecting the vast sea of blood from the wine press of God's wrath mentioned just before (14:20). This allusion, as well as the immediate mention of "the song of Moses the servant of God," and the entire picture of the triumphant host, show that the imagery is drawn from the triumph of Israel at the Red Sea. There the hosts of Israel, standing upon the further shore, safe from pursuit and persecution by Pharaoh, "saw the Egyptians dead upon the seashore" (Exo. 14:30).

Them that come off victorious from the beast (15:2). How like the victory of the Israelites who had escaped the persecutions of Egypt and, having made the passage of the Red Sea, triumphed gloriously as the saved people of Jehovah. In Revelation 12:4, 15–16, we have already noted allusions to this period of Israel's trial and triumph.

From his image and from the number of his name (15:2). This refers back to 13:17.

Standing by the glassy sea (15:2). Just as Israel stood by the Red Sea, or on its further shore and saw God's vengeance on their enemies. The preposition ἐπί (*epi*) with the accusative in the sense of *by* or *at*, is used here as it was in 3:20 and 7:1. **Having harps of God**. Like the multitude of exultant singers in 14:2. So the Israelitish song of triumph was accompanied with the sound of timbrels (Exo. 15:20).

They sing the song of Moses (15:3). That is, a song of victory like that of Moses in Exodus 15:1–18: "Then sang Moses and the children of Israel this song unto Jehovah, saying, I will sing unto Jehovah, for he hath triumphed gloriously: the horse and his rider he hath cast into the sea." But this strain of triumph is something more than that old song of Moses: it is also the song of the Lamb, who stood on Mount Zion with his redeemed Israel (14:1). These lofty designations of the song enhance in our minds the idea of its superior excellence and glory. The language of the song is a combination from Psalm 111:2; 139:14; Exodus 34:10; Amos 4:13 (Septuagint); Deuteronomy 32:4; Jeremiah 10:7, 10; Psalm 86:9; 145:17; Malachi 1:11.

The Procession of the Angels (15:5–8)

5 And after these things I saw and the temple of the tabernacle of the testimony in heaven was opened:
6 and there came out from the temple the seven angels that had the seven plagues, arrayed with precious stone, pure and bright and girt about their breasts with golden girdles.
7 And one of the four living creatures gave unto the seven angels seven golden bowls full of the wrath of God, who liveth forever and ever.
8 And the temple was filled with smoke from the glory of God and from his power; and none was able to enter into the temple, till the seven plagues of the seven angels should be finished.

After these things (15:5). The song of verses 3 and 4 is supposed to have occupied some time. Verse 1 serves to announce the entire subject of Revelation 15 and 16 and after the preliminaries of verses 2–4 the subject of the "seven angels having seven plagues" is formally taken up and their procession from the temple in heaven is described.

The temple of the tabernacle of the testimony in heaven was opened (15:5). This can be no other than the temple of 11:19, which was seen to contain the ark of the covenant of God. From the same temple went forth the angels of 14:15, 17. The phrase "the tabernacle of the testimony" appears in Acts 7:44 (cp. Septuagint of Exo. 29:10–11) and was so called because it contained as its most precious treasure the ark with the "two tables of testimony" (Exo. 25:16; 31:18). The "temple of the tabernacle of the testimony" is so called because it contained and represented all that was symbolized in the ancient tabernacle of the wilderness made after the pattern shown to Moses in the mount (Exo. 25:40).

There came out from the temple the seven angels (15:6). As in 14:17, the angel with the sharp sickle "came out from the temple "to execute his work of judgment. He was **arrayed with precious stones,**

pure and bright. This reading is remarkable and seems on the whole best attested. It is to be explained by comparison with Ezekiel 28:13. There the glory of the king of Tyre is set forth as a perfection of beauty, not the least of which was his covering of every precious stone. If, however, one prefer the reading "linen" (λίνον [*linon*] instead of λίθον [*lithon*]), he may find analogy in 19:8. Then he would think of these angels as clothed in priestly array (cp. Exo. 28:39) and performing a work as holy as the angel of the altar in Revelation 8:3–5.

Golden girdles (15:6). This imagery is like that of the Son of man in Revelation 1:13. The "angels of his power" (2 Thess. 1:7) are in apocalyptic symbolism appropriately arrayed in a glory like that of the Lord himself.

One of the four living creatures gave (15:7). The last recorded act of these living creatures was to call out the horses of the first four seals (6:1–8). It was appropriate that one of these also **gave unto the seven angels** the **seven golden bowls full of the wrath of God** now about to be poured out into the earth. The stability both of the temple and the throne of God in heaven calls for many judgments of wrath. Hence, the fitness of this act of one of the living creatures before the throne, as well as of the procession of the seven angels from the temple in heaven.

The temple was filled with smoke (15:8). This accords with Isaiah's vision of Jehovah's glory in his temple (Isa. 6:4). It was a sign of the invisible presence of God in his temple. The imagery is from Exodus 40:34 where it is written that "a cloud covered the tent of meeting and the glory of Jehovah filled the tabernacle." So this cloud of smoke proceeded from the glory of God and from his power. Compare 1 Kings 8:10–11. **None was able to enter** for the same reason that "Moses was not able to enter into the tent of meeting, because the cloud abode thereon and the glory of Jehovah filled the tabernacle" (Exo. 40:35).

No student can fail to see that the bowls of wrath, as depicted in Revelation 16, correspond in a striking manner to the seven trumpets in the first part of the book. Thus the first bowl like the first trumpet affects the earth, the second the sea, the third the rivers and fountains, the fourth the sun, the fifth the throne of the beast, the sixth the Euphrates, and the seventh the air, as if to clear the way for the kingdom of the heavens. But these correspondences are not exact repetitions, or a recapitulation, as some of the older expositors maintained.

No apocalyptic repetitions of symbolism are exactly parallel. The later imagery always adds somewhat to the earlier, so that the repetition is of the nature of a new and additional illustration. Thus it will be seen that the seven last plagues are more completely destructive than the trumpet woes. They are not limited to a third part of earth and sea and sun, but effect a total ruin. Nor are they divisible into groups of four and three, as the seven seals and the trumpets. Nor is any room allowed for side pictures and episodes between. Rather, the sevenfold tragedy moves right on without interruption until a great voice from the throne says, "It is done" (16:17). The climax is reached and the object of the plagues declared when it is said that "Babylon the great was remembered in the sight of God, to give unto her the cup of the wine of the fierceness of his wrath" (16:19).

The seven last plagues are therefore to be regarded as an intensified picture of consuming judgment. The imagery moves entirely in the realm of symbolism and metaphor and "literal interpretation" is not to be thought of. The seven trumpets have obvious suggestions of the trumpets that sounded the fall of Jericho and derive their general idea from there. Thus, the seven plagues derive much of their imagery from the plagues of Egypt, to which a number of the allusions are apparent. By means of these rapidly successive pictures of consuming wrath the same penal judgments are exhibited as in the seven trumpets. We are no more to seek different historical events to answer to these plagues than we are to suppose that Joseph's dream of the sun, moon, and stars depicted something entirely different from his dream of the sheaves of the field that bowed down to him.

The Pouring Out of the Bowls of Wrath (16:1–21)

First plague (grievous sore) (16:1–2)

> 1 And I heard a great voice out of the temple, saying to the seven angels, Go ye and pour out the seven bowls of the wrath of God into the earth.
> 2 And the first went and poured out his bowl into the earth; and it became a noisome and grievous sore upon the men which had the mark of the beast and which worshiped his image.

Voice out of the temple (16:1). The temple is the one just mentioned (15:8) and, as it was so filled with the cloud of the glory of God that none was able to enter, the voice must be understood as from God himself. **Pour out the seven bowls.** On the figure of pouring out of divine wrath compare Psalm 69:24; Jeremiah 10:25; Ezekiel 14:19; and Zephaniah 3:8. The bowls, or vials (φιάλας [*phialas*]), are conceived as containing ingredients of penal woe, like the cups of Revelation 14:10 and 16:19 (cp. also Isa. 51:17, 22; Eze. 23:32–33).

The first ... a noisome and grievous sore (16:2). Although the first bowl was poured directly into the earth, so corresponding to the first trumpet (8:7), it resulted like the ashes and small dust of the land of Egypt in producing a malarious sore, or ulcer (ἕλκος [*helkos*]), **upon the men which had the mark of the beast.** In this it was like the sixth Egyptian plague (Exo. 9:8–10), which brought boils and inflamed sores on man and beast and tormented the magicians as well as all the other Egyptians. The first trumpet was followed by hail and fire, mingled with blood, which, like the seventh plague of Egypt (Exo. 9:22–25), smote the land and herb and tree. But in both cases the sphere of operation was the earth as distinct from sea and waters and abyss and heavens.

Second plague (sea turned to blood) (16:3)

> 3 And the second poured out his bowl into the sea; and it became blood as of a dead man; and every living soul died, even the things that were in the sea.

The second ... into the sea ... blood (16:3). This plague and the following one result in the same calamity as that of the first Egyptian plague (Exo. 7:19–21) and is in noticeable analogy with the effects which followed the sounding of the second trumpet (Rev. 8:8–9). But the trumpet woe affected only a third part of the sea and its creatures; this affects the whole sea so that **every living** thing therein **died.**

Another notable feature was that the sea **became blood as of a dead man** (16:3). As Düsterdieck explains: "not a great pool of blood, as of many slain, but the horribleness of the fact is augmented in that the sea seems like the clotted and already putrefying blood of a dead man."

Third plague (rivers and fountains turned to blood) (16:4–7)

> 4 And the third poured out his bowl into the rivers and the fountains of the waters; and it became blood.
> 5 And I heard the angel of the waters saying, Righteous art thou, who art and who wast, thou Holy One, because thou didst thus judge:
> 6 for they poured out the blood of saints and prophets and blood hast thou given them to drink: they are worthy.
> 7 And I heard the altar saying, Yea, O Lord God, the Almighty, true and righteous are thy judgments.

The third ... rivers and the fountains ... blood (16:4). This third plague maintains the same distinction between the sea and the rivers and fountains as was observed in the third trumpet (Rev. 8:10–11). But while the result of the third trumpet was to make the waters bitter so as to cause the death of them that drank, the third plague, like the second, turns the waters into blood. This difference was designed, as is seen from what is added in verses 5–7: for in all this blood "the angel of the waters" (16:5) recognizes righteous retribution for "the blood of saints and prophets" (16:6).

The angel of the waters (16:5). Everything in apocalyptic vision appears to have a superintending angel, but the angel is to be conceived as the ideal personification of that which he represents. As the angel of a church is but a figure for the church itself, so "the angel of the waters" is but a personification of the waters themselves. It is as if the very waters cried out in acknowledgment of the righteous judgments of God.

Righteous art thou (16:5; cp. Psa. 19:9). As usual in such ascription of praise, the language is made up of choice selections from current expressions of devout worship (cp. 15:3–4). **Thus judge.** Or, "because you judged these things," namely, this judgment of blood, because it seemed so fitting a retribution for the shed blood of the saints.

They poured out the blood of saints (16:6). Who are they who "poured out the blood of saints and prophets"? The unmistakable answer is: They who are represented by the woman of 17:6, who was "drunken with the blood of the saints and with the blood of the witnesses of Jesus." That is, "Babylon the great" (14:8; 16:19), whose judgment is symbolized in all these plagues.

And blood hast thou given them to drink (16:6). This fulfills the prophecy of Jesus against the murderous Jerusalem "that killeth the prophets and stoneth them that are sent unto her" (Matt. 23:34–37). **Worthy are they**. That is, richly deserving such bloody retribution and therefore it was said that upon them should come "all the righteous blood shed upon the earth" (Matt. 23:35).

I heard the altar saying (16:7). This is the same as if he had written "the angel of the altar." For in this symbolism the one represents the other, as the "angel of the waters" in verse 5 above is the same as the waters themselves. Not only do the waters cry out in praise of God's **true and righteous ... judgments**, but also the altar at which the prayers of all the saints were mediated (8:3–5). It too utters the same acknowledgment before the **Lord God, the Almighty**. Compare the voices from the altar in Revelation 9:13 and 14:18.

Fourth plague (sun smitten) (16:8–9)

> 8 And the fourth poured out his bowl upon the sun; and it was given unto it to scorch men with fire.
> 9 And men were scorched with great heat: and they blasphemed the name of God who hath the power over these plagues; and they repented not to give him glory.

The fourth ... upon the sun (16:8; cp. the result of the fourth trumpet at 8:12). In the trumpet woe other luminaries were smitten and the third part was darkened. But the object of this plague was **to scorch men with fire**. This was the direct opposite of the ninth plague of Egypt (Exo. 10:21–23). But both were adapted to produce horror and torment. Thus, the result of the judgment was that the tormented ones **blasphemed the name of the God who has the power over these plagues** (16:9). Compare the corresponding impenitence of those "who were not killed with these plagues" (in 9:20, 21).

Fifth plague (throne of beast smitten) (16:10–11)

> 10 And the fifth poured out his bowl upon the throne of the beast; and his kingdom was darkened; and they gnawed their tongues for pain,
> 11 and they blasphemed the God of heaven because of their pains and their sores; and they repented not of their works.

The fifth ... upon the throne of the beast (16:10). Compare this to the fifth trumpet and the torments which followed it (Rev. 9:1–11). The tormenting locusts, which came out of "the pit of the abyss," have a king over them whose name is Abaddon and Apollyon. This king of the abyss is no other than the great red dragon of 12:3, "he that is called the Devil and Satan" (12:9) and he "gave his power and his throne and great authority" to the beast that came up out of the sea (13:2).

Now, by the pouring out of the fifth bowl of wrath, **his kingdom was darkened** and the consequent torment was even worse than that caused by the ninth Egyptian plague, which brought thick darkness over all the realm of Pharaoh (Exo. 10:21–23). Being poured upon the throne of the beast, this bowl of wrath seems to have tormented Satan himself and his fallen angels, as well as all the subjects of his infernal power (cp. Matt. 8:29; Mark 1:24; 5:7).

Gnawed their tongues for pain (16:10). This refers to all those subjects of Satan and the beast. These had been given over to believe a lie and persisted in their impiety in spite of all previous warnings and judgments. In pouring out the blood of saints (v. 6) they had inflicted many and great tortures. Now they are visited with demoniacal torment.

Blasphemed the God of heaven (16:11). Like the victims of the preceding plague (v. 9). **Because of their pains and their sores.** Each additional plague seems to increase the pains and sores (cp. v. 2) of all that went before. For these seven last plagues, like those of Egypt, increase in power as they advance and no respite is allowed between the successive strokes.

Repented not (16:11). Their hearts, like the heart of Pharaoh, became hardened and impenitent beyond recall. They had persistently hardened themselves until they had become "vessels of wrath fitted unto destruction" (Rom. 9:22).

Sixth plague (Euphrates-armies) (16:12–16)

> 12 And the sixth poured out his bowl upon the great river, the river Euphrates; and the water thereof was dried up, that the way might be made ready for the kings that come from the sunrising.
> 13 And I saw coming out of the mouth of the dragon and out of the mouth of the beast and out of the mouth of the false prophet, three unclean spirits, as it were frogs:
> 14 for they are spirits of devils, working signs; which go forth unto the kings of the whole world, to gather them together unto the war of the great day of God, the Almighty.

15 (Behold, I come as a thief. Blessed is he that watcheth and keepeth his garments, lest he walk naked and they see his shame.)
16 And they gathered them together into the place which is called in Hebrew Har-Magedon.

The sixth poured out his bowl upon the great river ... Euphrates (16:12). Compare the sixth trumpet and the armies from the Euphrates which it summoned for destructive war (9:13–19). The symbolic significance of Euphrates is the same here as in 9:14, where see note. The imagery is here changed to fit it to another point of view. Instead of four angels bound with their immense hosts and loosed at the divine mandate, we have the water of the great river **dried up, that the way might be made ready for the kings that come from the sunrising**. Thus the procedure of these kings is as truly under divine control as the march of Israel across the Red Sea and across the Jordan (cp. Josh. 4:23–24).

In the Old Testament, the Assyrian was employed as the rod of Jehovah's anger to execute his wrath upon a hypocritical nation (Isa. 10:5–6). Similarly are these "kings that come from the sunrising" (16:12) to execute like judgment upon the same nation. That nation is now utterly apostate and doomed to the fearful punishment here portrayed. Kings and armies that marched from the far East toward the West would naturally be spoken of as coming from the rising of the sun and they must necessarily cross the Euphrates on their western march. The analogy and self-consistency of the symbolism require that, though these are in some sense "the kings of the whole world" (v. 14), they march from that quarter from which the most terrible kings and armies came that of old desolated the land of Israel.

Three unclean spirits, as it were frogs (16:13). As so many of these plagues show a manifest reference to the plagues of Egypt we may, perhaps, see in this mention of "frogs" an allusion to the second Egyptian plague (Exo. 8:5–6). But the allusion is at most only incidental. The unclean spirits constitute a trinity by proceeding from the **dragon, beast**, and **false prophet**. Each is represented by a spirit and yet the three are "in demoniac concord joined." The "false prophet" is but another name for the second beast out of the land (13:11). He is so called on account of the deceitful signs and teaching ascribed to him in Revelation 13:13–14.

The trinity of Satanic forces are said to **be spirits of devils, working signs, which go forth unto the kings of the whole world, to gather**

them together unto the war (16:14). Here we see an obvious allusion to the vision of Micaiah. He saw "a lying spirit" go forth and speak through the mouth of the false prophets of Ahab, persuading the kings to undertake a disastrous war (1 Kgs. 22:19–23). For though this war **of the great day of God, the Almighty**, be a means of pouring out a bowl of wrath upon his enemies, his infinite wisdom and power can employ the agency of demons and military hosts to execute his punitive judgments. "The great day of God" is any day in which he executes the fearful judgments of his almighty power on wicked men and nations (cp. Joel 2:1, 11, 31; Isa. 13:6, 9; Zeph. 1:14–18; Amos 5:18). This was the great day of wrath foreshadowed by Jesus in the parable of the marriage of the king's son, when "the king was wroth and sent forth his armies and destroyed those murderers and burned up their city" (Matt. 22:7). These kings are the same as those more particularly described in 17:16–17.

Behold, I come as a thief (16:15; cp. 3:3; Matt. 24:42–44; Luke 12:35–40; 1 Thess. 5:2). **Blessed is he that watcheth** is an echo of Matthew 24:46 and Luke 12:37. **Keepeth his garments**. As suggested in 3:18 and 7:9, 14; compare 22:14. A failure to watch and keep their garments undefiled will expose to nakedness and shame at the coming of the Lord. This verse is a parenthesis and of the nature of an admonition occasioned by the mention of "the great day of God the Almighty" (v. 14). Compare the exclamation in Jacob's prophecy immediately after the mention of Dan as a serpent, biting the heels of the horse and throwing the rider (Gen. 49:18).

They gathered (16:16). The subject of the verb is the same as that of "go forth" (ἐκπορεύεται [*ekporeuetai*]) in verse 14, namely, the unclean spirits, who go forth to gather (συναγαγεῖν [*sunagagein*]) the kings together. There the subject is a neuter plural (ἅ [*ha*]) construed with a verb in the singular. Thus, the propriety of translating the συνήγαγεν (*sunēgagen*) of this verse as: "they gathered."

The place which is called in Hebrew Har-Magedon (16:16). The symbolical import of this name is to be sought in its Old Testament associations. Megiddo is first mentioned in Deborah's song as the place where the kings of Canaan came and fought (Jdgs. 5:19). It is again mentioned as the place where Josiah went up to war against the king of Egypt and was slain (2 Kgs. 23:29), a calamity so great that all Judah and Jerusalem mourned and perpetuated the lamentation for a protracted period (2 Chron. 35:24, 25; cp. Zech. 12:11). It seems therefore to have been associated in the songs of Israel with the great battlefield of nations, the plain of Esdraelon, and that battlefield came to be thought of in the later times as connected with sore lamentation in Jerusalem.

But the prefixed *Har*, or *Ar*, as some read it, is more difficult to explain. It may mean mountain (הר [*har*]) or city (עָר = עִיר [*ir* = *iyr*]) according as it is pronounced with a rough or smooth breathing. So we have the two readings Har-Magedon and Ar-Magedon. If we read Har-Magedon, that is, "Mount Magedon," we have a noticeable contrast with "valley of Megiddo" in Zechariah 12:11 and "waters of Megiddo" in Judges 5:19. If we read Ar-Magedon, that is, "city of Magedon," we may, perhaps, see a designed pointing to the great city Babylon, against which these armies march to make war. May not both meanings be allowed? This would suggest that the great war of these kings is to be fought in a mountain and about a city, the very city where the Lord was crucified (11:8). That war which destroyed the murderers and burned up their city (Matt. 22:7) caused "a great mourning in Jerusalem" like that of Zechariah 12:11 and to it a reference may be seen in 1:7.

It is to be noted that no account is here given of the actual "war of the great day of God," for which these kings are gathered together. In the woe of the sixth trumpet "the third part of men was killed" (9:18). So here we might naturally look for a complete slaughter to be accomplished by these kings from the sunrising, actuated by the foul spirits of demons. But it appears to be the plan of the writer to hasten on so rapidly to the end of these plagues that he does not pause to record separately the execution effected by the kings alone. Rather he combines it with the catastrophe consummated by the pouring out of the seventh bowl of wrath. Then earthquake and hailstones from heaven shake not only the great city, but the cities of the nations. The earth and the heavens thus are shown to unite with the forces of the kings and the elements take part in this war against the enemies of God. The art of the apocalyptist is notably displayed in thus reserving what will make the seventh and last judgment stroke the more tremendous.

Seventh plague (Babylon doomed) (16:17–21)

> 17 And the seventh poured out his bowl upon the air; and there came forth a great voice out of the temple, from the throne, saying, It is done: and there were lightnings and voices and thunders;
> 18 and there was a great earthquake, such as was not since there were men upon the earth, so great an earthquake, so mighty.
> 19 And the great city was divided into three parts and the cities of the nations fell: and Babylon the great was remembered in the sight of God, to give unto her the cup of the wine of the fierceness of his wrath.
> 20 And every island fled away and the mountains were not found.
> 21 And great hail, every stone about the weight of a talent, cometh down out of heaven upon men: and men blasphemed God because of the plague of the hail; for the plague thereof is exceeding great.

The seventh … upon the air (16:17). This is the elemental home of the "lightnings and voices and thunders" (v. 17) and the source of "the great hail" about to come down upon men (v. 21). The sounding of the seventh trumpet was followed by "great voices in the heaven" announcing the beginning of the reign of Christ (11:15). But the sounding of that trumpet was delayed by the revelation of many things which must come to pass before the end. Here, on the contrary, the plan of the writer is not yet to introduce the coming of the kingdom of Christ. Rather he depicts the signal judgments by which the end of the pre-Messianic age was consummated. The two events were essentially simultaneous. But the apocalyptic symbolism first portrays the fall of "Babylon the great" and shows how much was represented and implied in God's "giving unto her the cup of the wine of the fierceness of his wrath" (v. 19).

Hence the seventh plague displays the fearful end of these judgments. It is not until after the writer has amply described the fall of the bloody harlot and after the multitudes in heaven have sung their song of hallelujah over her righteous retribution that the "King of kings and Lord of lords" moves forth to his world-wide conquests and the new Jerusalem descends from heaven to earth.

Great voice out of the temple from the throne (16:17). The same voice which had commanded the seven angels to pour out the bowls of wrath (cp. v. 1 above). **It is done**. The Greek verb is Γέγονεν (*Gegonen*). It is not the same as the ἐτελέσθη (*etelesthē*; "it is finished") of 10:7.

Rather it refers more particularly to the completion of the seven plagues. This picture of sevenfold judgment is now done.

Lightnings ... voices ... thunders ... earthquake (16:18; cp. 11:19). The "earthquake" is here emphasized as something exceptional and unparalleled. All these movements of the elements are symbolic of a great revolution in the state of the world. And here, as in 11:19, they imply that the revelations of this book are not yet all given. Other and great apocalypses are to follow and the book itself, with its golden outlook into the future, is not to close with earthquakes and thunders and lightnings.

The great city was divided into three parts (16:19). This city is here, as elsewhere in the book, identical with **Babylon the great**. Already an apocalyptic angel has announced its fall (14:8). But the scheme of the book contemplates repeated pictures of its overthrow. The purpose of the repetitions is the same as that of Pharaoh's doubled dream (Gen. 41:32). The division into three parts is to be compared with the fall of the tenth part in 11:13 and shows a more effectual ruin.

The triple division of Ezekiel's symbolical act (Eze. 5:2–12) seems to have been in the writer's mind. For that was a prophecy against Jerusalem, whom God "set in the midst of the nations." Thus, according to the prophet's oracle,

> she hath changed my judgments into wickedness more than the nations that are round about her.... Therefore the fathers shall eat the sons in the midst of thee and the sons shall eat their fathers; and I will execute judgments unto thee.... A third part of thee shall die with pestilence and with famine shall they be consumed in the midst of thee: and a third part shall fall by the sword round about thee; and I will scatter a third part unto all the winds and I will draw out a sword after them.

Thus, in the fullness of time, was this once favored city, having made herself an abominable **Babylon, remembered in the sight of God to give unto her the cup of the wine of the fierceness of his wrath** (16:19). Compare the language of 18:5 and Psalm 9:12. On the figures of cup of wrath and wine of wrath see notes on 14:8, 10 and 16:1. All these figures set forth the doctrine of unfailing righteous retribution.

Every island fled ... mountains were not found (16:20). Apocalyptic metaphors like those of 6:14 are designed to produce an impression of the awful force and fierceness of the judgment.

Great hail about the weight of a talent (16:20). The incredibly great size of these hailstones is in keeping with the metaphorical picture of verse 20. The Jewish talent weighed more than a hundred pounds troy. Thus, every hailstone is to be conceived as a huge boulder as heavy as a man could well lift. Compare the Egyptian plague of hail (Exo. 9:23–26). In the statement that this great hail **cometh down out of heaven upon men** we may see a sign of "the war of the great day of God, the Almighty" (v. 14 above). There is an allusion here to the war at Gibeon, where Jehovah defeated the enemies of his people and "slew them with a great slaughter ... and cast down great stones from heaven upon them" (Josh. 10:10–11). Similarly the stars of heaven fought against Sisera and his host (Jdgs. 4:15; 5:20; cp. also Psa. 18:13–14; Isa. 28:2; 30:30).

It may be worthy of a passing notice that Josephus (*Wars* 5:6:3) speaks of stones of a talent weight hurled by the Romans on the men of Jerusalem. But to find in such a fact the fulfillment of our prophecy would be to belittle the sublime apocalyptic picture. The mind that is taken captive by such analogies and sees in them striking confirmations of prophecy, fails to appreciate the spirit of prophecy and misconceives both its purpose and method.

Men blasphemed (16:21) as they did under the fourth and fifth plagues (vv. 9 and 11). This statement in connection with the last plague sets in the strongest possible light the unchangeable obduracy of the people's hearts, upon whom these bowls of plagues were poured.

Chapter 9
BABYLON, THE GREAT HARLOT
(Rev. 17:1–19:10)

Although the seven angels have poured out the bowls of wrath, they have not yet finished their mission in this book. For the purpose of a fuller disclosure of "Babylon the great" one of these seven angels carries John away in the wilderness and shows him a vision of the great harlot. Her destruction must be accomplished before the Messianic King can fully introduce his kingdom and bring the new Jerusalem to the earth. For Babylon the Harlot and Jerusalem the Bride are the two great figures in the concluding portion of the Apocalypse. The one must be overthrown before the other can appear in her full glory. In the sequel, one of these same seven angels carries John away to a mountain and shows him the Bride, the wife of the Lamb (21:9).

Thus, it serves the scheme of the whole revelation that one of these angels first shows the character and judgment of "Babylon the great, the mother of the harlots and of the abominations of the earth" (17:5).

1. The Vision of the Harlot (17:1–6)

1 And there came one of the seven angels that had the seven bowls and spake with me, saying, Come hither, I will show thee the judgment of the great harlot that sitteth upon many waters;
2 with whom the kings of the earth committed fornication and they that dwell in the earth were made drunken with the wine of her fornication.
3 And he carried me away in the Spirit into a wilderness: and I saw a woman sitting upon a scarlet-colored beast, full of names of blasphemy, having seven heads and ten horns.
4 And the woman was arrayed in purple and scarlet and decked with gold and precious stone and pearls, having in her hand a golden cup full of abominations, even the unclean things of her fornication and upon her forehead a name written,
5 MYSTERY, BABYLON THE GREAT, THE MOTHER OF THE HARLOTS AND OF THE ABOMINATIONS OF THE EARTH.

6 And I saw the woman drunken with the blood of the saints and with the blood of the witnesses of Jesus. And when I saw her, I wondered with a great wonder.

One of the seven angels (17:1). It is fitting that one of these ministers of the judgments already symbolized **show ... the judgment of the great harlot**. The foregoing notes have already pointed out that "Babylon the great" is no other than the apostate "Judah and Jerusalem," more execrable now than when Isaiah cried over her, "How is the faithful city become a harlot!" The entire arraignment of the "sinful nation, a people laden with iniquity," found in the first chapter of Isaiah, might have been repeated against Jerusalem at the time this Apocalypse was written. In fact, the twenty-third chapter of Matthew is virtually such an arraignment by the Lord himself.

A "harlot" in the prophetical sense is one who has broken the vows and bonds of the marriage covenant by any infidelity to the obligations of such union. The idolatries of the older Jerusalem were one of her most infamous offenses against Jehovah. Nevertheless, extortion and falsehood and violation of many laws and ordinances of divine authority were also charged against her. Idolatry in the strict sense was not the crying sin of the Jewish people in the time of Christ and his apostles. Yet they were guilty of so many violations of the true spirit of God's law (cp. Acts 7:53) that the charge of infidelity to their covenanted bonds could be most justly made against them.

Their most flagrant crime was the open rejection of their Lord, who "came unto his own and they who were his own received him not" (John 1:11). They not only cast him off by such refusal, but were his "betrayers and murderers" (Acts 7:52). The crime of Clytemnestra in the betrayal and murder of her husband was not so enormous as that of the people who "denied the holy and righteous one and killed the Prince of life," preferring a murderer to him (Acts 3:14–15) and crying in blasphemous defiance, "His blood be on us and on our children" (Matt. 27:25). The Jerusalem and Judah which thus rejected the Christ of God were therefore guilty of the most criminal apostasy and are appropriately called "the great harlot." The shameful repudiation of her Lord was but the filling up of a long history of apostasy from the holy law, which was recognized as having been given by the ministry of angels (Acts 7:53; Gal. 3:19; Heb. 2:2).

That sitteth upon many waters (17:1). This is added to maintain the harmony of the figure with ancient Babylon, which is described by

Jeremiah as "dwelling upon many waters" (Jer. 51:13). But as these waters, according to verse 15, symbolize "peoples and multitudes and nations and tongues," so this harlot had her commerce with all the nations of the Roman empire and derived her revenues from them. She would not even hesitate for the sake of gain to make Jehovah's temple "a house of merchandise" (John 2:16).

Kings committed fornication (17:2). These are the same kings as those described in verse 12, but the reference is here without specific limitation. The language of this verse is in substance from Isaiah 23:17 and has allusion to a widespread commerce resembling that of ancient Tyre. Such commercial and political intercourse with heathen lands and rulers was inconsistent with the spirit of Mosaism (cp. Lev. 18:2; 20:23; Exo. 34:12) and is here figuratively called "fornication." Compare also Jeremiah 51:7 for the figure of being **drunken with the wine of her fornication**. Much intercourse with foreign peoples and ambition to be like them in power and glory, always produced among the Jewish people an infatuation like that of drunkenness and was the fruitful cause of their backslidings and calamities.

A woman sitting upon a scarlet-colored beast (17:3). Observe that the words sitting upon are the same as, in verse 1, are followed by "many waters." Not only does this harlot depend upon "peoples and multitudes and nations and tongues" for revenue and support, but also and most notably upon the **beast having seven heads and ten horns**, as described in 13:1. His heads bore **many names of blasphemy** and he received "his power and his throne and great authority" from the "great red dragon" of 12:3. Hence he may well be here called a **scarlet-colored beast and full of names of blasphemy**. The Jewish people, at the time this Apocalypse was written, had been dependent for their national existence a hundred years on Rome.

Arrayed in purple and scarlet (17:4). Notably the attire of a harlot. Contrast the array of the woman of 12:1. **Gilded with gold ... precious stone ... [and] pearls**. The corresponding extravagance of outward ornamentation befitting a harlot. **Golden cup full of abominations**. Compare Jeremiah 51:7. This allusion keeps up and complements the figure of uncleanness in verse 2.

A name written, a mystery (17:5). That is, a name that involved mystical significance symbolic of the woman's character. **Mother of harlots** is an allusion to Hosea's symbolical portraiture of the apostate Israel of his day (cp. Hos. 1:2; 2:1–5). **Abominations of the earth**, that is, "the land." All the evils of the land of Israel were the offspring of the people's apostasy from the Lord that bought them. The Lord Jesus came to the house of Israel and the men of Judah and, as in the times of Isaiah, "looked for judgment, but behold oppression; for righteousness, but behold a cry" (Isa. 5:7).

Drunken with the blood of saints (17:6). No clearer or more conclusive comment on these words could be asked than is furnished in the language of Jesus in Matthew 23:29–39; Luke 13:33–35. The **witnesses of Jesus** are to be understood as a direct reference to the μάρτυρες (*martures*) in 11:3. For these "witnesses" are no other than those slain by "the beast that cometh up out of the abyss." Their dead bodies were exposed "in the street of the great city ... where also their Lord was crucified" (11:7–8).

John reports **I wondered with a great wonder** (17:6) because he did not understand the mystery of the vision and the mystery seemed so very great. In this he was like Daniel, who confesses his astonishment in Daniel 8:27.

2. The Mystery Explained (17:7–18)

> 7 And the angel said unto me, Wherefore didst thou wonder? I will tell thee the mystery of the woman and of the beast that carrieth her, which hath the seven heads and the ten horns.
> 8 The beast that thou sawest was and is not; and is about to come up out of the abyss and to go into perdition. And they that dwell on the earth shall wonder, they whose name hath not been written in the book of life from the foundation of the world, when they behold the beast, how that he was and is not and shall come. Here is the mind which hath wisdom.
> 9 The seven heads are seven mountains, on which the woman sitteth:
> 10 and there are seven kings; the five are fallen, the one is, the other is not yet come; and when he cometh, he must continue a little while.
> 11 And the beast that was and is not, is himself also an eighth and is of the seven; and he goeth into perdition.
> 12 And the ten horns that thou sawest are ten kings, which have received no kingdom as yet; but they receive authority as kings, with the beast, for one hour.
> 13 These have one mind and they give their power and authority unto the beast.
> 14 These shall war against the Lamb and the Lamb shall overcome them, for he is Lord of lords and King of kings; and they also shall overcome that are with him, called and chosen and faithful.

15 And he saith unto me, The waters which thou sawest, where the harlot sitteth, are peoples and multitudes and nations and tongues.
16 And the ten horns which thou sawest and the beast, these shall hate the harlot and shall make her desolate and naked and shall eat her flesh and shall burn her utterly with fire.
17 For God did put in their hearts to do his mind and to come to one mind and to give their kingdom unto the beast, until the words of God should be accomplished.
18 And the woman whom thou sawest is the great city, which reigneth over the kings of the land.

I will tell thee (17:7). All this is modeled much after the manner of Daniel 8:15–19. It is designed to introduce an angel interpreter to make known the mystery.

The beast was and is not (17:8). The interpretation of the angel is itself cast in the form of an enigma. Thus, the demand for wisdom to comprehend it (see next verse) is like that prefixed to the riddle of 13:18, concerning the number of the beast. In his explanation the angel seems to point our attention particularly to the spirit which actuated the dragon, the beast from the sea, and the false prophet alike. So what is here affirmed of the beast has a special reference to the different and successive manifestations of Satan himself. He has his hour, when he wields the power of darkness (cp. Luke 22:53), now in one form, now in another. He was shown in the previous visions to have been in heaven (12:3). Then being cast out from there he seemed to disappear for a time (12:17). But soon he incarnated himself in the beast that came up out of the sea (13:1–2). And then yet again in the beast that came up out of the land, in whom he acted as the prophet of lies (13:13–15).

Hence, we understand by the beast that *was and is not* an enigmatical portraiture of the great red dragon of 12:3. He is the king of the abyss in 9:11 and the beast that killed the witnesses in 11:7. He appears for a time in the person of some great persecutor, or in the form of some huge iniquity, but is after awhile cast out. Then he again finds some other organ for his operations and enters it with all the malice of the unclean spirit who wandered through dry places, seeking rest and finding none until he discovered his old house, empty, swept and put in order as if to invite his return (Matt. 12:44).

So we are told this same beast is **about to come up out of the abyss** (17:8). So we can therefore believe that he is in some sense identical with the angel of the abyss, whose name is Abaddon and Apollyon (9:11), that is, "the old serpent, he that is called the Devil and Satan, the deceiver of the whole world" (12:9). His destiny is, as the sequel of the book will show, **to go into perdition**. For the beast and the false prophet and the devil himself are all ultimately to be "cast into the lake of fire and brimstone" (20:10). Such also was the fate of the terrible beast of Daniel's vision (Dan. 7:11).

They that dwell on the earth shall wonder (17:8). As they did in the case of the beast whose deathstroke was healed (cp. 13:3–5). The power and signs and lying wonders of Satan, however manifested, have never failed to attract wondering crowds and to command the admiration of such as have **not been written in the book of life**. For the ungodly world will love its own and bestow an idolatrous worship on that which panders to its lust of the flesh and lust of the eye and pride of life. The Roman world-power, filled with Satanic pride, possessed much to be thus admired and the apocalyptist saw in this perpetual command of idolatrous admiration the power of the infernal spirit, who **was and is not and shall come**. Disappearing with one imperial monster, who acts the part of a persecutor of the saints, before long he reappears in another, but always displaying the same Satanic spirit and power.

Here is the mind that hath wisdom (17:9). This is a notice that he is speaking in enigmas and furnishing occasion and subject-matter on which the wise mind may exercise its skill (cp. 13:18).

The seven heads are seven mountains, on which the woman sitteth. This statement has led most interpreters to believe that the woman must be Rome, the great city of the Tiber. This is because that city is said to have been built on the seven hills, known as the Palatine, Capitoline, Quirinal, Viminal, Æsquiline, Cœlian, and Aventine. But such a specific designation of Rome is not in harmony with the enigmatical character of the angel's interpretation. Glasgow well remarks: "The mountains are, like other terms, to be understood symbolically. If the woman is not literal why should the mountains be so thought? And to call the woman a literal city, built on seven hills, is equally gratuitous, whether a Protestant says it of Rome or a Romanist of Constantinople." And, we may add, if literal mountains are to be understood, we may find them at Jerusalem as well as at Rome. There were Zion, Moriah, Acra, Bezetha, Millo, Ophel, and the rocky eminence fifty cubits in height (see Josephus, *Wars* 5:5:8) on which the tower of Antonia was erected.

But these seven heads of the beast no more represent literal mountains than do the seven heads of the dragon in 12:3. And unless we insist on understanding the "waters" of verses 1 and 15 and the "scarlet-colored beast" of verse 3 as literal waters and a literal beast, we cannot consistently maintain that the mountains must be understood literally. For the woman sits on many waters, on a beast, and on seven mountains. Rather do mountains symbolize seats of power and political and governmental resources (cp. note on 13:3). This great Babylon had her seats of power and resources of various kinds and in various places. And so did the beast on which she was seated, so that for dependence and support, as far as she needed, the heads of the beast were her heads. She rested on them.

And there are seven kings (17:10). Not "they are seven kings, as if referring to the mountains. For such a rendering would work confusion in the whole picture. Kings are represented by the horns of a beast (see v. 12 below), not by its heads. Hence we should punctuate and read the beginning of this verse as a new and independent statement. The "seven kings" here referred to are generally understood as the first seven Cæsars and this we believe to be the true interpretation.

Five of these are fallen (17:10), having passed away before John wrote. These were (1) Julius Cæsar, (2) Augustus, (3) Tiberius, (4) Caligula, and (5) Claudius. **The one is** refers to the currently reigning Nero, the sixth of the list. And **the other is not yet come**, which refers to the seventh, who had not yet come when this book was written. Nothing is said about him, except that when he comes he, like all the rest, must continue **a little while**. So we are not concerned to know more about him. The controversies of exegetes over what emperors were the real successors of Nero is irrelevant and of no value in the true interpretation of John's Apocalypse. All that it concerns us here to know is that the succession would go on and not to a seventh only, but also "an eighth," as the next verse declares.

The beast that was and is not (17:11) is the same as in verse 8 above. The king of the abyss (9:11) comes up out of the abyss to make war on the witnesses of Jesus (11:7). He gives his throne and power (13:2) to every agent and system of organized force that will advance his foul purposes. He **is himself also an eighth**, as he is also the inspiring genius **of the seven**. He is the same red dragon, the same old serpent and deceiver of the whole world, that appears in one imperial persecutor after another. But his destiny is decreed, as we have seen in verse 8, for he goes into perdition and will drag there all his subjects and satellites along with him. So while the beast is the great Roman world-power as symbolized in 13:1–8, the angel interpreter of this vision of the great harlot points us especially to the Satanic spirit which gave the beast its great authority (13:2).

The superstitious fiction of *Nero redivivus*, found in many early writers, has been brought forward by some interpreters to explain "the beast that was and is not and shall come." Nero is held to be the wounded head of 13:3 and the healing of the stroke is supposed to be the reappearance of that monster after his death. The rumor was to the effect that Nero was not dead, but had only disappeared from Rome and was for the time dwelling among the Parthians, from which he would return again to the empire of the West. But this theory requires us to understand that Nero had already disappeared when this book was written. It also involves the utterly improbable, not to say preposterous, supposition that the writer of this sublime Apocalypse gave so conspicuous a place in his work to a fabulous and superstitious rumor. Düsterdieck well remarks: "The writer of the Apocalypse in no way betrays such impurity and limitation of faith and Christian culture that without injustice a superstition dare be ascribed to him which the Roman authors already had derided" (*Commentary* on 13:3).

It is far more likely that the rumor itself arose from an early misapprehension of this passage in John's prophecy. It could not have acquired its current form in Nero's time, when this Apocalypse was written, Therefore, with him it would have been an unthinkable anachronism. But the notion may have started from an early misunderstanding of the beast which "was, and is not" and yet shall come again as an "eighth" and be **also of the seven** (17:11). Once started, the fear of Nero and the superstition of the times might have easily spread it through many parts of the empire. In fact, many of the early writers affirm that it originated with an oracle of the soothsayers.

The ten horns ... are ten kings (17:12). The number ten is to be taken here as elsewhere symbolically and we need not cast about for ten particular persons to satisfy the import of the symbol. It is the totality of those allied or subject kings who aided Rome in her wars both on Judaism and Christianity. That they **have received as yet no kingdom** explains that they possessed no independent royalty and as yet exercise no kingly dominion. There seems to be here an appropriation of Daniel's language concerning the "ten kings that shall arise" (Dan. 7:24). **They receive authority as kings one hour with the beast.** This statement shows that these kings are not independent sovereigns, but exercise only a temporary authority, after the style of kings, in conjunction with the beast. Apart from the beast they held no power.

These have one mind (17:13). Beast and kings all have one and the same judgment, feeling, and purpose (γνώμην, *gnōmēn*) in the war against the Lamb (v. 14) and also in the destruction of the harlot (v. 16). So, in giving **their power and authority unto the beast**, these kings are not performing an altogether compulsory service. They are in full sympathy with the operations of the beast. For they are all alike inspired by the angel of the abyss and are in fact so many incarnations of his power. The ten horns, therefore, of this vision appear to represent the same power that was symbolized by the beast out of the land in 13:11–17. But they may include also the heads of all the allied tribes and nations which were associated with Rome in her acts of persecution and especially such as hated the harlot and helped to destroy her (v. 16).

These shall war against the Lamb (17:14) even as the dragon and his angels warred against Michael and his angels in 12:7. For having lost in that war, the dragon was enraged and went away to war with the rest of the woman's seed (12:17). This war against the Lamb and **those who are with him, called and chosen and faithful** is one phase of that war on the seed of the woman. But in their war on the Lamb and his followers **the Lamb shall overcome them** as triumphantly as Michael prevailed in the war of 12:7–9, for he is Lord of lords and King of kings. This will be more fully brought out in Revelation 19 and 20, after the destruction of the harlot has been fully shown.

The **chosen and faithful** (17:14) associates of the Lamb shall also overcome, as was done in 12:11, where it was announced by a great voice in heaven (12:10). Here as there we understand that they overcome "because of the blood of the Lamb and because of the word of their testimony" (12:11). "They conquer though they die," but not so the harlot, as the sequel shows.

The **waters** (cp. v. 1) are **peoples ... multitudes ... nations ... tongues** (17:15). This fourfold designation suggests the many and extensive affiliations of Jerusalem with the mixed populations of the Roman empire. The Jewish people had manifold connection with the provinces of the empire, as is seen in the fact that the devout from all these parts tended to come up to Jerusalem to the great feasts (Acts 2:5–10).

These shall hate the harlot (17:16). The bitterness of neighboring tribes and nations toward Jerusalem is noticed by Josephus (*Wars* 2:18). Their union with the armies of the empire in the final war against the hated city was an acceptable service. In this they displayed one mind with the beast (v. 13). The destruction of "the harlot" is set forth under the fourfold picture of making her **desolate and naked**, eating her **flesh**, and burning her **utterly with fire**. This is a vivid apocalyptic portraiture of the terrible judgments inflicted on Jerusalem by the Roman armies.

God put it into their hearts to do his mind (17:17). That is, as verse 13 above has already implied, God put it into the hearts of the ten kings to do the mind and will (γνώμην, *gnōmēn*) of the beast. So they readily **give their kingdom**, that is, contribute whatever their several dominions afford of a nature to assist the beast in executing on the harlot the judgments which had been foretold. **Until the words of God should be accomplished**. Such words as were uttered by the Son of God in Matthew 23:35-36.

The woman ... is the great city (17:18). Here, at the conclusion of the vision and its explanation, we have the most specific and formal definition of the import of the harlot. The term "great city" has already been applied to the place called in mystic language "Sodom and Egypt," where the Lord of the two witnesses was crucified (11:8). That city is allowed by the best exegetes to be Jerusalem and Josephus calls Jerusalem in one passage (*Wars* 7:8:7) "that great city." But it has generally been supposed that the concluding words, commonly translated **which reigneth over the kings of the earth**, cannot be appropriately applied to Jerusalem. Hence this verse, as well as the "seven mountains" of verse 9, are held by many to be conclusive that "the great city" intended must be Rome. But we believe that opinion to be erroneous and the following reasons to be conclusive of the soundness of the exposition given in these pages:

First, if our position is correct that the latter half of the Apocalypse (Rev. 12–22) is in the main a repetition of the first half (Rev. 1–11) under different symbols, "the great city" of this verse is presumably the same as that of 11:8. It comports with the variety of symbols employed that other symbolical names also be introduced; hence "Babylon the great," instead of "Sodom and Egypt."

Second, the latter part of verse 18 should be translated "which has dominion over the kings of the land." The meaning is, not that this city reigns over all the kings and kingdoms of the habitable world. Rather, it is the capital city of "the land" in which the great catastrophe of this book centers. "The kings of the land" is a phrase to be interpreted in the light of Acts 4:26–27, where it is evident that in the early Church "Herod and Pontius Pilate, with the Gentiles and the peoples of Israel," were the sort of kings and rulers of the earth contemplated in the second Psalm, there quoted. Such kings are represented by Josephus as subject "to the royal city Jerusalem," which, says he, "was supreme and presided over all the neighboring country as the head does over the body" (*Wars* 3:3:5). He goes on to designate ten "inferior cities," which were in the land of Judea. In another place he speaks of Jerusalem in the identical language of our writer and calls it "that great city" (*Wars* 7:8:7).

Third, if the beast is the Roman empire, the harlot must be something else than the city of Rome. For it cannot be said that the emperors or the chief princes of the empire hated Rome or ever sought to destroy that great city. For the empire to destroy its own capital is incongruous in thought and untrue in fact.

Fourth, it contravenes the analogy of biblical symbolism and usage to call pagan Rome a "harlot." The imagery, according to this scripture, implies that she had been in covenant relations with God, but this is totally untrue of any heathen city. The imagery of this whole section of the Apocalypse is appropriated from Ezekiel 16, 22, and 23, where the apostate people of Judah and Jerusalem are depicted. But they were a people unto whom Jehovah swore and entered into covenant (Eze. 16:8). Their sins were accordingly like those of "a woman that breaketh wedlock" (Eze. 16:38). But such imagery is wholly inapplicable to Rome. How unsuitable it would have been for Ezekiel to have employed the imagery of those chapters in reference to Assyria, or Babylon, or Egypt!

Fifth, many expositors have held that this "great harlot" is the Church of Rome, depicted as an apostate Church. In that case the imagery employed would not be inconsistent and the political affiliations and claims of the Roman papacy. For the bloody persecutions of which that Church has been guilty correspond well with the picture here drawn of "Babylon the great." But it is not true that the Roman empire or any kings or powers of earth have hated and destroyed that Church in any such sense as the statements of verse 16 require.

Sixth, finally, we may well discard any views which carry our thoughts far away from that great metropolis, the fall of which was the sign of the end of the old dispensation and the complete introduction of Christianity. Rome is but incidentally connected with this and figures only as one of the agents operating with other forces at the time. This revelation is not particularly concerned with the fall of the Roman empire as such. Rather, only as it rises and passes from view as an instrument used by the Almighty to accomplish what his own wisdom and counsel determined to have done. Its beastliness as symbolized in vision, together with all that works abomination and makes a lie, is destined to go into perdition. But this overthrow of "the mother of harlots and of the abominations of the land" is the fulfillment of what Jesus so emphatically foretold in Matthew 23 and 24 and is in perfect harmony with the scope of the Apocalypse.

3. The Angelic Proclamation (18:1–3)

The eighteenth chapter introduces no new subject, but is a continuous part of the apocalyptic portraiture of the fall of the harlot-city. Having described in prophetic form the judgment of the great harlot and given an interpretation of the "mystery," the writer aims to intensify the vividness of his picture by what follows as far as 19:8.

The dirges over this fall of Babylon and the exultations of the holy heavens over such righteous judgment of God, are largely of the nature of rhetorical embellishment. It is therefore unnecessary to enlarge on these symbolic pictures. They are a combination of the imagery and language which the author has carefully selected from the Old Testament. No better commentary can be furnished the student than a patient study for himself of the passages (referred to in the notes which follow) from which the imagery is drawn.

> 1 After these things I saw another angel coming down out of heaven, having great authority; and the earth was lightened with his glory.
> 2 And he cried with a mighty voice, saying, Fallen, fallen is Babylon the great and is become a habitation of devils and a hold of every unclean spirit and a hold of every unclean and hateful bird.
> 3 For by the wine of the wrath of her fornication all the nations are fallen; and the kings of the earth committed fornication with her and

the merchants of the earth waxed rich by the power of her wantonness.

Another angel (18:1). That is, one different from the angel mentioned in 17:1, 7, 15. **Having great authority**. No special significance is to be seen in this statement. Nor in the fact that **the earth was lightened with his glory** — other than that his authority and glory were in keeping with the great proclamation he was commissioned to make "with a mighty voice." Compare the announcement of the "strong angel" of 5:2.

Fallen, fallen is Babylon (18:2). Already in 14:8, this word of doom has been sounded forth and it is now repeated with even greater impressiveness. The language is from Isaiah 21:9 and Jeremiah 51:7–8. **Devils ... spirit ... bird**. The imagery is traceable to Isaiah 13:21; Jeremiah 9:11; 50:39; 51:37 and indicates a scene of utter desolation. How Jerusalem became infested with demoniacal exhibitions of wickedness, even before her fall, has been shown in notes on the woe of the fifth trumpet (9:1–11).

Wine of the wrath of her fornication (18:3). See note on this expression in 14:8 and for the imagery compare Jeremiah 25:27; 51:7.

4. The Voice from Heaven (18:4–8)

> 4 And I heard another voice from heaven, saying, Come forth, my people, out of her, that ye have no fellowship with her sins and that ye receive not of her plagues:
> 5 for her sins have reached even unto heaven and God hath remembered her iniquities.
> 6 Render unto her even as she rendered and double unto her the double according to her works: in the cup which she mingled, mingle unto her double.
> 7 How much soever she glorified herself and waxed wanton, so much give her of torment and mourning: for she saith in her heart, I sit a queen and am no widow and shall in no wise see mourning.
> 8 Therefore in one day shall her plagues come, death and mourning and famine; and she shall be utterly burned with fire; for strong is the Lord God who judged her.

Come forth, my people (18:4; cp. Isa. 48:20; 52:11; Jer. 1:8; 51:6, 9, 45). There was something analogous to this in Christ's command for the disciples to flee from Jerusalem when they should see the signs of her impending ruin (Matt. 24:16).

Her sins have reached even unto heaven (18:5). In substance, Jeremiah said this of Babylon (Jer. 51:9).

Render unto her even as she rendered (18:6; cp. Jer. 50:15, 29; Psa. 137:8). **The cup.** See on 14:10. **Double.** Compare Isaiah 40:2; Jeremiah 16:18; 17:18.

I sit a queen (Rev. 18:7). Compare Isaiah 47:5, 7–8.

In one day (18:8). That is, suddenly, as in Isaiah 47:9: "These two things shall come to thee in a moment in one day, the loss of children and widowhood: they shall come upon thee in their perfection for the multitude of thy sorceries, the great abundance of thine enchantments."

Strong is the Lord God (18:8). Compare Jeremiah 50:34: "Their avenger is strong; Jehovah of hosts his name."

5. The Dirges and Rejoicing over Her Fall (18:9–20)

> 9 And the kings of the earth, who committed fornication and lived wantonly with her, shall weep and wail over her, when they look upon the smoke of her burning,
> 10 standing afar off for the fear of her torment, saying, Woe, woe, the great city, Babylon, the strong city! for in one hour is thy judgment come.
> 11 And the merchants of the earth weep and mourn over her, for no man buyeth their merchandise any more;
> 12 merchandise of gold and silver and precious stone and pearls and fine linen and purple and silk and scarlet; and all thyine wood and every vessel of ivory and every vessel made of most precious wood and of brass and iron and marble;
> 13 and cinnamon and spice and incense and ointment and frankincense and wine and oil and fine flour and wheat and cattle and sheep; and merchandise of horses and chariots and slaves; and souls of men.
> 14 And the fruits which thy soul lusted after are gone from thee and all things that were dainty and sumptuous are perished from thee and men shall find them no more at all.
> 15 The merchants of these things, who were made rich by her, shall stand afar off for the fear of her torment, weeping and mourning;
> 16 saying, Woe, woe, the great city, she that was arrayed in fine linen and purple and scarlet and decked with gold and precious stone and pearl!

17 for in one hour so great riches is made desolate. And every shipmaster and every one that saileth any whither and mariners and as many as gain their living by sea, stood afar off,
18 and cried out as they looked upon the smoke of her burning, saying, What city is like the great city?
19 And they cast dust on their heads and cried, weeping and mourning, saying, Woe, woe, the great city, wherein were made rich all that had their ships in the sea by reason of her costliness! for in one hour is she made desolate.
20 Rejoice over her, thou heaven and ye saints and ye apostles and ye prophets; for God hath judged your judgment on her.

Kings of the earth (18:9). The entire picture of the wailing of kings, merchants, shipmasters and sailors (vv. 9–19) is taken from Ezekiel's prophecy of the fall of Tyre (Eze. 26 and 27). But it is not thence to be urged that this great city of the Apocalypse must needs be as celebrated for commercial enterprise as ancient Tyre. The imagery of the older prophet is appropriated in order to give the utmost sublimity and completeness to the picture of her fall.

Look upon the smoke of her burning (18:9). This imagery has its origin in such passages as Genesis 19:28 and Isaiah 66:24. **The merchants ... weep and mourn** (18:11). Compare Ezekiel 26:16, 17; 27:24, 36. **Merchandise of gold ... purple ... ivory ... spice** (18:12–13). This specification of various kinds of articles of commerce is in imitation of Ezekiel 27:12–22. **Shipmaster ... sailors** (18:17). Compare Ezekiel 27:26–33.

Rejoice over her, thou heaven (18:20). This sudden call for heaven, saints, apostles, and prophets to exult over the fall of Babylon is in striking contrast with the weeping and wailing of the earthly associates of the ruined harlot. Compare Isaiah 44:23; 49:13; and Jeremiah 51:48. This exultation, like the hallelujahs of 19:1–7, is the utterance of joy over the triumph of righteousness and the "judgment" celebrated is that for which the martyrs prayed (6:10).

6. The Symbolic Act and Word of Doom (18:21–24)

21 And a strong angel took up a stone as it were a great millstone and cast it into the sea, saying, Thus with a mighty fall shall Babylon, the great city, be cast down and shall be found no more at all.
22 And the voice of harpers and minstrels and flute-players and trumpeters shall be heard no more at all in thee; and no craftsman, of

whatsoever craft, shall be found any more at all in thee; and the sound of a millstone shall be heard no more at all in thee;
23 and the light of a lamp shall shine no more at all in thee; and the voice of the bridegroom and of the bride shall be heard no more at all in thee: for thy merchants were the princes of the earth;
24 for with thy sorcery were all the nations deceived. And in her was found the blood of prophets and of saints and of all that have been slain upon the earth.

Cast it into the sea ... thus with a mighty fall shall Babylon ... be cast down (18:21). The main figure in this symbolic act of doom is taken from Jeremiah 51:63-64, where Seraiah is commanded by the prophet to bind a stone to the book of the woes of Babylon and cast it into the Euphrates and say, "Thus shall Babylon sink and shall not rise from the evil that I will bring upon her." **Shall be found no more.** Compare Ezekiel 26:21.

Voice of harpers ... no more (18:22-23; cp. Eze. 26:13; Jer. 25:10). Observe the fourfold picture: **harpers, minstrels, flute-players, trumpeters.** The immediate mention of **craftsmen, sound of the millstone, light of the lamp,** and **the voice of the bridegroom,** forms a corresponding set of images of prosperity and joy (cp. Jer. 7:34; 16:9).

Thy merchants were princes. Compare Isaiah 23:8. **Thy sorcery.** Compare Isaiah 47:9; Nahum 3:4.

Blood of prophets and of saints (18:24). Compare Matthew 23: 34-35; Luke 11:49-51; 13:33-34. Needlessly do some expositors, in spite of Jesus's words, go outside of Jerusalem to find this martyr-blood.

7. The Heavenly Hallelujahs (19:1-8)

1 After these things I heard as it were a great voice of a great multitude in heaven, saying, Hallelujah; Salvation and glory and power, belong to our God:
2 for true and righteous are his judgments; for he hath judged the great harlot, which did corrupt the earth with her fornication and he hath avenged the blood of his servants at her hand.
3 And a second time they say, Hallelujah. And her smoke goeth up forever and ever.
4 And the four and twenty elders and the four living creatures fell down and worshiped God who sitteth on the throne, saying, Amen; Hallelujah.

5 And a voice came forth from the throne, saying, Give praise to our God,
6 all ye his servants, ye that fear him, the small and the great. And I heard as it were the voice of a great multitude and as the voice of many waters and as the voice of mighty thunders, saying, Hallelujah: for the Lord our God, the Almighty, reigneth.
7 Let us rejoice and be exceeding glad and let us give the glory unto him: for the marriage of the Lamb is come and his wife hath made herself ready.
8 And it was given unto her that she should array herself in fine linen, bright and pure: for the fine linen is the righteous acts of the saints.

The fall of the mystic Babylon, which we have shown to be identical with the great city called "Sodom and Egypt" (11:8), is the great catastrophe of this book. And Revelation 18 is a solemn prophetical dirge over that fearful fall. But now, in contrast with her "harpers and minstrels and flute-players and trumpeters," which have become silent (18:22), there is heard the sound of heavenly song, as if in answer to the call of 18:20. In sentiment it corresponds to the song of 12:10–12, over the casting out of Satan.

The position of this song between the fall of the great Babylon and the going forth of the King of kings to smite the nations and destroy the beast and false prophet is also worthy of note as a part of the artificial arrangement of the book. See the note at the beginning of Revelation 7. The fall of the blood-stained Harlot is essential to the manifestation of the Bride, the wife of the Lamb. Hence this heavenly song serves not only to celebrate the righteous judgment of God on the great Harlot, but also to open the way for the concluding visions of the triumph of the Lamb over all his enemies and his marriage with the beloved Bride.

After these things (19:1; cp. 18:1). The word **Hallelujah** occurs here for the first time in this book and it is repeated four times in verses 1–6. The Hebrew הַלְלוּ יָהּ *(hallalu Yah)* means "Praise ye Jehovah." It occurs in Psalm 104:35 and frequently thereafter, especially at the beginning and end of the last five psalms.

True and righteous are his judgments (19:2; cp. Psa.19:9; 119:137). For **judged ... avenged**, see Deuteronomy 32:43.

Her smoke goeth up forever (19:3). Compare Isaiah 34:10.

The four and twenty elders (19:4). This is as in 5:8, 14; 11:16–18.

A voice from the throne (19:5). This is distinct from that of the elders and the living creatures, but by whom uttered is not said. We see in this no special mystic significance. Rather it is only the art of the writer to give a profound impression of the number and variety of voices in the heaven.

Give praise to our God, all ye his servants (19:5–6). Compare Psalm 134:1; 135:1. **Ye that fear him.** Compare Psalm 22:23. **The small and the great.** Compare Psalm 115:13.

Voice of a great multitude (19:6). Compare Daniel 10:6. **Voice of many waters.** Compare Ezekiel 1:24; 43:2. **The Lord reigneth.** Compare Psalm 93:1; 99:1.

The marriage of the Lamb is come (19:7). In verse 9 below mention is made of "the supper of the marriage of the Lamb." The song being cast in a prophetic mold, things future are conceived as already complete and hence the aorists of this verse, "came" (ἦλθεν [ēlthen]) and "made ... ready" (ἡτοίμασεν [ētoimasen]). The marriage of the Lamb is the union of Christ with believers and is therefore essentially a fact of spiritual life.

The feast or supper of that marriage is a figure for the delightful fellowship, the blessed entertainment and fruition of such vital union with the Prince of life. The marriage of the Lamb is a process continually going on as long as such unions of Christ and his beloved and elect ones continue to be consummated. The glory and blessedness of life with Christ in heaven are but the perpetuation of the union formed by faith and love in this world. The marriage and feast of this apocalyptic song are accordingly to be understood as referring to the same spiritual fact as the parables of the marriage of the king's son in Matthew 22:2–13 and the great supper in Luke 14:15–24.

His wife hath made herself ready (19:7). In apocalypse as in parable facts or great truths which continue for ages are necessarily pictured in harmony with the figure employed. The union of one believer with Christ is a representative of all such unions of all time. But to conserve the figure of a marriage feast the entire process of ages is conceived as complete.

Fine linen, bright and pure (19:8). Compare the "bright pure stone" of 15:6. The fine, soft, white linen (βύσσινος [bussinos]) array, we are told, is **the righteous acts of the saints.** It is a symbol of that outward beauty and purity which must distinguish all who are truly Christ's. It shows itself in all labors of love and acts of righteousness (δικαιώματα [dikaiōmata]), which the saints perform in their devotion to their

Lord. We should compare the lesson of the wedding garment in Matthew 22:11–13.

[[The Angel's Words to John (19:9–10)]]

> 9 And he saith unto me, Write, Blessed are they who are bidden to the marriage supper of the Lamb. And he saith unto me, These are true words of God.
> 10 And I fell down before his feet to worship him. And he saith unto me, See thou do it not: I am a fellow-servant with thee and with thy brethren who hold the testimony of Jesus: worship God: for the testimony of Jesus is the spirit of prophecy.

The words immediately following the heavenly song (vv. 9–10) are analogous to those of 10:8–11 and are addressed personally to the seer (cp. also 22:6–9). He is admonished by the angel that he is the honored recipient of divine revelations of God. Before the closing scenes of the first part of the Apocalypse, he was commanded to eat the book received from the angel's hand and was told that he must "prophesy again over many peoples and nations and tongues and kings" (10:11). So now, before the closing scenes of the second part, he is admonished that vital union with Christ is unspeakably blessed and the witness of that holy fellowship is the very life and soul of all true prophecy. The angels have no higher honor.

Blessed are they who are bidden (19:9). Compare the beatitude of Luke 14:15. Compare also the other two beatitudes of this book (14:13 and 20:6), which are, in their essential blessedness, the same perpetual fruition as the marriage supper of the Lamb.

And he saith unto me (19:9). Observe the double statement. Twice over in this verse he repeats the fact that the angel addressed him thus personally. It was the same angel of 17:1, who had shown him the judgment of the great Harlot and now bids him write the heavenly blessedness of those who are in fact the wife of the Lamb. Here is the mystery within a mystery. "The wife" that "made herself ready" (v. 7) is truly no other than those blessed ones who are bidden to the marriage supper of the Lamb.

These are true words of God (19:9). Strictly, "these ... words" may refer to the beatitude which John has just been told to write. For that utterance of blessedness contained no conjecture or hope of the angel, but "true words of God" himself. The reference, however, is generally understood of all the foregoing communications of this angel from 17:1, onward to this point. And, indeed, all the words of this book of divine revelation will bear this commendation. Compare 21:5; 22:6.

I fell down ... to worship him (19:10). It seemed to him as if God himself had spoken and in the deep emotion of the moment he would have worshiped the messenger instead of the one who sent him. Compare 22:8.

Fellow-servant of thee am I and of thy brethren (19:10). This is not equivalent to saying, "I am one of thy brethren." Rather, he assures John that he is also himself a "servant." He serves the same God that John and his brethren serve. So every created intelligence of heaven capable of serving God is a fellow-servant along with men on the earth who love God and keep his commandments.

That hold the testimony of Jesus (19:10). These are the same form of words as found in 12:17. They are to be explained here, as there, of those who hold fast the word which Jesus had witnessed of himself. There is no sufficient reason for making "the testimony of Jesus" mean anything else in this passage than it means in 1:2, 9, where it is coordinate with "the word of God." The genitive is that of the subject, that is, the testimony which Jesus himself gives. He is preeminently "the faithful witness" (1:5) and his testimony in this book consists of "true words of God."

This testimony proceeding from Jesus and received and apprehended as God's truth in the heart of John or any of his brethren is the **spirit of prophecy** (19:10). Without it there can be no New Testament prophecy. It is the vital element, the life and soul and essence of prophecy. It is also a part of the office and work of the Holy Spirit to take this "testimony of Jesus" and make it clear to the consciousness of every true disciple of the Lord (John 16:14). Possessed of such inspired testimony one becomes gifted for the work of prophesying.

The last statement is not to be understood as an appended word of John, but a part of the personal announcement of the angel to John. Thus, it is an intimation, like 10:8–11, that he is yet to prophesy and publish this testimony of Jesus to the world. As a part of that testimony and one of its most inspiring words, he was commanded to write, **Blessed are they who are bidden to the marriage supper of the Lamb** (19:9).

Chapter 10
THE MILLENNIAL CONFLICT AND TRIUMPH
(Rev. 19:11–21:8)

In this section of the book we have a series of seven visions, each beginning with the words Καὶ εἶδον (*kai eidon*) "and I saw." It opens with the picture of a heavenly Conqueror going forth, in company with white-robed armies, to smite the nations with the sword of his mouth. And after a series of wonderful victories it concludes with the picture of a new heaven and a new earth, from which all evil-doers are cast out. From the seer's point of view it is an apocalyptic outlook into the Messianic era, the millennial age, during which "the law shall go forth out of Zion and the word of Jehovah from Jerusalem" (Mic. 4:2; Isa. 2:3). While disclosing an ideal outline of future Messianic triumphs, the prophet does not transcend the main purpose of his book, which is "to show the things which must shortly come to pass" (1:1). That purpose is accomplished when he depicts the overthrow of Judaism, the end of the old temple dispensation, and the consequent opening of the new era. That new era is the Messianic age, which is destined, according to the prophets, to make all things new.

His task is complete when he shows forth the beginning of the new age and a visional outline of what that age will bring. He furnishes no "continuous historical" record of the progress of Christianity in the Roman empire. We should no more look in the prophecies of this book for a syllabus of the petty feuds of mediæval Europe than for an account of modern missions in India, China, and Japan. Too long have false presumptions led men to search in apocalyptic pictures for predictions of such events as the French Revolution, the fall of Napoleon Bonaparte, the Protestant Reformation, and the Wars of the Roses. One might as well expect to find in scripture predictions of the discovery of America and the invention of the steam engine and the electric telegraph. The mind that gives itself to discover such things in biblical prophecy misapprehends the mind of the Spirit. The fallacy of such procedures in exegesis lies in a total misconception of the nature and scope of apocalyptic writing.

1. The Heavenly Conqueror (19:11–16)

11 And I saw the heaven opened; and behold, a white horse and he that sat thereon, called Faithful and True; and in righteousness he doth judge and make war.
12 And his eyes are a flame of fire and upon his head are many diadems; and he hath a name written, which no one knoweth but he himself.
13 And he is arrayed in a garment sprinkled with blood: and his name is called The Word of God.
14 And the armies which are in heaven followed him upon white horses, clothed in fine linen, white and pure.
15 And out of his mouth proceedeth a sharp sword, that with it he should smite the nations: and he shall rule them with a rod of iron: and he treadeth the wine press of the fierceness of the wrath of God, the Almighty.
16 And he hath on his garment and on his thigh a name written, king of kings and lord of lords.

I saw the heaven opened (19:11). Compare the language of Ezekiel 1:1. We are about to have a new apocalyptic picture of the Son of man coming in the clouds of heaven (1:7). It is the picture of an æonic struggle upon which he sets out, not a single historical event to which one can point and say, Lo here! or, Lo there! The **white horse** is the symbol of victorious procession here as in 6:2. But **he that sat thereon** is not the same as the rider on the white horse in the earlier vision. His title of **faithful and true** is sufficient to designate him as the Christ of 1:5 and 3:14. And the additional statement that **in righteousness he judges and makes war**, is appropriated from Psalm 96:13; Isaiah 32:1; Jeremiah 23:5–6. It shows that he is no other than the Messiah of Old Testament prophecy.

His eyes a flame of fire (19:12; cp. 1:14 and Dan. 10:6). The **many diadems** are symbols of many a triumph and of highest royalty. He is the Conqueror of Psalm 110:6, who "has smitten the heads (chiefs) over many a land." **A name written which no one knoweth but he himself.** So that he is a high priest of the holiest mysteries. Compare 2:17 and 3:12.

Arrayed in a garment sprinkled with blood (19:13). This, in connection with the figure of treading the wine press of God's wrath in verse 15, makes it evident that Isaiah 63:1–6 is before the mind of the writer. The victor has sprinkled his garments with the blood of his enemies, as he trod on them in his anger and trampled them in his fury (cp. Isa. 63:3).

His name is called the Word of God (19:13). He is the same Word which is so sublimely presented to our thought at the beginning of John's gospel (John 1:1–18). He is the beginning of the revelation as well as of the creation of God (3:14).

Armies which are in the heaven followed him (19:14). These are identical with the "called and chosen and faithful" associates of the Lamb spoken of in 17:14. His saints are with him in this glorious war and like the bride, the wife of the Lamb, are **clothed in fine linen, white and pure**. Compare verse 8 above.

Out of his mouth proceedeth a sharp sword (19:15; as in 1:16). **That with it he should smite the nations**. This is the same figure that we find in Isaiah 11:4, where it is said of the Messiah that "he shall smite the earth with the rod of his mouth and with the breath of his lips shall he slay the wicked."

Rule them with a rod of iron (19:15; cp. 2:27; 12:5; and Psa. 2:9). **Treadeth the wine press** (cp. 14:19–20 and Isa. 63:1–6). In all these allusions the great Conqueror is described as executing righteous judgment upon the enemies of **God, the Almighty**. It is the picture, not of a judge sitting on his throne and formulating a sentence, but of a fierce warrior who goes forth to execute judgment by treading the enemies of God under his feet.

King of kings and Lord of lords (19:16). This is the lofty title of the Messianic ruler and judge of the nations. Compare 17:14; 1 Timothy 6:15; Deuteronomy 10:17; and Daniel 2:47. All the kingdoms of the world are to become the kingdom of Jehovah and his anointed (11:15; Psa. 2:2–8).

The foregoing vision (19:11–16) is a most sublime apocalypse of the conquering Messiah, who "must reign until he has put all his enemies under his feet" (1 Cor. 15:25). The struggle may consume a million years. The details and chronology of its age-long history no prophet has foretold. But this unrivaled portraiture presents the conquering King, with his names, his insignia, and his works. Its comprehensiveness may be seen by tabulating the contents as follows:

His Names. (1) Faithful and True; (2) written but known only to himself; (3) the Word of God; and (4) King of kings and Lord of lords.

His Insignia. (1) Sitting upon a white horse; (2) many diadems; (3) blood-sprinkled garments; and (4) eyes of flame.

His Works. (1) In righteousness he judges and makes war; (2) he smites the nations with the sword of his mouth; (3) he rules them as with a rod of iron; and (4) he treads the wine press of the wrath of God.

There can surely be no question but that this glorious personage is the Christ of Old Testament prophecy and of New Testament revelation.

2. The Great Supper of Sacrifice (19:17–18)

> 17 And I saw an angel standing in the sun; and he cried with a loud voice, saying to all the birds that fly in midheaven, Come and be gathered together unto the great supper of God;
> 18 that ye may eat the flesh of kings and the flesh of captains and the flesh of mighty men and the flesh of horses and of them that sit thereon and the flesh of all men, both free and bond and small and great.

The symbolism of this passage is appropriated from Ezekiel 39: 17–20. There the prophet is commanded to "speak unto every feathered fowl and to every beast of the field," and to say unto them:

> Assemble yourselves and come; gather yourselves on every side to my slaughter which I sacrifice for you, even a great slaughter upon the mountains of Israel, that ye may eat flesh and drink blood. Ye shall eat the flesh of the mighty and drink the blood of the princes of the earth, of rams, of lambs and of goats, of bullocks, all of them fatlings of Bashan. And ye shall eat fat till ye be full and drink blood till ye be drunken, of my sacrifice which I have sacrificed for you. Thus shall ye be filled at my table with horses and chariots, with mighty men and with all men of war, saith the Lord Jehovah.

A literal interpretation of such a metaphorical passage must necessarily lead to absurdity and confusion. It is a symbolic picture of the fearful visitation of divine wrath on wicked men and nations and quite analogous to the figure of the wine press in verse 15.

An angel standing in the sun (19:17). This is the most appropriate place in the visible heavens for an angel to take his position for the purpose of addressing **all the birds that fly in midheaven.** Hence, we need not look for special allegorical significance in this statement. It is but an incidental feature of the vision.

The great supper of God (19:17). The idea is that of a sacrificial feast, in which the victims slain are so many propitiatory offerings to God.

Eat the flesh of kings (19:18). Six kinds of flesh are specified, but it seems to be mainly a human sacrifice. Kings, captains, and mighty men are specifications which show how largely the slaughter is to take the mighty ones. No kings or princes of the earth will be able to withstand the power of "the King of kings and Lord of lords." The other three are **horses** and **them that sit thereon** and **all men**. The enumeration is less comprehensive than that of Ezekiel 39:17–20. There mention is made of drinking blood as well as of eating the flesh of mighty men and princes, along with rams, lambs, goats, and bulls. But in both pictures the idea of a fearful slaughter is conveyed. And the addition in this verse of the words **free and bond and small and great** is designed to show that no class or condition of men will be able to escape the judgment of the great Conqueror of verses 11–16.

3. The Beast and False Prophet Destroyed (19:19–21)

19 And I saw the beast and the kings of the earth and their armies, gathered together to make war against him that sat upon the horse and against his army.
20 And the beast was taken and with him the false prophet that wrought the signs in his sight, wherewith he deceived them that had received the mark of the beast and them that worshiped his image: they twain were cast alive into the lake of fire that burneth with brimstone:
21 and the rest were killed with the sword of him that sat upon the horse, even the sword which came forth out of his mouth: and all the birds were filled with their flesh.

This picture stands in closest possible connection with the preceding one and in fact is the result of the angel's call to eat the flesh of kings and mighty men. It shows in few words the necessary and certain outcome of the conflict between Christ and his white-robed armies on the one side and the beast and his army on the other. The imagery is substantially identical with that of the overthrow of the beast in Daniel's vision (Dan. 7:11–12). Yet it is notably expanded and enhanced with various incidental features which show the genius of the New Testament apocalyptist.

Beast ... kings ... armies (19:19). This beast is obviously the one portrayed in 13:1–7 and **the kings of the earth** may be understood of the ten kings of 17:12. But in a general way beast, kings, and their armies also represent all hostile earthly forces which in any way "set themselves" — in the spirit of Psa. 2:2–3 — "against Jehovah and against his Messiah, saying, Let us break their bands asunder and cast away their cords from us."

The false prophet (19:20). Already mentioned in 16:13 and to be understood as another designation of the "beast out of the land" described in 13:11–16. **That wrought the signs** (see 13:14). **They twain were cast alive into the lake of fire.** Daniel saw the beast slain "and his body destroyed and given to the burning flame" (Dan. 7:11). But our author gives a more fearful touch to the picture by representing both beast and prophet as **cast alive into the lake of fire which burneth with brimstone**, which is a figure peculiar to this book (cp. 20:10, 14, 15; 21:8). It is doubtless to be understood as "the gehenna of fire" (Matt. 5:22; Mark 9:43–48).

But when in apocalyptic symbolism a beast is seen to be "cast into a lake of fire," or "given to the burning flame," coherency of figure requires us to interpret the entire statement on some general principle. If the beast is not a literal beast, the lake of fire is not to be explained literally. The idea conveyed is rather that of complete destruction.

The rest (19:21). Referring to the kings and armies of verse 19 and to all supposable allies that engage in war against Jehovah and his Christ. **Killed with the sword.** Thus verifying the prophetic word of 13:10 and also confirming the saying of Jesus that "with what judgment ye judge, ye shall be judged and with what measure ye mete, it shall be measured unto you" (Matt. 7:1).

All the birds were filled (19:21). This completes the picture outlined in verse 18. The two visions introduced by "I saw" in verses 17 and 19 constitute but one actual judgment. The vision of verses 17 and 18 is but an introduction to the vision of verses 19–21, but they are nevertheless presented as two separate visions.

4. The Devil Chained and in Prison (20:1–3)

1 And I saw an angel coming down out of heaven, having the key of the abyss and a great chain in his hand.
2 And he laid hold on the dragon, the old serpent, which is the Devil and Satan and bound him for a thousand years,

3 and cast him into the abyss and shut it and sealed it over him, that he should deceive the nations no more, until the thousand years should be finished: after this he must be loosed for a little time.

The harlot has fallen and the beast and false prophet are cast into the lake of fire. It now remains to show that Christ's victory is not complete until the great dragon, the old serpent, the deceiver of the whole world, is not only cast down to the earth (cp. 12:9), but cast into the abyss, his appropriate place.

An angel coming down out of heaven (20:1). Quite different from "a star fallen out of heaven" (9:1). No particular description of this angel is given, but it is evident that he is able to bind the strong adversary of God and man (cp. Matt. 12:29). **Having the key of the abyss**, for it is no longer in a fallen angel's hand (cp. 9:1). **A great chain**, like the key, is a figure to be compared with the statement of Jude 6 and 2 Peter 2:4.

Dragon ... serpent ... Devil ... Satan (20:2). Observe this notable accumulation of titles and names and compare 12:9. The old deceiver has made himself a name for evil. **Bound for a thousand years**. The period of the Messianic reign (cp. vv. 4–5). Observe that nothing is here said of the angels of Satan, who, according to 12:9, were cast down to the earth with him. They seem to have been left at large in the earth.

Cast him into the abyss (20:3). This is where the demons dread to go (Luke 8:31), but where they properly belong. **Shut and sealed over him**. Thus making his imprisonment secure and authoritative (cp. Matt. 27:66). This is so that he may **deceive the nations no more**. Thus, no more shall beasts or false prophets, of the character and likeness of those depicted in Revelation 13, appear to persecute the saints and trample down the rights of men.

This symbolic picture of the binding of Satan has been greatly misapprehended by supposing it to imply the cessation of all evil among men. It is too readily assumed that if Satan be shut up and sealed in the abyss, the angels of Satan and wicked men can have no more place in the world. This is a most unauthorized assumption. The passage presents only one phase of the triumph of Christ over all his enemies. The final defeat of the devil is described in verse 10 and the Messiah's triumph over the last enemy, Death and Hades, is told in verses 13 and 14. Hence it is of the first importance to a correct interpretation of these closely related visions to note that they constitute a series of victories which run through the entire period called symbolically **a thousand years** (20:3).

We must keep in mind that we are dealing with symbols, not pragmatic events marked off by definite chronological dates. The symbolism of 20:1–3, points to a suppression of personal Satanic agency. It is to be studied in the light of such sayings of Jesus as "I beheld Satan fallen as lightning from heaven" (Luke 10:18); "Now is the judgment of this world; now shall the prince of this world be cast out" (John 12:31); "The prince of this world has been judged" (John 16:11). None of these declarations imply the sudden and permanent cessation of wickedness among men.

In some of Jesus' statements and especially in the symbolism of this passage of the Apocalypse, we may understand the cessation of demoniacal possession, so conspicuous in the time of our Lord and of which we have so vivid a picture in 9:1–11. After the overthrow of Jerusalem the Harlot and the full inauguration of the kingdom of heaven things change. With the triumphant going forth of the Gospel that followed that momentous crisis of ages, no well-authenticated instance of such demoniacal possession is to be found. That crisis, moreover, marked a transition from the old barbaric civilizations to a new and better order of affairs in the world. All this is represented, symbolically, as a binding of Satan, the deceiver of the nations.

5. The Millennial Reign and Final Overthrow of Satan (20:4–10)

> 4 And I saw thrones and they sat upon them and judgment was given unto them: and I saw the souls of them that had been beheaded for the testimony of Jesus and for the word of God and such as worshiped not the beast, neither his image and received not the mark upon their forehead and upon their hand; and they lived and reigned with Christ a thousand years.
> 5 The rest of the dead lived not until the thousand years should be finished.
> 6 This is the first resurrection. Blessed and holy is he that hath part in the first resurrection: over these the second death hath no power; but they shall be priests of God and of Christ and shall reign with him a thousand years.
> 7 And when the thousand years are finished, Satan shall be loosed out of his prison,

8 and shall come forth to deceive the nations which are in the four corners of the earth, Gog and Magog, to gather them together to the war: the number of whom is as the sand of the sea.
9 And they went up over the breadth of the earth and compassed the camp of the saints about and the beloved city: and fire came down out of heaven and devoured them.
10 And the devil that deceived them was cast into the lake of fire and brimstone, where are also the beast and the false prophet; and they shall be tormented day and night forever and ever.

I saw thrones (20:4). Daniel prophetically beheld thrones set and the kingdom and dominion under the whole heaven given to the saints of the Most High (Dan. 7:9, 18, 27; cp. Matt. 19:28; 1 Cor. 6:2). **They sat upon them.** Who they were that sat upon the thrones is not expressly said. But the most natural inference from the context is that they were **the souls of them that had been beheaded for the testimony of Jesus and for the word of God and such as worshiped not the beast, neither his image and received not the mark upon their forehead and upon their hand.**

It was one part of the purpose of this book to encourage the martyr spirit in the early Church. It does so by portraying again and again the triumph and glory sure to come to them that "loved not their life even unto death" (12:11). It is pledged in the martyr scene of 6:9–11 and symbolized in the triumph of the witnesses of 11:11–12 and of the man child caught up to the throne of God (12:5).

The further statement that **they lived and reigned with Christ** (20:4), shows that the thrones were set for them to occupy. It is one essential part of the office and work of a king to exercise judgment (cp. Psa. 72:2; Isa. 11:2–4; 32:1) and reigning with Christ is to participate in the judgments which he makes and executes. So in 19:14, his white-robed armies follow with the King of kings as he goes forth to smite the nations and to rule with a rod of iron. So in 2:18, 26–27, "the Son of God, who hath his eyes like a flame of fire and his feet like unto burnished brass," promises to him "that overcometh" that he shall have "authority over the nations and shall rule them with a rod of iron." Compare also 3:21.

These martyrs do not reign on the earth in the forms of flesh and blood, as some have grossly imagined. Rather they are enthroned along with Christ in the place of his glory and are with all other saints permitted to behold his glory (John 17:24). Not only so but they are also given to sit down with him in his throne, as he also overcame by not loving his life unto death and sat down with his Father in his throne (3:21). Hence the encouragement given in 2 Timothy 2:11: "If we died with him, we shall also live with him: if we endure, we shall also reign with him."

The statement that **judgment was given unto them** (20:4) is capable of a double meaning. It may signify that these souls now received a judgment in their favor and were vindicated and avenged (cp. 11:18). But the context here favors the idea that to those who sat upon thrones was given the authority of exercising judgment — the power and right to judge. To them was given power to pass condemning sentence on the enemies of their Lord, as if they were constituted a jury or were made associate judges with the Christ himself.

The **thousand years** (20:4) is to be understood as a symbolical number, denoting a long period. It is a round number, but stands for an indefinite period, an æon whose duration it would be a folly to attempt to compute. Its beginning dates from the great catastrophe of this book, the fall of the mystic Babylon. It is the æon which opens with the going forth of the great Conqueror of 19:11–16 and continues until he shall have put all his enemies under his feet (1 Cor. 15:25). It is the same period as that required for the stone of Daniel's prophecy (Dan. 2:35) to fill the earth and the mustard seed of Jesus's parable to consummate its world-wide growth (Matt. 13:31–32).

How long the King of kings will continue his battle against evil and defer the last decisive blow, when Satan shall be "loosed for a little time," no man can even approximately judge. It may require a million years. But during all this time the enthroned martyrs, whose blood and ashes were the seed of the Church, live and reign with their glorified Lord. They are conceived as risen with Christ (cp. Rom. 6:5; Eph. 2:6; Col. 2:12; 3:1), seated with him in glory, sharing his triumphs, and exercising judgment with him as associate kings.

But those who live and reign with Christ during the thousand years are not the martyrs only. All such as **worshiped not the beast** (20:4), whether called to a martyr's death or not, share in the millennial glory. All those who overcome on account of the blood of the Lamb may expect to realize the blessed answer to the prayer and will of Jesus "that, where I am, they also may be with me, that they may behold my glory" (John 17:24).

The rest of the dead (20:5) are those not belonging to the class who live and reign with Christ. We may discern this from two observations. First, the benediction is pronounced in the next verse on those who have part in the first resurrection. Second, the judgment scene of verses 11–15 is concerned mainly, if not altogether, with the final doom of everyone who "was not found written in the book of life." Both of these observations leave us very naturally to infer that "the rest of the dead" are those who held not the testimony of Jesus, nor the word of God. Rather, they are those who worshiped the beast and his image and in some way received his damning mark.

Lived not until the thousand years should be finished (20:5). They came not into the apocalyptist's field of vision until he "saw the dead, the great and the small, standing before the throne," and "the sea gave up the dead which were in it and Death and Hades gave up the dead which were in them" (vv. 12–13). Those thus held under the dominion of Death and Hades are not they who are "dead unto sin and alive unto God through Jesus Christ" (Rom. 6:11) and of whom it may be said, as it is said of Christ himself, that "death has no more dominion over him" (Rom. 6:9; cp. John 11:26).

This is the first resurrection (20:6). That is, the living and reigning with Christ a thousand years is the first resurrection. This resurrection is evidently to be understood and explained as a part of a series of great symbolical pictures. Nothing is said, either here or in verses 12 and 13, of a rising up from the dust of the earth or a resuscitation of mortal bodies. The word "resurrection" may ordinarily imply this and what is here written does not necessarily exclude the thought. Yet it is simply a fact that these apocalyptic pictures do not represent "the general resurrection of the last day," as commonly apprehended. They represent the millennial living and reigning of the blessed with Christ on the one hand and the appearance of all the rest of the dead for judgment on the other.

All the dogmatic deliverances about "the plain literal sense" which interpreters like Alford have made concerning the "two resurrections" of this passage are irrelevant. The word "resurrection" is here no more to be pressed into a literal significance than the words "thrones" and "books" and "lake of fire." Indeed, the "first resurrection" is expressly shown in the context to be a living and reigning with Christ.

Blessed and holy is he that hath part in the first resurrection (20:6). Compare the beatitude of 14:13 and the note thereon. This benediction implies that those only who partake in "the first resurrection" are preeminently "blessed and holy." Then it is immediately added that over **these the second death hath no power**. Thus, we cannot but infer that those not partaking in the first resurrection are under the dominion of sin and of death and consequently exposed to the power of the second death. And according to verse 14, this is "the lake of fire." But all the "blessed and holy" that overcome the powers of evil "shall not be hurt of the second death" (2:11) ; **but they shall be priests of God and of Christ**, as already shown in 1:6 and 5:10.

The five scenes of the millennial period thus far presented form a closely connected series and are not to be thought of as chronologically successive. Rather they are simultaneous and supplementary in their logical relations. Thus, the moving forth of the great Conqueror (19:11–16) results in the great slaughter of the numerous enemies of God (19:17–18). This involves at the same time the destruction of the beast and the false prophet (19:19–21) and the binding of Satan (20:1–3). These are different aspects of a world-wide conquest, for the Messianic King of Old Testament prophecy is to "have dominion from sea to sea and from the river unto the ends of the earth" (Psa. 72:8).

The great events symbolized, however, are not sharply separated from each other in time. Most of them, if not all, are coetaneous and extend through the entire period of the Messianic era, the symbolical **thousand years** (20:6). We do not know through what historic stages the conflict is to pass. Nor what particular forms of government may arise and exhibit more or less of the spirit of the beast and the dragon. Nor what mysteries of iniquity may work against Jehovah and against his Anointed during the thousand years. These and such like are not written; their details do not seem to come within the scope of prophetic revelation. But the millennial era of conflict and triumph is prophetically presented in one great field of view.

When the thousand years are finished Satan shall be loosed (20:7). The millennial era is to end with the utter defeat and destruction of the old serpent, the Devil. This fulfills at the last the prediction of Genesis 3:15. With this final defeat of Satan all his allied forces are also destined to perish (cp. Matt. 25:41).

In order to enhance the final and decisive character of this victory over Satan, the writer represents him as loosed **out of his prison** (20:7), in which he had been shut up for the long period (cp. v. 3). The old enemy is thus granted a second probation in order to show that "the deceiver of the whole world" (12:9) is at the end, as from the beginning, "a liar and the father thereof" (John 8:44).

Now Satan goes forth once more **to deceive the nations which are in the four corners of the earth** (20:8). This implies that the millennial era, with all its world-wide triumphs, is not destined to eliminate all evil from among men. For at the very last, there will be found in all quarters of the earth those who can be deceived and led by Satan into conflict with the people of God.

These nations, which are thus marshaled **to the war** against the Most High, are called by the symbolical names **Gog and Magog** (20:8). These names are taken from a similar prophetic picture in the Book of Ezekiel (cp. Eze. 38:2). Any attempt to find in these symbolical names and pictures of battle a reference to particular peoples and provinces of the earth is utterly futile. Both here and in Ezekiel we have an ideal scene.

The number of those gathered for the final battle **is as the sand of the sea** (20:8). In Ezekiel they are represented as "many people," "a great company and a mighty army" (Eze. 38:15). They come up "against my people of Israel, as a cloud to cover the land" (Eze. 38:16). They are "gathered out of many people against the mountains of Israel."

The corresponding passage in Ezekiel (38:18–23) deserves transcription here, as showing beyond question its metaphorical character:

> It shall come to pass in that day, when Gog shall come against the land of Israel, saith the Lord Jehovah, that my fury shall come up into my nostrils. For in my jealousy and in the fire of my wrath have I spoken. Surely in that day there shall be a great shaking upon the land of Israel; so that the fishes of the sea and the fowls of heaven and the beasts of the field and all creeping things that creep upon the earth and all the men that are upon the face of the earth, shall shake at my presence and the mountains shall be thrown down and the steep places shall fall and every wall shall fall to the ground. And I will call for a sword against him unto all my mountains, saith the Lord Jehovah: every man's sword shall be against his brother. And I will plead[14] against him with pestilence and with blood; and I will rain upon him and upon his hordes and upon the many peoples that are with him, an overflowing shower and great hailstones, fire and brimstone. And I will magnify myself and sanctify myself and I will make myself known in the eyes of many nations; and they shall know that I am Jehovah. (Eze. 38:18–23)

---

[14] This is the same word as that employed in Joel 3:2. The pleading is an execution of judgment (שפט, *shaphat*) in vindication of God and his people.

Went up over the breadth of the land (20:9). The language has allusion to Habakkuk 1:6. There the Chaldean armies are spoken of as "marching through the breadth of the land to possess the dwelling places which are not their own."

Compassed the camp of the saints about (20:9). The imagery here is of a fortified camp rather than of a moving army, as in 19:14. This affords us with variety of description. At the same time it conforms to the corresponding picture in Ezekiel of Israel dwelling safely in the day when the armies of Gog come up against their land (cp. Eze. 38:14).

And the beloved city (20:9). The figure is that of a city with a camp outside of it, as if set there for defense. The "city" is the new Jerusalem, already mentioned in 3:12, but to be more fully described in following visions. It is called "the beloved city" in allusion to such scriptures as Jeremiah 11:15; 12:7; and Psalm 78:68. In point of fact, this beloved city is to be understood as descending from heaven to earth (21:2–3, 10) *during the entire period of the millennial era.* But the artistic proprieties of the book required that the full description of the city of the saints follow the record of the overthrow of all her foes.

Fire came down ... and devoured them (20:9). Allusion to the event in Elijah's history (2 Kgs. 1:10, 12), which has been already referred to in these visions (cp. 11:5). Thus these saints have only to stand still and see the miraculous judgment of God upon their enemies. Thus will God ultimately crush Satan under their feet (Rom. 16:20).

The devil ... was cast into the lake of fire (20:10). Not now "cast down to the earth" (12:9, 13), where he may still persecute the saints of God. But cast into final and irretrievable perdition and visited with the terrible fury which Ezekiel thus portrays: "I will rain upon him and upon his bands and upon the many people that are with him, an overflowing rain and great hailstones, fire and brimstone" (Eze. 38:22; cp. Gen. 19:24).

Where are also the beast and the false prophet (20:10). This is as described in 19:20. **Tormented day and night forever and ever** (literally, "unto the ages of the ages"). This is another form of expressing the *perpetual* torment so vividly portrayed in 14:10–11. See the notes on those verses.

These verses 7–10 depict the last great struggle of Satan and his forces to overcome the saints of God and their overwhelming defeat before the manifested power of heaven. The obvious purpose is to show the final and decisive victory of the seed of the woman over their ancient foe. It is a great symbolic picture and its one great teaching is clear beyond the possibility of doubt or misunderstanding: namely, that Satan and his forces must all ultimately perish. This is written for the comfort and confidence of the saints. But that final victory is in the far future, at the close of the Messianic age and it is here simply outlined in apocalyptic symbols. Any presumption, therefore, of determining specific events of the future from this grand symbolism must be regarded as in the nature of the case a species of worthless and misleading speculation.

6. The Final Judgment (20:11–15)

> 11 And I saw a great white throne and him that sat upon it, from whose face the earth and the heaven fled away; and there was found no place for them.
> 12 And I saw the dead, the great and the small, standing before the throne; and books were opened: and another book was opened, which is the book of life: and the dead were judged out of the things which were written in the books, according to their works.
> 13 And the sea gave up the dead which were in it; and death and Hades gave up the dead which were in them: and they were judged every man according to their works.
> 14 And death and Hades were cast into the lake of fire.
> 15 This is the second death, even the lake of fire. And if any was not found written in the book of life, he was cast into the lake of fire.

The kings and their armies have been defeated and the beast and the false prophet and Satan himself are cast into the lake of fire. But the apocalyptic scheme is yet incomplete. Thus, we have here a further vision of "the rest of the dead" (cp. v. 4) and of the destruction of the last enemy, even death itself (1 Cor. 15:26).

According to apostolic teaching, "we must all be made manifest before the judgment seat of Christ, that each one may receive the things done through the body according to what he hath done, whether good or bad" (2 Cor. 5:10). We have been shown a glorious picture of the judgment and honor of the martyrs and of all those who kept themselves untainted by any mark of the beast. It remains for us to be shown the judgment which will try every man's work, of what sort it is (1 Cor. 3:13). This final judgment shows that not one of all the dead, whether hidden in earth or sea or the vast realm of Hades, is to escape the retribution which tests "every man according to his works." The vision, like all the rest of this sevenfold series, is set in the form of apocalyptic symbol.

I saw a great white throne (20:11; cp. Isa. 6:1; Dan. 7:9). So far as the symbolism of the color points to anything, it may, as in the white horse and the white robes, suggest an ideal of divine triumph. This throne of judgment is associated with the thought of the final victory and vindication of righteousness. **Him that sat upon it** is the same "King of kings and Lord of lords" who was seen sitting upon a white horse (19:11).

From whose face the earth and the heaven fled away (20:11). The concept is an enlargement of Psalm 114:3, 7 and designed to give an awful impression of the majesty of the judge. The earth and the heaven above it are thought of as so terrified that they vanish utterly and so **there was found no place for them.** They disappeared from view.

The dead, the great and the small (20:12). These are most naturally understood as "the rest of the dead" referred to in verse 5. The words "the great and the small," repeated from 19:18, seem to classify them in general character with those there mentioned. It is notable that in this entire passage (vv. 11–15) there is no word indicative of blessedness to accrue to these dead, as in the case of those "that have part in the first resurrection" (v. 6). These dead of various grades do not sit on thrones and "live and reign with Christ." Rather they are seen **standing before the throne** as so many culprits and there is no evidence apparent that any one of them was found written in the book of life (see on v. 15).

The books were opened (20:12). The record of their works is conceived here, as in Daniel 7:10, to have been written in books or scrolls and the accurate record assures us that they are to be judged strictly according to their works. **And another book was opened** to afford them every possible means of evidence. It is implied in this description, when taken altogether, that no name was to be found written in the book of life which had a record in the other books.

The book of life (20:12), or of the living, in which the names of God's approved ones are written, is a familiar figure in the Scriptures (cp. Exo. 32:32; Psa. 56:8; 69:28; Dan. 12:1; Luke 10:20; Phil. 4:3). But **the dead**, whose judgment is here depicted, do not seem to have been written in the "book of life." For it is immediately added that **they were judged out of the things which were written in the books**, that is, the other books first mentioned above. And they are judged **according to their works** as in Rom. 2:6; 2 Cor. 5:10.

The sea ... Death and Hades gave up the dead (20:13). This reference is to all supposable places where the dead could be found. The enumeration of the sea in the same category with Death and Hades (see on 6:8) forbids any dogmatic inference from this text touching the resurrection of bodies from the grave. It is noticeable, also, that no mention is here made of the dust of the earth giving up its dead. For the thought conveyed is not so much of a resurrection of bodies from their graves as of a gathering together of all the dead (exclusive of those contemplated in v. 4) in conscious personality before the throne of final judgment.

But as it is immediately added that **they were judged, every man according to their works** (20:13), it is evident that we have here a picture of resurrection unto judgment. We may well call attention to the analogy of John 5:28–29. There Jesus declares that "the hour is coming, in which all that are in the tombs [ἐν τοῖς μνημείοις (*en tois menēmeiois*)] shall hear his voice and shall come forth; they that have done good, unto the resurrection of life; and they that have done ill, unto the resurrection of judgment." The first resurrection, as depicted in verses 4–6, is conspicuously a resurrection of life and this of the rest of the dead is as conspicuously a resurrection of judgment. The fourth gospel and the Apocalypse of John thus supplement each other.

Death and Hades were cast into the lake of fire (20:14). This is the apocalyptic equivalent for the statement of 1 Corinthians 15:26: "The last enemy that shall be abolished is Death" (cp. Isa. 25:8; Hos. 13:14). But taken in connection with what follows and compared with 21:8, the words "Death and Hades" seem also to be used by synecdoche for the subjects of these infernal powers. But the entire picture of judgment and perdition is wrapped in mystic symbolism. The one certain revelation is the final overthrow in remediless ruin of all who live and die as subjects of sin and death.

This is the second death, even the lake of fire (20:15). Observe that there is no specific designation of a "second resurrection" as distinct from the first. But in contrast therewith we have the second death, which involves the doom of being cast into "the lake of fire." It was promised to the martyr church of Smyrna, "he that overcometh shall not be hurt of the second death" (2:11). It was also written of those blessed and holy ones who have part in the first resurrection that the second death has no power over them (v. 6). But those who come to the judgment scene here described are impliedly of the characters enumerated in 21:8, whose "part is in the lake that burneth with fire and brimstone, which is the second death."

If any was not found written in the book of life (20:15). This statement is to be understood as a principle governing the judgment of the dead and not as implying that numbers of them were found written in the book of the living. There is nothing to indicate that any of those dead, "great and small," seen standing before the throne in verse 12 were found written in the book. Indeed, the whole passage and context imply the contrary. Their works (which seem to have been of the character specified in 21:8 and which accordingly made them the slaves of Death and Hades) were written in the other books that were opened and condemned them, And, as a further evidence against them, "the book of life" was also opened and no record of their names was found therein.

It will be seen that the foregoing exposition of "the first resurrection," and of the judgment before "the great white throne," removes this entire section of the Apocalypse (which has ever been regarded as the most difficult in the book) from what may be cited as specific revelation touching the question how the dead are raised and with what manner of body they come (1 Cor. 15:35). The doctrine of the resurrection of all the dead, as enunciated in John 5:28–29, is evidently assumed. But these apocalyptic pictures of "the first resurrection" and "the second death" are given, not to furnish a doctrine of resurrection from the dead. Rather they serve the purpose of showing most impressively the heavenly glory, on the one hand, of those who "overcome," and the certain judgment and final perdition, on the other, of all who are not found "written from the foundation of the world in the book of life of the Lamb that hath been slain" (13:8).

A faithful and true interpretation must follow the scope and artistic method of the entire book and not be concerning itself with specific dogmas about "the general resurrection of the last day." Nor the efforts to reconcile "two resurrections a thousand years apart" with other teachings of Christ and the apostles on the general subject. For the Apocalyptist employs the concept of resurrection of the dead only metaphorically and with special reference to the rewards awaiting the blessed and holy and the retribution sure to come on the unbelieving and unholy, whose names are not written in heaven.

7. New Heaven, New Earth and New Jerusalem (21:1–8)

1 And I saw a new heaven and a new earth: for the first heaven and the first earth are passed away; and the sea is no more.
2 And I saw the holy city, new Jerusalem, coming down out of heaven from God, made ready as a bride adorned for her husband.
3 And I heard a great voice out of the throne saying, Behold, the tabernacle of God is with men and he shall dwell with them and they shall be his peoples and God himself shall be with them and be their God:
4 and he shall wipe away every tear from their eyes; and death shall be no more; neither shall there be mourning, nor crying, nor pain, any more: the first things are passed away.
5 And he that sitteth on the throne said, Behold, I make all things new.
6 And he saith, Write: for these words are faithful and true. And he said unto me, They are come to pass. I am the Alpha and the Omega, the beginning and the end. I will give unto him that is athirst of the fountain of the water of life freely.
7 He that overcometh shall inherit these things; and I will be his God and he shall be my son.
8 But for the fearful and unbelieving and abominable and murderers and fornicators and sorcerers and idolaters and all liars, their part shall be in the lake that burneth with fire and brimstone; which is the second death.

This last vision of the series commencing at 19:11, is appropriately placed after the great judgment scene of 20:11–15. Although the "making of all things new" (v. 5) is a process going on through all the thousand years of the Messiah's reign. The new earth and heaven are never to pass away and the felicity of God's servants, as portrayed in this section, contemplates not only the life that now is, but also the eternal life of a glorified existence before the throne of God and of the Lamb.

New heaven and new earth (21:1). This ideal of a new creation is appropriated from Isaiah 65:17–18: "Behold, I create new heavens and a new earth: and the former shall not be remembered, nor come into mind. But be ye glad and rejoice forever in that which I create: for behold, I create Jerusalem a rejoicing and her people a joy." In this book, as in Isaiah, the reference is to the renovation of the world by the coming and reign of the Messiah. This new creation is "the regeneration" (παλινγενεσία [*palingenesia*]) referred to in Matthew 19:28

and the "restoration of all things" (ἀποκατάστασις πάντων [*apokatastasis pantōn*]) mentioned in Acts 3:21. This renovation, as Hebrews 12:26–27, shows, involves a removal or passing away of that which is old and shaken.

And the sea is no more (21:1). To interpret this statement literally would be to bring confusion into the whole picture. "Heaven," "earth," and "sea" are mentioned as including all the "elements" (cp. 2 Pet. 3:10) and is symbolic of what Paul calls "the fashion (σχῆμα [*schēma*]) of this world" (1 Cor. 7:31). The new creation, wrought by the truth and word and sword and rod of the great Conqueror of 19:11–16, will not be shaken by the wild restlessness and trouble which the Hebrew mind associated with "the sea" (cp. Isa. 57:20–21). There will be no more such sea as that from which the beast came forth (13:1).

The holy city, new Jerusalem (21:2). Jerusalem is called "the holy city" in Isaiah 48:2; 52:1 and here is called also "new" in order to harmonize with the new heaven and earth to which it belongs. The old Jerusalem became a harlot and is called "Babylon the great" (17:5). The seer has witnessed and recorded her miserable fall and now is permitted to behold a new and holy city, **coming down out of heaven from God, made ready as a bride adorned for her husband** (cp. Isa. 61:10).

How beautiful is the conception of the bride descending in glory from heaven after the abominable harlot has "fallen, fallen!" (14:8; 18:2, 21!) This new Jerusalem is the same as that which Paul in Galatians 4:26, calls "the upper Jerusalem, our mother" (cp. Heb. 12:22). It is a symbol of the new covenant and those embraced therein. It includes all which the redeeming work of Christ secures to them that believe in his name and by implication stands for "the general assembly and church of the firstborn, who are enrolled in heaven" (Heb. 12:23). For the bride is indeed the Church of Christ (Eph. 5:25–32).

A great voice out of the throne (21:3). Best understood as the voice of God and of the Lamb, who are so united as to possess one throne (22:1). **The tabernacle of God is with men**. The old tabernacle served its highest purpose when it conveyed to the true worshiper the profound uplifting thought that God would indeed dwell with men on the earth and commune with them (cp. Exo. 29:42–46; 1 Kgs. 8:27; Eze. 37:27; Zech. 2:10–11).[15] The New Testament dispensation brings the

---

[15] See my chapter on the symbolism of the Mosaic tent of meeting, in *Biblical Apocalyptics* (1898), pages 81–84.

symbolism of the tabernacle into blessed realization, for the believer now enters with boldness into the holy places by the blood of Jesus (Heb. 10:19). And he knows by the witness of the Spirit that he has passed from death into life, is an adopted child of God and dwells in God (Rom. 8:14–16; 1 John 3:24; 4:13–16). In view of these facts of the new covenant how significant the words, **he shall dwell with them and they shall be his peoples and God himself shall be with them**. Thus they become the temple and tabernacle of the living God.

Wipe away every tear (21:4; cp. 7:17; Isa. 25:8). With this comforting assurance is also connected the promise of the fourfold army of earthly woe: **neither shall there be mourning, nor crying, nor pain, any more**. This promise finds fulfillment in the believer's immortality and eternal life in Christ.

He who sitteth on the throne (21:5) is the judge seen in 20:11, "from whose face the earth and the heaven fled away." He is also the ruler of the ages, the great Conqueror of 19:11–16. And his throne is "the throne of God and of the Lamb" (22:1). In the renovation of the world, as in its original creation, God and his Word are one (cp. John 1:1–3).

I make all things new (21:5; cp. Isa. 43:19; 2 Cor. 5:17). In establishing and carrying out the provisions of the new covenant "he hath made the first old. But that which becometh old and waxeth aged is nigh unto vanishing away" (Heb. 8:13). It required a shaking of heaven and earth to effect the change from the old to the new and a "removing of those things that are shaken, that those things which are not shaken may remain" (Heb. 12:26–27). The crisis hour of transition from the old to the new was that of the ruin of the old Jerusalem, but the renovation of the world is the work of the millennial age. The words may well apply to what the Christ is doing during all this period and should be translated "I am making all things new," that is, a new heaven and a new earth, according to verse 1.

Write (21:6; cp. 14:13). Things of special note and comfort are thus emphasized by a definite command to put on record. **These words are faithful and true** for they proceed from the great Conqueror who is "called Faithful and True" (19:11).

They are come to pass (21:6). Regarding γέγοναν (*gegonan*). see the γέγονεν (*gegonen*) of 16:17. The vision and prophetic work treat the restoration of all things as already accomplished in the purpose of God. For the divine speaker immediately adds, **I am the Alpha and the Omega, the beginning and the end.** He is the one who "calls the generations from the beginning," inasmuch as he is "the first and the last" (Isa. 41:4; 43:10; 44:6; 48:12), the one "who is and who was and who is to come" (1:4). He accordingly beholds all the purpose both of judgment and of grace as accomplished from the very beginning. Compare 1:8.

Unto him that is athirst ... water of life (21:6; cp. Isa. 55:1; Zech. 14:8). The promise is not, after the manner of verse 4, "there shall be no more thirst." Rather, the bounteous provision for the satisfaction of thirst is named, for the "water of life [is] freely" given (cp. 22:17). This pledge virtually implies that there will be no more thirst because of the ample and free provision; and hence the passage is not essentially different from 7:16–17.

He that overcometh (21:7). Compare the promises appended to each of the epistles to the seven churches (2:7, 11, 17, etc.). The victor (ὁ νικῶν [ho nikōn]) is kept prominent in this Apocalypse as the associate of Christ and the sharer of his glory. "These are they who follow the Lamb whithersoever he goeth" (14:4) and they constitute the white-robed armies of 19:14. They know the felicity of "the first resurrection" and "live and reign with Christ a thousand years" (20:4–6).

Shall inherit these things (21:7). That is, all the blessedness and glory mentioned or implied in the preceding verses. For if children, sons of God, as is said immediately after, then are they "heirs of God and joint heirs with Christ" (Rom. 8:17). **I will be his God and he shall be my son.** Compare the language of 2 Samuel 7:14; Psalm 89:26–27; and Zechariah 8:8. The one who overcomes along with Christ is thus honored as a son of God and sits down with him on his throne as an associate prince and ruler (cp. 3:21; 2:26–27).

But for the fearful and unbelieving (21:8). Observe how the series of visions, begun with the εἶδον (eidon), *I saw* of 19:11, concludes with the solemn statement of the doom of all who have no inheritance in the new Jerusalem. The statement may be regarded as a solemn warning. The "fearful" are those timid souls who shrink away from the bloody struggle required of them that overcome. They are not willing to dare fierce conflict with the enemies of God. The "unbelieving" are those of perverse hearts who refuse to accept and act upon the truths of divine revelation. The **abominable** are all such as are in love with the "golden cup full of abominations" referred to in 17:4. The **murderers** are especially those who killed the prophets and stoned the messengers of God (Matt. 23:37; Acts 7:52). The **fornicators and sorcerers and idolaters** refer especially to such as made the harlot Babylon "a hold of every unclean spirit" (cp. 18:2–3 and 9:20–21).

All liars (21:8; cp. v. 27; 22:15). He that "loveth and maketh a lie" is last named as a character which is made up of the sum of all evils. For he shows himself to be a worthy son of the devil, who was a liar and a murderer from the beginning (John 8:44). Observe how the eight words of this category of evildoers compose four sets of two in each: (1) fearful and unbelieving; (2) abominable and murderers; (3) fornicators and sorcerers; and (4) idolaters and liars.

Their part is in the lake that burneth with fire and brimstone (21:8). They belong to the great body of enemies represented by the beast and the false prophet (19:20) and Satan and his angels (20:7–10). Compare with this the language of Matthew 25:41, 46.

At the risk of some repetition, we again call attention to the general character and scope of the seven visions, beginning with 19:11 and ending with 21:8. These are seven closely related pictures of the triumph of the holy heavens over the powers of earth and hell. They furnish a vivid outline of the entire period of the Messiah's reign. As a series of triumphs over all evil, preceding and introducing the everlasting fruition of the heavenly Jerusalem, they correspond in the apocalyptic scheme to the seven last plagues which issued in the fall of the great Babylon. Those plagues were of the nature of seven judgments on the corrupt and abominable harlot.

These visions are of seven victories over the various allied forces of the old serpent, the devil. After the rapid narration of the seven last plagues, there followed a detailed picture of the ruin of the great harlot, the mother of abominations of the land (17:1–19:10). We shall note the artistic formality with which these seven triumphs are followed by a detailed vision of the glorious bride, the wife of the Lamb (21:9–22:5).

But we shall miss the great purpose of John's Apocalypse if we presume to treat these seven last visions of triumph as a literal record of historic events. They are to be recognized as symbolical pictures, designed to indicate the ultimate victory of the Christ, "who must reign till he hath put all his enemies under his feet" (1 Cor. 15:25).

Accordingly, the first (19:11–16) is a magnificent representation of the coming and kingdom of the Christ of God. It is set in such symbolic figures and allusions as indicate his character and work. It is an ideal picture of what the Messiah is and what he does during the whole period of his reign — not of any one particular event of his coming.

To render the more impressive the certainty of his triumph, we next have the call to God's great sacrificial feast (19:17–18). This is set in a symbolical form, which is appropriated from the prophet Ezekiel. This call is appropriately followed by the vision of the overwhelming destruction of the beast and the false prophet, along with the kings and armies gathered to war against the King of kings (19:19–21).

Then this victory is made the more signal by the vision of Satan chained and imprisoned for a thousand years (20:1–3). But during all this period, the witnesses of Jesus, who overcome for the word of God, keep themselves unspotted from the beast, live and reign with Christ in his glory (20:6). And when at the end Satan is loosed and makes one more assault upon "the camp of the saints," he and his hosts are consumed by fire from heaven (20:4–10). Thereupon two additional pictures are given. The one (20:11–15) is descriptive of final judgment upon all who are not found written in the book of life. The other (21:1–8) gives a brief outline of the renovation of heaven and earth and the descent of the new Jerusalem as a bride adorned for her husband. These are all millennial pictures, set in one broad field of vision, but involving also the eternal issues of the Messiah's reign.

The coming and kingdom of Christ are accordingly to be conceived as continuing through the long indefinite period symbolized by "a thousand years." It is no sudden product of a night; no local scenic display of a day and an hour, as literalist interpreters have vainly imagined. But it was no part of John's purpose to write a detailed history of Christianity beforehand. He wrote of things destined to come to pass shortly, namely, the fall of Judaism, the ruin of Jerusalem, and the passing away of the old cultus. And he accordingly compassed all that was given him to know of the great future of the kingdom of God in a few vivid pictures, set in symbolic forms which the Old Testament prophets had already employed.

Chapter 11
JERUSALEM, THE GLORIOUS BRIDE
(Rev. 21:9–22:5)

We have now witnessed the pouring out of the seven bowls of the wrath of God. The seventh and last of these was accompanied by "a great voice out of the temple, from the throne, saying, It is done" (γέγονεν [*gegonen*]), "and Babylon the great was remembered in the sight of God" (16:17–19). Then there followed a vision of "Babylon the great, the mother of harlots and of the abominations of the earth" (17:5). This is so detailed and comprehensive as to occupy two full chapters of the book. That detailed portraiture was introduced by "one of the seven angels that had the seven bowls" (17:1). In notable analogy as an artistic counterpart, the seven visions of Messianic triumph (19:11–21:8) concluded with a picture of the new Jerusalem and a voice from the throne, saying, Γέγοναν (*gegonan*) "they are done."

Now there follows (21:9–22:5) a vision of the new Jerusalem, the wife of the Lamb. This is set in an elaborate symbolic framework corresponding to that of Babylon the harlot. This was a definite design of the writer. This fact appears further in the statement that one of the same seven angels showed him this picture of a woman so opposite in character and destiny.

So, after the manner of apocalyptic repetition, the seer now proceeds to take up the last preceding vision (21:1–8). As he does so, he expands it with manifold details appropriated largely from the abundant metaphors and symbols of the Hebrew scriptures.

1. The Vision of the New Jerusalem (21:9–14)

> 9 And there came one of the seven angels who had the seven bowls, who were laden with the seven last plagues; and he spake with me, saying, Come hither, I will show thee the bride, the wife of the Lamb.
> 10 And he carried me away in the Spirit to a mountain great and high and showed me the holy city Jerusalem, coming down out of heaven from God, having the glory of God:
> 11 her light was like unto a stone most precious, as it were a jasper stone,

12 clear as crystal: having a wall great and high; having twelve gates and at the gates twelve angels; and names written thereon, which are the names of the twelve tribes of the children of Israel:
13 on the east were three gates; and on the north three gates; and on the south three gates; and on the west three gates.
14 And the wall of the city had twelve foundations and on them twelve names of the twelve apostles of the Lamb.

There came one of the seven angels (21:9). Compare this with the identical language employed in 17:1. He declares to the seer: **I will show thee the bride.** This is to be a vision of glory, not of penal judgment (as in 17:1). It is a sight of **the wife of the Lamb,** not of a "great harlot sitting upon many waters." This is a figure of the Church and people of God or of Christ wedded in holy covenant relationship. This is a familiar Old Testament image and may be profitably studied in the light of Ephesians 5:23–32.

He carried me away in the Spirit to a mountain great and high (21:10). He did not carry him "into a wilderness," as when the harlot was seen (17:3). Ezekiel's corresponding vision of the temple of God was seen from "a very high mountain" (Eze. 40:2).

The holy city Jerusalem (21:10). This is a conspicuous contrast with Babylon, the mother of harlots and abominations (17:5). This holy city is the symbol of the Church of the new covenant. Paul seems to refer to this apocalyptic vision when he writes about "the Jerusalem that is above, which is our mother" (Gal. 4:26). Once united in living fellowship with Christ, believers are his own beloved for time and eternity. Hence the vision of the heavenly Jerusalem makes no distinction between those who are in the flesh and those who are perfected in heavenly glory. They all belong to one great family and constitute the one body of Christ. This idea, together with this whole picture of the holy city Jerusalem, appears to have prompted the language of Hebrews 12:22–24.

Coming down out of heaven from God (21:10). This is just as already stated in verse 2. The renovation of the world is to be accomplished by this "coming down" of the holy city. Thus is the prayer to be answered, "Thy kingdom come; thy will be done, as in heaven, so on earth" (Matt. 6:10). The infusion of heavenly truth and life into the hearts of men on earth is the great aim of the kingdom of Christ.

Having the glory of God (21:10). This is an allusion to the *shekinah,* the cloud of glory which covered and filled the tabernacle in the day of its erection (Exo. 40:34–38; cp. Isa. 58:8; 60:1, 19; Zech. 2:5). **Her light was like unto a stone most precious.** In 4:3, we were told that he who sat upon the throne was "to look upon like a jasper stone and a sardius." Here the comparison of the light, or brightness (φωστήρ [*phōstēr*]), of the holy city to a most precious stone is suggestive of the light of the glory of God himself (cp. v. 23).

It had a **wall great and high** (21:12) so as to be proof against all assaults or reproach of enemies (cp. Neh. 2:17). He also saw **twelve gates ... twelve angels.** Hence, so guarded that the powers of Hades cannot prevail against her (Matt. 16:18) or take her by surprise. That which was written on the twelve gates were **the names of the twelve tribes.** This agrees with the vision of Ezekiel 48:30–34, from which the statements of this verse and the following are fashioned.

Twelve foundations (21:14). The three gates on each side divided the entire circuit of the wall into twelve great sections, of which the four corner sections would be most prominent. Each of these twelve sections was supported by a massive foundation stone, the quality and material of which are enumerated in verses 19 and 20 below.

On them twelve names of the twelve apostles. In Ephesians 2:19–22, it is written:
> Ye are fellow-citizens with the saints and of the household of God, being built upon the foundation of the apostles and prophets, Jesus Christ himself being the chief corner stone; in whom each several building, fitly framed together, groweth into a holy temple in the Lord; in whom ye also are builded together for a habitation of God in the Spirit.

In connection with this general figure, we should compare what Jesus said to Peter about building his church upon the rock (πέτρα [*petra*]) of a confessing disciple. We should also consider what Peter says (in 1 Pet. 2:5) about being built up as living stones into a spiritual house. By such we may obtain a more complete conception of the new Jerusalem as the Church of Christ. The Church of the prophets and apostles hears the names of the twelve tribes of Israel as well as the twelve apostles of the Lamb. Hence, as we have observed elsewhere, the twenty-four elders before the throne of God (4:4).

2. The Measuring of City and Walls (21:15–17)

15 And he that spake with me had for a measure a golden reed to measure the city and the gates thereof and the wall thereof.
16 And the city lieth foursquare and the length thereof is as great as the breadth: and he measured the city with the reed, twelve thousand furlongs: the length and the breadth and the height thereof are equal.
17 And he measured the wall thereof, a hundred and forty and four cubits, according to the measure of a man, that is, of an angel.

Had for a measure a golden reed (21:15). This measurement of the city with a reed is modeled after Ezekiel 40:3, 5. The measurement is not carried out to the extent that is detailed in Ezekiel's successive chapters, but is said to have compassed city, gates, and wall. The result of the measurement is announced in the next verse and is there seen to serve a symbolic purpose.

Twelve thousand furlongs (21:16). This figure represents about fifteen hundred miles. But the number, as well as the measure, is symbolical. Thus, it is of no great importance to determine whether the twelve thousand stadia are the measure of the entire circuit of the city or only of one of the four sides. The main result of the measurement is to show that the city was immense and that **the length and the breadth and the height thereof are equal**. Its form is accordingly shown to be a perfect cube, like the holy of holies in the tabernacle. The symbolism thus suggests that this holy city was to the new earth and heavens what the holy of holies was to the congregation and camp of Israel.

The wall [was] a hundred and forty and four cubits (21:17). That is, the height of the wall was twelve times twelve cubits, about two hundred and sixteen feet. Thus, we have the picture of a vast city, in the form of a perfect cube, surrounded by a comparatively low wall.

The measure of a man, that is, of an angel (21:17). The only natural meaning these words can bear is that the angel who showed these things to John and measured the city and wall, employed the measure commonly adopted by men. The measure reckoned by man and angel were alike.

3. The Materials of its Structure (21:18–21)

> 18 And the building of the wall thereof was jasper: and the city was pure gold, like unto pure glass.
> 19 The foundations of the wall of the city were adorned with all manner of precious stones. The first foundation was jasper; the second, sapphire; the third, chalcedony; the fourth, emerald;
> 20 the fifth, sardonyx; the sixth, sardius; the seventh, chrysolite; the eighth, beryl; the ninth, topaz; the tenth, chrysoprase; the eleventh, jacinth; the twelfth, amethyst.
> 21 And the twelve gates were twelve pearls; each one of the several gates was of one pearl: and the street of the city was pure gold, as it were transparent glass.

The building of the wall (21:18). This speaks of the material of which the wall was constructed. **Jasper**, which is like the appearance of him who sat upon the throne (4:3). **The city was pure gold, like unto pure glass.** This is designed to enhance the splendor of the city to the uttermost in the thought of the reader. The comparison with glass implies that the gold was so pure as to be even transparent as glass.

The foundations of the wall (21:19). These are mentioned in verse 14 as being twelve in number and bearing the names of the twelve apostles. Already Isaiah had prophesied of Zion that God would lay her foundations with sapphires (Isa. 54:11).

The enumeration of **all manner of precious stones** (21:19) in this verse and the following is modeled after the four rows of similar stones which were set in the breastplate of the high priest (Exo. 28:17–21). Those bore the twelve names of the tribes of Israel. No special and separate significance attaches to each stone. But the enumeration as a whole is designed to produce the effect of something beautiful and exquisite in the extreme. All the precious stones referred to in Holy Writ are named to give the impression of the superior glory of the heavenly city.

Is there not a profound symbolical suggestion in foundations that bear both the names of the twelve apostles and the precious stones of the ephod? "The city which hath the foundations" (Heb. 11:10) is a symbol of "the church of the firstborn who are written in heaven" and is built upon the apostles and prophets. To each of these is given to know and publish the mysteries of the kingdom of heaven, even as the high priest learned the will of Jehovah by means of the precious stones of the ephod.

The twelve gates were twelve pearls (21:21). Most appropriate portals of a city, of which the foundation stones were of jasper and amethyst and the city itself pure gold. The Talmud has a saying that "God will give gems and pearls thirty cubits long and just as broad and will hollow them to the depth of twenty cubits and the breadth ten and place them in the gates of Jerusalem."

The street of the city (21:21). The singular is employed for the entire street system of the city. All the streetways were of **pure gold transparent as glass**, as if forming a part of the solid material of the city itself (cp. v. 18).

4. The Temple and Its Light (21:22–23)

22 And I saw no temple therein: for the Lord God the Almighty and the Lamb, are the temple thereof.
23 And the city hath no need of the sun, neither of the moon, to shine upon it: for the glory of God did lighten it and the lamp thereof is the Lamb.

No temple therein (21:22). This is stated because his golden city is in fact the reality of which the old temple and tabernacle were outward symbols. They were fashioned after the pattern shown to Moses in the mount (Exo. 25:40), but this holy city is itself the true Israel dwelling in God. For all that the temple symbolized in its highest ideal is realized by those whose lives are hidden with Christ in God (Col. 3:3) and who understand the blessed truth that "God is love; and he that abideth in love abideth in God and God in him" (1 Jn. 4:16). Hence the announcement that **the Lord God the Almighty and the Lamb, are the temple** of this new Jerusalem. When God is all and in all there is no place for outward symbol, for the saints behold the glory of God, like cherubim in the holy of holies.

No need of the sun (21:23). This realizes the fulfillment of Isaiah 60:19–20:
> The sun shall be no more thy light by day; neither for brightness shall the moon give light unto thee; but Jehovah shall be thine everlasting light and thy God thy glory. Thy sun shall no more go down; neither shall thy moon withdraw itself; for Jehovah shall be thy everlasting light and the days of thy mourning shall be ended.

Not only is God Almighty the giver of **light** to the new Jerusalem, but the **lamp** of it is the **Lamb**. This association of the Lamb with God as the source of heavenly light and also as the temple of heaven itself, exalts him to the dignity and glory of Jehovah himself.

5. The Character of its Inhabitants (21:24–27)

> 24 And the nations shall walk amidst the light thereof: and the kings of the earth do bring their glory into it.
> 25 And the gates thereof shall in no wise be shut by day (for there shall be no night there):
> 26 and they shall bring the glory and the honor of the nations into it:
> 27 and there shall in no wise enter into it anything unclean, or he that maketh an abomination and a lie: but only they who are written in the Lamb's book of life.

The nations shall walk by means of its light (21:24). Compare Isaiah 60:3: "The nations shall come to thy light and kings to the brightness of thy rising." This statement implies that the new Jerusalem coexists with nations and is not essentially different from "the mountain of Jehovah's house," unto which "all the nations flow" (Isa. 2:2). This is the "desire of all the nations," to which "all the nations shall come" and bring their precious things (Hag. 2:7–8).

The gates shall in no wise be shut by day (21:25). So Isaiah's picture of the future of Zion: "Thy gates shall be open continually; they shall not be shut day nor night; that men may bring unto thee the wealth of the nations" (Isa. 60:11). There will be **no night there**, which statement will be repeated in 22:5, as an important feature of the city of everlasting light.

Bring the glory and honor of the nations into it (21:26). So that it will be a treasure city of all that can contribute to its glory and beauty. Compare Isaiah 60:5–10; 66:12; Haggai 2:7–8.

There shall in no wise enter into it anything common (21:27). Compare Isaiah 52:1, when "Jerusalem, the holy city," is told that "henceforth there shall no more come into thee the uncircumcised and the unclean." The last part of this verse is in substance a repetition of verse 8 and of Revelation 20:15.

6. The River and Trees of Life (22:1–2)

> 1 And he showed me a river of water of life, bright as crystal, proceeding out of the throne of God and of the Lamb, in the midst of the street thereof.
> 2 And on this side of the river and on that was the tree of life, bearing twelve manner of fruits, yielding its fruit every month: and the leaves of the tree were for the healing of the nations.

A river of water of life (22:1). Here the imagery is taken from Ezekiel 47:1 and Zechariah 14:8. But the picture furnished by John is most choice and beautiful. The river as seen by him was **bright as crystal**, a most entrancing sight. And it was seen **proceeding out of the throne of God and of the Lamb**. Hence it must be from an inexhaustible fountain and a most sacred stream (cp. John 4:14). It is also seen to flow **in the midst of the street** of the city, for these words are best connected with the preceding and show the position of the river, not the tree of life, as many have read it.

On this side of the river and on that (22:2). That is, on each bank of the river. The language is equivalent to that of Ezekiel 47:7, 12 and Daniel 12:5. **The tree of life** (22:2). This suggests that paradise is to be fully restored (Gen. 2:9). Compare 2:7: "To him that overcometh will I give to eat of the tree of life, which is in the midst of the paradise of God." The words "tree of life" may here be taken as a collective, like the street of the city (see note on Rev. 21:21) and denote a collection of trees.

Bearing twelve fruits (22:2). That is, yielding twelve crops of fruit, because of its yielding its fruit every month. Compare the like statement in Ezekiel 47:12. **The leaves ... were for the healing of the nations**. Compare Ezekiel 47:12: "The fruit thereof shall be for food and the leaf thereof for a medicine." As the nations walk by the light of this golden city, so also have they their bruises and diseases cured by the leaves of its tree of life.

7. The Eternal Reign in Glory (22:3–5)

> 3 And there shall be no curse any more: and the throne of God and of the Lamb shall be therein: and his servants shall serve him;
> 4 and they shall see his face; and his name shall be on their foreheads.

5 And there shall be night no more; and they need no light of lamp, neither light of sun; for the Lord God shall give them light: and they shall reign forever and ever.

There shall be no curse any more (22:3). As Zechariah also prophesied (Zech.14:11). The original curse brought on the world of man by sin (Gen. 3:16–19, 23) is thus removed and all the nations have access to the tree of life. This truly points to the regeneration and restoration of all things (Matt. 19:28; Acts 3:21), a heavenly paradise regained.

The throne of God and of the Lamb shall be therein (22:3). This is so that all who enter may stand before the throne, like the elders and the cherubim of 4:4–6. Like so many royal ministering servants shall they not only worship him but **shall serve him**.

They shall see his face (22:4; cp. Psa. 17:15; Matt. 5:8; 1 Cor. 13:12; 1 John 3:2). This beatific vision of the saints of God supplants the cherubim. For as this city has no temple, so, as the holy of holies is in heaven, it has no symbolic cherubim. For the glorified servants of God and the Lamb, who have washed their robes and obtained authority over the tree of life (v. 14), now take the places of "the living creatures." Thus, they realize all the life and glory which those forms of living being symbolized.

his name shall be on their foreheads (22:4). Compare Revelation 3:12; 14:1.

Night no more (22:5). Therefore eternal day. **Need no light of lamp ... neither light of sun.** For the same reason as that given in 21:23 (cp. Psa. 36:9).

They shall reign forever and ever (22:5), literally, "for the ages of the ages." So that the reign of the thousand years (20:4–6) is but the beginning of a regal life and felicity which are to continue through all the æons to come. So the kingdom of the saints of the Most High will be most truly, as Daniel wrote, "an everlasting kingdom" (Dan. 7:27). This is the "eternal life" of Matthew 25:46, just as the second death, the lake of fire, is the "eternal punishment" into which the "cursed" go away. But no curse shall come any more to those who stand before the throne and inherit the kingdom prepared for them from the foundation of the world.

Thus, ends the vision of the new Jerusalem, the wife of the Lamb. What follows is of the nature of a conclusion to the book.

This glorious picture of the new Jerusalem, the Bride, the wife of the Lamb, is the New Testament Apocalypse of what the last nine chapters of Ezekiel portray in a more minute and detailed description peculiar to that prophet. Taken as a whole, it is a symbolical picture of the Church of Christ in time and eternity, but especially in its ultimate glorification. We have repeatedly called attention to the fact that the New Testament conception of the believer's life in Christ leaves the matter of death quite out of account. He who lives and believes in Christ never dies (John 11:26). Having died with Christ, he is also raised with him and, as in the case of his risen Lord, he conceives that "death no more hath dominion over him" (Rom. 6:8–11; Col. 3:1).

So the entire Church is also conceived as the living body of Christ. Thus, all the ideals of triumph and glory which the Old Testament prophets associated with the Messianic reign are in the New Testament Apocalypse associated with the Church and kingdom of Christ. The members of this sanctified body

> have already come unto Mount Zion and unto the city of the living God, the heavenly Jerusalem and to the innumerable hosts of angels, to the general assembly and church of the firstborn who are enrolled in heaven and to God the Judge of all and to the spirits of just men made perfect and to Jesus the Mediator of the new covenant and to the blood of sprinkling that speaketh better than that of Abel. (Heb. 12:22–24)

This is a vivid conception of identification with God and Christ and all the holy ones. It leaves for the moment all other things out of sight and associates with the blessed life in Christ the vision of eternal fellowship in his glory.

Chapter 12
CONCLUSION
(Rev. 22:6–21)

The conclusion of the Apocalypse appears upon close analysis to be a sevenfold epilogue. It affirms and confirms at the close the fact that this is truly the book of the revelation and testimony of Jesus Christ, as announced at the beginning (1:1–3). For we have (1) the angel's testimony to the truthfulness of the words of this book (vv. 6–7). Then follows (2) John's own testimony of his intercourse with the angel (vv. 8–9). (3) Then a testimony of solemn admonition and counsel, in view of the revelations given (vv. 10–15). (4) Next we have Jesus's own personal testimony (v. 16), followed by (5) the great invitation to partake of the water of life freely (v. 17), And then comes (6) the final prophetic warning, confirmed by the Lord himself (vv. 18–20) and finally (7) a brief benediction (v. 21).

1. The Angel's Testimony (22:6–7)

> 6 And he said unto me, These words are faithful and true: and the Lord, the God of the spirits of the prophets, sent his angel to show unto his servants the things which must shortly come to pass.
> 7 And behold, I come quickly. Blessed is he that keepeth the words of the prophecy of this book.

He said unto me (22:6). That is, the angel of 21:9, who has just shown him the vision of the new Jerusalem. **These words**, i.e., the entire prophecy of this book (cp. v. 7 and Rev. 21:5). **Faithful and true.** Like the Lord from whom they came (1:5; 3:7).

The God of the spirits of the prophets (22:6). The God who inspired the spirits of the ancient prophets and made them the vehicles of communicating his truths to men. He **sent his angel**, as stated in 1:1 and shown repeatedly during the progress of the revelations.

Behold, I come quickly (22:7). Everything relative to the great catastrophe of this book and the coming and kingdom of the Christ, is represented as about to come to pass. The great event is in the immediate future (cp. vv. 10, 12, 20 and 1:1, 3, 7).

Of this same momentous crisis and its related signs and woes Jesus spoke most solemnly to his disciples on the Mount of Olives. There he assured them that their generation should not pass till all these things were fulfilled (Matt. 24:34). It was coincident with the collapse of Judaism and its temple. For the kingdom of God, as represented in the Gospel of Jesus, was destined to supersede the old covenant, grow like the mustard seed (Matt. 13:31–32), and fill the whole earth like the stone of Daniel's prophecy (Dan. 2:35). The judgment of Judah and Jerusalem and the consequent coming and kingdom of Christ were events near at hand when John wrote.

Blessed is he that keepeth the words (22:7). Compare the like beatitude in 1:3.

2. The Angel and John (22:8–9)

> 8 And I John am he that heard and saw these things. And when I heard and saw, I fell down to worship before the feet of the angel which showed me these things.
> 9 And he saith unto me, See thou do it not: I am a fellow-servant with thee and with thy brethren the prophets and with them who keep the words of this book: worship God.

I John am he that heard and saw these things (22:8). We repeat here what we have said elsewhere (on 1:4, 9) that no other John known to the Church could write these words so properly as the well-known apostle and disciple of Jesus.

I fell down (22:8), as also recorded in 19:10. The repetition of this attempt to **worship before the feet of the angel** shows what a profound impression the revelation made upon the seer. Notwithstanding the previous rebuke and admonition to worship God only, the abundance of the revelations and their magnitude so overwhelm him that he forgets for the moment that it is only an angel that shows him the visions.

3. The Solemn Admonition (22:10–15)

> 10 And he saith unto me, Seal not up the words of the prophecy of this book; for the time is at hand.
> 11 He that is unrighteous, let him do unrighteousness still: and he that is filthy, let him be made filthy still: and he that is righteous, let

him do righteousness still: and he that is holy, let him be made holy still.
12 Behold, I come quickly; and my reward is with me, to render to each man according as his work is.
13 I am the Alpha and the Omega, the first and the last, the beginning and the end.
14 Blessed are they that wash their robes, that they may have the right to come to the tree of life and may enter in by the gates into the city.
15 Without are the dogs and the sorcerers and the fornicators and the murderers and the idolaters and every one that loveth and maketh a lie.

Seal not up the words (22:10). This is quite unlike the command given to Daniel (Dan. 12:9). The Old Testament prophet's revelations were not to come to pass shortly, but "closed up and sealed till the time of the end." But of the fulfillment of John's revelation he is assured that **the time is at hand** (cp. vv. 7, 12, 20; Rev. 1:1, 3).

He that is unrighteous, let him do unrighteousness still (22:11). The language and sentiment of this verse are those of exhortation, mixed with a conspicuous element of judicial declaration. The passage is to be studied and understood in the light of scriptures of similar tone and spirit in Isaiah 6:10; Ezekiel 3:27; Matthew 26:45.

My reward is with me, to render to each man according to his works (22:12). So that much of that judgment which is depicted in 20:11–15, is a continual process, coming quickly and certainly to every man. Neither Lazarus nor Dives wait indefinite ages to receive, each according to his works. Often in this life, but always after death sure judgment comes (Heb. 9:27).

I am the Alpha and the Omega (22:13). Thus he repeats at the end what he declared at the beginning (cp. 1:8).

Blessed are they that wash their robes (22:14). Like those beatified ones described in 7:14–17. For besides the glory there mentioned, they also **have the right to come to the tree of life**. Or, more literally, their authority may be *over* the tree of life. This implies a restoration of all that was lost in Eden and an elevation to the position and glory of the cherubim (Gen. 3:24).

Enter in by the gates (22;14). Which are ever open to those whose names are written in the Lamb's book of life (21:25–27).

Without are the dogs (22:15). The dog being an abomination according to the law (Deut. 23:18). It is an animal of many odious habits, and so was naturally associated in the Jewish mind with that which is vile. Hence the word is used metaphorically for the vicious and the unclean. In oriental cities dogs are notorious for prowling in the darkness of the night and for fighting and devouring one another. Hence the horror of the thought of "the outer darkness, where is gnashing of teeth" (Matt. 22:13).

Düsterdieck suggests that in view of the prominence of the word "without" (ἔξω [exō]) and standing as it does in the true text without a connecting particle, we should translate, "Let dogs be without." The other impious characters named in this verse are the same as those of 21:8.

4. The Personal Testimony of Jesus (22:16)

> 16 I Jesus have sent mine angel to testify unto you these things for the churches. I am the root and the offspring of David, the bright, the morning star.

I Jesus have sent mine angel (22:16). Here is the self-testimony of Jesus to the fact stated in 1:1. **To testify unto you**, i.e., unto all you who "read and hear the words of the prophecy of this book" (1:3).

For the churches (22:16) means "for the good of the churches". Compare the sending of the book to the seven churches (1:11). Instead of for "the churches," other authorities read "in the churches." The book is not to remain a sealed one, but to be read in the churches for their comfort and hope.

The root and the offspring of David (22:16). The word "offspring" is here but epexegetical of "root," which is to be understood in the light of Isaiah 11:1, 10 (see on Rev. 5:5).

The bright, the morning star (22:16). Introducing the eternal day, in which there shall be no more need of lamp or sun, "and there shall be night no more" (v. 5; cp. 2 Sam. 23:4; Num. 24:17).

5. The Great Invitation (22:17)

> 17 And the Spirit and the bride say, Come. And he that heareth, let him say, Come. And he that is athirst, let him come: he that will, let him take the water of life freely.

The Spirit (22:17). Who is no other than "the seven spirits before the throne" (1:4), omniscient and omnipresent.

The bride (22:17). This is the whole body of Christ's beloved people, whom he has purchased with his own blood. The general assembly and church written in heaven are ever inviting to "come unto Mount Zion and unto the city of the living God, the heavenly Jerusalem" (Heb. 12:22).

He that heareth (22:17). The one who hears the Spirit and the bride say, **Come** and who hears this book read in the churches, is not only to come himself, but to extend the invitation to others.

He that is athirst (22:17; cp. 21:6; John 7:37). And when he is guided by the Lamb "unto fountains of waters of life" he shall thirst no more (7:16–17). The fullness and freeness of this invitation, intensified further by the words **he that will, let him take the water of life freely**, represent the spirit of the everlasting Gospel. These good tidings are to be announced during the entire millennial age.

6. The Prophetic Warning (22:18–20)

> 18 I testify unto every man that heareth the words of the prophecy of this book, If any man shall add unto them, God shall add unto him the plagues which are written in this book:
> 19 and if any man shall take away from the words of the book of this prophecy, God shall take away his part from the tree of life and out of the holy city, which are written in this book.
> 20 He who testifieth these things saith, Yea: I come quickly. Amen: come, Lord Jesus.

I testify (22:18). These are most naturally understood as the words of John himself. But he speaks as the prophet of God and his testimony is also that of Jesus and the Spirit.

If any man shall add unto or **shall take away from** (22:18–19). The solemn warning given in these two verses is in substance like that of Moses in Deuteronomy 4:2. But it is cast in an impressive form, after the apocalyptic style and spirit of the whole book. The writer thus most solemnly guards against any unlawful adding to or taking from the words of the book of this prophecy, that is, this book of Revelation (as in vv. 7, 9 and 1:3, 11).

He who testifieth these things (22:20). That is, Jesus Christ himself; so that the Apocalypse is, as announced at the beginning, the "testimony of Jesus Christ" (1:2).

Yea: I come quickly (22:20). This emphasizes in the conclusion the great theme of the book as announced in 1:7. And we know that he did come in that generation to which John belonged. This is the great Conqueror of nameless secret power, who is called Faithful and True, the Word of God, and King of kings and Lord of lords (19:11–16). He is also now coming and will continue to come in his kingdom and power and glory, until he shall have put all his enemies under his feet.

To his words, "I come quickly," the seer at once responds, **Amen: come, Lord Jesus** (22:20). This prayer is but another form of saying, "Thy kingdom come. Thy will be done, as in heaven, so on earth" (Matt. 6:10). This is the continual prayer of every true servant of God and of Jesus Christ. And in answer to it, Jehovah shall give unto his Anointed the heathen for an inheritance and the uttermost parts of the earth for a possession (Psa. 2:8).

7. The Benediction (22:21)

21 The grace of the Lord Jesus be with the saints. Amen.

The grace of the Lord Jesus be with the saints (22:21). This final benediction is a brief repetition of what is more fully and rhetorically drawn out in 1:4–5. It is not strange that very early copies contain also the words "Christ" and "all": "The grace of the Lord Jesus Christ be with all the saints." In either form the benediction appropriately closes this word of God and testimony of Jesus.

APPENDICES

Appendix 1
Approaches to Revelation
Kenneth L. Gentry, Jr.

Since Revelation is such a difficult book, we discover many different approaches to it in church history. But to subscribe to a particular school of interpretation is not a matter that we can decide *prior* to our exposition. For as Mounce notes: "it is difficult to say what anything means until one has decided in a sense what everything means."[1]

As we look at the history of approaches to Revelation "most scholars summarize the options under four headings."[2] Each of these four schools of interpretation have representatives ranging from conservative evangelicals to radical critical scholars.[3] Thus, Johnson makes an important observation on this matter: "Since there have been evangelicals who have held to each of the four views, the issue is not that of orthodoxy but of interpretation."[4] Oddly enough, all evangelical millennial schools are represented (to varying degrees) among these various approaches, as we see in the merging of elements of preterism and futurism in G. R. Beasley-Murray, George E. Ladd, Robert Mounce, and Marvin Pate.[5]

We should note also that although there are four leading schools of thought or interpretive classifications, oftentimes an author might hold to a merged or blended view. Consequently, as Beckwith observes

---

[1] Robert H. Mounce, *The Book of Revelation* (NICNT) (Grand Rapids: Eerdmans, 1977), xiii.

[2] Grant R. Osborne, *Revelation* (BECNT) (Grand Rapids: Baker, 2002), 18.

[3] For a helpful, lay-oriented comparison of the views, see: Gregg, *Revelation: Four View* (1996).

[4] Alan F. Johnson in *The Expositor's Bible Commentary*, ed. Frank E. Gaebelein (Grand Rapids: Zondervan/Regency, 1981), 12:410.

[5] George R. Beasley-Murray, "The Revelation" in *The Eerdmans Bible Commentary*, ed. by D. Guthrie and J. A. Motyer (Grand Rapids: Eerdmans, 1970). George E. Ladd, *A Commentary on the Revelation of John* (Grand Rapids: Eerdmans, 1972). 14. Mounce, *Revelation*, 29–30. C. Marvin Pate and Calvin B. Haines, Jr., *Doomsday Delusions: What's Wrong with Predictions About the End of the World* (Downer's Grove, Ill.: Inter-varsity. 1995), 40–44.

"such a classification, however, is not to be carried out on rigidly fixed lines, for most of the interpreters combine, at least to some degree, elements belonging to different systems."[6]

Nevertheless, historically interpretations divide among four basic schools. I will briefly survey these and mention their strengths and weaknesses.

Historicism: All History

The *historicist* school is sometimes called "continuous-historical" or "ecclesiastical-historical." This view promotes a continuous fulfillment of the prophetic drama in Revelation. In it we see a panorama of Church history from the apostolic era and the foundation of Christianity to the return of Christ at the conclusion of history. As Collins expresses it:

> This approach sees the Revelation as a forecast of the progress and destiny of the church in its conflict with Rome and the Roman Antichrist power forecast in Daniel seven. Its prophecies pertain to events from the time of the New Testament church to the end-time consummation .... It focuses on the course of church history depicting the victory of Christ over the Antichrist, the redemption of His bride, the Church, the ultimate destruction of evil, and the establishment of Christ's everlasting rule at His second coming.[7]

Historical continuity is the main focus of this approach. Thus, historicists deem Revelation as something of a divinely-written almanac or compendium of church history that provides a prophetic outline of certain key elements in that history. They apply the numerous judgment scenes to various wars, revolutions, and socio-political and religious movements (e.g., the rising of Roman Catholicism, the birth of Islam, the Crusades, the Inquisition, the French Revolution, etc.), as well as important historical persons (e.g., various Popes, Muhammed, Charlemagne, Saladin, Napoleon, Hitler, etc.).

Today we are witnessing a precipitous decline in advocacy of historicism. Desrosiers speaks of it as "on the brink of completely disap-

---

[6]Isbon T. Beckwith, *The Apocalypse of John: Studies in Introduction with a Critical and Exegetical Commentary* (Grand Rapids: Baker, 1919 [rep. 1979]), 335.

[7]"The Book of Revelation" in John J. Collins, ed. *The Encyclopedia of Apocalypticism*; vol. 1: *The Origins of Apocalypticism in Judaism and Christianity* (New York: Contiuum, 2000), 11.

pearing."[8] Significantly, Zondervan does not even include it as an option in its *Four Views on the Book of Revelation* (1999). Historicists are so scarce today that in his rather complete listing of historicist commentaries O. Collins has to leap from E. P. Cachemaille's commentary in 1931 to Francis Nigel Lee's in 2000.[9] Boring seems to be correct when he notes that "although widely held by Protestant interpreters after the Reformation and into the twentieth century, no critical New Testament scholar today advocates this view."[10] Consequently, "there are few historicists today."[11] Two recent commentaries, however, do support the position: Francis Nigel Lee's *John's Revelation Unveiled* (2000) and Oral E. Collins' *The Final Prophecy of Jesus* (2007).

Oddly enough, we may often find traces of historicism mixed with futurism in the dispensational approach to Revelation. Though dispensationalism strongly advocates futurism (see below), many dispensationalists view the seven churches from an historicist perspective as representing seven stages of church history.[12]

Historicism's strengths

This view has several strengths that have attracted adherents. (1) The very concept has a certain contextual plausibility: Revelation 1–3 clearly opens with events in John's day and Revelation 21–22, wherein we find the *new* creation, seems to present the consummate state coming at the conclusion of history. This suggests that chapters 4–20 should cover the time in between. In fact, early in John's record at 1:19 we learn that he must write the things "which you have seen, and the

---

[8] Gilbert Desrosiers, *An Introduction to Revelation: A Pathway to Interpretation* (New York: Continuum, 2000), 27.

[9] Oral E. Collins, *The Final Prophecy of Jesus: An Introduction, Analysis and Commentary on the Book of Revelation* (Eugene, Ore.: Wipf & Stock, 2007), 11n, 13, 120n).

[10] M. Eugene Boring, *Revelation: Interpretation: A Bible Commentary for Teaching and Preaching* (Louisville: John Knox, 1989), 49.

[11] J. Daniel Hays, J. Scott Duvall, and C. Marvin Pate, eds., *Dictionary of Biblical Prophecy and End Times* (Grand Rapids: Zondervan, 2007).

[12] Charles Caldwell Ryrie, *Revelation* (Chicago: Moody, 1968), 21, 24. John F. Walvoord, *The Revelation of Jesus Christ* (Chicago: Moody, 1966), 52. Tim LaHaye and Ed Hindson, eds., *The Popular Encyclopedia of Bible Prophecy* (Eugene, Ore.: Harvest House, 2004), 42, 352–53. *New Scofield Reference Bible* at Revelation 1:20.

things which are, and the things which shall take place after these things."

(2) Its interest in chronological succession seems to fit well with Revelation's several series of events (first trumpet, second trumpet, third trumpet, etc.) and statements about things occurring "after" this or that (7:1; 9:12; 15:5; 18:1; 19:1; etc.). (3) It also suggests the contemporary relevance of Revelation's prophecies to our own day, since it is mapping the flow of history until the end — which obviously has not occurred yet.

Historicism's weaknesses

Despite these appealing strengths, several debilitating weaknesses undermine the system. These explain why "the majority of modern scholarly exegesis no longer sustains such an application."[13] (1) Its most glaring deficiency lies in the fact that John writes Revelation to a first-century Church under siege. Yet in this view he is writing to them mostly about distantly future, detailed events of which they could have absolutely no understanding. And this despite John's stated concern for his contemporary audience under duress (1:9) as they fear what they are "about to suffer" (2:10). In addition, he promises a special blessing to them if they heed the things within (1:3) so that they might be "overcomers" (2:7, 11, 17, 26; 3:5, 12, 21).

(2) Historically, most historicists have assumed that they are living at the conclusion of history and are about to witness Revelation's finale. For instance, this view is quite prominent in the Middle Ages when millennialism began to flourish once again and historicism is employed to show that "the millennium was about to dawn."[14] To take but one example, Josephus Mede (1586–1639) notes in his commentary: "While I write, news is brought of a Prince from the North (meaning Gustavus Adophus) gaining victories over the Emperor in defence of the German afflicted Protestants."[15]

---

[13] John M. Court, *Myth and History in the Book of Revelation* (Atlanta: John Knox, 1979), 8,

[14] D. A. Carson, Douglas J. Moo, and Leon Morris, *An Introduction to the New Testament* (Grand Rapids: Zondervan, 1992), 482.

[15] From Elliott, *Horae Apocalypticae* (London: 1845), 474. Cited in Henry Barclay Swete, *Commentary on Revelation* (Grand Rapids: Kregel, 1906 (rep. 1977), ccxiv (n 1).

A comment on recurring problems in eschatological debate in general would apply to historicism in particular: historian F. Roy Coad well states that "almost invariably interpretation has been vitiated by the reluctance or incapacity of commentators to visualise their own age as other than the end time."[16] Thus, Ehrman scornfully observes that most such Revelation interpreters "have been concerned to show that the beast has finally arisen in their own day. Rarely are the interpretations put forth as conjectures, of course, but almost always with the confidence of those who have the inside scoop."[17]

(3) As a consequence of the preceding problem, the historicist interpretation is in a constant state of flux because it "was under the necessity of revising its result with the progress of events."[18] As history grows longer, older varieties of this interpretive school experience a great number of failed expectations exposing the system to great embarrassment. This problem can be easily demonstrated by simply picking up an historicist commentary over 100 years old. Court wonders how this view long remained "strangely attractive in spite of the recurrent anguish and disappointment it causes."[19]

(4) Brady highlights the underlying reason for both of the preceding problems: "Revelation was at the mercy of an almost complete subjectivism, for the symbols could be made to represent just whatever feature of notoriety the expositor desired to extract from the records of the Church's history."[20]

Thus, historicism can easily lead to flimsy interpretations. For instance, in O. Collins' (2007) recent commentary we find the following dates presented as prophetic fulfillments of Revelation: The first seal's white horse "was remarkably and uniquely fulfilled in the era extending from A.D. 98–180."[21] The second seal's red horse speaks of "the

---

[16] F. Roy Coad, "Prophetic Developments: A Christian Brethren Research Fellowship Occasional Paper" (Pinner, England: 1966), 10.

[17] Bart D. Ehrman, *The New Testament: A Historical Introduction to the Early Christian Writings* (New York: Oxford, 2000), 436.

[18] Henry Barclay Swete, *Commentary on Revelation* (Grand Rapids: Kregel, 1906 (rep. 1977), ccxv.

[19] Court, *Myth and History*, 7.

[20] David M. Brady, *The Contribution of British Writers between 1560 and 1830 to the Interpretation of Revelation 13.16–18 (The Number of the Beast): A Study in the History of Exegesis* (Tübingen: Mohr, 1983), 298.

[21] O. Collins, *Final Prophecy of Jesus*, 128.

accession of the Emperor Commodus in A.D. 180 until the death of Carinus in A.D. 284)" which events "strikingly fulfill the prophetic imagery of this second seal" (p. 132). "The black horse [fourth seal] era produced a particularly remarkable illustration of the conditions dramatized by the symbols of the third seal . . . . When the deflation of the *choenix* in the period of Alexander Severus [A.D. 222–235] is factored in, [it] accurately represents the prices then stipulated" in this seal (pp. 138–39). "The period from A.D. 248 to about A.D. 270, beginning with the rule of the Emperor Philip and ending with the Emperor Aurelianus, is aptly characterized by the rider, 'Death.'" (p. 141). The fifth seal prophesies "Diocletian in A.D. 303 announced his determination to eliminate Christians and Christianity from the Empire." (p. 146).

(5) As a result of its subjectivism, historicists demonstrate an almost complete lack of agreement with one another. Wherever two or three historicists are gathered together, chaos is in the midst. (6) Historicism generally deals with Revelation's prophecies as occurring in a linear fashion, despite strong evidence of its employing recapitulation. It tends to hold John's "after" statements as asserting chronological succession in *historical fulfillment* rather than *John's experience* in receiving the visions in a particular order.

(7) Rather than providing a truly global view of history, its relevance is confined to the Western world with the progress of history traced only in a westerly direction. "Historicist readings, however, are highly Eurocentric. Rarely if ever does a historicist reading take the church in Asia or the southern hemisphere into account."[22]

Idealism: Supra-history

The *idealist* school is also called the "timeless symbolic" and the "poetic-symbolic." This view sees a "repeated pattern of fulfillment."[23] This approach is ahistorical — or perhaps better supra-historical — in that it sees the point of Revelation as not so much painting an objective, historical portrait at all. Rather, John's concern is to provide a nonhistorical, allegorical summation of various significant redemptive truths or historical principles. It attempts to provide the scene behind

---

[22] David A. deSilva, *Seeing Things John's Way: The Rhetoric of the Book of Revelation* (Louisville, Kent.: Westminster John Knox, 2009), 3.

[23] Vern S. Poythress, *The Returning King: A Guide to the Book of Revelation* (Phillipsburg, N.J.: P & R, 2000), 29.

the scenes. That is, it offers a look at the philosophical/spiritual issues working themselves out in history, rather than at historical events themselves.

Consequently, idealism presents the ongoing struggle between good and evil, showing God's work for good and his victory over evil by presenting "transcendent truths that are valid in every generation."[24] Advocates of idealism include William Milligan (1889), R. C. H. Lenski (1943), William Hendriksen (1967), Paul S. Minear (1968), and R. J. Rushdoony (1970), as well as modified (blended) idealist-preterists such as G. K. Beale (1999), and Vern S. Poythress (2000).

Milligan argues that "we are not to look in the Apocalypse for special events, but for an exhibition of the principles which govern the history both of the world and the Church."[25] It provides "the action of great principles and not special events."[26] Thus, John's great work serves virtually as a theological poem regarding historical struggle, providing a philosophy of history. The symbols of Revelation reveal God in his sovereign control over men and nations, despite man's warring resistance.

Idealism's strengths

Idealism has several appealing strengths. (1) It seems to fit well with the obvious symbolic nature of the book and with the frequent involvement of heaven with its "events" (e.g., 4:1–2; 9:1; 10:1; 11:19; 12:3). (2) It provides an important framework for the Christian worldview regarding historical development in that it shows God's governing hand ultimately at work. It thereby establishes a central place to theology in one's historical outlook. (3) Unlike historicism, it is not subject to failed expectations since it does not expressly deal with concrete historical individuals or events. Thus, "it spares the devout the needless pains of following the course of vain calculations and questions of idle curiosity."[27] (4) It does not ignore John's original audience in that it is always applicable at any time in history.

---

[24] deSilva, *Seeing Things John's Way*, 5.
[25] Mounce. *Revelation*, 28.
[26] Cited in Carson, *Introduction to the New Testament*, 483.
[27] Abraham Kuyper, *The Revelation of St. John*, trans. by John Hendrik de Vries (Grand Rapids: Eerdmans, 1935), iii.

(5) It also is amendable to the other interpretive approaches. For in a certain sense this view could be held simultaneously with any one of the other views. After all, history *is in fact* the outworking of divinely-established principles. Carrington writes of his own view (a merged preterism-idealism): "The best commentaries of recent years have been those in which the Spiritual [i.e., idealist] and the Present-Historical [i.e., preterist] methods have been combined; the Revelation represents great principles working themselves out in actual history."[28] Thus, even premillennialist Ladd recognizes that there is "some truth in this method."[29] Keener cites Tenney's statement regarding idealism: "almost any interpreter of Revelation could give assent regardless of the school to which he belongs."[30]

(6) It encourages Christians to look beyond this vale of tears to ultimate issues controlling history. This, of course, is a recurring practice in all of biblical revelation.

Idealism's weaknesses

Idealism is not without some weaknesses. (1) By all appearance Revelation appears to be so concerned with concrete history that wholly to overlook historical events seems to defy the strong impression the book leaves. In fact, the oracles to the seven churches clearly show a knowledge of and concern with their actual historical settings (see works on the seven letters by W. M. Ramsay; Colin Hemer; Roland H. Worth; Edwin M. Yamauchi).

(2) Revelation is so long and complex that it would seem such a view as idealism could better be presented in a shorter space and without giving such an appearance of historical reality. (3) It downplays the time-frame indicators of the book which clearly assert that its primary intent is to deal with events that "must shortly take place" (1:1) because "the time is near" (1:3). Thus, deSilva complains: "a purely idealist approach, however, runs afoul of John's own perspective on the

---

[28] Philip Carrington, *The Meaning of the Revelation* (Eugene, Ore.: Wipf & Stock, 1931 (rep. 2007),viii–ix.

[29] Ladd, *Revelation*, 11.

[30] Craig S. Keener, *Revelation* (*NIV Application Commentary*) (Grand Rapids: Zondervan, 2000), 27.

imminence, and therefore special relevance, of the material for his immediate audience."[31]

Futurism: End of History

The most widely prevalent interpretive approach in American evangelicalism today is *futurism*. Futurism is sometimes designated the "pure eschatological," "end-historical," or "ultimate-eschatological" view. It understands Revelation's prophecies (beginning after 4:1) as presenting remotely distant events, well beyond John's own historical setting. This view understands Revelation as dealing with the ultimate historical issues that the world and/or the church will face just prior to Christ's return.

Most scholars agree with Court that "the pioneer, and a notable exponent, of this method of exegesis was the Spanish Jesuit Ribera." He was responding to "the bombardment of anti-Catholic exegesis from the Protestant Reformers who used the Apocalypse as ammunition for their attacks on the Papacy and the Church of Rome."[32]

It is difficult to class some of the very early premillennialists as futurists, despite the obvious predilection for futurism among present-day premillennialists. The reason for this is because the several early church fathers who are premillennial think they are already in the very end times. Thus, they have no thought of a distantly future second advent, since they believe that they exist on the event-horizon itself. Certainly the original audience was close enough to the writing of Revelation that some form of historicism could explain their views.

While mistaken regarding the historical origins of futurism, even futurist John Walvoord laments:

> Though the premillennial conclusions of the futuristic view seem to have been held by the early church, the early fathers did not in any clear or consistent way interpret the book of Revelation as a whole in a futuristic sense. In fact, it can be demonstrated that the principal error of the fathers was that they attempted to interpret the book of Revelation as being fulfilled contemporaneously in the trials and difficulties of the church.[33]

---

[31] deSilva, *Seeing Things John's Way*, 5.
[32] Court, *Myth and History*, 9.
[33] Walvoord, *Revelation*, 22.

Futurism is very popular today due to the widespread influence of dispensationalism. Popular evangelical proponents of dispensationalist futurism in Revelation include: C. I. Scofield (1907), John F. Walvoord (1966), Charles C. Ryrie (1968), Hal Lindsey (1973), Robert L. Thomas (1995), and John F. MacArthur, Jr. (1999).

This view also is strongly held by Reformed amillennialist theologian Abraham Kuyper (1935). Kuyper claims that nothing in Revelation is prior to the events building up to the Second Advent: "The Apocalypse of St. John treats exclusively of what will come to pass when the ordinary course of things shall be broken up, and the concluding period of both the life of the church and the life of the world is ushered in."[34] He adds that Revelation "shows even at great pains that the Return of the Lord will almost immediately be preceded by extremely important and very striking events" (18–19). Still further: "These Apocalyptic prophecies do not refer to the past, they are no history of the past twenty centuries, but forecast *what is to come at the beginning of the end*" (23).

Futurism's strengths

Certain seeming strengths of futurism make it appealing to many today. (1) It seems to allow for the apparent universal and catastrophic events of Revelation, in that these are so destructive they could not occur prior to the very end time. After all, "most natural disasters . . . pale into insignificance when compared with the Seer's descriptions of the sixth seal."[35] In this light Walvoord (21) states that "the futuristic position allows a more literal interpretation of the specific prophecies of the book."

(2) It encourages fidelity among God's people at all times due to the potential outbreak of the judgments in Revelation as the end suddenly begins erupting on the scene. Therefore it keeps Christians looking ahead to God's completing his plan for history. (3) It informs us how history will end and under what circumstances, making an appropriate conclusion to the biblical canon which starts with the very beginning of history (Gen. 1).

---

[34] Kuyper, *Revelation*, 18.
[35] Court, *Myth and History*, 78.

Futurism's weaknesses

Despite its seeming strengths, several debilitating weaknesses undermine it. (1) Futurism almost totally removes the relevance of Revelation from John's original audience, and at a time of great suffering. This approach virtually renders Revelation as a time capsule sent to the twenty-first century (or later!). Koester amusingly complains that many seem understand Revelation 1:1 as if it read: "John, to the Christians in North America, who live in the twenty-first century."[36] Walvoord himself admits that (on his view) Revelation "could be only dimly comprehended by the first readers of the book."[37] But John is writing to a persecuted Church (even beyond the seven churches of Asia; 2:7, 11, 17, 23, 29; 3:6, 13, 22) about things they themselves must heed (1:3, 9; 3:10; 6:9–11). Yet futurism claims that the prophesied events lay off in the distant future.

Futurist Kuyper sees this weakness as a strength when he writes: "Meanwhile, however, as really the Apocalypse gives no data with respect to history, but presents solely an account of the wondrous events that will herald the parousia, immediately precede it, and prepare the way for it, the church has not been able to give instant currency to this only correct understanding of the Apocalyptic prophecies."[38]

(2) Futurism requires the current-day reader of Revelation to re-interpret its phenomena (which are drawn right out of the historical context of John's day) to make them fit modern times. This includes such ancient military issues as bows-and-arrows, sword-fighting, mounted cavalry, walled cities, and so forth. Populist dispensationalists, for instance, will transpose these ancient weapons with modern weapons — despite their vigorous assertions that they are literalists. Thus, the system (within the dispensationalist branch) is torn by dialectical tension.

(3) The futurist must wholly re-interpret Revelation's claims of the nearness of its events, despite their introducing and concluding the whole work (1:1, 3; 22:6, 10). As deSilva observes:

---

[36] Craig R. Koester, *Revelation and the End of All Things* (Grand Rapids: Eerdmans, 2001), 26.
[37] Walvoord, *Revelation*, 8.
[38] Kuyper, *Revelation*, 22.

The distance created between the first hearers and the fulfillment of Revelation's visions stands in stark contrast to the consistent emphasis throughout Revelation that 'the time is near' (1:3; 22:10) and that the visions are imminently relevant (coming to pass *quickly*: 1:1; 3:11; 22:7, 12, 20). Particularly problematic is the claim by "prophecy experts" that the message of Revelation is finally being revealed in current events, when John himself regarded the message of Revelation to stand "unsealed," open to be understood by his immediate readers (22:10p; contrast Dan. 12:9).[39]

Indeed, "John gives a clear signal that Revelation is to be read as a letter, specifically a pastoral letter . . . . John therefore intended his letter to be understood by *them*, shape *their* perceptions of *their* every day realities, and motivate a particular response to *their* circumstances" (deSilva, p. 9).

(4) Futurism too often involves exegetical subjectivity despite its claims to involving a "more normative" approach to Scripture,[40] "the plain, literal or normal principle of interpretation."[41] After all, new technologies will arise in our future that will require a re-interpretation of Revelation's already altered imagery. For instance, Hal Lindsey's Cobra helicopter interpretation of Revelation 9 could eventually give way to the newer, remote-controlled drone warfare technology.

Preterism: Ancient History

Finally, we have the *preterist* view, also known as the "contemporary imminent" or "contemporary historical" or "imminent historical" viewpoint. It is a strongly redemptive-historical approach highlighting the transition from the old covenant to the new covenant as the concluding phase of redemptive history, though also including God's judgment on the Roman Empire. Thus, it sees Revelation's fulfillment in our past. Basically this school understands the great majority (not *all*, e.g., 20:11–15; see Terry's discussion in the commentary) of the prophecies in Revelation 4–22 to be dealing with issues and events beginning in John's own day or within just a couple of centuries thereafter. From our perspective, these matters lie in the distant past. Hence, the

---

[39] deSilva, *Seeing Things John's Way*, 4.
[40] Walvoord, *Revelation*, 22.
[41] Ryrie, *Revelation*, 9.

designation "*prete*rism," from the Latin word *praeteritus* meaning "gone by," i.e., past.[42]

The opening and closing statements in Revelation provide key evidence for the preterist interpreter. In those passages John declares the events "must soon take place" (1:1; 22:6) for "the time is near" (1:3). Consequently, the angel commands him "do not seal up the words of the prophecy of this book, for the time is near" (22:6). The fact that Revelation is in letter form also underscores its direct significance for the original audience.

According to Charles, traces of preterism may be found in some early church fathers, such as Irenaeus, Hippolytus, and Victorinus.[43] For instance, premillennialist Victorinus counts the five dead emperors beginning with Galba and sees Nero as the beast. We certainly see its influence in Andreas of Caesarea (AD 611) where he interprets some of the judgment scenes as referring to Vespasian and the Jewish War. Even Walvoord admits: "some in the early church may have had similar views."[44]

Preterism seems to become a major interpretive force in 1547 when Johannes Hentenius of Louvain (1499–1564) edits the commentary on Revelation by Arethas of Cappadocia.[45] It is held by Hugo Grotius (1583–1645) and Henry Hammond (1605–60), but its most influential systematizer is the Spanish Jesuit Luis De Alcasar (1554–1613) who is "the first to attempt a complete exposition of the entire premillennial [i.e., pre-Revelation 20] part of the book, as a connected and advancing whole falling within the Apocalyptist's age and the centuries immediately following."[46] Many liberals hold this view, though stripped of the supernaturalism of evangelical preterism.

Two basic views exist within the preterist camp. One holds that the events of Revelation focus almost equally on the destruction of Jerusalem with its temple (AD 70) *and* the collapse of Rome (AD 410). For

---

[42] For a helpful summary of preterism's modern history among commentators, see Wainwright, ch. 8: "Contemporary-Historical Criticism and Mythology."

[43] R. H. Charles, *Studies in the Apocalypse: Lectures Delivered Before the University of London* Edinburgh: T & T Clark, 1913), 8.

[44] Walvoord, *Revelation*, 17.

[45] Court, *Myth and History in Revelation*, 11. Arthur W. Wainwright, *Mysterious Apocalypse: Interpreting the Book of Revelation* (Nashville: Abingdon, 1993), 63.

[46] Beckwith, *Apocalypse*, 332.

instance, McClintock and Strong write: "We are inclined to adopt that which regards the first series of prophetical visions proper (ch. iv–xii) as indicating the collapse (in part at the time already transpired) of the nearest persecuting power, namely, Judaism; the second series (ch. xiii–xix) as denoting the eventual downfall of the succeeding persecutor, i.e., Rome" (with the final persecutor conquered in the final visions).[47]

The other preterist perspective sees John's primary focus to be on the events surrounding AD 70. It includes both the destruction of the temple and the Roman civil wars in the Year of the Four Emperors (AD 68–69. Yet it says nothing about the collapse of Rome centuries later. Beagley summarizes this position, noting that: John is

> concerned with the situation of the Church and its conflict with Judaism and with the Roman government, and particularly with the alliance between these two powers which sought to crush the growing Christian movement. . . . The book depicts primarily judgments which come upon the Jewish people because of their rejection of Jesus' Messiahship and their persecution of the Christian community, the climax being reached in the description of the fall of Jerusalem (symbolized by the harlot/city, "Babylon").[48]

The predominant preterist position is the dual Jerusalem and Rome view. It is held by such writers as Moses Stuart (1845), Friederich Düsterdieck (1884), Philip Schaff (1910), David S. Clark (1922), Philip Mauro (1925), Ray Summers (1951), Martin Hopkins (1965), Andrè Feuillet (1965), Jay Adams (1966), G. B. Caird (1966), William Barclay (1976), Greg L. Bahnsen (1977), M. E. Boring (1989), Wilfred J. Harrington (1991), and Roland H. Worth (1999).

The view holding that Revelation more narrowly focuses on the AD 70 era is held by Milton Terry (1898), J. Massyngberde Ford (1975), Cornelis Vanderwaal (1979; 1990), Alan James Beagley (1987), David Chilton (1987), Kenneth L. Gentry, Jr. (1989), J. E. Leonard (1991), Bruce J. Malina (2000), Margaret Barker (2000), Michael Barber (2005), Sebastian Smolarz (2011), and Douglas F. Kelly (2012).

For instance, Cornelis van der Waal states: "the fact that a whole book is devoted to the fall of Jerusalem proves how dominant this

---

[47] John McClintock and James Strong, eds., *Cyclopedia of Biblical, Theological, and Ecclesiastical Literature* (Grand Rapids: Baker, 1981 [rep. 1867]), 8:1067.
[48] Alan James Beagley, *The "Sitz im Leben" of the Apocalypse with Particular Reference to the Role of the Church's Enemies* (New York: Walter de Gruyter, 1987), 113.

theme is in the New Testament. . . . In Revelation the controversy is: church versus synagogue."[49] For the most part it is also held by Philip Carrington (1931), Eugenia Corsini (1983), Edmondo Lupieri (1999), and probably Paul T. Penley (2010) who intentionally suppresses his viewpoint but frequently defends the position.

I call the Rome + Jerusalem position "historical-preterism" in that it deals with both the destructions of sacred Jerusalem and secular Rome as significant world-historical episodes. Whereas the Jerusalem-focus view (my own) I designate as "redemptive-historical preterism."[50] I draw this distinction in that it emphasizes the *theological* and *redemptive* — not simply historical and experiential — significance of AD 70 as concluding the old covenant when it finally, fully, and forever establishes the new covenant. Just as Beale, Smalley and others call themselves "modified idealists," perhaps redemptive-historical preterism could be deemed "modified preterism," as over against the majority preterist view.

Preterism's strengths

The leading strengths of preterism are: (1) It retains and emphasizes the relevance of Revelation for John's first-century audience (the seven churches in Asia Minor and apostolic Christianity more broadly). That audience is enduring a worsening period of persecution and oppression (Rev. 1:9; 6:9–11; 14:13; 17:6) that would require Christians to strive to "overcome" (2:7, 11, 17, 26; 3:5, 12, 21). John writes to a particular people at a particular time, and those people are urged to carefully "hear" (1:3) what Revelation presents.

As Beckwith well notes: "Like 'every scripture inspired of God' the Apocalypse was certainly meant to be to those to whom it first came 'profitable for teaching' (2 Tim. 3:16), and so the writer must have counted on its being understood in its chief lessons."[51] This differs

---

[49] Cornelis Vanderwaal, *Search the Scriptures* (St. Catherines, Ont.: Paideia, 1979), 10:125.

[50] Beale (48) deems his view as "a "Redemptive-Historical Form of Modified Idealism," which he calls "eclecticism." But his reason for this designation is too broad, pointing to what virtually all commentators hold, i.e., that the events "finally issue in the last judgment and the definitive establishment of his kingdom."

[51] Beckwith, *Apocalypse*, 319.

radically from futurism which must argue that "as history unfolds and as prophecy is fulfilled in the future, much will be understood that could be only dimly comprehended by the first readers of the book."[52]

(2) Preterism takes seriously Revelation's time-frame indicators: "the things which must shortly take place" (Rev. 1:1, 22:6) and "the time is near" (1:3; 22:10). These temporal qualifiers appear in the introduction and the conclusion of Revelation. Thus, any unprejudiced original reader should expect that what he will hear and what he should understand is a prophecy about fast-approaching events. Not only so but these temporal delimiters appear well before and immediately after the perplexing symbolic visions. That is, they appear in the more didactic and less dramatic sections.

(3) It dramatically presents major redemptive-historical matters: the demise of Judaism and the temple system (after 2000 years of Jewish focus and 1500 years of tabernacle/temple worship) and the universalizing of the Christian faith as it permanently breaks free of its maternal bonds to temple-based Israel.[53] During its earliest years Christianity gravitates to the temple (e.g., Acts 2:46; 3:1; 5:20, 42; 21:26; 22:17; 24:11) and Jerusalem (e.g., Acts 1:4; 6:7; 8:1; 15:2; 19:21). Thus, this covenantal transition is a major, recurring theme in the New Testament. We see this especially in Hebrews which has this as its central, controlling point: John "depicts the replacement of the Old Covenant by Christianity in language reminiscent of the epistle to the Hebrews."[54] But we also witness numerous allusions to AD 70 in many texts in the Gospels (e.g., Matt. 8:11–12; 21:43; 22:1–7; 23:35–38;

---

[52] Walvoord, *Revelation*, 8.

[53] We must understand that "the patriarchal family was only a stage in the development of the people of God, so national and territorial Israel in the Old Testament period was a stage toward the development of an international and global people of God. This is not just a 'Christian idea' but intrinsic to the Old Testament itself." N. T. Wright, "Jerusalem in the New Testament" in Peter W. L. Walker, ed., *Jerusalem Past and Present in the Purposes of God* (2 ed.: Grand Rapids: Baker, 1994), 2. Wright notes the OT evidence, citing especially Zec 2:11a: "And many nations will join themselves to the Lord in that day and will become My people." See also: Gen. 12:3; Psa. 22:27; 47:8ff; 72:17; 86:9; 87:1ff; 102:13–22; Isa. 11:1–9, 10, 12; 19:19–25; 25:1ff; 42:6; 44:5; 45:22ff; 49:6; Jer. 16:19; Amos 9:12; Hag. 2:6ff; Zech. 8:20—23; Mal. 1:11.

[54] Martin Hopkins, "The Historical Perspective of Apocalypse 1–11," *CBQ* 27 (1965): 44.

24:1–34) as well as elsewhere (Acts 2:16–21, 37–40; 7:48–53; 1 Thess. 2:14–16).

(4) By enduring such catastrophes as appearing in Revelation, the first-century church serves as an example of Christ's providential protection of his people — giving hope for not only that day but all ages. If Christ can deliver the church in its infancy during its weakest stage of development from two ubiquitous enemies, then the future looks bright with hope.

Preterism's weaknesses

Preterism's weaknesses. Non-preterist scholars detect certain elements in the system that they believe render it inoperable.

First, preterism's focus on the first century seems to limit its usefulness to us today. But this complaint is just as true regarding most Old Testament books and much of the contemporary focus of the New Testament epistles (see 1 Corinthians, for instance). Besides preterism's strengths (see above) more than make up for this perceived problem.

Second, preterism's focus on first-century events must apply apparent end-time prophecies to those events. But this problem is mitigated by realizing that John is using apocalyptic language, which is fundamentally dramatic and symbolic.

Third, preterism's interpretation of Revelation makes apparently worldwide events apply to local matters. But again, this characterizes apocalyptic language. Hyperbolic images serve to drive home ethical warnings — just as they do in the Old Testament prophets (see Isa. 13 and 34).

Conclusion

Although a great number of sub-varieties exist within each of the four basic interpretive schools, we should be aware of their fundamental distinctives. I do not present the currently popular "eclectic" approach of Beale and some others because, as Beale notes: "the majority of the symbols in the book are transtemporal in the sense that they are applicable to events throughout the 'church age,'"[55] consequently, "no specific prophesied historical events are discerned in the book." Thus, this "eclectic" view is simply another version of idealism.

---

[55] G. K. Beale, *The Book of Revelation* (Rapids: Eerdmans, 1999). 48.

I would also note that the different interpretive schools seem to arise from our historical distance from Revelation's original setting. As Mounce notes: John "wrote out of his own immediate situation, his prophecies would have a historical fulfillment, he anticipated a future consummation, and revealed principles that operated beneath the course of history."[56] Consequently, we may actually surmise that as he writes Revelation, John is simultaneously a futurist, historicist, idealist, and preterist!

And finally, as an evangelical Christian I would point out that each view has evangelical adherents within it. Unfortunately, some dispensationalist-futurists dismiss the other approaches as dangerously trending toward liberalism — though they conveniently never mention the cultic versions of premillennialism (Mormonism; Jehovah's Witnesses).

---

[56] Mounce, *Revelation*, 29.

Appendix 2
A Brief Study on "The Land" in Revelation
Kenneth L. Gentry, Jr., Th.D.

As Terry occasionally notes, in Revelation John often employs the term *gē* as a reference to "the Land," i.e., of Israel. Unfortunately, most versions translate this as "earth" in every appearance in the book. I would point out, however, that the interlinear translations of Revelation 1:7 by Robert Young and Alfred Marshall properly translate it "land."

Terry's commentary understands this in several key passages, though he does not consistently work this out in the whole commentary. I believe that the majority of its appearances refer to the Land for the reasons to follow. Stuart states that *gēs* like (the Hebrew) *eretz* "is more or less extensive, as the nature of the context demands.[1] Here [at 6:4], not the whole earth, but *the land of Palestine* is especially denoted."

I would point out the following suggestive evidence for this translation in Revelation.

First, redemptive-history's 2000 year-old focus on the Land (beginning with Abraham, Gen. 12) which dominates the 1500 years of old covenant revelation (beginning with Moses) when coupled with John's abundant use of the OT as his major image source. This suggests that John himself could be referring to this fundamental reality of biblical revelation, especially in that:

Second, John's intentionally Hebraic presentation mimics the old covenant prophets. And they frequently focused on Israel and her land-promises to explain her banishment from it. When we compare Revelation with John's Gospel, we see that John can write Greek in a more polished and acceptable form. Something is going on in Revelation to account for his solecisms. We should recall that John was called to labor among "the circumcised" (Gal. 2:9) which would have kept alive his dealing with the matter of the Land.

---

[1] Moses Stuart, *Commentary on the Apocalypse* (Andover: Allen, Morrill, Wardwell, 1845), 2:154; cp. 161.

Third, his clear and repeated near-term expectations (Rev. 1:1, 3; 22:6, 10) introducing this earth-shaking, universe-collapsing prophecies. Since he expects something fast approaching to fulfill his prophecies, this requires events of dramatic historical consequences. This would fit with the collapse of the 1500 years of formal, centralized Jewish sacrificial worship, first by means of a tabernacle, then for the remaining 1000 years in a temple. When we look in the first century we can find nothing else on that order of magnitude for redemptive-history. In fact, with the coming of Jesus as the center point of redemptive history and the hinge of the covenant leading to the firm establishment of the new covenant, we should expect his interest in the question of the Land as the place where the old covenant people and worship operated.

Fourth, Revelation reaches its climax in the appearing of "new Jerusalem" (Rev. 21:2, 9). In that this is a "new" reality it must be replacing the old, original, historical Jerusalem in the Land (cp. Gal. 4:25–31; Heb. 12:22–24). Jerusalem and the Land dominate the old covenant experience as the historical setting of the promises of God. Fifth, as Terry argues at 1:7, John's theme is Christ's (metaphorical) judgment-coming against Israel. In his Olivet Discourse warning of this same event (cp. Revelation 1:7 with Matt. 24:30), he urges his followers to depart Judea as hastily as possible (Matt. 24:16–19).

Malina argues similarly from a social-science perspective:

> The Greek word *gē* may mean either "land," "earth," "territory" or the like. The meaning of the word depends on the social system and point of view of the speaker. Since the prophet John is of Israelite background, concerned with a cosmic lord called Jesus Messiah (an exclusively Israelite category), uses Israelite scripture for his groups found in Israelite enclaves (whose presence is indicated by references in the letters to Smyrna and Philadelpia [2:9; 3:9]), and looks to the emergence of a new Jerusalem (capital of Judea), there is little reason to expect any concern with non-Israelites.[2]

Then he adds regarding Revelation 8:5: "As we have repeatedly indicated, there simply is no solid reason for [translating *gē* as "earth"]. The focus is the house of Israel, specifically Judea."

All of this explains a statistical peculiarity regarding Revelation: the word *gē* occurs eighty-two times in Revelation, almost a full third of

---

[2] Bruce J. Malina and John J. Pilch, *Social-Science Commentary on the Book of Revelation* (Minneapolis: Fortress, 2000), 122.

the times it appears in the entire NT (250 x).[3] The translation "the Land" should appear more frequently than it does in most commentaries.

By way of quick sampling, we should note some rather obvious "Land" uses of *gē* in the following Revelation passages. At 3:10 the whole world is contrasted to the Land when it speaks of "the hour of testing, that hour which is about to come upon the whole world, to test those who dwell upon the *earth*." When God holds back the "four winds of the *earth*" (Rev. 7:1) it is so he can seal the 144,000 from the twelve tribes of the sons of Israel (7:3–4). The 144,000 are immediately contrasted to an uncountable multitude from "every nation and all tribes and peoples and tongues" (7:9). These 144,000 are later said to have been "purchased from the *earth*" (14:3). This reflects the historical reality of Christianity beginning in Israel where it was initially made up almost entirely of Jews. The angel preaches the gospel "to those who live on the *earth*, and to every nation and tribe and tongue and people" (14:6). The widely recognized image of Israel as a vine appears in 14:19 where the sickle gathers "the clusters from the vine of the *earth*."

These appearances of *gē* represent the more obvious evidence for its application to the Land. In my forthcoming commentary on Revelation (*The Divorce of Israel: A Redemptive-Historical Interpretation*), I will demonstrate the contextual demands for an even wider use of *gē*. In the following Table I will sort out the uses of *gē* in Revelation as I understand it. I would note that the term appears eighty-two times in Revelation with 64% speaking of "the Land."

---

[3] Surprisingly, Burge notes this statistical fact but then states that "in each case it points to the earth and never to the Holy Land" Gary M. Burge, *Jesus and the Land: The New Testament Challenge to "Holy Land" Theology* (Grand Rapids: Baker Academic, 2010), 104–05. This despite the fact that he argues "in Revelation it is the Holy Land that becomes a land of violence toward the people of God and in the end the subject to judgment and devastation" (108). And this just after noting that Revelation's harlot is Jerusalem (105–06)!

App. 2: A Brief Study on "The Land" in Revelation

Uses of *Gē* in Revelation

"The Land" (of Israel) 52x (64+%)	Not meaning "the Land" (of Israel) 24x (29+%)	Uncertain, indifferent, or double significance 5x (6%)
1:5, 7; 3:10; 6:4, 8a, 10; 6:15; 8:5, 7 (2x), 13; 9:1, 3a; 11:6, 10 (2x); 11:18; 12:4, 9, 12(?); 13:8, 11, 12, 13, 14 (2x); 14:3, 6, 15, 16 (2x), 18, 19 (2x); 16:1, 2; 17:2 (2x), 5, 8, 18; 18:3 (2x), 9, 11, 23, 24; 19:2, 19; 20:9; 21:24	5:3 (2x), 6, 10, 13 (2x); 7:1b (2x), 2, 3 (4x); 9:4; 10:6; 11:4; 13:3; 14:7; 16:18; 18:1; 20:8, 11; 21:1 (2x)	6:8b, 13; 7:1a; 9:3b; 12:16 (2x)

In my forthcoming commentary I will demonstrate the dramatic significance of the translation "the Land" for *hē gē*. Though "the Land" itself is significant, its significance intensifies when it appears in the two most important phrases involving it: "the kings of the earth" (1:5; 6:15; 17:2, 18; 18:3, 9; 19:19; 21:24) and "those who dwell [*katoikeō*] on the earth [*epi tēs gēs*]" (3:10; 6:10; 8:13; 11:10; 13:8, 12, 14; 17:2, 8).

At 1:7 Beale disputes this interpretation arguing that "*gē* ("earth, land") cannot be a limited reference to the land of Israel but has a universal denotation."[4] Though here he does so at 1:7 because of that verse's associating the land with "all the tribes," he never allows this word to signify simply the Land of Israel anywhere in Revelation. I would point out, though, that some of Beale's own methods allow this use and can be used to counter his argument. For instance, regarding

---

[4] G. K. Beale, *The Book of Revelation* (NIGTC) (Grand Rapids: Eerdmans, 1999), 197.

Revelation 3:9 Beale (94) notes that "promises given to Israel, who are prophesied to be persecuted by the nations, are now ironically applied to and understood to be fulfilled in Gentile believers persecuted by Israel." But this ironic re-application of prophecy can also explain the ironic re-application of the OT phrase "the kings of the earth" in order to refer to Israel's high-priestly. This would be an especially significant rhetorical irony since he is focusing on Israel whose synagogue is no longer "the synagogue of the Lord" (LXX: Num. 16:3; 20:4; 31:16; cf. Pss. Sol. 17:18; cp. Philo, *Post.* 19 §67) but a "synagogue of Satan" (2:9; 3:9) and whose "holy city" (11:2) Jerusalem becomes "mystically . . . Sodom and Egypt" (11:8).

Furthermore, Beale (p. 91) argues along with Vanhoye and Vogelgesang and many others for John's practice of "universalization." By this method John "has a tendency to apply to the world what the OT applied only to Israel or to other entities." I agree. But I would argue that John can also employ an opposite method in Revelation, which we might call "localization." That is, since John's focus is on Christ's judgment of Israel (cf. 1:7), he can re-orient global judgment language and apply it to Israel as a local reality. After all, "John creatively reworks the OT and changes its application" (p. 92). If he can universalize some passages and prophetic concepts, why may he not also *localize* other passages and prophetic concepts? Thus, John may engage in more than one form of "inverted or ironic use," "polemical irony," and "retributive ironies" as a "reversal phenomenon" (pp. 92–93).

Appendix 3
Why I Am a Preterist
Jay Rogers

At age 23, I was converted to saving faith in Jesus Christ while attending a small evangelical church in Boston, Massachusetts. Although I had read the Bible for many years in high school and college, I soon developed a greater hunger for the Scriptures as my understanding was opened by the Holy Spirit. Numerous guest speakers visited our church in that first year. One of the most interesting preachers was a "leading prophecy expert" in our denomination. This man assured us that the Antichrist was alive somewhere on planet earth and the rapture would surely come at any moment. Each night, this man would give a list of candidates who he thought the Antichrist *might be*.

**"Come back tomorrow and I'll tell you
who is my number one candidate for the Antichrist!"**

During this three-night seminar, I began to realize how absurd end times predictions could be. I cautiously told one of our assistant pastors that I disagreed with some of what this evangelist said. He just stared at me and said, "Only *some*? I disagree with more than *half* of what he said!" That led me to wonder why we had invited this "expert" to teach in our church for three nights in the first place.

I resolved to listen to an audio recording of the Book of Revelation striving to hear with "open ears" — to understand what it was all about. As a teenager, I had read the bestselling book, *The Late Great Planet Earth* and had seen the film. However, as I listened to the audio of Revelation, I could not for the life of me imagine that I would ever have come up with the dispensationalist model on my own unless it had been taught to me. I also discovered that the discussion on eschatology in many evangelical circles often revolves around this question:

"Are you pre-trib, mid-trib or post-trib?"

As if these are the only three forms of eschatology! It is difficult to show some Christians that there is another way of looking at the end times that emphasizes earthly victory prior to Jesus' return.

After I rejected dispensationalism, I would ask Christians I knew what they thought about the books of Daniel and Revelation. They would often say, "I stopped trying to figure that out! I'm a *panmillennialist*! I believe it will all *pan out* in the end!"

The problem for me was that I could not accept that God would give us an inspired, inerrant book of Scripture that was impossible to understand. Further, if we begin with the wrong presuppositions, we will draw the wrong conclusions. The Bible is misunderstood and misinterpreted, not because it is impossible, but because believers often do not seek to understand biblical texts in their original literary and historical context in consideration of immediate audience relevance.

A few years later, I came across *Christ's Victorious Kingdom: Postmillennialism Reconsidered* by John Jefferson Davis. This was for me 150 pages of dynamite. Davis proves that the postmillennial doctrine is not only supported by many passages in both the Old and New Testaments, but it also has a strong pedigree among the great Christian missionary leaders and theologians throughout history.

Submission to the Lordship of Jesus Christ and doing Kingdom work is a necessary requirement for all Christians. We ought to gladly take part in the Great Commission with an eye toward winning. The message of earthly victory for the Gospel has great appeal. God did not preprogram His Church for defeat in an ever-darkening world. I asked myself the following question:

Are we, the Church of the living God, to be losers in history only to be rescued at the Second Coming?

Much to the contrary, postmillennialism teaches that Jesus is Lord over the whole world and the Church is destined to enjoy earthly victory in time and on earth. The "millennium" is seen as a metaphor for a long period of time in which the Gospel is ever advancing. Jesus will come again to judge the living and the dead after the "millennial" reign of Christ from heaven is completed. His Second Coming will be *post*-millennial, literally *after* the millennium. During the millennium, righteousness, peace, and prosperity will result from the Church's influence in society. God will increasingly bless the "seed of Abraham" to bless in turn all the nations of the earth (Gen. 12:3; 18:18; 22:18, Matt. 1:1, Luke 3:34, Acts 3:25, Gal. 3:16).

Although I accepted postmillennialism as a young Christian, I did not immediately know what to think about the Book of Revelation.

Then in 1999, I co-produced a video called, *The Beast of Revelation: Identified* presented by Kenneth Gentry and Eric Homberg. I began to see that many well-known theologians were shifting toward a preterist postmillennial eschatology. Among the more notable was R. C. Sproul, a renowned Reformed scholar and founding pastor of the Saint Andrew's Chapel, a church I later joined as a member. Until I produced Gentry's video teaching on the Beast of Revelation as found in Revelation 13 and 17, I did not understand it well enough to know whether I agreed fully.

I found it odd that some interpret Daniel and the Mount Olivet Discourse one way, but then shift gears when they encounter the Book of Revelation there they begin using a different hermeneutic. For example, many interpreters are preterists when they encounter Matthew 24, seeing its fulfillment mainly in the destruction of the Temple at Jerusalem in AD 70. But they are either historicists, futurists, or idealists on Revelation, which deals with largely the same events and with the same prophetic language.

Have you been bitten by the preterist bug?

I have observed many Christians understanding preterism for the first time go through a "cage stage" in their eschatology. They become full-time evangelists for preterism. Or worse, a small minority become hyper-preterists and assert that the whole Bible is about AD 70. The destruction of Jerusalem becomes a grid through which they filter *every* biblical prophecy.

But preterism is a hermeneutic, not a doctrine. Our focus ought to be the Lordship of Jesus Christ. Difficult apocalyptic passages found in Daniel, Ezekiel, Zechariah, Matthew 24, and Revelation are made clearer when we understand that the theme is the victory of Christ over the world. Biblical apocalyptic literature also emphasizes the Dominion Mandate — the work that God has given to His people to accomplish in history even in times of trial and persecution. Preterism then helps make sense out of controversial passages that speak of the Great Tribulation, the Beast of Revelation, the Lord "coming quickly," and so on.

In the New Testament, one of several Greek words translated as "coming" is *parousia* (Matt. 24:3, 27, 37, 39; 1 Cor. 15:23; 1 Thess. 2:19; 3:13; 4:15; 5:23; 2 Thess. 2:1, 8, 9; Jms. 5:7, 8; 2 Pet. 1:16; 3:4, 12; 1

John 2:28). The numerous "coming" passages in the New Testament may speak of the following things.

- The incarnation, birth and earthly ministry of Jesus Christ
- The physical coming on the scene of any person in a biblical narrative
- The coming with the power of the Holy Spirit at Pentecost
- The ascended Lord seated on a throne coming in temporal judgment on nations
- The bodily Second Coming of Christ

To interpret all of the Lord's "coming" passages to speak of AD 70, as some preterists maintain, is shortsighted. However, on the other end of the spectrum, it is also an error to assume that all "coming" passages speak of the Second Coming. In this way, pietistic premillennialism pushes many Christians to become monastic and inwardly focused. As fallen creatures, we have a fleshly inclination to think that Bible prophecy applies to us directly. It is the height of self-centeredness to assume that every "last days" prophecy refers to the time we live in. One of the problems of pietistic thinking in our time is that it neglects the emphasis on the great victories God has won for His people and focuses on how bad things are in the here and now.

True Revival comes when our focus on prayer and Bible study directs us to see God's purposes in the whole world in all of history. A right understanding of the historical background of the Bible will help us to cultivate a total biblical worldview. We will understand that history has a meaning and a purpose. History is not, as the Marxists have taught, a list of dates and wars chronicling the political struggles between the economic classes. Rather, we must preach and teach a providential view of history – a perspective that sees the hand of God directing the entire earth toward a glorious destiny. It is God, not man, who decides which nations must rise and fall. He does so to fulfill the promise of His kingdom coming on earth as it is in heaven.

One of the most difficult aspects of studying the prophecies of Daniel, Mathew 24 and Revelation is that some portions prompt wide ranging disagreement. Therefore, nearly all Bible scholars throughout history must be woefully wrong about some aspects of these difficult parts of the Bible. This is troubling because as Christians we see the Bible as an inspired and inerrant book. This prompts the following question.

Would the Holy Spirit speak through the prophets in a way that is incomprehensible to nearly all Christians?

The main reason that Revelation remains obscure in our time is due to the rise of futurism in the past century especially through dispensational premillennialism. The preterist view of Revelation along with the study of the prophecy's background history is too often neglected.

In the 1800s, there was a time, at least among scholars, when it looked as though preterist postmillennialism had won the day. Postmillennial optimism fueled world missions, evangelism and social reform. Preterism as a hermeneutic helped many make sense of some of the most difficult prophetic passages in the Bible. By the end of the 1800s, many scholars who had once held to a late date of the writing of Revelation had changed their view to agree that it had been written during the Neronian persecution prior to AD 70. This included the noted authority on the Church Fathers, Philip Schaff:

> "The early date is now accepted by perhaps the majority of scholars. In its favor ... may be urged the allusion to the temple at Jerusalem (11:1), in language which implies that it yet existed, but would speedily be destroyed; and, further, that the nature and object of the Revelation are best suited by the earlier date, while its historical understanding is greatly facilitated. With the great conflagration at Rome, and the Neronian persecution fresh in mind, with the horrors of the Jewish war then going on, and in view of the destruction of Jerusalem as an impending fact, John received the visions of the conflicts and the final victories of the Christian Church. His book came, therefore, as a comforter to hearts distracted by calamities without a parallel in history."[1]

Preterism is the view that most of the prophecies of Revelation were fulfilled by the cataclysmic events that occurred in Judea in AD 70, one generation after Jesus preached the Mount Olivet Discourse. Yet even more work needs to be done in order to bring the preterist view into unity. The Book of Revelation is difficult, but it is not impossible to understand with the correct presuppositions. Books such as Milton S. Terry's *Biblical Apocalyptics* were often difficult to obtain for many decades until the advent of electronic digital media. My hope is that this

---

[1] *History of the Christian Church*, rev. ed., vol. 1. 834–837. Quoted in: Philip Schaff, ed., *A Religious Encyclopedia: or Dictionary of Biblical Historical, Doctrinal, and Practical Theology* (1891), 3:2086 n. 1).

stand-alone portion of Terry's book will further help to convince the unconvinced and bring preterist studies into clearer focus.

Notes

Notes

Notes

Notes

Notes

Notes

www.ingramcontent.com/pod-product-compliance
Lightning Source LLC
Chambersburg PA
CBHW070959160426
43193CB00012B/1844